CONTENTS

T5-AWK-764

THE DYNAMICS OF AMERICAN PUBLIC OPINION

PATTERNS AND PROCESSES

THE DYNAMICS OF AMERICAN PUBLIC OPINION

PATTERNS AND PROCESSES

John C. Pierce
Washington State University

Kathleen M. Beatty
University of Colorado,
Colorado Springs

Paul R. Hagner
Washington State University

Scott, Foresman and Company

Glenview, Illinois

Dallas, Tex.   Oakland, N.J.   Palo Alto, Cal.   Tucker, Ga.   London, England

Library of Congress Cataloging in Publication Data

Pierce, John C.
   The dynamics of American public opinion.

   Includes index.
   1. Public opinion—United States.   I. Beatty,
Kathleen.   II. Hagner, Paul R.   III. Title.
 HN90.P8P52   303.3'8'0973   81-13585
ISBN 0-673-16055-6   AACR2

Some of the data and tabulations utilized in this book were made available by
the Inter-University Consortium for Political and Social Research. The data
for the CPS 1976 American National Election Study were originally collected
by the Center for Political Studies of the Institute for Social Research, the
University of Michigan under a grant from the National Science Foundation.
Neither the original collectors of the data nor the Consortium bear any responsibility for the analyses or interpretations presented here.

ISBN: 0-673-16055-6

Printed in the United States of America

1 2 3 4 5 6-KPF-86 85 84 83 28 81

PREFACE

Little more than a decade ago, most political scientists felt they had a relatively clear picture of American public opinion. Relying on a series of landmark studies of the public's political beliefs and political behavior, many scholars tended to describe public opinion with a set of rather static characteristics. Much recent scholarly work, however, suggests that public opinion has changed in numerous significant ways, that it is not as immutable as it once was thought to be. Public opinion is dynamic. It is responsive to changes in the political and social environment and to the actions and attitudes of political leaders. Yet these changes make sense only when viewed against the backdrop of the stability in opinions and in their causes, both of which are occasionally overshadowed.

Throughout this book we maintain these themes: patterns of stability and change; alternative explanations of those patterns; the methodological and conceptual problems in assessing the patterns and their explanations; and the importance of the changes for the democratic nature of the political system and for the democratic character of the American public.

Part One consists of three chapters designed to serve as background for the substantive chapters that follow. Chapter 1 is an overview of the nature of public opinion and its importance. Chapter 2 reviews the major kinds of explanations for recent patterns of public opinion and explores the dynamics of opinions at the individual and the aggregate levels. Chapter 3 examines the conceptual and methodological problems inherent in the study of opinion patterns.

The chapters in Part Two consider two major influences on political learning. Chapter 4 discusses political socialization and changes in the patterns of socialization. Chapter 5 covers the role of the mass media in opinion formation and change. Many readers will observe that Part Two omits several topics traditionally treated as separate chapters in public opinion texts (e.g., personality and opinions, and social group characteristics and public opinion). Those concerns (as well as several others) are dealt with throughout the book as they appear as explanations for various patterns of public opinion or change in public opinion.

Part Three contains a series of chapters about the expression of public opinion. Chapter 6 discusses the cognitive structure underlying expressions of public opinion. Chapter 7 focuses on the structure of the public's political thinking and the relationships among the public's opinions. Chapter 8 is the first of two that examine important elements of the American political cul-

ture. That chapter looks at changes in the American public's political tolerance — an essential element of a democratic political culture. Chapter 9
examines the steep decline in the American public's trust in government and
the alternative explanations for its occurrence. Chapter 10 considers the public's orientations to political parties, focusing on the decline in support for
parties and on the changes in the sources of party choice. Chapter 11 presents
data showing the changes in the public's opinions about two major social
movements: the civil rights movement and the women's movement.

Part Four examines the consequences of public opinion. Chapter 12 looks at
political behavior. Chapter 13 considers the public's involvement in interest
groups (particularly those public interest groups that have exhibited a vast
increase in membership in the past decade) as a means of pressing opinions
on the political process. Chapter 14 concludes the book with an evaluation of
the impact of public opinion on the political system. The major concern here
is with political linkage and changes in political linkage over the past few
decades.

We hope this book will stimulate in the student a sensitivity to the importance of public opinion and to the intrinsic interest inherent in its study.
Similarly, we believe that students of public opinion must be open to the
possibility of changing patterns of opinions as the political system changes
and as political leaders change. Ignoring the extent to which the public is
responsive to what goes on around it will lead neither to an understanding of
the nature of public opinion nor to an enhancement of its impact in politics.

ACKNOWLEDGMENTS

The authors owe many debts for assistance in the preparation of this book. Our colleagues at Washington State University, Terry Cook, Frank Mullen, Nick Lovrich, Chuck Sheldon, and Taketsugu Tsurutani, have read drafts of several of the chapters of the manuscript or have endured and responded to our discussions of their (the chapters') contents. Carol Lowinger read four of the chapters with great care; much of whatever clarity is found in those chapters is attributable to her fine hand. Philip Converse, William Flanigan, and Pinky Wassenberg were of special help in obtaining data for Chapter 7. Many of the chapters include data originally collected by the Center for Political Studies of the Institute for Social Research (ISR) at the University of Michigan and distributed through the Inter-University Consortium for Political and Social Research (ICPSR). Neither the ISR nor the ICPSR are responsible for the presentation or analysis of these data. Many of our colleagues throughout the scholarly community have allowed us to use some of their findings in this book. We are grateful to them and to all students of public opinion whose efforts are reflected here. Jim Boyd, our Editor, has been most cooperative in the development of the book. Laurie Greenstein has been the Production Editor for this enterprise. Her skill and tact are quite extraordinary, and helped make the drudgery of the final stages of the book as pleasant as possible. Dell Day, Joyce Lynd, and Cynthia Avery have contributed their skill and their constant good-humored cooperation to the preparations of the manuscript. For their various personal contributions to our thinking about public opinion over the years, we would like to acknowledge William Flanigan, Leroy Rieselbach, Doug Rose, and John Sullivan. As is customary, we assume, however reluctantly, responsibility for the errors and omissions in the contents of this book.

PART I

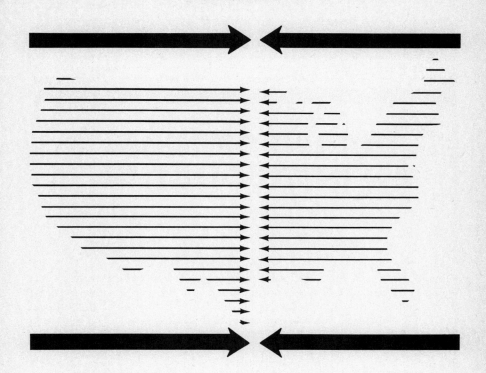

DYNAMICS OF
PUBLIC OPINION

CHAPTER 1

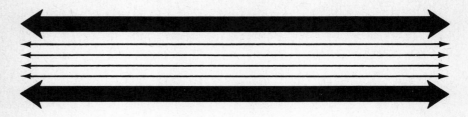

PUBLIC OPINION: AN INTRODUCTION

Current pictures of American public opinion produce sharply contrasting images. On the one hand, a rather abrupt break with the past is widely heralded as the hallmark of contemporary public opinion.[1] Many studies suggest that the public is politically more sophisticated than in earlier years, and other research points to major changes in the public's attitudes about political parties, issues of public policy, and the fundamental rights of minorities. These apparent changes, as well as many others, have been seen to be so pervasive that they mount a serious challenge to a traditional picture of the public sketched by several decades of pathfinding scholarly work. On the other hand, during this same period of seeming change, many characteristics of public opinion displayed remarkable stability. Some changes seemed surprisingly short-lived. And in some cases what were thought to be changes turned out to be merely illusions of change, simply the outgrowth of different research techniques producing different results.

This book is about changes in public opinion, reasons put forward for their occurrence, and why they are so important. It is also about the continuity and stability in American public opinion. Juxtaposing the themes of stability and change enhances our understanding of each. The linchpin for the analysis will be the *dynamics* of public opinion: a focus on dynamics incorporates themes of change as well as stability. The study of public opinion in recent years has centered on the explanation or the debunking of apparent changes, and the dynamics of the change process provide the key to understanding how opinions are formed and the extent to which they persist through time.

This book is intended to provide a context for the interpretation both of recent developments in public opinion and of those in the coming years, whatever combination of stability and change they turn out to be. As a backdrop to the remainder of the book, this chapter first provides an overview of the importance of public opinion. It then turns to a consideration of the major characteristics of public opinion that provide the dimensions along which major stability and change can be charted.

WHY STUDY PUBLIC OPINION?

Scholars, newspaper and television journalists, politicians, interest groups, government agencies, and interested citizens all try to fathom American public opinion. Why do such diverse groups share this passion for public opinion? This section discusses some of the most important answers.

Intrinsic Interest

Many people study public opinion because they find it intrinsically interesting. As V.O. Key has noted,

> depiction of the distribution of opinions within the public, identification of the qualities of opinion, isolation of the odd and of the obvious correlates of opinion, and ascertainment of opinion formation are pursuits that excite human curiosity.[2]

There is something about trying to find out why people believe what they do that creates an intriguing and often fascinating puzzle. Much of this intrinsic interest in public opinion stems from a personal involvement in the results. That is, when we study public opinion, and when we reach conclusions about the nature of public opinion, we are making conclusions about ourselves, for each of us is a part of some public. When we hear about the role of the family in political education, for example, we can reflect on how we acquired our own political attitudes and how they developed out of our own family situation. Thus, learning about public opinion can help people learn about themselves, and most people (rightly or wrongly) find themselves quite interesting.

Public opinion often has the aura of theater about it. It can be a dynamic and entertaining display of the roots of human emotion. In response to political assassination, public opinion can be dramatic and explosive; in reaction to the changing tides of life-style and social mores, it can be subtle and silent. Public opinion reveals the best characteristics of a people when it comes closest to matching the normative ideal of the democratic citizen; and it reveals the worst of a people when it expresses racism and bigotry. All of these — the personal nature of public opinion, its theatrical elements, its intellectual puzzles — combine to make public opinion an attractive and engaging subject.

Understanding Politics

Studying public opinion heightens our understanding of how the political system works. The public now plays an important role in many theories of the political process. The emphasis on the opinions and behavior of the individual in the understanding of politics surfaced in the "behavioral revolution" in political science in the 1950s. Within that context, Heinz Eulau gave the following defense of the study of public opinion and political behavior:

> The root is man. I don't think it is possible to say anything meaningful about the governance of man without talking about the behavior of man — his acts, goals, drives, feelings, beliefs, commitments and values. . . . Politics is concerned with the conditions and consequences of human action. A study of politics which leaves man out of its equations is a rather barren politics.[3]

The concept of public opinion thus is crucial to understanding political institutions, such as legislative bodies, the courts, presidents, and governors. How, for example, can one best explain the politics of the United States Congress? One answer argues that it is best explained in terms of the motives of individual members, and that one motive stands out: reelection.[4] Reelection depends to large degree on the attitudes and behaviors of the members' public. Therefore, much of the legislator's behavior can be understood as an attempt to respond to and/or shape the beliefs and perceptions of the public.

Influencing Politics

Understanding public opinion also can help people achieve political goals. How can knowing about public opinion help one politically? Perhaps the most obvious place is electoral politics. Clearly, to win an election it is advantageous to know how people make up their minds in choosing among candidates and how opinions about issues affect that choice. If such opinions are important in the way people vote, then parties and candidates need some information about the sources of those opinions and how the opinions might be changed or reinforced in politically profitable ways.

Presidents likewise understand the political importance of public opinion.[5] They recognize public opinion as a constraint on the alternatives available to them in particular policy areas. They know that certain kinds of solutions may be unacceptable because of public opinion. At the same time, presidents attempt to influence public opinion through fireside chats, press conferences, town meetings, and special addresses to the nation.

Interest groups similarly are sensitive to public opinion. These political organizations rely on people who share certain opinions for much of their membership,[6] and in fact often claim to represent public opinion when they make their political demands on policymakers. Interest groups also attempt to create or influence public opinion through advertising, in the hope that the public then will influence those people who make public policy.

Making Public Policy

An understanding of public opinion can be crucial to people involved in making formal public policy.[7] Decision makers need to consider public opinion as they formulate and implement policy. An inaccurate knowledge of public opinion, or an inability to alter it, may cause a policy to fall short of its intended impact. Clearly, the role of public opinion in making policy is coupled with its role in influencing politics.

How might public opinion be crucial to effective policymaking? One case would be when public policy is designed to elicit certain kinds of behavior from the public. Public opinion about the policy, or about the legitimacy of the government making the policy, can be critical to the level of public compliance with that policy. If public opinion clearly does not support that policy, and there is an absence of intensive enforcement, there will be little compliance with it.

Thus, the reasons people study public opinion vary widely, ranging from a personal interest in the dynamics of a highly fluid process to the pursuit of policy and political goals. These reasons attest to the many political implications of public opinion and to the importance of its role in American politics. Up to this point, however, we have ignored perhaps the most important normative rationale for studying public opinion: its centrality to the character of American democracy.

PUBLIC OPINION AND DEMOCRACY

Perhaps no reason for studying public opinion has been cited more frequently than its relevance to democracy. This relationship between public opinion and democracy is multifaceted. On the one hand, the extent to which public policy matches public opinion is used to judge the extent to which a political system is democratic. On the other hand, public opinion also is used to evaluate the public's fitness for participation in democratic politics. As one might expect, there are substantial disagreements among scholars about the answers to each of these questions.

Many of the characteristics of public opinion are important for judging both the democratic nature of the political system and the democratic qualities of the American public. Thus, we now turn to the relationship between public opinion and democracy. We return to this relationship throughout the book, not only when describing public opinion but also when examining the nature of changes in it. If public opinion is related to democracy, and it surely is, then changes in public opinion and the sources of those changes must have democratic implications.

Public Opinion and Political Linkage

One standard frequently employed for judging the presence of democracy in a political system is the extent to which public policy reflects the public's preferences. Congruity between public policy and the public's preferences is taken as evidence of the public's control over those in positions of power. As Gabriel Almond and Sidney Verba comment, "unless there is control of government elites by nonelites, it is hard to consider a political system democratic."[8] The importance of this relationship is underscored by V.O. Key:

> Consideration of the role of public opinion drives the observer to the more fundamental question of how it is that democratic governments manage to operate at all. Despite endless speculation on that problem, perplexities still exist about what critical circumstances, beliefs, outlooks, faiths, and conditions are conducive to the maintenance of regimes under which public opinion is controlling, at least in principle, and is, in fact, highly influential.[9]

One author has recently argued that the relationship between public opinion and public policy is the key to democracy. He defines democracy as "the extent to which public opinion influences public policy. In other words, democracy is the correlation between what the people ask for and what they get from the political process."[10] Although this position clearly represents a circumscribed view of the meaning of democracy, it illustrates an increasingly common focus in the study of public opinion.[11]

The conception of democracy as opinion-policy concurrence has centered considerable attention on those instruments through which the public can ensure that policymakers are responsive to its preferences. These instruments of policy responsiveness are *linkage* processes. A linkage process is "any means by which political leaders act in accordance with the wants, needs, and demands of the 'public' in making governmental policy."[12] Linkage processes, then, are essential to that conception of democracy as the relationship between public opinion and public policy.

What linkage mechanisms are available for communicating public preferences to political leaders and thereby enhancing democracy in America? Many have been defined, but perhaps the most frequently cited is the electoral process. Through elections the public has the formal opportunity to reject public officials who fail to respond to its policy preferences. The public exercises an informed choice among candidates with opposing policy positions and votes for the candidate with the position closest to that of individual voters in the public.

Political parties play an important intermediary role in the electoral linkage process. The public can choose among parties with competing platforms, and the candidates contesting under each party label share the party policy positions. Voting for the party with the appropriate policy positions considerably lessens the effort required of the individual citizen to identify and evaluate the policy positions of each specific candidate. Moreover, the party organization provides a vehicle for the channeling of demands from the public. Because of the possible role of parties in linking public opinion to policy, as well as for other reasons, political parties are seen by many commentators as crucial to the operation of the American democracy. E.E. Schattschneider's classic *Party Government,* for example, begins thus: "It should be stated flatly at the outset that this volume is devoted to the thesis that the political parties created democracy and that modern democracy is unthinkable save in terms of the parties."[13]

A number of writers are critical of the assumptions and conclusions in the party and electoral linkage models. They argue that democracy is not enhanced through the electoral process, nor particularly promoted through the two-party system. Elections are seen only as symbolic events, having little, if any, impact on important policy outcomes. The parties have no control over officeholders. They are seen as differing little from each other, and therefore are regarded as incapable of offering policy alternatives to the public that can be translated into the individual citizen's self-interest.[14]

Another possible linkage mechanism of considerable importance is the group process. In its simplest form, political linkage occurs when individuals with similar interests band together in organizations that then press claims on the government. The government responds to the shared opinions of group members in shaping public policy.[15] The range of interests articulated by all of these groups is alleged to correspond to the range of interests in the general public. The process of interaction among the group leaders and between the group leaders and the policymakers is said to result in a "pluralist democracy."

Considerable criticism has been directed at the effectiveness of this group process as a linkage mechanism and at its contribution to this conception of democracy (congruence between public opinion and public policy). Critics have argued that the existing constellation of groups has failed to provide representation for all important interests in society. Rather, the dominant economic interests in the society are better organized and have greater access to policymakers, while those with fewer resources continue to be excluded from having their opinions heard. Others claim that the leaders of the traditionally powerful interest groups are unresponsive to their group members. And it is said that the traditional group process provides representation for only narrow interests, while ignoring general "public" interests. In partial response to the latter, recent years have seen the development of "public interest groups."

The concern that government is unresponsive to public opinion through existing linkage mechanisms has led to pressure for alternative means of influencing policy. One of these is the "citizen advisory committee" (CAC). These committees mushroomed under the policy of "maximum feasible participation" during the Great Society programs of the 1960s, particularly in the attempted renewal of urban areas.[16] Citizen advisory committees subsequently took root in environmental and natural resource policy areas, primarily in response to environmental interests' complaints about the closed nature of the policy process.[17] The premise for the CAC is that public officials and established interests cannot be representative of the interests of many people directly affected by government policies. Therefore, it is argued, the public has the right to be directly represented in policy formation. Citizen advisory committees are the vehicle for that representation. Individuals chosen from different interests in the community participate directly with public officials in making policy. They are chosen in several ways, including election by the members of the community affected by the policy, selection by government officials, and nomination by organized interests in the community. Of greatest importance is the choice of representatives of interests that would not otherwise participate in the policy process as it normally operates.

The desire for direct public involvement in policy formation has deep historical roots. Early in the 1900s this desire took form in the Progressive movement's successful enactment of provisions for the initiative and referendum, particularly in the western states.[18] The initiative process allows the public to place on the ballot and enact legislation; the referendum process enables the public to accept or reject measures passed by the legislature. Both the initiative and the referendum demand that a certain proportion of the voters sign a petition asking for a specific measure to be placed on the ballot. As Frank P. Weaver and Charles H. Sheldon note,

> the theory underlying the processes reflects the tenets of the Progressive movement. Direct democracy constitutes its foundation. When the legislature or other officialdom fail to observe the will of the people, the citizenry assumes direct responsibility for governing. . . . These forms are perhaps the purest forms of direct democracy remaining to the people today.[19]

In recent years, initiatives and referenda have been employed in some widely publicized issues, such as tax limitations, the rights of homosexuals, and the salaries of public officials.

One of the more innovative proposals for direct linkage between public opinion and policymakers is a continuing initiative-referendum process through cable TV.[20] Cable TV provides a direct link between a television studio and individual homes. What has been recently realized is that it also enables people to send messages in the other direction, from the home to the studio. This direct connection provides the opportunity for a kind of instant democracy, an adaptation of the town meeting concept to the realities of a modern technological society. Public issues are debated in a television studio and viewed on the screens of every connected home. At the conclusion of the debates, and after viewer input into the deliberations, the citizens relay their votes on the issues. The votes of many people can be almost instantaneously tallied to provide an indication of the public's will.

All procedures or proposals for the direct involvement of the public in policy formation stimulate consideration of the "quality" of public opinion. Is the public sufficiently informed to make decisions about important questions of public policy? Can the public make rational decisions, or will it be swayed by appeals to emotion? Can the public rise above individual concerns and see the public interest? What about bypassing the moderating effects of policy making in formal deliberative bodies (i.e., the legislature)? The answers to these questions, of course, must be weighed against the criticisms of the traditional political process that led to the direct involvement mechanisms, namely that public policy has been unresponsive to citizen preferences.

Defining democracy as the extent to which public policy matches public opinion clearly raises several critical questions. Some of these questions are definitional, while others are methodological. As a definitional question, one must ask whether there is not more to democracy than the match between public opinion and public policy. To be sure, one would question the democratic nature of a system in which the political leaders' actions and the government's policies rarely were consistent with the preferences of the public. Yet there are considerations in determining the extent to which a system is democratic that are independent of public opinion-public policy congruence. Democracy entails a process that includes the opportunity for the regular and unrestricted participation of the public in the selection of political leaders, the right to express political views, and the guarantee of political and civil rights of minorities. Moreover, other definitions of democracy consider the distribution of economic and social values in a society, and the level of government involvement in the lives of citizens.

Clearly, definitions of such important and value-laden terms as *democracy* will always generate disagreement. In certain cases what we commonly think of as democracy may be absent even though public opinion matches public policy. If a majority of the public prefers the abolition of the right of some minority to participate in the political process, can a democracy be said to be present if that abolition in fact occurs? The answer must be no. Nevertheless, that the match between public opinion and public policy fails to encompass all there is to democracy does not eliminate the fundamental importance of that relationship.

It is important to realize that simply finding agreement between public policy and public opinion reveals little about the process through which that concurrence developed. The use of concurrence as a criterion for democratic linkage assumes that the public's preferences have caused the policy, that policymakers have responded to public opinion either willingly or through threat of political sanction; but there are at least two other possible explanations. The first is that there is no direct *causal* relationship between the two. The policy outcome and the public's preferences are the same, but neither caused the other.

Another explanation is that the public's preferences are brought into line with public policy. That is, government policy and political leaders influence public opinion rather than vice versa. Opinion may be created where none existed before. Weakly formed opinions may be crystallized. Existing opinions may be linked to new situations or may even be reversed. John E. Mueller has argued that the president is a very important source of public opinion in the areas of war and foreign policy, suggesting that

> *there exists, particularly in the area of foreign affairs, an important group of citizens — they can be called "followers" — who are inclined to rally to the support of the president no matter what he does.*[21]

For example, in September 1965, 70 percent of the public opposed the bombing of Hanoi and Haiphong harbor in North Vietnam; that figure dropped gradually to 50 percent in opposition in May 1966. However, once the president initiated the bombing, opposition to it plummeted to 15 percent in July 1966, only two months later. Recently it has been argued that the mass media (and television in particular) even set the political agenda for the public.[22] That is, the public is told what the important political issues are, rather than defining those issues for itself.

One also unavoidably encounters certain methodological problems in deciding whether public opinion matches public policy.[23] Public policy is complex. On many technical issues it may be impossible to reduce the alternatives to a form understandable by the general public. Moreover, if there are more than two alternatives, as often is the case, it is very likely that no majority opinion will surface. Suppose the largest percentage favoring any alternative is 30 percent and public policy matches the preferences of that 30 percent. Does that mean that there is democracy? What about the 70 percent that chose alternatives not reflected in the policy? Should one employ the modal preference (the position with the greatest number of supporters) or the average preference?

While there are no clear answers to these questions — and in spite of substantial criticism — linkage remains relevant to the evaluation of American democracy, for if public policy consistently fails to respond to the public's preferences on important issues one would be hard pressed to conclude that democracy is present. The major problems stem from the argument that concurrence is all there is to democracy, and that it is susceptible to straightforward and value-free measurement. Perhaps concurrence of opinion and policy should be considered one of several criteria for evaluating a system calling itself democratic. It should be employed as a standard, but only in conjunction with other standards, such as the procedures for decision making, the distribution of democratic values in the society, and the rights granted to those interests in the public that currently are out of power.

The Democratic Attributes of Public Opinion

Many scholars contend that for a democratic system to persist the public must support democratic principles.[24] Research examining the public's support for democratic principles has concentrated on political tolerance — the public's willingness to support general principles of freedom of speech and activity, and whether those principles should be extended to minorities in the system (e.g., atheists or communists). The major examinations of public support for democratic principles were conducted in the 1950s. The results suggested that nearly all Americans expressed support for the general principles of democracy, but that support often deteriorated when these principles were applied to specific groups.[25] That is, Americans exhibited a willingness to support the general principle of freedom of speech, but many found it difficult to support freedom of speech for communists in public school classrooms. These early studies found elites to possess attitudes substantially more democratic than the general public's when applying those principles to specific groups and situations. The conclusion was then forwarded by some that the American democratic system is not dependent on the opinions of the public, but rather on the opinions of the elite — those who are in power. The system is said to remain democratic precisely because those with the democratic attitudes are in power; the public's support for democratic principles provides only some general boundaries within which any elite nondemocratic tendencies are constrained.

The question of support for democratic principles is treated in much greater detail in Chapter 8. At this point, though, it is important to note that the above picture of the electorate's support for democratic principles has been challenged on a number of fronts. Some scholars have reinterpreted the earlier studies, arguing that the conclusions are incorrect that elite attitudes are more democratic than public attitudes, either because the public is better than it was described or because the elite is not as "good" as described. Other authors suggest that the earlier outline of the public was correct, but that now the public is much more democratic.[26] Regardless of the substantive conclusions, the frequency and tenor of the discussions about public support for democratic principles provide yet another link between public opinion and democracy, and therefore another reason to examine the implications of changes in public opinion for democracy.

Conceptions of democracy rarely fail to include some public participation in the political process. Through that participation, appropriate policy is produced, usually in line with the public's preferences. Yet it is often argued that for desirable policies to result, members of the participating public must meet the requirements of democratic citizenship. The "good" democratic citizen is supposed to be active in politics, to be well informed, to hold opinions about public issues and to relate those opinions to others in a consistent manner, and to employ rationally those opinions when evaluating political parties and candidates. In many people's minds, the extent to which the public meets those criteria determines the extent to which it is capable of playing its proper role in a democratic polity.

How well do Americans fit into this mold? The earliest studies of public opinion and voting behavior suggested to many observers that a large portion of the public was ill equipped to take up its prescribed role.[27] Compared to other western democracies, turnout in American elections was low. Half of all Americans were unable to identify their congressional representative. Americans were thought by some scholars to express their opinions about many major issues in a random fashion, reflecting no true underlying attitudes; to hold inconsistent opinions about important political issues; and to be unable to conceptualize politics in a relatively sophisticated manner. These early studies also found that the individual's choice among political parties was something handed down from parent to child, rather than derived from a systematic evaluation of the policy positions of the parties and their proximity to those of the individual. Similarly, individuals selected candidates based on party or group affiliation rather than on the candidates' positions on the issues.

As with other characteristics of the electorate, researchers are altering their conception of the public's unsuitability for participation in a democratic system. Many recent studies argue that the public does possess attitudes about political issues, that those attitudes are related to each other in a consistent manner, and that the public relates political issues to its choices of parties and candidates.[28]

What do these changes mean for ideal democratic citizens? One approach argues that the public now more fully meets the democratic ideal than it did before. Thus, it is suggested that the public has changed in a desirable direction. Another approach states that the public has been miscast, that the early picture of it as lacking in the appropriate democratic characteristics was drawn from misguided research methods and faulty theoretical concepts. Using the appropriate methods, researchers today can more accurately assess the public's favorable characteristics. A third explanation suggests that the nature of American politics has changed; politics is now more relevant to the public. Because it is more relevant, the public is more likely to exhibit the characteristics of an involved and capable democratic citizenry. Indeed, the public may in fact be demonstrating its rationality, its capacity for democratic citizenship, when it chooses not to respond to an irrelevant politics. A fourth approach contends that while the public has indeed changed, these changes are only superficial and do not suggest that the public is any more rational or democratic than in previous years. Rather, the public is only responding to different stimuli in the political environment and those stimuli happen to contain more acceptable cues than before.

This relationship between the characteristics of public opinion and participation in democratic political processes has two faces. On the one hand, we have been describing arguments about the public's fitness for that participation. On the other hand, there is the contention (which can be traced back at least as far as Jefferson) that participation in a democratic political process actually enhances the public's ability to meet the demands of a democratic citizenry.[29] That is, political participation is said to contribute to the public's understanding of politics and political issues, to its support for democratic principles and processes, and to its feelings of worth and competence. It is suggested that the more the public participates the better able it becomes to participate intelligently and effectively and, consequently, the more desirable will be the policies and the system that result.

Debate over the democratic qualities of the public continues, much of it centering on the nature and reasons for stability and change in those qualities. This book considers many of those elements of public opinion that have particular relevance for the "democratic citizen." In order to understand their nature, though, it is necessary to understand the meaning of the term *public opinion*. The next section takes up that concern.

WHAT IS PUBLIC OPINION?

The *concept* of public opinion has been in use for well over a thousand years.[30] In the course of that use, public opinion has been both praised and damned. It has been given reverential status and has been relegated to the back shelf of politics. Even with such a long history behind it, there still is no single, exact meaning of public opinion.

What is public opinion? Even though definitions abound, [31] it is difficult to mark public opinion's precise boundaries; the very frequency and variety of the term's use in scholarly discourse, political rhetoric, and everyday conversation obscures its meaning. Indeed, the meaning attached to public opinion depends on who uses it and why. The public official may think of the public as supporters in the last election. The leader of an interest group may see the public as the members of that organization. A voter may consider the public to be those like-minded people with whom he or she works and associates informally. Scholarly definitions likewise range broadly, from all individuals within a geographic boundary to all people interested in a specific issue, regardless of their geographic location.

Just as it is difficult to find a common meaning for public opinion, it also may be undesirable to offer a rigid definition. Such rigidity may lend an artificial inflexibility to an important part of a fundamentally fluid political process. The objects of public opinion — issues, events, groups, individuals, institutions — move in and out of the political arena. Moreover, our very conception of what constitutes politically relevant objects changes with time. A definition of public opinion, then, must be sufficiently fluid to encompass a range of *political* phenomena on which most observers and participants would agree at any given time. A definition of public opinion also will help set the scope and the limits of this book's discussions. It tells us what to look at and where to begin that search. Thus, we offer public opinion as a *collection of individual opinions about a political object*. While this definition is not unusual, it does raise some difficult questions. How does one decide which individuals should be included or excluded as part of the public (the collection of individuals)? What is meant by the term *opinion*?

The Public

There is no simple answer to the question of just who should be included in "the public." In order to answer the question one must establish some boundaries, so that some people are included and others are excluded. There is often disagreement about the appropriate way to demarcate these boundaries.

The most obvious criterion for including and excluding people from a public is the boundaries of governmental units: the public includes those people who live within recognized governmental boundaries. Thus, when one talks about "American public opinion" it is assumed that one is including people who live within the boundaries of the United States and excluding people who live elsewhere. The same is true of studies that describe public opinion in a particular state or compare opinions across the states. At least part of the working definition is the residence of the individual within the boundaries of the political unit with which the observer is concerned. One variation of this definition might focus on citizenship rather than residence. Thus, one could argue that the American public includes all citizens of the United States, regardless of where they live, and excludes noncitizens, even if they reside within the United States.

Sometimes not all people who live within the political boundaries of the United States or of specific states are included in the "public" of public opinion. People who are ineligible to vote may be excluded from the working definition of public. Studies of public opinion about major political issues or candidates usually do not include people who are too young to vote. On the other hand, there are cases in which young people become a legitimate object of inquiry for students of public opinion. Scholars often examine the opinions and preferences of young people when they are trying to determine the persistence of opinions from childhood through adulthood, or when the young are particularly active in politics.[32]

Some definitions of public specify the appropriate boundary as surrounding only those people who are affected by an issue. An example might be the issue of parity in agricultural prices for farmers. One rather restrictive meaning of the public would include only the people in agriculture who would benefit directly from an increase in income; yet others are affected by the issue in varying degrees. Change in the prices of agricultural products has an impact on processors, distributors, retailers, and consumers. Thus, when assessing the affected public one still is confronted with the question of where to draw the line in terms of the issue's impact.

A variation on the above distinction defines the public as those people who demonstrate an interest in a particular issue or in politics generally. More precisely, distinctions are made among different types of publics. Some scholars identify "issue publics," composed of people identifying an issue as one they especially care about, or lines are drawn between an "attentive public" and the remainder of a population, which is less concerned about politics.[33] The opinions of the attentive public may differ from those of the inattentive public. The attentive public is more likely to engage in political activity and to try to get its opinions translated into public policy. Thus, the opinions of the attentive public may have much more to do with what policies are adopted by government. The extent to which government decisions can be said to respond to public opinion, then, may depend on whether one is measuring the opinions of the attentive public or public opinion in general.

Pollsters and scholars often are circumscribed in their definition of public by the techniques they employ for obtaining and measuring opinions. Certain methods of acquiring public opinion data sometimes must be employed due to financial or physical restrictions. Thus, rather than personal interviews, many public opinion surveys are telephone interviews; the people interviewed are selected from existing telephone directories.[34] Such procedures automatically exclude people who have no telephone, who have unlisted numbers, or who have changed residence since the telephone directory was issued. To compensate for these problems, some survey companies employ random-digit dialing for survey purposes.[35] Telephone numbers are randomly generated by a computer, and in this way people with unlisted numbers or with new numbers have an equal chance for inclusion. Likewise, surveys based on face-to-face interviews of people permanently residing in households may eliminate potential members of the public, such as transients and residents of institutions. And one who is interested in finding out why the American public exhibits a certain opinion characteristic may be able to survey only the public in one city.

Thus, one is faced with a number of differing conceptions of "the public" in public opinion, and we have touched only some of them. The differences are important because the definition one chooses will determine the resulting description of public opinion. That is, the people excluded from the public may hold opinions that differ from those of the people included, and that exclusion may alter the overall distribution of opinions.

Differences in the definitions of the public also can hamper efforts to systematically build knowledge about the nature of public opinion. Studies with different definitions (because of different research concerns) are difficult to link to each other. Scientific research development is harder to achieve when the findings of different studies are based on the opinions of different publics.

What, then, is the appropriate criterion for including people in the public? For our purposes, there is no such thing as *the* public. Who makes up the public in any particular case depends on the purposes of the analyst; and the analyst must make clear both the purposes and the nature of the public. The analyst who is interested in explaining why nonvoting is on the increase may have a different working conception of the public than one who is interested in the changes of opinions and behavior of southern blacks. The relevant public also will depend on whether the concern is children's attitudes about government or Californians' attitudes about the rights of homosexuals. Any particular public is thus a consequence of what is politically important and what the observer is trying to explain.

Opinion

A second question deals with what constitutes an "opinion." For the purposes of this book, we employ a broad conception of opinion: a political opinion is any orientation of an individual to politics, *except for explicit behavior*. Some conceptions see an opinion as the simple expression of support for or opposition to a particular issue, policy, group, candidate, or event. Other views contain *any expression* of an individual, including such behaviors as voting or violent protest. Although behavior and opinion are related in many ways, we see them as distinct.[36] While excluding behavior, our definition includes many other kinds of individual orientations to politics within the concept of public "opinion." Our definition includes many different terms, such as personal values; political ideologies; evaluations of political organizations, individuals, and political issues; perceptions of one's role and impact in politics; and attitudes about the political system and its underlying principles.

Public opinion is a collection of individual opinions about some aspects of politics. The opinions of individuals — their orientations to politics — have certain attributes. Likewise, aggregations or collections of individual opinions possess certain important characteristics. Thus, we now turn to a discussion of the characteristics of individual opinions and of aggregate public opinions.[37]

Individual Opinion Characteristics

An initial distinction that should be made is whether or not people actually hold an opinion about a particular object. Rarely does one find an aspect of politics on which all individuals in a given public are willing to express themselves. And there surely are some esoteric or highly technical issues on which most people will admit to holding no opinion. Thus, people can be compared according to whether they hold opinions on a given issue and the number of issues on which they hold opinions.

A more difficult question with which scholars have wrestled is whether people *expressing* an opinion really *hold* an opinion. It has been suggested that many expressed opinions are simply responses to the stimulus of the interview, with the respondent trying to please the interviewer or to save face by not seeming uninterested or uninformed.[38] As a result, some survey organizations include questions designed to screen out people with no previously formed opinion on an issue. Others attempt to assess the presence of an opinion by panel studies, studies in which the respondent is asked the same question at different times. Unstable responses (those in which the individual expresses a different opinion on the same issue at different times) are suspected of representing random expressions and not real attitudes.[39] Chapter 6 will consider some of the problems in segregating these "nonattitude" responses from those that represent true opinions. For the moment, though, it is sufficient to note that in most public opinion studies the individual's expressed opinion is considered valid.

The *direction* of an opinion is whether it is favorable or unfavorable toward its object, or if choosing among alternatives, which choice is made. If one is asked to identify with a political party, either Republican or Democrat, direction is the choice between the two. Similarly, one may identify in the liberal or conservative direction. Direction also is present in the evaluation of policy statements, when the individual indicates that he or she is favorable or unfavorable, pro or con, agrees or disagrees, or favors more or less spending.

The *extremity* of an opinion reflects how far the individual favors going in a particular direction. Extremity indicates how liberal or conservative the ideology, how Democratic or Republican the partisan identification, how favorable or unfavorable the position on the political issue, or how much more or less spending is preferred.[40] Thus, for example, Figure 1–1 shows how in 1976 the ideological orientations of the public were arrayed along a single dimension, the poles of which are extreme liberal and extreme conservative, and the middle of which is moderate. The direction of the individual's ideological feeling is indicated by the sign (+ or −), and the extremity is shown by the number attached to the sign. Clearly, then, people who share the direction of an opinion may differ considerably in the extremity of that opinion.

FIGURE 1–1   The Distribution of the Direction and Extremity of the American Public's Ideological Identification in 1976

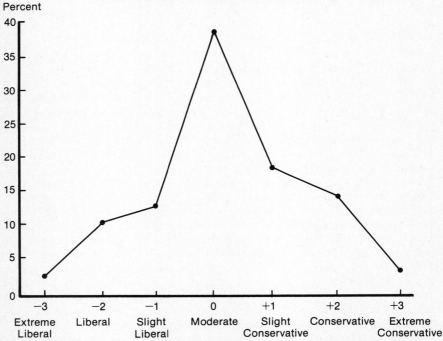

Source: Center for Political Studies. American National Election Study, 1976 [machine-readable data file].

Opinions also differ in their *centrality* — their psychological importance to the individual.[41] Central opinions play a greater role in determining opinions about other objects.[42] For example, for many people religious opinions are very central and thus they shape or "color" many of their opinions about nonreligious objects. For other people an opinion about the political party with which they identify may be quite central to their opinions about political candidates (they like the candidates of their own party) or political issues (they like the issues promoted by their political party). On the other hand, an opinion about a particular issue of public policy may be so central that it governs the individual's choice of political party or electoral candidate.

Aggregate Opinion Characteristics

The aggregation or grouping of individual opinions into a public also has distinguishing characteristics. One aggregate opinion characteristic is the percentage of people in a given public with opinions on an issue. Just as people can be compared according to whether or not they have an opinion on an issue, or the number of issues on which they have opinions, the percentage of people within publics who hold opinions also can be compared. These comparisons can be made across time, across issues, and across publics. Thus, the percentage having opinions about environmental protection may be greater after a major oil spill. Greater percentages of a given public may have opinions about whether the president is doing a good job than have opinions about some complex and intricate alteration in the tax code. And the public in Idaho certainly will be more likely than the public in Louisiana to have opinions about the diversion of Snake River waters to the arid Southwest.

Another major aggregate opinion characteristic is the *distribution* of opinions among a public. This is the number or percentage of individual opinions in each category of direction and extremity. On a question of the public's evaluation of the job performance of the incumbent president, the distribution of opinions might appear in a form similar to the following:

Excellent	40%
Good	30
Fair	20
Poor	10
Total	100%

The distributions of a public's opinion preferences can be compared in several ways. The distribution for a single question can be compared across publics, as in comparing the distributions of the American public to that of the Canadian public in their preferences for the involvement of government in social welfare activities. The distribution of the same public can be compared at different points in time for the same opinion, as in the percentage opposing the Vietnam War in 1965 and 1972. Figure 1–2 shows how the same public's distribution can be compared across different issues.

The direction and extremity of public opinions are described in terms of the level of *consensus* and the level of *polarization*. Consensus refers to the degree to which a public agrees in the direction and extremity of opinions on a particular object, while polarization refers to the nature of the dispersion or disagreement among a public's opinions. Just how much agreement there must be to conclude that a "consensus" exists is unclear. Some authors have suggested that 75 percent agreement might be an appropriate figure.[43] The crucial question, however, is not what precise figure constitutes a consensus, but whether differences in consensus levels have any political consequences. For example, are countries with higher levels of consensus less likely to experience significant amounts of political violence?

FIGURE 1 – 2 The Percentage Distribution of the American Public's Opinions on Four Issues: 1976

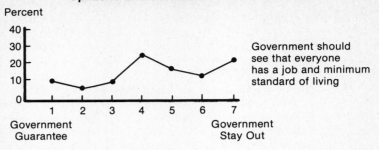

Government should see that everyone has a job and minimum standard of living

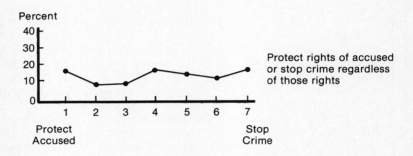

Protect rights of accused or stop crime regardless of those rights

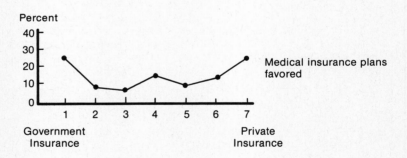

Medical insurance plans favored

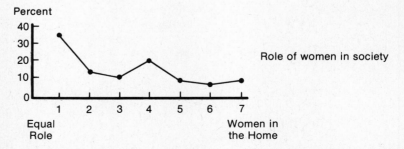

Role of women in society

Source: Center for Political Studies. American National Election Study, 1976 [machine-readable data file].

Again we return to V.O. Key, Jr., who has argued that there are different kinds of consensus, and that they do have different political implications.[44] According to Key, "supportive" consensus is that which "underpins existing politics and practice"; "permissive" consensus allows the government to formulate policy without fear of negative reactions from the public; and "decisive" consensus is where the government responds directly to the public's preferences.[45] Thus, the same distribution, such as widespread agreement on an issue of public opinion, can have widely differing political implications, depending on the nature of the consensus, and this nature is largely a function of the intensity with which the individuals in the public hold their opinions. Intensely held consensual opinions may force the government into action consistent with the direction of the opinions, while weakly held opinions may allow the government to engage in certain formulations of policy, but not demand that it do so.

Estimating the level of consensus also has political uses. That is, participants in the political process may employ the perception of a consensus in public opinion supporting their views as one of the reasons for the superiority in their position. Terrence Cook describes this use of public opinion as

> an appeal to the quantity of persons holding the view, with any qualitative distinctions largely limited to defining the relevant public rather than assessment of the relative merits of members of that public. Subtypes may be categorized in terms of the scale of the public (e.g., national opinion, world opinion) or its location in time (present oriented appeals, bandwagon appeals to a supposedly emerging majority opinion, or historical absolution appeals to such a majority expected to crystallize in the future). Or subtypes could be distinguished as informal or formal, with the latter referring to the legally binding concurrence within the electorate as public.[46]

Whether for appeals in political arguments or for assessments of the impact of public opinion on public policy, measuring the level of consensus in public opinion is subject to some arbitrary methodological manipulations. The level of consensus can be a function of the number of categories on which public opinion is distributed. For example, one may be interested in the level of consensus regarding the proper role for women in American society. As shown in Figure 1-3, each respondent was asked to indicate an opinion on a scale from one to seven. No category receives support from more than a third of the public. However, a much larger consensus can be created by combining categories. One might, for example, combine categories 1, 2, and 3 into a "support" category, categories 5, 6, and 7 into an opposition category, and leave category 4 as an undecided or middle category. Such collapsing would result in 60 percent in the "equal role" category and the appearance of much greater agreement. Thus, consensus in collective opinions of a public is a function not only of the opinions of the public, but also of the instrument measuring those opinions.

Polarization in an opinion is the extent to which the opinions are both divided and concentrated at the extremes of the opinion dimension. In Figure 1-2 the polarization is greatest on the issue of medical insurance policies.

Only on that issue of the four are there substantially greater percentages at *both* extremes than in any of the intervening categories. One might conclude, then, that there is potential for great conflict in the public on the issue, and that there is little room for compromise, since the two sets of opinions are widely separated. Yet the level of conflict generated by the polarization will also depend on how strongly the public feels about its opinions and on the opportunity for the opinions to be converted into political action, such as the issue being important in a presidential election campaign. If the opinions are not strongly held or there is no opportunity for political action based on them, then polarization may not create conflict.

The level of polarization one finds in the public, like the level of consensus, depends both on the public's opinions and on the questions eliciting the responses. If only two alternative responses are provided to the respondents, and the public splits 50-50, one might conclude that the public is polarized. However, if six alternative positions are allowed and the public is distributed among the six alternatives with 30 percent at each of the two middle positions ("3" and "4"), 15 percent in positions "2" and "5," and 5 percent in the two extreme positions, one would not interpret the presence of polarization. Yet dividing the latter distribution down the middle would suggest that there is a split of major proportions in the public, even though a majority of the public resides in adjacent locations ("3" and "4").

Another characteristic of opinion aggregates is the extent to which a public's opinions on one issue are related to its opinions on another issue. The question here is whether people who share an opinion on Issue A also share an opinion on Issue B. For example, do we find that people who oppose nuclear power production are more likely to support wilderness preservation than are people who support nuclear power production? Framed another way, in a given public, what is the level of *consistency* among the public's responses on different issues?[47] If the opinions on different issues are related to each other, if people who share an opinion on one issue share an opinion on another issue, those issues *may* be seen by members of the public to share some common elements or dimension. An example of a perfect relationship, where everyone who shares an opinion on one issue also shares an opinion on another issue is shown below.

Issue A

		Agree	Undecided	Disagree
	Agree	100%	0	0
Issue B	Undecided	0	100%	0
	Disagree	0	0	100%
		100%	100%	100%

In this example, everyone who agrees with issue statement A also agrees with issue statement B, and likewise for the undecided and disagree positions. At the aggregate level, then, there is consistency in the relationship among opinions on different issues.

Table 1-1 shows examples of cases in which opinions are unrelated (low consistency) and moderately related for a public. In Table 1-1, knowing a person's ideology is very little help in determining whether that person agrees or disagrees that government wastes a lot of taxes. There is very little consistency, for people whose opinions differ on one issue do not necessarily differ on the second issue.

TABLE 1-1   Examples of Low and Moderate Aggregate Consistency Among Opinions: Ideology and Two Issues in 1976

Low Aggregate Consistency

Government Tax Waste	Ideology		
	Liberal	Moderate	Conservative
Not Much	0%	2%	0%
Some	27	21	19
A Lot	72	77	81
TOTAL	99%	100%	100%
N	(958)	(714)	(724)

Moderate Aggregate Consistency

Government Guarantee School Integration	Ideology		
	Liberal	Moderate	Conservative
Pro Government Involvement	59%	35%	28%
Government Stay Out	41%	65%	72%
TOTAL	100%	100%	100%
N	(327)	(455)	(511)

Source: Center for Political Studies. American National Election Study, 1976 [machine-readable data file].

CONCLUSION

Contrasting patterns of stability and change provide the focal point for recent analyses of the dynamics of American public opinion. In this chapter we have reviewed the reasons why these patterns are important to study. We also have identified several characteristics of opinions — both for individuals and for groups of individuals — that are used to plot patterns of change and stability. The following chapter explores the major kinds of explanations for recent patterns in American public opinion and describes the processes through which different combinations of change and stability take place.

NOTES

1. For examples, see the following more extended treatments of various aspects of that change: Philip E. Converse, "Change in the American Electorate," in *The Human Meaning of Social Change,* Angus Campbell and Philip E. Converse, eds. (New York: Russell Sage, 1972), pp. 263–337; Philip E. Converse, "Public Opinion and Voting Behavior," in *Handbook of Political Science,* vol. 4, Fred Greenstein

and Nelson Polsby, eds. (Reading, Mass.: Addison-Wesley, 1975), pp. 75–171; Ronald Inglehart, *The Silent Revolution* (Princeton: Princeton University Press, 1977); Warren E. Miller and Teresa E. Levitin, *Leadership and Change* (Cambridge, Mass.: Winthrop, 1976); Norman H. Nie, Sidney Verba, and John R. Petrocik, *The Changing American Voter* (Cambridge, Mass.: Harvard University Press, 1976); and Gerald Pomper, *Voters' Choice* (New York: Dodd, Mead & Co., 1975).

2. V.O. Key, Jr., *Public Opinion and American Democracy* (New York: Alfred A. Knopf, 1965), p. 535.

3. Heinz Eulau, *The Behavioral Persuasion in Politics* (New York: Random House, 1963), p. 3.

4. David Mayhew, *Congress: The Electoral Connection* (New Haven, Conn.: Yale University Press, 1974).

5. Richard E. Neustadt, *Presidential Power* (New York: John Wiley & Sons, 1960); George C. Edwards, *Presidential Influence in Congress* (San Francisco: W.H. Freeman, 1979).

6. See the discussion of incentives to organizational membership in James Q. Wilson, *Political Organization* (New York: Basic Books, 1973), pp. 30–55.

7. See the discussion of the relationship between public policy and public opinion (especially in Chapters 2 and 3) in George C. Edwards III and Ira Sharkansky, *The Policy Predicament: Making and Implementing Policy* (San Francisco: W.H. Freeman, 1978).

8. Gabriel Almond and Sidney Verba, *The Civic Culture* (Boston: Little, Brown & Co., 1965), p. 341.

9. Key, *Public Opinion and American Democracy*, p. 536.

10. Alan D. Monroe, *Public Opinion in America* (New York: Dodd, Mead & Co., 1975), p. 6.

11. For an example of recent textbooks on public opinion concentrating on the relationship between public opinion and public policy, see Robert Weissberg, *Public Opinion and Popular Government* (Englewood Cliffs, N.J.: Prentice-Hall, 1976). Perhaps the most extensive analysis of the conditions under which concurrence between public opinion and the opinions of leaders develops is found in Sidney Verba and Norman H. Nie, *Participation in America: Political Democracy and Social Equality* (New York: Harper & Row, 1972).

12. Norman R. Luttbeg, ed., *Public Opinion and Public Policy* (Homewood, Ill.: Dorsey Press, 1974), p. 3.

13. E.E. Schattschneider, *Party Government* (New York: Holt, Rinehart and Winston, 1942), p. 1.

14. See the critique of the American party system in Michael P. Lerner, "The Future of the Two-Party System in America," in *1984 Revisited: Prospects for American Politics*, Robert Paul Wolff, ed. (New York: Alfred A. Knopf, 1973), pp. 113–38.

15. For the classic statements of the group process, see: Arthur F. Bentley, *The Process of Government* (Evanston, Ill.: Principia Press, 1908); and David B. Truman, *The Governmental Process* (New York: Alfred A. Knopf, 1951). For recent analyses, see: Wilson, *Political Organizations;* and Mancur Olson, Jr., *The Logic of Collective Action* (Cambridge, Mass.: Harvard University Press, 1965).

16. Richard L. Cole, *Citizen Participation and the Urban Policy Process* (Lexington, Mass.: Lexington Books, 1974).

17. John C. Pierce and Harvey R. Doerksen, eds., *Water Politics and Public Involvement* (Ann Arbor, Mich.: Ann Arbor Science, 1976).

18. Charles M. Price, "The Initiative: A Comparative State Analysis and Reassessment of a Western Phenomenon," *Western Political Quarterly* 28 (June 1975), pp. 243–62.

19. Frank P. Weaver and Charles H. Sheldon, *Politicians, Judges and the People: The Politics of Participation* (Westport, Conn.: Greenwood Press, 1980).
20. Robert H. Cushman, "Real-Time, Two-Way Communications Between Citizens and Leaders," *EDN Magazine* (June 1, 1969), pp. 28, 112–13; Robert Paul Wolff, *In Defense of Anarchism* (New York: Harper & Row, 1970), pp. 34–37.
21. John E. Mueller, *War, Presidents and Public Opinion* (New York: John Wiley & Sons, 1973), p. 69.
22. Maxwell E. McCombs and Donald L. Shaw, "The Agenda-Setting Function of Mass Media," *Public Opinion Quarterly* (Summer 1972), pp. 178–87; Byron Shafer and Richard Larson, "Did TV Create the 'Social Issue'?," *Columbia Journalism Review* II (September/October 1972), pp. 10–17.
23. See the discussions in Verba and Nie, *Participation in America*, pp. 302–4; Weissberg, *Public Opinion and Popular Government*, pp. 81–93; and Anne L. Schneider, "Measuring Political Responsiveness: A Comparison of Several Alternative Methods," in *Water Politics and Public Involvement*, Pierce and Doerksen, eds., pp. 87–115.
24. See the analysis of this position in Robert Dahl, *Who Governs?* (New Haven, Conn.: Yale University Press, 1961), pp. 311–25.
25. McClosky, "Consensus and Ideology in American Politics," *American Political Science Review* 58 (June 1964), pp. 361–82; James W. Prothro and Charles M. Grigg, "Fundamental Principles of Democracy," *Journal of Politics* 22 (Spring 1960), pp. 276–94; and Samuel A. Stouffer, *Communism, Conformity and Civil Liberties* (Garden City, N.Y.: Doubleday, 1955).
26. See the review of critiques of the traditional view in Chapter 8.
27. For one example, see Bernard R. Berelson, Paul F. Lazarsfeld, and William N. McPhee, *Voting* (Chicago: University of Chicago Press, 1954), p. 311.
28. Pomper, *Voters' Choice*.
29. See the discussion in Carole Patemen, *Participation and Democratic Theory* (London: Cambridge University Press, 1970).
30. George Boas, *Vox Populi: Essays in the History of an Idea* (Baltimore: Johns Hopkins University Press, 1969).
31. For various approaches, see the discussions in Converse, "Public Opinion and Voting Behavior," and Bernard C. Hennessey, *Public Opinion,* 3rd ed. (North Scituate, Mass.: Duxbury Press, 1975), pp. 3–11.
32. See Chapter 4, which discusses changes in patterns of political socialization.
33. See Donald J. Devine, *The Attentive Public: Polyarchical Democracy* (Chicago: Rand McNally, 1970).
34. Don A. Dillman, *Mail and Telephone Surveys: The Total Design Method* (New York: John Wiley & Sons, 1978).
35. Paul A. Scipione, "Random Digit Dialing," *Sampler* (Fall 1978), p. 3.
36. Milton J. Rosenberg, Carl I. Hovland, William J. McGuire, Robert P. Abelson and Jack W. Brehm, *Attitude Organization and Change* (New Haven, Conn.: Yale University Press, 1960), p. 3.
37. See the related discussion in Robert E. Lane and Robert O. Sears, *Public Opinion* (Englewood Cliffs, N.J.: Prentice-Hall, 1964), pp. 5–16.
38. Philip E. Converse, "Comment: The Status of Nonattitudes," *American Political Science Review* 68 (June 1974), p. 650.
39. Philip E. Converse, "The Nature of Belief Systems in Mass Publics," in *Ideology and Discontent,* David E. Apter, ed. (Glencoe: Free Press, 1964), pp. 238–45.
40. There are two conceptions of extremity in an opinion, absolute and relative. Absolute extremity is based on the assumption that the ideological dimension is "real," with real end points. Extreme opinions are those near the end points. The labeling

of an opinion as extreme is in reference to the absolute nature of the opinion object. The relative extremity of an opinion is determined in reference to the distribution of opinions. An opinion is extreme if it is distant from the bulk of other opinions expressed by the public. If the bulk of the public's opinions are at an end-point (e.g., extreme liberal), someone extreme in an absolute sense would not be extreme in a relative sense.

41. Carolyn W. Sherif, Musafer Sherif and R.C. Nebergall, *Attitude and Attitude Change: The Social Judgment Approach* (Philadelphia: Saunders, 1965).

42. Milton Rokeach, *Beliefs, Attitudes and Values* (San Francisco: Jossey-Bass, 1972), p. 5.

43. McClosky, "Consensus and Ideology in American Politics," p. 363.

44. V.O. Key, Jr., *Public Opinion and American Democracy,* pp. 27–53.

45. Ibid., pp. 29–37.

46. Terrence E. Cook, "Political Justifications: The Use of Standards in Political Appeals," *Journal of Politics* 42 (1980), pp. 515–16.

47. See Chapter 7 on political thinking for an extended discussion of recent inquiries into the public's belief consistency across issues.

CHAPTER 2

THE DYNAMICS OF PUBLIC OPINION

Public opinion reveals much about the impact of events, issues, and personalities on a political system. It provides a basis for evaluating the responsiveness of a political process and conveys information about the democratic qualities of the American public. Yet, if we are to fully understand public opinion we must probe its *dynamics*. The analysis of public opinion's dynamics pivots on three key concepts: the *patterns* of public opinion, the *explanations* of those patterns, and the *processes* through which those patterns are produced.

The *patterns* of public opinion refer to stability and change in the individual and collective shape or distribution of opinions. An example of a stable pattern has been the constant level of public support for and opposition to school integration over the past twenty years. A fluid public opinion pattern has been the electorate's declining confidence in political parties. The next section provides a brief overview of recent patterns in American public opinion.

The *explanations* of opinion dynamics are the reasons offered for the particular patterns by researchers attempting to answer the question, Why? What forces produced the decline in public support for American political parties? Was it because of television, or was it because of Watergate? Why have opinions about school integration remained stable in the face of sweeping legal and social changes in the past two decades? The second section of this chapter examines the major kinds of explanations for recent opinion patterns, grouping them into three categories: systemic, leadership, and individual.

The *processes* of opinion dynamics refer to the *way* in which the forces driving public opinion are translated into patterns of opinion change and stability. Do we find that the decline in support for political parties is the result of a large number of people changing their opinions about the parties? Or, instead, has there been an entry into the electorate of groups of voters with

more cynical attitudes about the parties? Is the stability of individual opinions about school integration the result of a rational evaluation of information, or does it stem from some deep-seated personality needs? The third section of this chapter examines these and other processes through which patterns of opinion change and stability are produced.

PUBLIC OPINION PATTERNS

Many characteristics of public opinion seem to have changed in recent years.[1]
This pattern of change has dominated scholarly discourse. At the same time,
however, significant elements of stability remained. This section provides an
overview of some of the major public opinion patterns.

The Political Agenda

The past two decades have seen a continual evolution in the issues dominating the public's political agenda.[2] There has been a constant flux in the issues
the public perceives to be the most important and around which their political evaluations and behaviors revolve. The 1950s and early 1960s were dominated by concern with New Deal issues and international conflict growing out
of the aftermath of World War II. But the New Deal issues were largely displaced in the mind of the public as civil rights issues assumed a place of
prominence in the mid-1960s. The Vietnam War also came to dominate much
of the issue agenda. Environmental issues soared to the forefront of public
attention, and women's liberation and the equal rights movement became the
center of much conflict and controversy. There has been relatively consistent
dispute over rather pervasive changes in life-style and fundamental political
values, often manifest in the "new politics."[3] The public has become cynical
and skeptical about the honesty of public officials and about the power and
ability of government to solve major problems.[4] The size of government and
the "tax revolt" are major items of public discussion. In the late 1970s, pre-
saged by the oil boycott of 1973, the energy crisis captured public concern.
In the early 1980s, much of the 1970s agenda remained intact, but newly
prominent issues also clamored for attention — e.g., Iran, Afghanistan,
and inflation, the latter refocusing attention on some of the old themes
of the New Deal days.

There is little question, then, that in the mind of the public the agenda of
American politics has undergone substantial redefinition. Many new issues
captured the attention of the American public. Some of those issues were
rather short-lived, while others have become permanent fixtures, sharing the
limelight with the ebb and flow of traditional public concerns.

Public's Political Thinking

According to many scholars, the public has changed the *way* it thinks about
politics; it has become more consistent and sophisticated.

Although there is disagreement, and chapter 7 will discuss the bases for
that disagreement, a number of studies suggest that in the 1960s and 1970s
the public's opinion became more consistent.[5] There is some indication that

knowing how someone feels about one issue seems to provide a better prediction of how that person will feel about other issues. Some people say the public has become more enlightened, while others believe scholars now more accurately measure opinions and their consistency with each other. Moreover, there apparently was an increase in the public's political sophistication in recent years.[6] There is clear evidence that in the 1960s and 1970s greater numbers of Americans evaluated political figures and issues in ideological terms, particularly when the candidates and parties proffered ideological alternatives during elections.

Party Support and Vote Choice

The public's attachment to the two major political parties has declined substantially.[7] The public has grown more negative about the political parties. Many more people now call themselves "Independent," rejecting association with the Republicans and Democrats. They think the parties do little to help control government, and that the parties cannot be trusted. People are less likely to use the party label as a reason for voting for or against a candidate. Instead, more people focus on individuals, defecting from their own party and voting for candidates of both parties.[8]

Consistent with the decline in party support there has been a shift in the reasons people choose to vote for a particular candidate. One's party identification had been the best predictor of a person's vote during the 1950s and early 1960s. In the 1960s and early 1970s the public's views of candidates' abilities and the public's opinions on issues rose to explain a considerable share of the vote choice.[9] In the later 1970s, though, there is some indication that the parties regained some of their importance in people's choices. The fluctuations in the causes of people's votes, and the changing character of candidates and issues, has created less predictability as to how any particular person will vote. It also has created less certainty about the outcome of a particular election.

Opinion Sources

There also have been some major alterations in the ways people acquire their opinions. The growth in the importance of television as a source of political information is well documented.[10] The role of television newspeople in forming opinions became an issue in the early 1970s. The mass media are said to play an important role in setting the political agenda—deciding which issues are important topics of discussion. Television advertising is a central element in election campaigning. Concurrently, some observers argue that in many areas the family's influence on the opinions of children apparently has weakened, being supplanted by television and peers.

Stability and Change: A Review

Considerable evidence suggests that the public has redefined the political agenda. It has changed the direction of some important opinions, altered the way it thinks about certain issues, changed its feelings about the parties, shifted its emphases in making candidate choices, and substituted some new sources of opinions for old ones.

This picture of a changed and changing public in the 1960s and 1970s stands in rather stark contrast to the portrait painted in the 1950s. The 1950s public seemed to be predictable and stable in its political opinions and in its political behavior. This stability was thought to be one of the strengths of the American system, protecting it from sudden political and social upheavals. These relatively fixed characteristics of the public also provided a constant base on which political organizations — parties and interest groups — could operate. Political activists could find certainty in the political arena, at least where the public was involved. One of the differences of the new public is that it is less predictable. Political interests may be less certain of their support in the public. New issues may strike a responsive chord, providing the basis for third parties, public interest organizations, and single-issue movements.

This discussion has emphasized changes in public opinion patterns, particularly in the last two decades. Despite these changes, however, there remains an underlying current of stability. This stability prevails in two areas.

First, stability *is* present in the opinions of the American public. While many people changed their opinions, many others did not. Changes in the opinions of a relatively small portion of the public may have substantial political implications, and we understandably tend to focus on the change. For example, one-fifth of the public may forgo the Democrats and become Republicans, clearly altering the American political system in rather substantial ways. Yet we cannot ignore the fact that four-fifths of the public has remained stable, and that their stability is important for the political system. It also is important to remember that just as the glare from the changes of a small segment of the public may blind us to a much larger but less dazzling display of stability in the rest of the public, so may the changes in a particular opinion obscure stability in many others. Instability in party identification may be so engrossing that we overlook little change in the distribution of the public's political ideology. We must be wary of some well-documented and highly touted changes leading to a misplaced conclusion that nothing has stayed the same.

Second, stability and continuity also exist in the *explanation* of changes in opinions. To explain *why* change has occurred one must assume some persevering relationships between public opinion and its sources. The reasons for public opinion's transformations and for its persistence provide a constant in American public opinion. The public's beliefs about political issues may have become more consistent. This change in consistency may be explained by a change in the consistency of the positions on issues as they are argued in the political arena. Thus, the increase (change) in opinion consistency is explained by the *stable* relationship between public opinion and the world of politics. What is constant is that the relationship among opinions will reflect the content of politics.

EXPLANATIONS OF OPINION PATTERNS

How can we explain the recent patterns of stability and change in American public opinion? As one would expect, explanations are almost as numerous as the identifiable patterns of public opinion. Some of the explanations are far-reaching, linking public opinion to the fundamental characteristcs of society, while others are substantially more modest in scope. This section summarizes the major kinds of explanations of recent opinion patterns: environmental, leadership, and individual.

Environmental/Systemic Explanations

Many analyses of public opinion center on the importance of the social and economic environment within which opinions are formed and expressed. In these views, public opinion can be understood only or largely in terms of the system-wide environment that surrounds it. As the character of those systems changes, so will public opinion.

One example of an environmental explanation of recent patterns of public opinion is *postindustrialism*.[11] According to this view, Western society has changed considerably in recent decades. It has become a postindustrial society characterized by

> *affluence; advanced technological development; the central importance of knowledge, national communication processes, the growing prominence and independence of culture; new occupational structures, and with them new lifestyles and expectations. . . .*[12]

These changes in society are important because they have altered the public's fundamental values (what people most want out of life and how they want to get it).[13] These changes in what people want — what they value — profoundly affect public opinion.[14] The public's political opinions express what people value and how they want to obtain those values in politics. The relationship can be summarized this way:

Environmental/   Public
Systemic Conditions⟶Values⟶Public Opinion

A person's values are said to reflect the extent to which fundamental needs have been satisfied, and the level of that satisfaction often depends on the political, social, and economic environment within which one lives.[15] If basic physiological needs are unmet, the individual will place a high value on objects that will satisfy those needs. If basic needs are met, then one will value higher-level needs, such as self-esteem, belonging, and aesthetics. But people's present values often reflect environmental conditions at the time they first acquired and cemented their fundamental orientations to the world — during childhood and youth. Even if environmental conditions change, a person is likely to retain values acquired under the earlier system. Thus, people who acquired their values in times of economic need and global warfare will express political preferences designed to satisfy physiological and safety needs, even if peace and prosperity now reign. However, people who acquire their values during peace and prosperity will emphasize issues and preferences designed to obtain satisfaction of needs for belonging, self-esteem, or aesthetics, and will de-emphasize political alternatives meeting physiological and safety needs.

In periods of long-term stability in environmental conditions, there will be stability in the distribution of political preferences. However, when environmental conditions change the stage is set for conflict. People raised under different environmental conditions will have different values and different opinions as to how to achieve the preferred values.

This postindustrial explanation has been used to explain much of the conflict among generations in the 1960s and 1970s.[16] It was argued that the younger generation — particularly the favored portions in higher education — had been raised in a period of relative peace and economic security. Thus, they held "higher-level" values emphasizing a beautiful world, political and social equality, and other public concerns. On the other hand, the "older" generation's values for the most part were rooted in the Great Depression of the 1930s and in World War II. They were more concerned with national and economic security than with social and political freedom and equality — at least when the two were seen to directly conflict with each other. Thus, conflicts over civil rights, women's liberation, the Vietnam War, the physical environment, and more open political processes were all seen to grow out of difference in political values rooted in sharply contrasting environmental conditions.

Postindustrialism is only one of a number of explanations of public opinion that emphasize the role of the political, social, and economic environment. Yet it is a good example of how these environmental explanations attempt to account for stability and change in patterns of public opinion.

Political Leadership

Many studies identify political leaders as key causes of public opinion. Political leaders can contribute both to stability and to change in public opinion, although recent explanations have concentrated on the role of leaders in opinion change. Thus Warren Miller and Teresa Levitin write that

> issues became more structured and opinions became more abstract with the electorate principally because the quality of political leadership changed between the early 1950s and the late 1960s.[17]

Through what processes do political leaders exercise such control over public opinion, and how did they create such changes in recent public opinion?

Political leadership explanations argue that the public is fundamentally dependent on others, especially leaders, for guidance through the maze of political issues, events, and personalities. There just are too many issues and events with which to deal for the average American to be expected to make much sense out of them. Not only are there many issues, but a lot of them are very technical and complex. Who in the general public has the motivation, the time, or the expertise to come up with a reasonable opinion on each important issue? Certainly not the average citizen. Thus, each individual turns to someone who can be trusted for guidance as to how best to respond to a political issue. People turn to political leaders who have been reliable guides in the past, who seem to have their general best interest at heart.

Political leaders do more than just provide cues to their followers in the general public. They also structure the political world to which the public must respond. The public's evaluations of politics are at least partially determined by the actions of the political leaders who structure that politics.

The nature of political conflict, the foundations of divisions among competing interests, the clarity of the political choices available to the public, the responsiveness of the political system to public opinion — these and many more consequences of political leaders' performance have the potential to affect public opinion.

Many of the recent patterns in public opinion are traced directly to leadership behavior, especially in the search for the reasons for apparent *changes* in public opinion.

What was the nature of the change in leadership behavior that occasioned such a widely heralded response in the general public? Many writers suggest that the most important leadership action was an increasing clarification and polarization of issue positions, particularly within the context of presidential election politics.[18] In 1964 Barry Goldwater made "A Choice, Not an Echo" his campaign theme, and he staked out policy positions distinct from those of Lyndon Johnson. For the first time in over a decade substantial policy differences between the two major candidates were emphasized and became the major focus of the campaign. This made it easier for the public to distinguish between the two major parties on political issues.[19] The ideological rhetoric of Republican conservatism triggered an increase in the percentage of the electorate evaluating the parties and candidates in ideological terms.[20]

In 1968 two presidential candidates, Eugene McCarthy and George Wallace, formed additional issue-based alternatives. While neither captured the nomination of one of the two major political parties, both based their campaigns on issues — Vietnam for McCarthy, law and order for Wallace — and both struck a responsive chord in portions of the public. Moreover, a nation watched as the Democratic convention was torn by conflict among its leaders. During the same period, many other issues became the basis for conflict among political leaders: the power of government, the environment, civil rights and race relations, solutions to the problems of the inner cities.

In the 1972 election the McGovern candidacy continued the issue-based themes of the previous two elections. McGovern claimed rather distinct policy positions on Vietnam, national defense, social welfare, and equal rights for blacks and women. The public again was offered a clear choice. The 1972 presidential election was followed in short order by the Watergate revelations, and the issue of leadership morality dominated the 1976 campaign.

This same period witnessed heightened activity by new kinds of groups and organizations. This activity took two main forms. First, there developed a series of "public interest groups," the most prominent being Common Cause and those headed by Ralph Nader.[21] These groups focused on a number of specific political issues and attempted to raise the public consciousness about those issues. They became an additional source of information and positions on important political issues. Similarly, there was a great expansion of membership in environmental organizations and the creation of many new environmental groups.[22] These groups lobbied government in support of particular public policies and tried to influence the beliefs and perceptions of the American public. The leaders of these organizations became important sources of views of the political world for both their followers and their opponents.

Second, there also was a substantial increase in ethnic consciousness, most notably among black Americans. Black activism and organizational support for the civil rights movement heightened awareness of racial issues. Central to this movement and to the articulation of major policy positions were the leaders of the civil rights movement. Similar phenomena occurred in the women's rights movement, the Chicano movement, and the Native American movement. In each area major figures emerged who provided a focus for the attention and allegiance of followers, as well as a clarification of policy alternatives for all Americans. Thus, through their organizations and through the media, these nonelectoral leaders played a major role in the changing response of the public to politics.

During the last decade and a half political leaders took distinct and firmly anchored policy positions. These policy positions were clearly communicated to the public, and the conflicts among the leaders were framed in precise and ideologically coherent packages. The development of television as a medium of mass communication clearly enhanced the ease and the ability with which political leaders' positions on issues could be transmitted to the public. Consequently, it is argued, it was easy for the public to identify the issue and ideological bases of political conflict among the leaders and to follow the cues provided for them in that conflict.

The public appeared to respond to the leaders' changes in many ways. It followed cues as to the most important problems facing the country, such as the law-and-order argument of George Wallace. The public increased in ideological thinking, or at least in employing ideological terms to evaluate parties and candidates. Better able to distinguish the issue positions of the major political parties, the public was more likely to employ issues in their choices among political parties and candidates. It became critical of the political parties, seeing them as ineffective in solving the problems identified by leaders or providing unacceptable answers to those problems. The public's positions on a number of political issues became substantially more consistent with each other than in prior years. And the public, apparently in response to the inability of government and political leaders to deal with the issues, exhibited rapidly growing cynicism.

The widespread agreement about the importance of political leaders does not extend to interpretations of the leader-public relationship. On one side is the position that the public's response to leaders has been an informed one, based on a rational reaction to the leaders' political activities.[23] The public needed only to have available a clear picture of the country's politics in order to evaluate the political alternatives, to relate them consistently to individual interests, and to relate issues consistently to each other. On the other side is the theme that the public has indeed responded to changes in leadership behavior, but not because of its rationality. Instead, the public depends on leaders to define the political questions *and* to provide the appropriate response to the alternatives.[24] The public's changes are merely responses to changes in the kinds of cues offered by political leaders; the public responds by adopting and articulating the positions that their favored political leaders provide for them. The change reflects neither an underlying shift in the public's abilities nor a rational response to changes in the political realities.

Public dependence on leaders does not inevitably lead to change, even in a time of social and political upheaval. In periods of political stability leaders will likely continue to disseminate similar cues, and the public's response will remain unchanged. In periods of change — new issues, new social forces — some leaders will articulate new positions for their followers, while others will not. Many in the electorate will attend only to those leaders who emphasize unchanged positions, while still others apparently remain insulated from any meaningful political stimuli.

Thus, political leaders are important in public opinion. To be sure, they are objects of opinions. They also provide important sources of cues for public response to issues and events by people who share the leaders' particular interest or group identification. Leaders can generate change in public opinion and they can act as a barricade against that change. In the last several decades leaders have played out both roles, contributing both stability and change to American public opinion.

Individual Characteristics

Many aspects of public opinion are explained by the personal characteristics of the people expressing the opinions. Scholars often find that people who share an individual characteristic also share an opinion characteristic. For example, it is commonplace to find comparisons of opinions in different age groups (are the young more liberal?), religious groups (are Protestants more Republican?), socioeconomic categories (are the working class more Democratic?), and education levels (are the better educated better informed politically?). The argument is that there is something about the shared individual characteristics that lead to shared opinions. People with common characteristics may have the same stakes in a political issue, they may listen to the same political leader, and they may have the same life experiences.

Not surprisingly, individual characteristics have been widely used to explain recent patterns of public opinion, particularly in those cases where change has occurred. One example is education. The individual's level of formal education has been linked to a number of opinion characteristics. Research has shown that people with higher education have been more likely to think they have an impact on politics, to trust the political system, to be politically informed, to vote, to hold consistent opinions, to support the environmental and women's liberation movements, and to hold different political values.[25]

The level of formal education has increased in recent years. Changes also occurred in characteristics of public opinion to which education has been linked. Thus, according to some scholars, the rising levels of education may account for those changes. Nie et al. note that the percentage of the public employing sophisticated levels of conceptualization rose substantially during the same period as the increase in education. They suggest that "in terms of both magnitude and timing, it seems possible that the rise in conceptual level within the mass public is the consequence of an increasingly educated and thus more knowledgeable and sophisticated public."[26] However, people became more sophisticated at *all* levels of education even though those people with more education are still more likely to have the highest level of conceptualization.

Nunn et al. note that the public's tolerance for nonconformity increased during the same period as the level of education increased.[27] Since level of education is strongly associated with political tolerance they thought the increase in tolerance might stem from the increase in education. Yet it turns out that the increase in education accounts for only part of the increase in tolerance. While both in 1954 and 1973 the higher educated were more tolerant, there was an increase in tolerance at all levels of education (see Table 2 – 1), albeit rather small among those with only grade-school education. If education were the primary cause of the increase in tolerance the level of tolerance would have remained the same in each education category, but the overall increase in tolerance would stem from the presence of many more people in the higher education levels.

TABLE 2 – 1   Percentage "More Tolerant" at Each Education Level in 1954 and 1973[a]

Education	Percent "More Tolerant"		Change
	1954	1973	
College Graduates	65	84	+19
Some College	53	75	+22
High School Graduates	40	58	+18
Some High School	27	40	+13
Grade School	14	19	+5

[a]The term "more tolerant" is the group at the highest levels of an index measuring tolerance. This table is reformulated from a table that also included the percentages less tolerant and in-between, found on p. 60 of Clyde Z. Nunn, Harry J. Crockett, Jr., and J. Allen Williams, Jr., *Tolerance for Nonconformity* (San Francisco: Jossey-Bass, 1976), p. 60. Used by permission.

This discussion has segregated and simplified the kinds of explanations for recent patterns in American public opinion. Yet the "real world" of public opinion is quite complicated and does not easily admit of simple solutions. The public is highly diverse, and one should not expect all people to respond to the same forces or in the same direction. Some people may have opinions that are more open to influence by leaders and their behaviors. Some people's opinions are less responsive to changes in the political and social environment. Specific reference groups or political leaders are more important to some people than to others, and the impact of changes in cues provided by those reference groups will vary. That there has been considerable stability in the opinions of some people while those of others have changed is testimony to these varied responses of the public.

OPINION PROCESSES

The first chapter distinguished between public opinion at the individual level — the characteristics of an opinion held by a person — and public opinion at the aggregate level — the opinion characteristics of a group or collection of people, a public. Patterns of opinion dynamics — stability and change — occur at both levels. Many people may change their opinions (the individual level), and the overall distribution of opinions may change. But change or stability at one level is not necessarily accompanied by the same pattern at the other. Moreover, the processes through which opinion dynamics take place at the two levels are distinct. This section explores those processes and their relationship to each other.

Individual Level Processes

What is the process through which individual opinions persist or change? There have been many answers forwarded, three of which have been most commonly employed to explain individual political opinions: consistency theories, functional theories, and rational theories.

CONSISTENCY THEORIES. Although the label "consistency theory" applies to a wide range of approaches to opinion processes, there are some common elements.[28] Underlying consistency theories is the proposition that people have a fundamental aversion to holding opinions that are inconsistent with each other. The Watergate affair vis-à-vis opinions about Richard Nixon is a recent example of inconsistency and resulting discomfort. Many Americans had very positive feelings about Nixon, at least before Watergate. But revelations of his role in Watergate created negative perceptions that did not mesh with the positive ones already held. The result surely was inconsistency and discomfort for many Americans. A ready way to reduce the inconsistency was to change the previously held positive feelings so that they became consistent with the new information. From 1972 to 1974, the American public's evaluation of Nixon on a hundred-point scale dropped from 64.4 to 37.3, suggesting substantial effort to reinstitute consistency.[29]

An example of a consistency theory will illustrate further. One such approach shares the widely held assumption that an attitude is an underlying psychological predisposition that is itself unobservable.[30] However, there are three observable properties reflecting that attitude: affect, cognition, and behavior. *Affect* is the individual's emotional, pro or con orientation to the attitude object (how much one likes or is positive toward Richard Nixon) and is the property usually measured in public opinion polls. *Cognition* is the individual's perceptions of the characteristics of the attitude object (is Nixon seen as honest or dishonest?). *Behavior* is the person's action toward the object (such as voting for Nixon). The ordinary state, according to the theory, is consistency among the components, so that one will feel positive about and behave positively toward something about which one has positive perceptions. Change in one of the components of the attitude will result in an inconsistency. There will be pressure either to alter the other components or to return the changed component to its initial position, providing the level of inconsistency passes the individual's threshold of tolerance.[31]

Consistency theories have been used to explain the relationship among beliefs in belief systems, opinions about issues of public policy, and reactions to political events and figures.[32] How might consistency theories identify the processes through which opinion patterns in recent years took place? In cases where opinion change exists we might look for the sources of inconsistency in the political and social environment, in the actions of leaders, or in individual characteristics. Each of those may establish inconsistency leading to opinion change. On the other hand, the consistency theories might also explain the insulation of many people to opinion change. People may reject a certain negative perception of a political figure (e.g., Nixon) because it would create a great deal of inconsistency with other perceptions and opinions. Rather than change other opinions it may be more comfortable to prevent the inconsistency from developing.

FUNCTIONAL THEORIES.   According to functional theories, each individual's personality has certain basic needs that must be satisfied. Many of these needs can be satisfied through the expression of certain opinions about politics. Political opinions, in this framework, satisfy certain of those needs and thereby perform "functions" for the personality — they help it to function.

M. Brewster Smith, Jerome Bruner, and Robert White suggest that opinions perform three functions for the personality: social adjustment, object appraisal, and externalization.[33] The *social adjustment* function is performed because each individual has some need to affiliate with other people, to be liked, to have a feeling of belonging. Consciously or unconsciously, a person may hold certain political opinions in order to help him- or herself to adapt to a particular social group and to be more highly regarded by that group. Robert Lane, for example, reports

> *the case of a young man who says that when he got to college he quickly decided he would have to adopt the prevailing norms of the college because, being Jewish, being from a little-known school, being physically small, and having no real dynamic qualities of his own, he would need to do this in order to get along.*[34]

Although for many other people the adjustment of opinions in order to find acceptance may not be quite so overt, it surely occurs.

The function of *object appraisal* arises because of the individual's need to conserve effort in evaluating politics. One cannot take the time and the effort to completely evaluate an object each time one confronts it. Holding an opinion about the object (e.g., a political figure or a political issue) provides one with a ready response to it, without going through the evaluation process each time. The holding of an opinion also provides an economical response to groups of objects sharing a particular characteristic. One may hold a favorable opinion of the Republican party. Each time the Republican party is confronted the opinion is there to apply to it. The same general opinion may be applied to issues and people that are associated with the Republican party (such as its presidential candidate).

The third function of opinions is *externalization*. An individual may have some unresolved internal problem. The opinion formed about a political object (a person, issue, or group) may help with the problem. Suppose someone does not think very highly of him- or herself. This may create internal conflict. The individual may try to resolve the conflict by forming an opinion that raises his own position in relation to some group of people. Some have argued that this is the basis for racist attitudes — that people form certain negative opinions about other races because of their own inability to view themselves favorably, and thereby elevate their own self-perception.

The functions opinions perform can be used to explain both opinion stability and opinion change. In a stable environment, with stable political leadership behavior and with no individual changes, the opinions an individual holds would be expected to continue to perform the same functions for the personality and therefore to remain unchanged. Yet the personality relevance of opinions may make them relatively immune to changes in the political environment, leadership behavior, or individual characteristics. Because certain opinions are deeply rooted in someone's personality, that person may resist change even in the face of a political world to which the opinion may seem starkly inconsistent.

The functional process also can explain opinion change. Opinion change occurs when something alters the functional relationship between the opinion and the personality. For example, one may no longer feel a particular need (with the disappearance of feelings of low self-esteem one may no longer need to denigrate the position of others). Or something in the environment may change so that a particular opinion no longer performs the same function (someone may change social environments and enter a new one dominated by people with a different set of opinions). Changes in the functional relationship between opinions and someone's personality may stem from a variety of sources, including changes in the political and social environment, in the alternatives presented to the public by leaders, and in the individual.

RATIONAL THEORIES.   Rational opinion theory begins with the proposition that people seek to maximize their self-interest.[35] According to this approach, alternative opinions are evaluated according to their impact on the achievement of that self-interest.[36] The potential costs and benefits of each alternative are weighed; the alternative with the greatest net benefit, or least net cost, is preferred. In choosing a political party, for example, individuals will define their self-interest, evaluate the parties' positions in terms of their consequences for the self-interest, and choose the party that is expected to provide the greatest benefits. How much the choice actually benefits the self-interest will be determined by the information available to the individual and the certainty about the alternatives' implications. Moreover, in many cases it may be rational not to obtain complete information, for the information cost may be greater than the potential benefit to be obtained from having the information.[37]

If a particular opinion is the result of someone's cost-benefit calculation, the opinion is likely to remain unaltered as long as the information remains substantially the same and the definition of the self-interest is unchanged. However, the person might redefine his or her self-interest so that a previously beneficial opinion no longer is so. Or the opinion object (policy, person) itself may change, so that it no longer provides the same benefits as before.

Aggregate Level Processes

Aggregate level processes refer to the dynamics producing opinion patterns
for a public as a whole (a collection or aggregation of people). Thus, aggregate
processes are at work when we try to explain the *percentage of the public*
approving of the president at two different points in time, rather than trying
to explain the opinion pattern of a particular individual. Through what kinds
of processes do these aggregate patterns prevail? Three major answers are
described below.

CUMULATIVE INDIVIDUAL PATTERNS. A cumulative individual pattern is simply the sum total of individual patterns of stability and change
across a public. The outcome of no change at the individual level is fairly
clear at the aggregate level also — no change. However, there are different
aggregate outcomes from different patterns of individual change. The
cumulative individual change can be symmetrical or it can be asymmetrical.
If there is symmetrical individual change, the changes have balanced — say
25 percent moving from pro to con and 25 percent moving from con to pro.
Asymmetrical change means that many individuals have changed their position on an issue and that change is predominantly in the same direction.
As a result, the overall distribution has changed. For example, asymmetrical change occurred in the public's reaction to Richard Nixon in the
wake of Watergate.

REPLACEMENT. The idea of replacement is most relevant to relatively
long-term opinion patterns. Replacement is based in a conceptualization of
the public as a dynamic collection of individuals whose composition constantly is changing. There is a constant flow of people exiting the public
through death or emigration, and there is a constant influx of new members
through immigration and individual maturation. Moreover, on occasion the
boundaries of the public will be expanded, a new group will be gathered in —
as when the age limit for voting was lowered to eighteen.

   When the opinions of the entering group are similar to the existing public
and to any exiting portion there will be stability in the distribution of opinions. But if the entering group is different in its opinions there will be an
overall change in the aggregate opinion patterns. If the group leaving the
public is comprised mainly of conservatives, and the group entering the public is predominately liberal, the overall distribution will become more liberal
even though no individuals have changed their opinions. In recent years the
American public has become more independent; smaller and smaller percentages of the public are willing to align themselves with one of the two
major political parties. Some of that pattern comes from people formerly calling themselves Republicans or Democrats, but now identifying with neither.
Most scholars, though, believe the change to result predominately from replacement. That is, the younger groups entering the electorate are much
more likely to be Independents, while the older groups leaving the electorate
are more likely to be party identifiers. The overall impact is to increase the
percentage of Independents in the public.

OPINION AROUSAL. At any given time there is a certain proportion of the electorate not holding opinions about a particular issue or public figure. The percentage not having an opinion will vary from issue to issue, depending on the issue's salience to the public, and will vary for any issue through time. Changes in the environment or in the actions of political leaders may stimulate the formation of opinions where previously they were not held. This arousal may alter the aggregate distribution if the newly formed opinions differ from those already present in the public. The public holding opinions about an issue may split 50–50, but this may constitute only half of the *potential* opinion-holding public. A sudden crisis or spectacular event may arouse those people without opinions to form them. These newly formed opinions may be distributed 100 percent in a single direction. This new group of opinions would then alter the aggregate distribution to 75–25, with no change in the direction of opinions by any individual.

CONCLUSION

The beginning of this chapter noted that according to many scholars recent public opinion has undergone substantial change. Although many individuals have changed their opinions, and the overall distribution of opinions in the public has been altered, stability and change at the two levels do not necessarily go hand in hand. To bring together the previous distinctions, the conclusion describes a typology of opinion dynamics based on the patterns of change and stability at the individual levels and the processes that may produce those dynamics. The basis for the discussion is shown in Table 2–2.

TABLE 2–2   The Dynamics of Public Opinion: Patterns and Processes of Individual and Aggregate Public Opinion

Individual Level Pattern	Aggregate Level Pattern	
	Change	**Stability**
Change	A. Asymmetrical Individual Change	B. Symmetrical Individual Change
Stability	C. Asymmetrical Replacement/ Arousal	D. Symmetrical Replacement/ Arousal

Aggregate Change/Individual Change (Cell A)

In this type there is both widespread individual change and widespread aggregate change. Many individuals have altered their opinion, and the alteration is sufficiently asymmetrical that there is a change in the overall distribution of opinions in the public. A number of people might change their opinion about medicare and this individual-level change is predominately in the direction of favoring medicare—the aggregate distribution of opinion also becomes more favorable to medicare than before. This particular pattern is what most people have in mind when considering change in public opinion.

Aggregate Stability/Individual Change (Cell B)

In this case there is widespread individual-level change but aggregate-level stability. The overall distribution of opinions remains undisturbed because the large-scale changes among individuals cancel out each other. In other words, the individual change is symmetrical. The forces producing individual change push different people in different directions. The recognition of this pattern is important for understanding the dynamics of public opinion. Too often our analyses of public opinion consider only the distribution of opinion at the aggregate level. On some issue there may be relative stability in the distribution of public opinion, and we may conclude that little of interest is taking place. Observers sensitive to the possibility of this pattern will probe beneath the aggregate distribution, searching for individual patterns of stability and change. A great deal of turbulence may be hidden beneath the apparently calm surface of public opinion. That turbulence may have long-term consequences for a country's politics if the individual changes in opinions are linked to other important characteristics, such as class, age, race, religion, or party affiliation. For example, both Democrats and Republicans may be composed of 50 percent favorable to a policy position and 50 percent opposed to it. Thus, there will be no partisan basis for conflict on the issue. However, Republicans may change so that all favor the policy, and the Democrats change so that all are opposed to it. If the groups are of equal size the aggregate distribution will remain the same. However, the character of the individual changes may result in the issue now becoming a major source of division and competition among the two political parties.

Aggregate Change/Individual Stability (Cell C)

At first blush, the presence of aggregate change with no individual change may seem unlikely, if not impossible. How could the number of people favoring or opposing a particular issue position change when there is little or no change on the part of individuals? The answer is found in asymmetrical replacement or arousal. The distribution of opinions among new cohorts or among people newly forming an opinion may differ substantially from the distribution already in the public. If the change is a consequence of replacement — the entry of new and distinct cohorts — then the new pattern of public opinion is likely to persist for some time unless succeeding cohorts also differ significantly. Arousal, on the other hand, may reflect abrupt short-term changes in opinion.

Aggregate Stability/Individual Stability (Cell D)

Oddly enough, no individual change along with no aggregate change may not reflect complete stability in the public's opinions. Symmetrical patterns of replacement or arousal would result in unchanged opinion patterns and would result from no individual change. However, there would be a change in the particular people who hold many of the opinions. Thus, there may be a change in the politics surrounding the opinions. That is, replacement may result in precisely the same distribution of opinions, but the *kinds* of people holding particular opinions may change. Among the existing public there may be substantial differences between Republicans and Democrats in their opinions about an issue, with the Democrats taking the "pro" position and the Republicans holding the "con" position. In the entering cohort there also may be substantial partisan differences on the issue, but with the Republicans taking the "pro" position and the Democrats holding the "con" position. If the two groups (the Republicans and Democrats in the new cohort) are of equal size their entry into the public will leave the aggregate distribution of opinions undisturbed. However, the nature of partisan conflict over that issue will be substantially altered.

SUMMARY

In order to understand the dynamics of public opinion it is important to understand both the patterns and the processes. What appears to be opinion stability may be only disguised change. What appears to be opinion change may hide consistencies in the explanations for opinions, or may stem from changes in the methods employed to study those opinions. Indeed, in almost every instance where this chapter has described changes in public opinion there are a number of observers who attribute the changes to poor or inconsistent methodology — unreliable measures that produce different results when applied to the same people, or different measures designed to measure the same opinion but do not. The following chapter explores in much greater detail the conceptual and methodological problems in measuring opinions and opinion change.

NOTES

1. Many of the patterns described in this section are not uniformly accepted by students of public opinion. We will not treat the substance of those disagreements at this point. Rather, they are reviewed in the chapters that follow.
2. Alden S. Raine, "Change in the Political Agenda: Social and Cultural Conflict in the American Electorate," *Sage Professional Papers in American Politics,* vol. 3, no. 04-035 (Beverly Hills: Sage Publications, 1977).
3. Warren E. Miller and Teresa E. Levitin, *Leadership and Change* (Cambridge, Mass.: Winthrop Publishers, 1976), pp. 5–6.
4. Robert S. Gilmour and Robert B. Lamb, *Political Alienation in Contemporary America* (New York: St. Martin's Press, 1975).
5. See Norman Nie with Kristi Andersen, "Mass Belief Systems Revisited: Political Change and Attitude Structure," *Journal of Politics* 36 (August 1974), pp. 540–91.
6. John O. Field and Ronald E. Anderson, "Ideology in the Public's Conception of the 1964 Election," *Public Opinion Quarterly* 33 (Fall 1969), pp. 380–98; Norman H. Nie, Sidney Verba, and John R. Petrocik, *The Changing American Voter* (Cambridge, Mass.: Harvard University Press, 1976), pp. 110–22.
7. Jack Dennis, "Trends in Support for the American Party System," *British Journal of Political Science* 5 (April 1975), pp. 197–230.
8. Walter DeVries and Lance Tarrance, Jr., *The Ticket-Splitter: A New Force in American Politics* (Grand Rapids, Mich.: William B. Eerdman's Publishing Co., 1972).

9. Gerald M. Pomper, *Voters' Choice* (New York: Dodd, Mead & Co., 1975), pp. 186–209.

10. Roper Organization, Inc., *What People Think of Television and Other Mass Media: 1959–1972* (New York: Television Information Office of the National Association of Broadcasters, 1973), p. 2.

11. See Daniel Bell, *The Coming of Postindustrial Society* (New York: Basic Books, 1973); and Leon N. Lindberg, ed., *Politics and the Future of Industrial Society* (New York: David McKay, 1976).

12. Everett Carll Ladd, Jr., with Charles D. Hadley, *Transformations of the American Party System,* 2nd ed. (New York: Norton, 1978), p. 184.

13. Milton Rokeach, *The Nature of Human Values* (New York: Free Press, 1973).

14. Ronald Inglehart, "The Nature of Value Change in Postindustrial Societies," in *Politics and the Future of Industrial Society,* p. 57. See also his "The Silent Revolution in Europe: Intergenerational Change in Postindustrial Societies," *American Political Science Review* 65 (December 1971), pp. 991–1017; and *The Silent Revolution* (Princeton, N.J.: Princeton University Press, 1977).

15. Abraham Maslow, *Motivation and Personality* (New York: Harper & Row, 1954). See also Jeanne N. Knutson, *The Human Basis of the Polity* (Chicago: Aldine-Atherton, 1972).

16. Inglehart, *The Silent Revolution.*

17. Miller and Levitin, *Leadership and Change,* pp. 17–18.

18. Benjamin I. Page, *Choices and Echoes in Presidential Politics: Rational Man and Electoral Democracy* (Chicago: University of Chicago Press, 1978).

19. Gerald M. Pomper, "From Confusion to Clarity: Issues and American Voters, 1956–1968," *American Political Science Review* 66 (June 1972), pp. 415–28.

20. John C. Pierce, "Party Identification and the Changing Role of Ideology in American Politics," *Midwest Journal of Political Science* 14 (February 1970), pp. 25–42.

21. Andrew S. McFarland, *Public Interest Lobbies* (Washington: American Enterprise Inst., 1976).

22. Walter A. Rosenbaum, *The Politics of Environmental Concern,* 2nd. ed. (New York: Praeger, 1977), p. 76

23. Pomper, *Voters' Choice.*

24. Philip E. Converse, "Public Opinion and Voting Behavior," in *Handbook of Political Science,* vol. 4, Fred Greenstein and Nelson Polsby, eds. (Reading, Mass.: Addison-Wesley, 1975), pp. 75–169.

25. See the summary of the impact of education on a number of variables in Lester W. Milbrath and M.L. Goel, *Political Participation,* 2nd ed. (Chicago: Rand McNally, 1977), pp. 98–102.

26. Nie, Verba, and Petrocik, *The Changing American Voter,* p. 119.

27. Clyde Z. Nunn, Harry J. Crockett, Jr., and J. Allen Williams, Jr., *Tolerance for Nonconformity* (San Francisco: Jossey-Bass, 1978).

28. See the selections describing various consistency theories in Martin Fishbein, ed., *Attitude Theory and Measurement* (New York: John Wiley & Sons, 1967), pp. 293–365.

29. Center for Political Studies 1972–74–76 panel study.

30. Milton J. Rosenberg et al., *Attitude Organization and Change* (New Haven, Conn.: Yale University Press, 1960), p. 1.

31. Ibid., p. 22.

32. See Milton J. Rosenberg, Sidney Verba, and Philip E. Converse, *Vietnam and the Silent Majority* (New York: Harper & Row, 1970).

33. M. Brewster Smith, Jerome S. Bruner, and Robert W. White, *Opinions and Personality* (New York: John Wiley & Sons, 1955).

34. Robert E. Lane, *Political Thinking and Consciousness* (Chicago: Markham, 1969), p. 35.
35. Anthony Downs, *An Economic Theory of Democracy* (New York: Harper & Row, 1957).
36. Arthur Goldberg, "Social Determinism and Rationality as Bases of Party Identification," *American Political Science Review* 63 (March 1969), p. 5; Page, *Choices and Echoes in Presidential Elections,* pp. 3–9.
37. Page, *Choices and Echoes in Presidential Elections,* p. 150.

CHAPTER 3

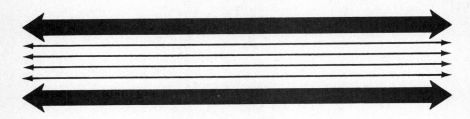

APPROACHES AND PROBLEMS IN THE STUDY OF OPINION DYNAMICS

As the preceding chapters indicate, widespread change is a major theme of much recent literature about public opinion. A great deal of scholarly effort has been dedicated to the analysis of these recent patterns, but that effort has resulted in little agreement. Over a decade ago a series of debates began about the seeming changes in public opinion, and these debates continue largely unabated today. The number and the nature of these controversies reflect different approaches and pose some fundamental problems for students of public opinion. This chapter describes those approaches and addresses several of these major problems. How one deals with them will affect one's conclusions about public opinion and its recent patterns.

Every student initially must cope with the question of whose opinions to study, when, and how. The first section of this chapter evaluates some alternative approaches to analyzing information about the change in public opinion. The discussion then turns to the importance of conceptual frameworks in the study of change. Hazy definitions of concepts, or changes in definitions of concepts, may result in the appearance of change where none exists.

Building a solid conceptual framework is only a beginning. The concepts must be measured before they are useful in opinion research.[1] The measurement of public opinion poses some problems, two of which are *reliability* and *validity*. The sensitivity to measurement error is particularly important in the study of change.

The chapter next turns to problems in the *interpretation* of changing opinions. Very similar evidence of change yields widely varying interpretations. In part, those different interpretations may reflect the subjective viewpoints of the researchers; however, they also may result from researchers not employing the most scientific methods.

Despite a lengthy discussion devoted to "problems," this chapter does not end on a pessimistic note. The last section mentions some of the challenges and benefits that come from studying public opinion stability and change.

APPROACHES TO THE ANALYSIS OF OPINION DYNAMICS

Opinion stability and change are part of a dynamic process. To study them one needs information about public opinion gathered at different times. At first glance this seems a simple proposition: survey opinions once before and once after a change is hypothesized to have taken place. However, selection of the appropriate data base is rarely a simple matter. There are several kinds of longitudinal studies, and each has its own advantages and disadvantages.[2] The following sections describe trend analysis, cohort analysis, and panel analysis.

Trend Analysis of Aggregate Public Opinion

In the trend analysis of aggregate public opinion one compares the *distribution* of opinions at different times — that is, the opinions of a sample of the public are compared at two points in time. Although different people make up the different samples, each sample is a cross section of the same public. An example of this kind of data is found in Figure 3–1, which presents the percentage of the public approving of President Carter's performance in office at a number of different time points.

FIGURE 3–1   An Example of Trend Analysis of Aggregate Opinion Data: Harris and CBS/NYT Poll Approval Ratings of President Carter

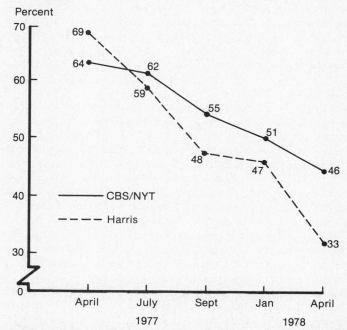

Source: *Public Opinion* (May/June 1978), p. 33. Used by permission of the American Enterprise Institute.

Aggregate-trend analysis provides a basis for comparing the distribution of opinions in the public at different times, but it cannot reveal much about individual-level stability or change. That the percentage of the public approving of the president's performance may have stayed about the same from one time to another (September 1977 to January 1978 in the Harris figures) tells us little about the percentage of people whose opinions were unchanged. Recall that the *distribution* of public opinion may remain the same when large numbers of people change their opinions and those changes balance out (are symmetrical). Equal numbers may have switched from approval to disapproval and vice versa. Thus, aggregate-trend statistics can hide elusive "components of the net trend."[3] One treatment of the dangers of aggregation and the pitfalls of trend analysis points out that

> no change or little change in the aggregate may conceal a radical change in one subgroup which is but a fraction in the total collectivity and therefore submerged in the aggregate findings. Little net change in the aggregate can come about through many larger changes in several subgroups who may have been moving in opposite directions and therefore balance each other out.[4]

Clearly, then, the use of trend analysis limits a researcher's legitimate interpretations.

In the absence of alternative data sources, the judicious use of trend analysis of aggregate-level data can provide some important information.[5] That information, however, is confined to descriptions of the public as a unit. Except in extreme cases, it cannot generally be employed to make statements about change or stability in the opinions of individuals. Two major alternative strategies for the study of change in public opinion are designed to overcome the limitations in the trend analysis of aggregate data: cohort analysis and panel studies.

Cohort Analysis

The technique of cohort analysis shares many of the characteristics of aggregate-level-trend studies and is subject to some of the same limitations. Cohort analysis consists of over-time comparisons of people who share a "significant life event,"[6] usually a period of birth. That is, the opinions of people born in a given period (say, 1952–1956) are compared at two or more points in time (say, 1972 and 1976) to see if the members of that cohort have changed in their opinions. Again, the same people do not comprise the cohort sample in the different time periods. Rather, at the first time period (1972) one obtains the opinions of a sample of those people born between 1952 and 1956 — between sixteen and twenty years old in 1972. Four years later one measures the opinions of a sample of the public aged twenty to twenty-four (still the same cohort: people born between 1952 and 1956). Thus, cohort studies draw upon several cross-sectional studies.

An example of cohort analysis is presented in Figure 3–2, which shows the percentage of Independents in two different age cohorts for the period from 1952 through 1972. Those two cohorts are the "New Voters of 1952" and the "New Voters of 1964." Of the new voters in 1952, 26 percent were Independent. In 1956, 29 percent of that same cohort (the new voters in 1952) were Independent; and in 1960, 32 percent of that cohort were Independent. The figures for that cohort remain the same through 1968, and then increase in 1972 to 37 percent Independent. The other cohort, the new voters in 1964, began with about the same percentage of Independents in 1964 (34 percent), but by 1968 had increased to 45 percent. Thus, between 1964 and 1968 there was a much greater aggregate-level change in the percentage of Independents in the younger cohort. However, just as in the aggregate-trend analysis, the stability in the cohorts shown by aggregate figures may mask a great deal of individual change. That is, from 1960 to 1964 there was no change in the percentage of the "New Voters of 1952" cohort identifying themselves as Independents (32 percent in each year). However, those figures *could* be explained by a great deal of individual change — equal numbers of people becoming independent and leaving independence for partisanship.

FIGURE 3 – 2   An Example of Cohort Analysis: Proportion of Independents in Two Age Cohorts, 1952 – 1972

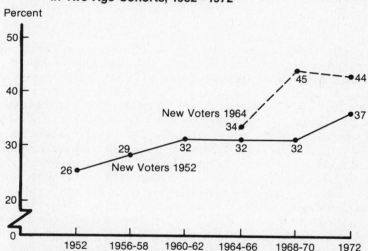

Source: Norman H. Nie, Sidney Verba, and John R. Petrocik, *The Changing American Voter*, enlarged ed. (Cambridge, Mass: Harvard University Press, 1979), p. 63. Copyright © 1976, 1979 by the Twentieth Century Fund. Reprinted by permission.

Cohort studies draw on several cross-sectional surveys to "simulate" studies of the same people at different times.[7] Frequently, the cohort design has been used to investigate the relationship between opinion change and aging. Do people change their opinions as they get older mainly because they are aging? A single cross-sectional survey cannot answer that question. Even though one may find that in 1981 older people are more conservative than younger people, we do not know whether the older people always have been conservative, even when young, or whether they were liberal as youth and then became more conservative as they aged. Opinion differences associated with age may have several sources: life-cycle effects, generational effects, and period effects.[8] *Life-cycle* effects are changes thought to be "endemic to the life course" as the individual passes through the aging process.[9] Thus, a life-cycle effect would be present if in fact people become more conservative as they get older. *Generational effects,* however, result from forces causing distinctive opinions peculiar to one birth cohort, which is a group born within a given time period. Differences in opinions among different age groups, then, may be a result of distinct forces at work when those age groups acquired their opinions. Again, older people may be more conservative than younger people in a given study of public opinion. If generational effects are at work, this difference would result from the older people always having been more conservative — even when they were young. And members of this younger generation may retain their liberal opinions throughout their lives. *Period effects* stem from major political events and forces, which cause opinion change across the entire public, not simply within certain age groups. Thus, the Watergate crisis might be expected to have affected the opinions of all age cohorts.

The puzzle of whether opinion change has been caused by life-cycle, generational, or period effects can be partially pieced together with cohort analysis. Thus, if opinion change is the result of life-cycle effects, younger cohorts should become more like older cohorts as they move through time. On the other hand, if generational change is present, a constant gap should be present between the opinions of young and old cohorts, regardless of when the comparison between them is made. Finally, if period effects account for opinion change, that change should be observed in all cohorts simultaneously, regardless of age.[10]

The trend toward weakening party attachments in the public is one place where cohort analysis has been used to try to untangle life-cycle, generational and period effects. A young person's partisan attachments usually are weaker than those of older persons. Early interpretations suggested that party identification increases in intensity with increasing age.[11] Age, in this case, stood as a surrogate for length of attachment to the party. Recently, however, scholars have challenged that interpretation, arguing the possibility that generational or period effects might better explain the changes.

Paul Allen Beck suggests that the alternative explanations of partisan decline can be tested by the cohort analysis of general cross-sectional studies.[12] Beck finds "virtually no support for the life-cycle explanation."[13] Other studies lend further support to a generational explanation because they all fail to find evidence that young persons develop stronger partisanship as they age.[14] Similarly, Figure 3–2 of this chapter (while an abbreviated cohort analysis) suggests an interaction of generational and period effects, but not life-cycle effects. The younger cohort is consistently less partisan than the older cohort (generational effects); and both cohorts became less partisan during the late 1960s (period effects).

Even though cohort analysis is a valuable tool, its limitations should not be overlooked.[15] As previously discussed, cohort studies employ a form of aggregate analysis; inferences about individual patterns must be drawn very cautiously, if at all.[16] Although one can reduce the problems of aggregate-trend analysis by looking at age cohorts, the pitfalls cannot be eliminated totally.

Panel Studies

Panel studies involve measurements taken on the *same people* at two or more points in time. They are used to detect changes across a whole sample (aggregate changes) and to determine whether people who hold an opinion at the first time also hold that opinion at the second time (individual changes).[17] Thus, panel studies provide information about both the stability in the distribution of opinions in the public *and* the stability of individual opinions. Panel studies have a great advantage over cohort analysis and aggregate-trend analysis; the latter two cannot provide reliable information about individual-level stability and change.

TABLE 3–1   Panel Study Data Showing Individual and Aggregate-Level Stability and Change in Opinions: Party Identification in 1956 and 1958*

| | 1958 | | | | | |
1956	Strong Demo-crat	Weak Demo-crat	Indepen-dent	Weak Repub-lican	Strong Repub-lican	Total
Strong Democrat	16.7%	4.2%	.3%	.1%	.3%	21.6%**
Weak Democrat	7.9	12.5	2.1	.5	0.0	23.0%**
Independent	2.1	4.7	13.3	3.2	1.5	24.8%**
Weak Republican	.3	1.2	2.2	8.7	2.5	14.9%**
Strong Republican	.5	.4	1.0	4.6	9.4	15.9%**
Total	27.5%	23.0%	18.9%	17.1%	13.7%	100.2%**

*The figure in each cell is the percentage of the total sample with that combination of responses in 1956 and 1958. Thus, 16.7 percent of the sample called themselves "Strong Democrats" in both 1956 and 1958. The figures in the marginals show the *distribution* of party identification in the two years. Thus, 21.6 percent called themselves "Strong Democrats" in 1956, but that figure rose to 27.5 percent in 1958.
**Rounding error.

Source: John C. Pierce and Douglas D. Rose, "Nonattitudes and American Public Opinion: The Examination of a Thesis," *American Political Science Review* 68 (June, 1974), p. 632.

Table 3–1 presents an example of results derived from a panel study. The cells of the table show what percentage of the sample held each *combination* of party identification at the two time periods. The figures in the diagonal cells moving from top left to bottom right contain those people who expressed the same identification in both interviews. Adding the figures in those diagonal cells provides an estimate of the amount of perfect individual stability in opinions (60.6 percent). The aggregate-level stability can be assessed by looking at the percentages on the outside of the table. At the right of the table are the percentages in each category of party identification at the first interview, and on the bottom are the percentages in each category at the second interview.

With all of their advantages panel studies often also have some drawbacks.[18] Because of expense and technical difficulties, panel studies frequently are used only for short-term studies, or they are limited to studies of small groups.[19] Moreover, the study itself may cause opinion change; this has been labeled "control," "reactive," or "interaction" effect.[20] The danger is that the initial survey may "increase or decrease a respondent's sensitivity or responsiveness."[21] A person's opinions about abortion may be unfocused or ambiguous when asked about it in an initial survey. Altered to the presence of the issue, the respondent's ideas may become more focused, with the issue assuming more importance precisely because the interview took place.

Donald Campbell and Julian Stanley also note a problem labeled sample "mortality."[22] Some people interviewed in the first wave of a panel study will not be available for the second- or third-wave interviews. The researcher cannot assume that respondents remaining available for all three waves are complete representative of the initial group. Changes in the opinions of people present for all of the interviews may be different from the changes among those people who were lost to the study after the first wave.

Another possible difficulty posed by panel studies occurs when change is incorrectly attributed to an event of interest when it really results from other events peculiar to the time frame of the study. These are called "history" effects.[23] Say, for example, one had wanted to look at the impact of a new civics curriculum on high school students' trust of political authorities, and that the opinions initially had been measured in 1972. Then the new curriculum was introduced and the students exposed to it for the next year. At the end of that time those same students were again surveyed, and the results showed a big drop in their trust of public officials. Can one attribute that change to the civics curriculum? Probably not, for there is a strong indication that history effects were present: it was during that period that many of the Watergate revelations occurred.

Another hazard of the panel study is maturation.[24] Maturation effects are present when changes in respondents' opinions are due to the passage of time itself, and not due to specific political events or conditions. For example, a panel study of college students may show that the respondents are substantially more liberal as graduating seniors than they were as entering freshmen. One would be tempted to conclude that the reason for the change is the students' exposure to college education. On the other hand, the students have grown older during that period, and the increased liberalism may just be a consequence of that aging.

Another impediment to the use of panel studies where they seem most appropriate is that scholarly concern with opinion change often is after the fact.[25] We often do not recognize the need for a panel study approach until it is too late to use it, and only aggregate or cohort data may be available. Recent evidence documenting the decline in the American public's support for political parties has inspired numerous questions about the nature and importance of changing party support. However, those questions became interesting only *after* notable evidence of aggregate change. Panel data during the period of rapid change are unavailable. If we rely solely on panel data, "many important questions will be made inaccessible to research."[26] Thus, the realities of research, both in terms of the availability of data and in terms of the costs of acquiring it, often dictate the use of aggregate-trend analysis or cohort analysis when panel designs may seem more appropriate.[27]

In spite of the difficulties they pose, panel studies are uniquely appropriate to some types of opinion research. Kent Jennings and Richard Niemi, for example, employed a panel design in their study of political socialization.[28] They surveyed adolescents and their parents in 1965 and again in 1973, with the same people being interviewed at both points. Thus, they were able to find out whether the distribution of opinions of the two groups remained the same, whether individual stability was greater among the adolescents or among the parents, and whether the opinions of individual adolescents moved closer to or farther away from those of their parents.

In summary the study of opinion stability or change demands a data base that provides information about public opinion at two or more points in time. The researcher has three major options in selecting the appropriate study design: aggregate-trend analysis, cohort analysis, and panel analysis. The design of the study and the selection of the data base are, however, only the first steps in the study of opinions and opinion change.

CONCEPTUAL PROBLEMS IN THE STUDY OF OPINION DYNAMICS

The selection of a design appropriate to the study of opinion change certainly is important. However, that enterprise must be guided by sound conceptualization. Before research can proceed, conceptualization, precise definitions of the terminology used, must be developed first.[29] Earl Babbie explains that "conceptualization is the refinement and specification of abstract concepts," and that it must be accompanied by "the development of specific research procedures (operations) that will result in empirical observations representing those concepts in the real world."[30] Defining and measuring concepts seems straightforward; yet public opinion research includes frequent disagreement on the definition and measurement of basic concepts. Caution is needed when comparing studies of opinions or when comparing public opinion over time. The comparison of findings based in dissimilar definitions of the same general concept or term can be misleading.

Studies of the American public's belief systems provide a good example of how different starting points and initial definitions of a concept may lead to different results. An individual's belief system is his or her set of *related* opinions about politics. Robert Lane and Philip Converse both conducted studies of public belief systems in the 1950s, but their conceptualizations were quite different.[31] Lane's conceptualization allowed individuals to possess relatively idiosyncratic belief systems — the opinions could be related to each other in unique ways and still qualify as a belief system. Converse, on the other hand, viewed a belief system as when the relationships among opinions are *shared* across the public — when people who share an opinion on one issue share an opinion on a second issue. Lane concluded that belief systems were widely present in the public, while Converse concluded that they were relatively rare. This difference can be traced, at least in part, to the initial differences in conceptualization.

The conceptual starting points of opinion research assume even greater significance when considering *changing* public opinion. Comparing public opinion analyses conducted by different people with different assumptions at different times cannot help but be troublesome. Lance Bennett refers to this problem as "conceptual slippage."[32] Conceptual slippage is the variation among studies in the meaning of basic concepts. It appears often in some areas of public opinion research, including the study of ideology and belief systems, political tolerance, political trust and alienation, and support for political parties. All are areas in which substantial change in public opinion has been noted in recent years and in which substantial conceptual slippage occurs.

The main point to be made here is that different definitions of the same concept may lead to different hypotheses tested in different ways. Thus, the public opinion researcher must be cautious when comparing the conclusions of different studies, particularly those conducted at different time periods. Differences in conclusions may stem from divergent definitions rather than from some "real" change in the public.

Yet the danger of conceptual slippage should not be overestimated. Alternative conceptualizations may open new directions in our knowledge of public opinion. That knowledge would be limited drastically if only one definition of belief system or party support had been universally accepted from the beginning. Initial conceptualizations (definitions of a concept) may be too narrow, restricting our knowledge of public opinion; if so, expanded definitions may be required. Thus, multiple definitions of a single concept become a problem only when one fails to distinguish among them, concluding that opinion change has occurred when none is clearly indicated. The warning to be sensitive to conceptual slippage, then, simply cautions the student of public opinion to make longitudinal comparisons with care and to understand why different conceptualizations produce different results.

THE MEASUREMENT OF PUBLIC OPINION

Precisely defining key concepts is critical for opinion research. Another integral part of that research process is developing measures that reflect those concepts. That is, upon defining a concept the researcher must develop specific research procedures (operations) for measuring it. Formally, the measurement of opinions is "the rigorous classification or quantification of things observed."[33] Measurement involves precisely defining the concepts and setting up a scheme for assigning numbers to the opinions in a way that reflects the definition. Thus, one may define party identification as psychological attachment to a political party. In an effort to measure party identification researchers may ask respondents about their party choice and the intensity of their preferences. A respondent can be classified as a strong Republican, a weak Republican, an Independent Republican, an Independent, an Independent Democrat, a weak Democrat, or a strong Democrat. Finally, numbers are assigned to each of those categories, and the numbers are used in subsequent analysis.[34]

Even though the process seems manageable, the measurement of opinions rarely is straightforward, largely because of variations in conceptualization. Given the widespread disagreement on the appropriate definitions of many concepts, it is not surprising that there are many measurement schemata for any given concept. In fact, even scholars who agree on basic definitions of concepts sometimes measure those concepts differently.

Measurement problems usually are grouped into two categories: measurement validity and measurement reliability. Measures are *valid* when they measure what they purport to measure; they are *reliable* if they consistently produce the same outcome. We consider each of these in a little more detail.

Measurement Validity

The question of measurement validity refers to whether a measure is assessing what it claims to be measuring. This addresses the match between the concept and the more specific measurement of the concept. The question is this: Are the measures chosen really appropriate to the concept? In some cases the answer is "no." One example of a challenge to a concept's validity is the measurement of political tolerance in the public. Support for the general democratic norm of tolerance has been said to be more prevalent among the political elite and the highly educated.[35] However, one observer argues that the measure of political tolerance is invalid:

> *The well educated are more likely to have genuinely "learned" abstract democratic principles, but that learning is relatively superficial. When democratic principles are contemplated in isolation from other factors, the well educated are more likely to recognize those principles, to know the "right" answers, and to believe sincerely in those answers. Such learning, however, is not very deeply embedded. In an applied situation, those principles are no more likely to influence the orientation of the well educated than of the poorly educated.*[36]

Mary Jackman thus concludes that overly abstract measures of political tolerance may not really measure tolerance; instead, they reflect the relative sophistication of the respondents.[37] The measures may be invalid.

Questions of measurement validity surface often in the study of public opinion and are particularly relevant to the study of change in public opinion. How can one be confident that changes in public opinion are "real" when there are doubts about the validity of the measures assessing those changes? Increases in political tolerance tapped by an allegedly invalid measure, as described above, may reflect only an increase in superficial learning rather than actual changes in tolerance.

Measurement Reliability

A second challenge to the assessment of public opinion questions the reliability of measures. Reliability is a question of measurement consistency, of whether the repeated use of the same measure or the use of different measures of the same concept yield consistent responses from the same individuals.[38]

The matter of reliability has been of grave concern in public opinion research. Christopher Achen argues that opinion measures of an individual at two different points in time often suggest opinion change or instability when none is present.[39] He also suggests that survey questions often are so vague that they elicit responses inaccurately reflecting the respondents' true opinions. He stresses:

> *A subject may "strongly agree" one time and "agree" the next, simply because of the ambiguity of the questions asked or because he is uncertain how strong is "strongly."*[40]

Thus, the responses given by the same individual at two points in time may be different not because he or she has changed an opinion but because of measurement error or unreliability.[41]

There are four other common sources of unreliability in opinion measurement: (1) the use of multiple items to assess single opinions; (2) a lack of centrality in the opinion being measured; (3) problems with the subjects of opinion research; and (4) problems of recall. Each source of unreliability is introduced below.

MULTIPLE ITEMS. Frequently, "multiple-item measures" (a series of questions, the answers to which are combined to create one measure) are used to assess an opinion of the public. One example is the measurement of the concept of *political efficacy.* Political efficacy has been defined as

> *the feeling that individual political action does have or can have an impact upon the political process, i.e., that it is worthwhile to perform one's civic duties.*[42]

The presence or absence of political efficacy often is tested with a set of four questions, the answers to which are combined into a single index. The presence or absence of political efficacy often is tested with a set of four questions, the answers to which are combined into a single index. Recent studies have challenged the reliability of the political efficacy measure. George Balch argues that the traditional measure of efficacy actually taps two types of efficacy.[43] One is internal efficacy (the person's views of his or her own ability), and the other is external efficacy (the view of the responsiveness of the political system). The single measure produced by multiple questions may be combining two different attributes of individuals. Because the two attributes may not be perfectly associated with each other, changes in one of the components will result in a change in the overall measure, even though the other component has not been altered. Thus, in multiple-item measures one or more of the items may not assess the concept that the group of items is designed to measure. Changes in those nonfitting items will produce changes in the overall measure, even though the actual opinion attribute (e.g., efficacy) has not changed.[44]

OPINION CENTRALITY. Measurement reliability may be influenced by the degree of centrality of an opinion. Even answers to relatively straightforward questions may have low reliability if the topic is not very important to the public. Herbert Asher has suggested that this may be a problem in the political efficacy measure, because efficacy may not be a topic of central concern for many people.[45] People may give different responses to questions at different times simply because the question is about something unimportant to them.

RESEARCH SUBJECTS. A third source of unreliability stems from the subject of the research — the respondent to the question. One example is the use of young children as respondents in studies of political socialization. Reliability may be a problem for several reasons. First, there are doubts about the degree to which young children really possess opinions about political issues, particularly on rather remote issues. If the children do not have opinions about the issues, but are instead merely responding to a test and guessing about the appropriate "answer," then there is likely to be little consistency in the responses over time. Second, reliability problems sometimes surface in the attempt to determine the level of correspondence between children's opinions and those of their parents. Such studies often survey only the children and not their parents, relying on the child's report of his or her parents' opinions or party affiliation.[46] Recent research findings illustrate the danger of relying on children's reports of parental opinions, insisting that such reports are extremely unreliable and should be used only in specific and rare instances.[47]

RECALL. A final caution on measurement reliability recognizes the temptation to study opinion change with recall items. Opinion change sometimes is assessed by asking people whether they have changed. People may not know whether they have changed, and their report of their previous opinion or behavior may be inaccurate. To assess partisan change, researchers have asked people their party affiliation during the previous presidential election and then compared that with their current party affiliation. However, people may not accurately remember their previous party identification. One recent study compared recall data for people who had participated in the 1956, 1958, 1960 panel study of the Survey Research Center to the actual opinions they had reported at the prior time.[48] That study showed that there are many people who over time come to believe that they voted for a candidate other than the one they had actually chosen. Recall data thus proved unreliable; survey respondents simply rationalized their current opinions by readjusting their memories of prior opinions. This problem is particularly important. Because panel studies are rarely used, recall data may provide the only information for assessing stability and change in the public's opinions.

Reliability problems are common in survey research, and they must be avoided if possible. However, there are several strategies useful in counteracting problems of reliability.[49] They include such obvious things as asking clear questions that are relevant to the respondent. One may also attempt to measure the same opinion with several different questions; then, if the responses to one question differ considerably from responses to the others, the reliability of that question is in doubt. These are only a few of the techniques available for determining and improving the reliability of measures of public opinion.

The Refinement of Measurement Techniques

In recent years measures of public opinion have become more accurate. New measures have increased the validity and reliability of questions. Unfortunately, in some instances the apparent changes in the public's opinions are in fact the result of improvements in measurement instruments. Some recent research argues that precisely this type of faulty attribution may be responsible for some claims that the public has become more ideological in recent years. For example, a study by John Sullivan et al. indicates that apparent increases in ideological constraint in the American public may be rooted less in real opinion change than in changes in measures of political issues:

> *The pattern of these results suggests that the level of constraint in the mass public has not increased greatly over the past two decades, as others have argued, but rather that it merely* appears *to have increased because of the ways in which it has been measured. . . .*
>
> Our own view is that the questions used in the national surveys before 1964 did not adequately capture the liberal-conservative dimension, and therefore it is not surprising that studies using these items should have found lower levels of constraint in this period than in the later period during which more reliable measures were used.[50]

Bishop et al. concur that conclusions about change in the public's ideological consistency may simply be "methodological artifacts," stemming from changes in issue-item wording and format.[512] Clearly, findings of this sort challenge the comparability of issue-opinion data gathered in the 1950s and issue-opinion data gathered since 1964.

Measurement poses difficult — but certainly not insurmountable — problems for the study of public opinion. Most of these problems affect the study of public opinion at one point in time as well as in over-time studies; but they are intensified in the study of change. Not only does the researcher of change have to deal with measurement problems at two or more time points (rather than one), but he or she must take special precautions to ensure that the change noted is real change and not simply evidence of measurement error compounded over time, and that genuine change is not hidden. Numerous tactics are available to help insulate findings from measurement errors. These strategies include careful selection of research subjects or respondents, the use of several alternative measurement strategies to tap the same opinion characteristics, careful attention to comparisons, and the use of identical measurement procedures in over-time studies. Overall, an awareness of the pitfalls of measurement error and the cautious interpretation of change are the best guards against drawing faulty conclusions.

INTERPRETING THE EVIDENCE FOR OPINION CHANGE

Although the decisions to be made prior to and during opinion research are of crucial importance, perhaps the most interesting problems are those found in different interpretations lent to the same factual findings. Bennett calls these differences "cutting edge effects" — or the "analyst's rendering of broad interpretive frames in which to place findings."[52] The reader, then, must develop a sensitivity to the possibilities for differing interpretations. This ability to search out and compare alternative interpretations becomes even more important when the focus of study is *change* in public opinion. For change can be (and has been) interpreted in widely varying ways.

Asher notes that traditional public opinion literature paints a rather negative picture of the electorate.[53] More recent research challenges that image, but there is disagreement in how to interpret the new findings. Asher groups the "revisionist" interpretations of change into two broad categories: those who attribute change in the electorate's abilities to faulty methodology in earlier studies; and those who attribute the noted changes to the "nature of the times."[54]

The argument of the "faulty methodology" school is that the early findings paint an inaccurate picture because they are based on unacceptable techniques and measures; more recent studies present a more optimistic view of the public simply because of the methods they employ. Early studies of the public found that people voting for different presidential candidates held fairly similar views on political issues. However, these issues were selected for the public by the scholars. David RePass argues that the only reasonable way to investigate the connection between vote choice and issue opinion is to let the public define the issues that are important to them. In particular, RePass notes that when allowed to pick issues that are salient or important to them, the public demonstrates an ability to base their party choice on those issues.[55] The faulty methodology argument has been widely applied in recent years, including studies of how many people have opinions on issues, the level of political tolerance, and the level of political ideology.

The "nature of the times" position similarly criticizes the early literature's dim view of the public. Here the argument is that the political calm of the 1950s inhibited the issue instincts of the public, and that the findings of studies conducted during that period are time-bound. In their classic work, *The American Voter,* Angus Campbell et al. found that in 1956 only 12 percent of the public looked at politics in ideological or "near" ideological frames of references.[56] This finding was taken by many to suggest that most of the public *could not* think ideologically, that there were some constant limitations inherent to the public's abilities. Yet studies of the 1964 election, with the presence of an ideological candidate (Goldwater), showed many more ideologues to be present. One author offers this "nature of the times" explanation:

> As well as stimulating an increase in the number of ideologues in 1964, the apparent ideological rhetoric of the campaign stimulated an increase in the participation and psychological involvement of ideologues, and consequently compounded the influence of ideological factors on the election outcome.[57]

Similarly, increases in the consistency of the public's opinions have been explained by increases in the salience and consistency of politics:

> Indeed our data suggests that not only specific political attitudes but the structure of mass attitudes may be affected by politics in the real world. The average citizen may not be as apolitical as thought.[58]

These studies, as well as others, suggest that many apparent changes in the characteristics of public opinion are not the result of fundamental changes in the public, but rather in the politics to which the public responds.

Clearly, then, the results of studies describing change in public opinion are interpreted within different contexts, even from the same sets of data developed by the same measures. These interpretations are structured in part by the personal and political assumptions and perspectives the scholar brings to the data. The variety of interpretations also stem from the absence of studies conducted in tightly controlled experimental settings. The subjects of public opinion research are usually the general public, and the focus is its behavior and opinion within a political setting. Students of public opinion frequently must employ cross-sectional, aggregate-level survey research results that bear little resemblance to carefully controlled experimentation. This chapter will not describe the list of research designs that attempt to simulate experimentation in opinion research; many methodology texts do that at some length.[59] Rather, at this point, it is sufficient to emphasize that the nature of the public opinion laboratory — the political world — leads to broad leeway in the interpretation of findings.

CONCLUSION

This chapter has described some of the problems facing students of change in public opinion. Many of these problems are not peculiar to the study of opinion change; on the contrary, the precautions noted here are equally relevant to other concerns in opinion research. Comparing public opinion at different points in time merely underscores the importance of these problems. Yet the precautions described in this chapter should not be interpreted only as discouraging features in the study of opinion change; they are better viewed as challenges. The process of scientific research, regardless of the substantive area of that research, is seldom clear-cut and problem-free. As Babbie points out,

> Scientific research is anything but a cut-and-dried progression of steps in the search for truth. It is a constant adventure and a constant challenge.[60]

The study of public opinion is no exception.

DATA COLLECTION: AN ADDENDUM ON SURVEY SAMPLES AND QUESTION WORDING

The student of public opinion must guard against the possibility that the data may be a set of jumbled, and useless, responses to a poorly designed project. All too often responses to public opinion polls are taken at face value, as if simply because some group of people is asked some sort of question, the responses must mean something. However, unless great care is taken in selecting both the people in the survey and the questions to be asked, the results of the survey will have little meaning. This section describes some of the most important considerations.

Survey Samples

The decade of the seventies may be remembered as the time when public opinion surveying went "public." Before 1970, large-scale public opinion surveys were generated primarily for the use of academics, merchandisers, or politicians. In the last ten years, however, the mass media have incorporated commissioned public opinion polling into their normal news-gathering process. The expansion of the use of public opinion surveys means that the reader of a newspaper can almost daily check to see what the public's opinion is on some type of issue.

While survey results have become a regular part of the individual's information about the outside world, people tend to be a bit suspicious of them. A good example of this suspicion is when one's favorite television program has been canceled because it did not receive a high enough viewership from use surveys conducted by the Nielson research company. The anger may become even greater when it is discovered that the survey that led to the cancellation was conducted in less than a thousand households. The impression left is that a small number of people dictate what everyone will and will not see on television.

Nevertheless, the survey practices of Nielson and others are, in fact, relatively valid ways of *approximating* the tastes and opinions of an entire population. Survey studies employ *samples* that, if correctly selected, represent a larger population, within a certain margin of error. The method by which the sample is drawn from a general population determines the degree to which it represents that larger population. Unless the population is very small, there is little choice but to select only a part of it to examine.

It has been argued, in fact, that the use of samples is more accurate than the use of general population surveys.[61] First, in order to contact (interview) a total population, one would have to hire and train a very large number of interviewers. The more interviewers hired, the greater the chance of including inexperienced or incompetent people who will not collect the interview material correctly. Second, with a larger number of people to interview the survey will take much longer. During the time the survey is "out in the field" all sorts of events may shift people's opinions. The result could be a survey in which half the respondents gave an opinion before an important event and half of them gave it after the event. In most surveys, it is important to get a "snapshot" of what is on the public's mind while it is seeing the same things.[62] Finally, interviewing a large population would be an enormously complex enterprise. As with most human endeavors, the more complex an action the more likely it is that errors will occur. Using a sample decreases the chance that errors will be introduced through the data collection process. It is for these and other reasons that the Bureau of Census uses a sample survey to check on the accuracy of its complete census of the population.

While the use of samples does provide insights into large populations and their opinions, the sample must be selected in a way that accurately reflects the characteristics of the members of a given population and minimizes the error that comes from generalizing from a small group to a large collectivity.

SAMPLING ACCURACY. Sampling accuracy is the degree to which a sample *represents* a larger population. If the method of choosing the sample is biased then the resulting sample will be a poor representation of the general population, and inferences based on that sample will not be accurate. To illustrate the relationship between sampling method and accuracy, consider the following situation. You are the mayor of Tinytown, with an adult population of 2,000. You are considering sponsoring a leash-law ordinance at the next city council meeting that would control the free-running dog population. You are worried, however, that there might be a strong "pro-free-dog" sentiment in the community that would not like the ordinance and that could turn you out of office in the upcoming election. You decide to conduct a survey using a sample of 200 Tinytown citizens to gauge the reaction to the proposed leash law. You consider a number of different sampling strategies.

1. *Strategy 1* is to have an interviewer stop people on Tinytown's Main Street and interview them until 200 have been questioned. While this is an easy way to obtain the interviews, you must remember that your goal is to acquire a representative sample, not an easy one. There are two strong sources of *sampling bias* involved in this strategy. First, since the interviewer is left alone to decide who to interview he or she will tend to select those people who look "approachable." It is possible that "nonapproachable" types tend to be in favor of strong leash laws. If so, then a "no-leash" majority found in the sample would be incorrect. Another problem is the choice of location. Are you sure that Main Street is frequented by *all* Tinytown residents? Perhaps residents who want strong leash laws are much more likely to walk up and down Main Street. If so, they will be overrepresented in the sample.

2. *Strategy 2* is for the interviewer to talk with every tenth person on Main Street. This sampling strategy introduces the method of *random selection* and eliminates the bias that comes from letting the interviewer talk to whomever he or she wants. The bias introduced by the location, though, still makes the strategy unattractive.[63]

3. *Strategy 3* is to use the telephone book, select every tenth name, and send the individual a questionnaire to fill out and return. This strategy is a great improvement over the second, for it retains random selection and eliminates the bias of interviewing at a specific location. However, it still can provide an inaccurate sample. While the *target population* remains all Tinytown adults, the *sample population,* that group from which the sample is actually drawn, does not include all Tinytown adults. Some people are systematically excluded from the sample population (the very poorest residents who cannot afford phones, and other adults in households with unlisted numbers, most notably, women.) An additional complication is that this method relies on the interviewee to send back the completed questionnaire. It might well be the case that those who are most upset about the dog problem, and who therefore are in favor of the leash law, are more highly motivated to return the questionnaire. Again, the sample results would not accurately reflect the attitudes of the general population.

4. *Strategy 4* is to randomly select city blocks, then randomly select house-holds on each of the selected blocks and have the interviewer talk with a randomly chosen resident within that household.[64] This strategy is called *multistage sampling*. At every point in the sample-selection process the decision to include or not to include some element is random. This means that no one is *systematically* excluded from the final sample since everyone has an equal chance of being interviewed. The sample population also comes very close to being the same as the target population, since the *sampling unit* is based on household residents. A sample chosen in this manner provides the best chance of approximating the opinions of the entire population of the town.

There are other methods of drawing samples for surveys as well. In general, though, the two main elements in improving sample accuracy are, first, to select a sample population that looks like the target population and, second, to make sure that every individual within the sample population has an equal chance of being interviewed. If these two requirements are not met, the results of a poll most likely will represent only a particular subunit of a population, rather than the population as a whole.

SAMPLING ERROR.   After the example given in the last section one may ask, "Even if the sample is accurate, how does one know that the responses of the 200 people are the same as those of the entire town?" This is a valid question. Unfortunately, the answer is not as straightforward as the discussion on sample accuracy, for it involves an understanding of the laws of probability. While this subject will not be treated in full, the following discussion will show how results from samples do, in fact, represent a larger population *within certain defined limits*.

Let us start with a simple excursion into probabilistic thinking, one where the distribution of something in the "real world" is known. If a quarter is flipped an infinite number of times, 50 percent of the time a head will appear and 50 percent of the time a tail will appear (assuming, of course, that the quarter is true and that the flips are done randomly). So, the *population average* or mean for flipping a quarter is 50 percent. Now imagine that a researcher decides to see how often a quarter will come up heads on fair flips. Since the researcher cannot flip the quarter an infinite number of times (thus obtaining the true population mean) a finite number of trial flips must be selected to ascertain the frequency of heads coming up. The finite number of flips can be thought of as the *sample size* of the research. The researcher decides to conduct five complete experiments for five days, one each day. On each successive day the number of flips (his sample size) is increased. Table 3–2 presents the results of these five experiments.

Table 3–2 reveals an important truth in the field of sampling: the larger the sample size the closer the sample results will be to those of the entire target population. As one can see, when the number of flips is increased, the sample results come more and more to approximate the real probability figure—50 percent. The difference between what a sample produces and what is really "out there" in the population is called *sampling error*. Another way, then, of casting the basic sampling axiom is that as the sample size increases, the sampling error decreases.

TABLE 3 – 2   Hypothetical Results of Five Coin Flipping Experiments

Day	Number of Flips	% Heads Turn Up
1	1	100%
2	10	70%
3	100	58%
4	1,000	52%
5	10,000	51%

Public opinion polls, unlike coin flips, do not have predetermined population figures. If the population characteristics were known, then there would be no reason to conduct a survey in the first place. How does one know that a survey result is a good representation of a population figure? If the sample is randomly selected, probability laws allow one to establish *confidence intervals* for the survey estimates, which tell within given margins of error how closely the survey result comes to the true population figure. Confidence intervals are established by calculating the average sampling error for a survey. For example, a survey asked a sample of 1,500 people how they stood on the Equal Rights Amendment (ERA). The sampling error for a survey of that size is about plus or minus 2.5 percent. This means that if 55 percent of the sample approves of the ERA, the real population approval has a high probability of falling within a confidence interval of 52.5 percent and 57.5 percent. Samples thus are approximations of real population values, and scientific sampling allows one to state how good an approximation the sample provides.

Recall that as the survey sample size increases, the sampling error decreases. This means that the confidence interval decreases as the sample size increases. A small confidence interval means that the sample estimates are more exact. To show the relationship between sample size and the size of the confidence interval, consider Table 3 – 3. That table presents the size of the confidence intervals associated with a survey response of 50 percent agreement to a question on the ERA. It is quite clear that as one increases the sample size the confidence interval decreases and the accuracy of the estimate increases.

TABLE 3 – 3   Confidence Intervals for a 50% Sample Approval of the ERA for Different Sample Sizes

Size of Sample	95% Confidence Interval (50% Approval of ERA)
50	36.1% — 63.9%
100	39.7% — 60.3%
300	44.2% — 55.8%
500	45.5% — 54.5%
1,000	46.8% — 53.2%
1,500	47.4% — 52.6%
2,000	47.8% — 52.2%
5,000	48.6% — 51.4%
10,000	49.0% — 51.0%

If a sample of fifty people has a 50 percent approval of the ERA, there is a 95 percent chance that the real population ERA approval could be as low as 36 percent or as high as 64 percent. That is quite a range and should not instill much confidence in the survey result. If the sample is 2,000, then there is 95 percent confidence that the actual population figure is no lower than roughly 48 percent and no higher than 52 percent. So, the 50 percent sample result would, in all probability, be not far off the mark.

The student of public opinion should therefore pay close attention to the sample size used in public opinion polling and to understanding the meaning behind statements such as, "We are 95 percent confident that the real value falls between —— percent and —— percent." Such statements are necessary before one can safely use survey data to generalize to larger populations.

While there has been a general improvement in the methodology of survey research in the past twenty years, the device can still be badly misused. Two such misuses occurred during the coverage of the 1980 election.

- After the debate between Jimmy Carter and Ronald Reagan, a major network asked its viewers to record their determination of the debate "victor" by calling one of two special phone numbers (at a cost of fifty cents). The result of the "poll" was an overwhelming victory for Reagan.
- Two weeks before the election, a poll was taken by a major network with a sample size of 1,562. The reported sampling error for the poll results was plus or minus 3 percent. In the news report it was related that 92 percent of the black voters polled indicated a preference for Carter.

Of these two examples, the first is the least valid: the respondents were not contacted randomly; the "interview" cost each "respondent" some money; individuals could vote as many times as they wished; the average Reagan supporter had a more intense support of his or her candidate than did the average Carter supporter; and people living in rural areas had an easier time in getting their interviews counted. Thus, the "poll" results were worthless. The sample had so many sources of bias (most of which favored a higher Reagan "victory") that the results cannot be used. The second example presents a slightly more subtle form of the problem. While the total sample size was 1,562, the total number of blacks interviewed was around 160. Generalizations about the attitudes of blacks are based on a number of 160, and not 1,562. The sampling error associated with 160 for that question response percentage is roughly plus or minus 5 percent (although it would be much larger were the distribution not quite so skewed). So, the confidence interval for this question actually was 87 percent to 97 percent approval of Carter. Careful reading of the reporting of other polling results will reveal many such errors of interpretation.

Question Wording and Placement

It often has been said that while designing a sampling scheme is a science, developing the questions to be asked in an interview is an art. While this is an overstatement, it does make an important point: even if a scientific sample is drawn, it still does not ensure that the responses to questions will be useful. As Seymour Martin Lipset and William Schneider argue, *most people believe that if polls are truly scientific, the results should not be open to alternative interpretations, that all reliable surveys should yield similar results, comparable to the results of a referendum.*[65]

Several aspects of questionnaire design can contribute to survey responses that make little, if any, sense.

QUESTION WORDING. In survey research, just as in everyday life, if one asks a stupid question one should be prepared for a similar answer. If a question is confusing or vague, the response to that question may not tap whatever it was that provided the original impetus for asking the question. Consider, for example, the following three questions involving Israel and Palestine. The questions were asked in two surveys collected within two months of each other.

- *Harris 12/74:* Israel should give back the territory it gained from the war of 1967. Agree: 25 percent.
- *Harris 12/74:* Israel should give up the occupied Palestinian Arab territory and let Arafat rule it. Agree: 11 percent.
- *Cambridge Research Center 2/75:* The Israelis ought to give up all of the territory they have captured since 1967 if the Arab states agree to peace. Agree: 36 percent.

At first glance the questions seem to be asking about the same thing: the individual's opinion on what the Israelis should do with the territory gained in the 1967 war. But a closer look makes it obvious that there are at least three different questions being asked. The first question deals specifically with the main issue. The second question asks the respondent two things: should the Israelis give up the land and should Arafat rule it. The 11 percent agree rate does not tell us which part of the question is generating the response — either agree or disagree. While the first and third questions seem to be asking the same thing, the inclusion of the word "peace" in the third seems to have produced a stronger sentiment of support, even though that might be tacitly assumed in the first question by some respondents.[66]

RESPONSE CATEGORY WORDING. Even if a question is clearly formed, the response alternatives presented to the respondent may play an important role in the resulting opinion distribution. Consider the responses to two different survey questions collected in the same month.

- *Gallup 2/75:* Do you approve or disapprove of the way Ford is handling his job as president?

Approve	55%
Disapprove	28%
Don't Know	17%

- *Harris 2/75:* How do you rate the job President Ford is doing as president — excellent, pretty good, only fair, or poor?

Excellent/Pretty Good	46%
Only Fair/Poor	52%
Don't Know	2%

Here, two questions that seem to be straightforward and tapping the same opinion have widely different opinion distributions. The reason is that given the larger number of response alternatives in the Harris question, people who were unsure about a clear-cut "yes" or "no" or "approve" or "disapprove" opinion on Ford's performance were more willing to give an opinion. When analyzing survey results, the student should be wary of questions that force a decision upon the respondents. Questions that allow a fuller breadth of opinion expression are much better instruments with which to gauge public opinion.

QUESTION PLACEMENT.   The last area of concern here is the most difficult to detect. Sometimes when and where one places a question in the survey can influence the responses to that question. This has been termed the *context effect*.[67] If one asks a series of questions about the problems facing society (inflation, unemployment, energy costs, and the like), and then asks for an evaluation of the job performance of a political decision maker such as the president, one may discover a lower approval rating than if the evaluation question had been asked *before* the problems questions. Context effects are difficult to discover, since it is rare that a full text of a survey questionnaire will accompany the reporting of the survey results.

SUMMARY

In summary, one must critically analyze the reporting of public opinion survey results. Many people have become so used to hearing and reading the results of surveys that they neglect to look deeper and discover whether or not the samples are accurate, the sampling error is acceptable, and the design of the questionnaire is straightforward and simple. The answers to those questions are crucial to one's interpretation of the outcome of the public opinion poll.

NOTES

1. Abraham Kaplan points out that the development of the concepts used in scientific research is inextricably bound to the operations used to measure those concepts. For a more detailed discussion see Abraham Kaplan, *The Conduct of Inquiry* (Scranton, Penn.: Chandler Publishing, 1964), pp. 34–50.
2. A longitudinal study is one that incorporates two or more observations over a given time span.
3. Herbert H. Hyman, *Secondary Analysis of Sample Surveys: Principles, Procedures, and Potentialities* (New York: John Wiley & Sons, 1972), p. 224.
4. Ibid.
5. Douglas Dobson and Duane A. Meeter, "Alternative Markov Models for Describing Change in Party Identification," *American Journal of Political Science* 18 (August 1974), p. 488.
6. Norval D. Glenn, *Cohort Analysis* (Beverly Hills: Sage Publications, 1977), p. 8.
7. G. David Garson, *Political Science Methods* (Boston: Holbrook Press, 1976), p. 169.
8. M. Kent Jennings and Richard G. Niemi, "Continuity and Change in Political Orientations: A Longitudinal Study of Two Generations," *American Political Science Review* 69 (December 1975), pp. 1316–35.

9. Ibid., p. 1317.
10. Ibid., pp. 1317–19.
11. Angus Campbell et al., *The American Voter* (New York: John Wiley & Sons, 1960), pp. 161–65.
12. Paul Allen Beck, "A Socialization Theory of Partisan Realignment," in *Controversies in American Voting Behavior,* Richard G. Niemi and Herbert F. Weisberg, eds. (San Francisco: W.H. Freeman & Co., 1970), pp. 396–411.
13. Ibid.
14. See the following: Paul R. Abramson, *Generational Change in American Politics* (Lexington, Mass.: D. C. Heath, 1975); Norval D. Glenn, "Sources of Shift to Political Independence: Some Evidence from a Cohort Analysis," *Social Science Quarterly* 53 (December 1972), pp. 494–519; Norval D. Glenn and Tedd Hefner, "Further Evidence on Aging and Party Identification," *Public Opinion Quarterly* 36 (Spring 1972), pp. 31–37; David Knoke, *Change and Continuity in American Politics: The Social Bases of Political Parties* (Baltimore: Johns Hopkins University Press, 1976).
15. The present treatment fails to note some complex methodological difficulties involved in the use of cohort analysis. For a detailed discussion of the difficulties of untangling age, period, and cohort effects see the following: Karen Oppenheim Mason et al., "Some Methodological Issues in Cohort Analysis of Archival Data," *American Sociological Review* 38 (April 1973), pp. 242–58.
16. William G. Vanderbok, "Cohorts, Aggregation Problems and Cross-Level Theorizing: The Case of Partisan Stability," *Western Political Quarterly* 30 (March 1977), pp. 104–11.
17. Eleanor Maccoby and Ray Hyman, "Measurement Problems in Panel Studies," in *American Voting Behavior,* Eugene Burdick and Arthur J. Brodbeck, eds. (New York: Free Press, 1959), p. 77.
18. Donald T. Campbell and Julian C. Stanley, *Experimental and Quasi-Experimental Designs for Research* (Chicago: Rand McNally, 1963), pp. 16–24.
19. See Hyman, *Sample Surveys,* p. 60; and Garson, *Political Science Methods,* p. 429.
20. Garson, *Political Science Methods,* pp. 433–34.
21. Campbell and Stanley, *Designs for Research,* pp. 5–6.
22. Ibid., pp. 7, 16–24.
23. Ibid.
24. Ibid.
25. Garson, *Political Science Methods,* p. 429.
26. Eric A. Hanushek, John E. Jackson, and John F. Kain, "Model Specification, Use of Aggregate Data, and the Ecological Correlation Fallacy," *Political Methodology* 1 (Winter 1974), pp. 100–1.
27. Numerous other threats to the correct interpretation of panel results are present. Although they will not be discussed at length here, they include technical aspects of the survey questions, regression effects, selection biases, and problems with generalizing the findings of panel studies. The student who plans to use a panel design should certainly explore these problems more thoroughly.
28. M. Kent Jennings and Richard G. Niemi, "The Persistence of Political Orientations: An Over-Time Analysis of Two Generations," *British Journal of Political Science* 8 (July 1967), pp. 333–63.
29. Earl R. Babbie, *The Practice of Social Research* (Belmont, Calif.: Wadsworth, 1979), p. 270.
30. Ibid., p. 137.
31. Robert E. Lane, "The Fear of Equality," *American Political Science Review* 53 (March 1959), pp. 35–51; Philip E. Converse, "The Nature of Belief Systems in Mass Publics," in *Ideology and Discontent,* David E. Apter, ed. (New York: Free Press, 1964).

32. W. Lance Bennett, "Epistemology and the Analysis of Mass Beliefs: Assumptions, Methods, and Meanings in Opinion Research" (Paper presented at the 1975 Annual Meeting of the American Political Science Association, San Francisco), pp. 16–20.
33. Babbie, *The Practice of Social Research,* p. 54.
34. Certainly an all-important consideration in the assignment of numbers to observations is the level of measurement appropriate to the forthcoming analysis. For a discussion of levels of measurement, see Kaplan, *The Conduct of Inquiry.*
35. Herbert McClosky, "Consensus and Ideology in American Politics," *American Political Science Review* 58 (June 1964), pp. 361–82; James W. Prothro and G. W. Grigg, "Fundamental Principles of Democracy: Bases of Agreement and Disagreement," *Journal of Politics* 22 (May 1960), pp. 276–94.
36. Mary R. Jackman, "General and Applied Tolerance: Does Education Increase Commitment to Racial Integration?" *American Journal of Political Science* 22 (May 1978), pp. 322–23.
37. Ibid.
38. David C. Leege and Wayne L. Francis, *Political Research* (New York: Basic Books, 1974), p. 149.
39. Christopher H. Achen, "Mass Political Attitudes and the Survey Response," *American Political Science Review* 69 (December 1975), pp. 1218–31.
40. Ibid., p. 1220.
41. John C. Pierce and Douglas D. Rose, "Nonattitudes and American Public Opinion: The Examination of a Thesis," *American Political Science Review* 68 (June 1974), pp. 629–49.
42. George I. Balch, "Multiple Indicators in Survey Research: The Concept 'Sense of Political Efficacy,'" *Political Methodology* 1 (Spring 1974), pp. 1–44.
43. Ibid.
44. Herbert B. Asher, "The Reliability of the Political Efficacy Items," *Political Methodology* 1 (Spring 1974), p. 57. The problem addressed by Balch and Asher is *also* a validity problem. If they are correct, the political efficacy scale confounds the measurement of internal and external efficacy. Therefore, that scale is both unreliable *and* invalid.
45. Ibid.
46. One notable exception is Jennings and Niemi, *Political Orientations.*
47. Kent L. Tedin, "On the Reliability of Reported Political Attitudes," *American Journal of Political Science* 20 (February 1976), pp. 117–24.
48. Blair I. Weir, "The Distortion of Voter Recall," *American Journal of Political Science* 19 (February 1975), pp. 53–61
49. Babbie, *The Practice of Social Research.*
50. John L. Sullivan, James Piereson, and George E. Marcus, "Ideological Constraint in the Mass Public: A Methodological Critique and Some New Findings," *American Journal of Political Science* 22 (May 1978), pp. 241–42.
51. George F. Bishop, Alfred J. Tuchfarber, and Robert W. Oldendick, "Change in the Structure of American Political Attitudes: The Nagging Question of Question Wording," *American Journal of Political Science* 22 (May 1978), p. 267.
52. Bennett, "Analysis of Mass Beliefs," p. 72.
53. Herbert B. Asher, *Presidential Elections and American Politics* (Homewood, Ill.: Dorsey Press, 1976), p. 80 ff.
54. Asher, Ibid., p. 100 ff.
55. David E. RePass, "Issue Salience and Party Choice," *American Political Science Review* 65 (June 1971), pp. 389–400.
56. Campbell et al., *The American Voter,* Chap. 10.
57. John C. Pierce, "Party Identification and the Changing Role of Ideology in American Politics," *Midwest Journal of Political Science* 14 (February 1970), p. 41.

58. Norman Nie with Kristi Andersen, "Mass Belief Systems Revisited: Political Change and Attitude Structure," *Journal of Politics* 36 (August 1974), p. 580.

59. Campbell and Stanley, *Designs for Research;* Leege and Francis, *Political Research;* Garson, *Political Science Methods;* Babbie, *The Practice of Social Research.*

60. Babbie, *The Practice of Social Research.*

61. Ibid., p. 162.

62. This is especially true in campaigns where events may occur at any time and disrupt an ongoing survey.

63. One journalistic mainstay, the "man-on-the-street" interview, is particularly subject to this problem.

64. For simplicity, we assume that Tinytown has residential blocks of equal population density. For a useful way of randomly selecting someone to interview once a residence is selected, see Raymond L. Gorden, *Interviewing* (Homewood, Ill.: Dorsey Press, 1980), pp. 243–45.

65. Seymour Martin Lipset and William Schneider, "Polls for the White House, and the Rest of Us," *Encounter* 49 (November 1977), p. 24. Examples of survey questions in this section are taken from this article.

66. For a good overview of question and response wordings *see* Gorden, *Interviewing,* Chap. 12.

67. For examples of this effect, *see* Lipset and Schneider, "Polls for the White House."

PART II

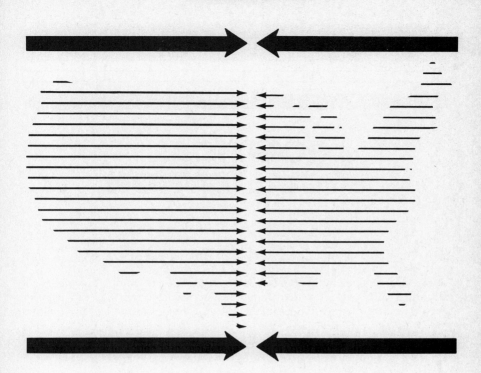

SOURCES OF
PUBLIC OPINION

CHAPTER 4

POLITICAL SOCIALIZATION

At the age of five, many kindergarten students can recite the pledge of allegiance (although often with humorous variations), and they can identify the pictures of George Washington and Abraham Lincoln on their classroom walls.

A major study of the development of children's political attitudes reported that by the fourth grade, 63 percent could articulate a preference among the major political parties.[1]

Sporting events, particularly those associated with high schools and colleges, ordinarily begin with the singing of the national anthem, and sometimes with prayer.

Campbell et al. report the following conversation between an interviewer and a respondent during a study of the public's political attitudes and behavior:

Interviewer: (Is there anything you like about the Democrats?)

Respondent: No Ma'am, not that I know of.

Interviewer: (Is there anything you dislike about the Democrats?)

Respondent: No Ma'am, but I've always been a Democrat just like my daddy.[2]

These examples illustrate a fundamental process called *political socialization:* the learning of political attitudes and behavior.

One definition of political socialization emphasizes the learning of political orientations that *support* the existing political system. Political socialization, in this approach, is the process by which the system transmits its dominant norms and values to individuals. Roberta Sigel takes this perspective when she defines political socialization as "the process by which people learn to adopt the norms, values, attitudes, and behaviors accepted and practiced by the ongoing system."[3] In this definition, political socialization is usually described as fundamentally a conservative process, directed at stability and the preservation of the status quo.[4] Attention focuses on those institutions and processes that strive to create and reinforce positive feelings about American symbols, processes, institutions, events, and personages.

A more inclusive and popular definition of political socialization is "the learning of political values, norms, perceptions, and identifications."[5] This chapter adopts this more general approach, viewing political socialization as the process by which people acquire *any* political beliefs and behavior. This conception shifts the focus from the political system to the individual and includes the study of all sources of the individual's political orientations, regardless of whether he or she supports the system, is critical of the system, or has no opinion of the system.

Political socialization is a process of interaction beween the *individual* who learns and the *sources* that provide the material being learned. The outcome of that interaction depends on what the source communicates, either directly or indirectly, and on the individual's response.[6] The sources of communication are called *agencies* of political socialization, and include parents, schools, peer groups, mass media, and political experiences. The person's response depends on several conditions, including his or her existing political orientations, which screen new messages; the context in which the response takes place (e.g., the way the child feels about his or her parents or the structure of a school's curriculum); and the individual's level of cognitive development.[7]

That children learn political attitudes rather early in life is thought to have some important long-range implications. While there is little conclusive evidence that adults possess political orientations closely resembling those they acquired as children, there are suggestions that these early beliefs are difficult to displace. Because they develop so early, beliefs may carry an inertial weight that works against change. These early tenets also may structure beliefs that the individual later acquires,[8] screening or filtering information, and allowing beliefs consistent with those already held, while excluding those that would not fit easily into the existing belief system. The classic example of this process is the development of party loyalty. It has been widely argued that for most Americans party identification is acquired quite early in life and persists throughout it.[9] These partisan orientations become a long-term force in the individual's behavior, and they "perform for the citizen an exceedingly useful evaluative function."[10]

In contrast, some political orientations acquired early in life may be changed, displaced, or forgotten in the daily context of politics decades later. For example, most children acquire a positive orientation to the American political system, but many adults express cynical attitudes about politics and government. In times of stress or perceived danger to the country, positive attitudes may be called to the surface again. The positive orientations may override the cynicism and provide a reservoir of support that the system can tap in times of need.

THE DEVELOPMENT OF SYSTEM SUPPORT

Building on the pioneering work of David Easton and Jack Dennis,[11] scholars have identified four major patterns in the development of children's attitudes about government and politics: politicization, personalization, idealization, and institutionalization.[12] *Politicization* occurs when the child learns that there is an authority above and beyond family and school figures.[13] Niemi cites the case of the child who becomes aware of the parent's compliance with traffic regulations. *Personalization* means that children are likely to think of individuals rather than institutions when choosing pictorial representations of government.

A third process is *idealization,* wherein "to most children political authority seems trustworthy, benevolent and helpful."[14] One researcher reports that as early as the fourth grade, children develop remarkably benevolent attitudes toward political authority.[15] He speculates that those benevolent attitudes about political authority stem from "adults — even cynical adults — [who] more or less unconsciously sugarcoat the political explanations they pass on to children."[16] These positive orientations about political authority may spring from positive attitudes the child develops about the first authority figures it faces — its parents:

> *Figures in the latter setting (political), for instance the president, are unconsciously (i.e., in a way not accessible to conscious awareness) perceived as analogues of parents and other immediate environment authorities. The public figure becomes invested with powerful private feelings; response to him assumes some of the qualities of response to family members and others in the face-to-face environment.*[17]

Dennis et al. found that 72 percent in their youngest age group of American children (fifth graders) agreed that "American citizens have the chance to express their opinions about the way our country is run." Forty-six percent of that same group could agree with the statement that "Democracy is the best form of government."[18] These benevolent orientations to the political world — to government, to forms of government, to figures of political authority — developed long before they could be based on some systematic evaluation of the political world. Thus, it is clear that the beliefs must be learned, either directly or indirectly.

Institutionalization, the fourth process, is the gradual identification of government as institutions (e.g., Congress) and processes rather than as individuals (President Reagan). The child learns to distinguish between the *position* in government and the person in the position — that is, the difference between the presidency and a particular president. As the child matures, many of the positive attitudes earlier oriented toward the personalized position become transferred to the institutionalized position. This transfer allows negative attitudes to surface toward the person in the position while positive attitudes are maintained toward the position itself.

While the landmark studies of political socialization depict a generally benevolent and positive view of government by children, subsequent studies suggest that this view may no longer be accurate. David O. Sears notes that the studies of the late 1960s showed children's views of government as less benevolent than earlier studies, particularly in the case of black children. Sears poses the question: "How can the idealization of earlier studies be reconciled with the mixed attitudes characteristic of so many that have appeared subsequently?"[19] He suggests that the answer may come from the kind of political environment in which children acquire their political orientations.

> *Let us argue here that to some extent the earlier findings were merely a historical accident. The Easton and Hess and the Greenstein projects were conducted during the Eisenhower and Kennedy administrations — the first, a time of relatively little partisan controversy around an extremely popular president, and the second, we will argue, a president unusually appealing to children."*[20]

During the middle and late 1960s, American politics and society were the stage of considerable political turmoil and increasing doubts about the efficacy of government. The sharp decline in adult support for the political system attests to the widespread impact of those patterns.[21] Moreover, those "environmental" events appeared to have some different effects on black and white children. In earlier studies, black children had positive attitudes towards politics similar to those of white children; by the late sixties, they were substantially more cynical than whites. Sears suggests that this may result from changes from the rural southern socialization patterns of the older age groups to northern urban patterns of the youngest groups, with increasing disaffection, black pride, sophistication and political activism, and some exposure to "more cynical and militant views" by civil rights protests and riots.[22]

The Watergate affair generated a new set of studies about children's attitudes towards government and politics. The question here was whether a major political event could alter the tendency of children to idealize government and political leaders. The general answer found in these studies is "yes," that even the overwhelmingly positive attitudes found among white children in the earlier studies had been largely erased.

Jack Dennis and Carol Webster studied children in Tacoma, Washington, comparing responses in a 1974 study with those observed in 1962.[23] They found that in 1974 children were substantially more critical of government and of the major political figure, the president. Table 4–1 shows the changes in two important questions. The children of 1974 were much less likely to idealize government than were the 1962 children. The difference is most striking at the higher grade levels. In 1962, 71 percent of the sixth graders agreed that the president keeps his promises, but in 1974 that figure was only 25 percent. Similar figures exist for perceptions that "what goes on in the government is all for the best."

Christopher Arterton also has shown that among third-, fourth-, and fifth-grade students in Boston, the percentage agreeing that the president is the child's favorite person declined precipitously in 1973, with only 5 percent of the Boston fifth graders agreeing, compared to 50 percent agreeing in a 1962 national sample.[24] Arterton concludes that "the once benevolent leader has been transformed into the malevolent leader by the impact of current events,"[25] and that "the effect of Watergate has been to transform the president from a positive, morally good symbol into a negative object to be affectively and morally rejected."[26] This rings close to Dennis and Webster's conclusion that "an age cohort of disbelievers has been created in response to what has lately been widely evaluated as a failure of leadership and in some senses a failure of the system as well."[27]

TABLE 4 – 1   Changes in Children's Attitudes About Government and the President

		Grade				
		2	3	4	5	6
Percentage saying president "always keeps his promises" or "almost always"	1962	89	82	83	82	71
	1974	61	54	40	29	25
Percentage agreeing that "what goes on in the government is all for the best"	1962				85	83	77
	1974				43	40	27

Source: This table is drawn from "Children's Images of the President and of Government in 1962 and 1974," by Jack Dennis and Carol Webster, and is reprinted from *American Politics Quarterly* Vol. 3, No. 4 (October 1975), pp. 397, 399, by permission of the Publisher, Sage Publications, Inc.

One important caveat to these patterns is found in the work of Fred Greenstein, who, in part of a cross-national study, looked at the attitudes of American children in 1969–1970 and 1973 and compared those findings to his work of the early 1960s. Contrary to some other studies in the same time period, he found that "to my surprise, the first-term Nixon-Administration counterparts of children in the Eisenhower-Kennedy Administration studies — namely the white American respondents — *were extraordinarily positive in their spontaneous descriptions of the President.*"[28] Greenstein does find that in later studies black children were only about half as likely to articulate favorable views of the president as they had been earlier. Greenstein also conducted interviews with children after Watergate and found some decline in positive feelings about the president, but nowhere near the precipitous drop suggested in the other post-Watergate studies.

These studies describe some important changes in the aggregate distribution of political orientations in American children: black children of the late sixties were less likely than whites to idealize government and political figures; and post-Watergate children are substantially different from those of the early sixties.[29] The decline in children's idealization and perceptions of benevolence in leaders appears to be a response to several concurrent patterns in their environment. First, during the decline there were similar changes in adult political attitudes. Second, there occurred events and patterns in the country's political life — racial disorder, antiwar protest, Watergate — that are directly related to the changes in attitudes. In part, at least, the changes in the children's orientations need not have been a *direct* response to political events. Rather, they may have been a reaction to those events as they were interpreted by political leaders and by relevant authority figures, such as parents and teachers. Even when some adults "sugarcoated" their interpretations of politics, there may have remained sufficient alternative sources of information to create change in the beliefs of many children.

THE SOURCES OF SOCIALIZATION

Much of the effort in the study of political socialization has been directed at disentangling the sources of the child's beliefs. That is, if the child is doing the learning, who is doing the teaching? A readily identifiable set of "teachers" has appeared in the literature, and they have been labeled the "agents" of socialization.

The Family

The family is thought by many scholars to be the most important source of political socialization. The family has the first opportunity to cement its norms in the child's mind. Parents need not override or manipulate beliefs built up through time. They are the focus of the child's initial social interaction and the predominant, if not the only, source of early cues for appropriate responses to their environment. James C. Davies summarizes the importance of the family in the following passage:

> The family provides the major means for transforming the mentally naked infant organism into the adult, fully clothed in its own personality. And most of the individual's political personality — his tendencies to think and act politically in particular ways — have been determined at home, several years before he can take part in politics as an ordinary adult citizen or as a political prominent.[30]

There are several processes by which the child may acquire the same political orientations as the parent. One is the direct transmission of political attitudes. That is, the parent explicitly indicates to the child the appropriate political orientation, and the child responds by adopting that orientation. The parent's definition of the correct political response is clear and intentional. Parents also may unintentionally transmit political attitudes to the child. Without their knowledge the child may mimic the parents' beliefs, much like the young boy or girl who pretends to be the mother or the father.

Even less directly, the parent may affect the child's orientations to non-political institutions and ideas (e.g., a church), which later act as positive or negative cues for political orientations. Also, as noted earlier in this chapter, the child's attitudes about the parents may be generalized to political authority figures, resulting in idealized and benevolent perceptions. Finally, the parents may influence the development of the child's personality, and that personality may stimulate certain kinds of political attitudes. Frank A. Pinner has shown in Belgium and the Netherlands that children who in their formative years have been overprotected by their parents are less trustful of the political world.[31] In the United States, Greeley has shown that different ethnic subcultures with different family environments differ in the extent to which parents and children agree on political questions.[32]

Recent studies show considerable variation in the magnitude of the correspondence between the opinions of children and their parents. Political party identification almost uniformly shows the strongest correspondence between the parents' political orientations and those of the children.[33] In recent years the increased percentage of Independents in younger age groups points to the declining influence of parents on the party choice of their offspring. In 1972, for example, a majority of the eighteen- to twenty-one-year-olds (50 percent) aligned themselves with neither of the two parties.[34] Jennings and Niemi found over a period of eight years that in a group of high school seniors the percentage of parents identifying with a political party remained stable.[35] And the percentage with the same partisanship as their parents dropped from 59 percent in 1965 to 47 percent in 1973.[36] Thus, the younger generation moved away from their parents' partisan attachment during the period of their lives when they should have exhibited greater partisanship.

What might account for the declining influence of parents on their children's party identification? Several possibilities emerge. First, American parents may now view party identification as less important and hence make less effort to ensure that their offspring possess the "correct" party identification. Second, it may be that other sources of learning that do not emphasize party identification, such as television, have increased in importance, providing communications that drown out those of the parents. Third, much in the politics of the post-Kennedy sixties and seventies have emphasized political issues with particular attraction for young people: civil rights, ecology, Vietnam, life-styles. According to some scholars, because the parties were not seen to offer coherent and distinct alternatives to those issues, many young people turned away.[37]

Parents are less successful in transmitting to their children their beliefs about specific issues than their partisanship. Indeed, the level of correspondence falls far short of what one might expect if the family were an overriding agent of political socialization.

What factors may account for greater agreement between parents and children in some families than in others? Kent Tedin examined the contribution of three conditions to increased parent-child agreement: the accuracy with which the child perceives the views of the parent; the importance of the issue to the parents; and the attractiveness of the parents to their children.[38] Tedin found that accurate perceptions substantially increase the agreement; where perceptions are accurate, agreement on issue positions is at the same level as that for party identification. A similar pattern holds for the importance of the issue to the parents. With high salience, the correspondence scores are much higher. Likewise, except for attitudes about marijuana laws, as parental attractiveness increases so does parent-child agreement.

Jennings and Niemi have compared the aggregate distributions of a sample of high school students and their parents at different points in time — 1965 and 1973.[39] Substantial differences (a "generation gap") were found in the two samples in 1965, paticularly in their attitudes on political issues. In the ensuing years the differences between the two generations remained in some cases (e.g., the younger generation remained more liberal). However, in

some important areas the children drew closer to their parents (e.g., in political cynicism), and in others both generations moved in the same direction.
Overall, Jennings and Niemi concluded that

> the flow of the two generations over time has, if anything, worked to bring
> them closer together now than they were eight years earlier. Only in certain
> issue areas and in regard to partisanship were the generations noticeably
> pulling apart.[40]

Thus, there is some indication that when the parents' socializing power
weakens, producing apparent splits between them and their children, the
political and social forces to which both groups are exposed will eventually
draw them together.

Parents can indirectly influence children's attitudes through the literature
they select for them. Children's literature carries with it both explicit and
implicit messages about political figures and political roles. Flattering biog-
raphies of such major historical figures as Washington and Lincoln are clear
examples. There is also explicit political content in many nonpolitical
stories,[41] and in the communication of sex-role stereotypes. The traditional
picture of the woman's role as housewife and mother is widely depicted. In
recent years, however, a number of children's books explicitly convey alternative roles for both men and women.[42]

The actual impact of literature on children's political attitudes is not
known at the present. Indeed, it would be extremely difficult to distinguish
its impact on children's attitudes from the impact of the parents' attitudes
that led to the selection of the literature. That is, correspondence between
children's attitudes and the content of the literature to which they are exposed may result from the parent having caused both of them.

How much influence, then, does the family have on the socialization of its
children? It apparently depends on the relationship between the child and the
parents, on the structure of the family unit, and on the character of the politics and society within which the family operates. Moreover, there is some
evidence that the socializing power of the family is declining. For reasons,
one might look to changing relationships between parents and children,
changing family structures with more single-parent families, the emergence
of powerful competing sources of cues for children, and differences in the perceptions of children and parents in the relevance of particular political issues.
Because of the apparent decline in the family's influence, other agents of
socialization are perhaps becoming more influential in the child's political
learning. Indeed, some authors argue that the schools are more important
than the family.

The Schools

Schools are the major rival of the family in political socialization. Contrast
the statement of Davies, cited earlier, that "most of the individual's personality — his tendencies to think and act politically in particular ways — have
been determined at home," with Robert Hess and Judith Torney's conclusion
that "the school stands out as the central, salient and dominant force in the

political socialization of the young child."[43] The schools do have access to the child for extended periods of time through the formative years. Yet although most studies of political socialization document extensive opinion changes during the years the child is in school, more evidence is needed to affirm the preeminence of the schools. One must be able to demonstrate that the changes would not have occurred anyway, and that the family's influence does not determine the nature of the child's response to the schools.

RITUALS AND SYMBOLS.   Almost from the moment of entry into school the child is faced daily with symbols and rituals designed to develop loyalty to the country. Starting with kindergarten, the schoolchild salutes the American flag and recites the pledge of allegiance — long before being able to understand the content of those words repeated from memory. The pledge often is followed by the group singing of the national anthem or "America." The walls of the classroom carry pictures of national heroes — George Washington, Abraham Lincoln, the incumbent president. The birthdays of Washington and Lincoln are occasion for a school holiday, and the telling of their childhood exploits is standard grade-school curriculum.

What is the consequence of this early and regular exposure to political symbols and rituals? Hess and Torney argue that it develops awe for government, submission, respect, and dependence, and that it is reinforced by its group nature.[44] They also report that second graders perceive the pledge of allegiance to be a prayer offered to God.[45] Reid Reading shows that 80 percent of second graders agree that "The American Flag Is the Best Flag in the World" and 84 percent agree that "America Is the Best Country in the World."[46] These positive orientations to the system may then act as a foundation upon which subsequent learning and experience can be built.

THE CURRICULUM.   Rare is the school curriculum that does not contain at least one course that loosely can be labeled as "civics," although these go under a variety of specific names, including American government and social studies. Civics courses traditionally are designed to convey information about the political process, to generate good citizenship, and to develop loyalty and respect for the system. Hess and Torney argue that the civics course in elementary schools focuses on *compliance* to rules and authority and "underemphasizes the rights and obligations of a citizen to participate in government."[47] Discussing civics textbooks, Patrick concludes that

> *loyalty, duty, order and obedience have seemed to be highlighted rather than ideas and information about how the political system works, how different individuals and groups might derive more benefits from it, and how it might be improved.*[48]

There is some dispute over the impact of traditional civics courses. Dawson and Prewitt conclude that "the classroom curriculum stands as a key means through which schoolchildren acquire knowledge about political life and loyalty to the nation."[49] Edgar Litt's study of civic education showed that "students in the civic education classes were more likely to endorse aspects of the democratic creed and less likely to hold chauvinistic political sentiments than students not exposed to the program."[50] On the other hand, a recent review of the literature suggests that "although the traditional approaches have dominated the public schools, the impact of these courses in the political knowledge domain (as suggested by various survey studies) has been meager."[51]

Kenneth Langton and Kent Jennings have conducted the most detailed analysis of the impact of civics courses.[52] Among high school students, those taking a civics course exhibit a higher level of political knowledge, interest, exposure to political content in media, amount of "political discourse," level of political efficacy, and amount of civic tolerance. Yet, they write, "it is perfectly obvious from the size of the correlations that the magnitude of the relationships are extremely weak, in most instances bordering on the trivial."[53] Why should civics courses be relatively ineffective in altering the way American students approach political questions? Langton and Jennings suggest the concept of redundancy; that is, the modern American student receives political cues from many sources, of which the high school civics course is only one. The content of the civics course may only duplicate that received from other sources, and hence add little to the student's store of information or political orientations.

Langton and Jennings compared the impact of civics courses on black and white high school students. While they found only minimal effects on whites, rather substantial effects were observed for blacks. Civics courses appeared to close the gap between black and white students in political efficacy and civic tolerance. The redundancy effect is not present for black students because they do not receive these cues from other sources.

What about civics courses in recent years? A study shows that the content and focus of most textbooks of the seventies differed little from those of earlier years.[54] At the same time, however, there were some attempts to develop more innovative curricula. Patrick cites examples of courses and textbooks developed in the late sixties and early seventies designed to "stress knowledge based on related social science concepts pertinent to political phenomena," and which "emphasize learning of generalizations about the political behavior of groups rather than details about institutions and legal documents."[55] Still others focus on the development of rational and informed beliefs, or "high moral reasoning."[56] Do these approaches make any difference? They are relatively successful in conveying different types of *information* to the students, information more in line with modern political science's concerns, such as voting behavior, political recruitment, political conflict and compromise, and role orientation.[57] However, they have little impact on the political attitudes of the students.

TEACHERS. It is widely recognized that "teachers are also disseminators of political values and skills in their own right,"[58] over and above the content of the curriculum they employ. Dawson and Prewitt describe the teacher as "an authoritative spokesman of society" with a position of respect.[59] Teachers ordinarily disseminate political values consistent with those dominant in the community, for the teacher is the product of the same socialization processes. Moreover, teachers are said to accept and discuss consensual values and to avoid talking about partisan topics. These discussions need not occur explicitly within the context of civics courses. Rather, they may occur at any time the teacher chooses to interpret learning material or current events in the classroom. It also has been suggested that the teacher indirectly socializes students through the establishment of a "learning culture."[60] The social system of the classroom emphasizes compliance to rules and authority and competitiveness among students. However,

> *a relatively permissive classroom rather than a structured and authoritarian one, an environment in which students participate in the formulation of decisions rather than merely receiving them from an authoritative source, is supposed to contribute to the development of critical, "reflective" and informed citizens.*[61]

Hess and Torney compared the attitudes of a large sample of teachers with the responses of children in the eighth grade. They noted that with rare exceptions the aggregate distributions of the children's attitudes were very similar to the aggregate distributions of their teachers' attitudes. For example, "the ideal citizen's role was viewed in a similar fashion by eighth-grade children and teachers. . . . Despite marked age changes across grades, children grow to resemble their teachers in this area."[62]

Jennings et al. challenge these results, arguing the presence of an ecological fallacy.[63] That is, showing that the aggregate distribution of attitudes among students is moving closer to the distribution among teachers does not mean that individual students are necessarily moving closer to their particular teachers. Moreover, both the students and the teachers may be responding to the same outside forces, in which case the relationship between student and teacher attitudes would be spurious. The students "may be developing in the direction of the other adults with whom they have had the most contact, viz., their parents."[64]

Jennings et al. assessed the relative impact of parents and teachers by matching students to their *own* parents and to their *own* teachers. Across nineteen attitudes, nowhere is the relationship between the students and their teachers higher than the relationship between the students and their parents. In almost all cases the student-parent correlations are substantially higher than the student-teacher correlations. The absence of *any* case where the teachers are more influential than the parents serves to cast considerable doubt about the *systematic* impact of teachers on the political attitudes of their students.

One of the rationales for extracurricular school activities is that they prepare the student for participation in parallel activities in the adult world. Student government, for example, is designed to "teach the student the values of self-government and to familiarize him with the forms and procedures he will face in the adult political world."[65] Yet David Ziblatt found no direct relationship between extracurricular participation and attitudes about politics.[66] Rather, a much more complex process appears to be at work. Extracurricular activities influence political attitudes only when students have positive feelings about the school social system and feelings of social trust.

Peer groups are an additional source of attitudes. The potential for peer-group influence, of course, is not confined to the school environment, but it is in the schools that the individual first interacts intensively with peers. Yet peer groups seem to be important in socialization only "under special circumstances."[67] For the most part, peer influences appear to be in the same direction as those of the parents and the school. When influential people and institutions pull in different directions, the peer will dominate only on issues that are "novel" or of particular relevance to the youth culture. On most political orientations peer groups come into play *after* the influence of the parents has been cemented: "peers have little left to teach in a field which has largely been preempted by earlier socialization."[68] Thus, peers are left with issues of special interest to the generation, such as life-style concerns, while parents maintain their influence in such things as party identification. One study found that when parents disagree with friends, "the parents are the clear 'winners' in the partisan areas of party preference and presidential choice. . . . On the other hand, friends are the easy 'victors' with respect to political efficacy and the eighteen-year-old vote question."[69] The impact of peers increases as their attractiveness increases and the duration of interaction with them increases.[70] The marginal impact of peers is true for college as well, even in the face of the contrary impressions of the sixties and early seventies:

> Despite all the special circumstances of college friendship, there is little evidence that the college experience molds large numbers of students into new directions of political thought through peer or other forms of influence.[71]

In spite of these conclusions, peer groups may have a special role in times of rapid political and social change, when new or novel issues become important. If it is the new or generational issue that stimulates peer-group influence then peer groups may increase in importance in times of political "novelty." Thus, the sixties and the seventies were the times of the new politics; peer groups may have played significant roles in how young people interpreted these issues. And to the extent that the children affected by the peer groups in that novel period alter the distribution of attitudes in the public, the peer groups themselves may have been a significant force in change in American public opinion.

THE DEVELOPMENT OF COGNITIVE SKILLS. Some scholars argue that the primary impact of education is on the *way* people think, rather than on *what* they think. Education is supposed to supply "the citizen with the information, cognitive capacities, motivation and values needed for involvement in the political arena."[72] Many studies show that as the grade level of a child increases so does the child's level of political information and his or her ability to deal critically with political questions. In part, at least, these developments are attributed to the general learning experience in the schools. Better-educated people are supposed to deal better with the complexities of the democratic political process, choosing among the alternatives available on public policy questions and at election time, and perceiving the importance of participation in the political process.

The most important impact of formal schooling may be on the individual's adaptability to change. The information and cognitive skills that accompany education *may* provide some people with greater resources to respond to change in politics. Again, the better-educated individual may be more flexible, better able to adjust personal political positions to changes in politics.

The Mass Media

The impact of the mass media on the attitudes of children has received increasing attention in recent years, with topics ranging from the effect of advertising for breakfast cereals to the consequences of violence in television shows.[73] Indeed, much publicity has been given claims that television shows have played a significant role in teenage crimes.

The media seem to have great opportunity to influence children's attitudes, for children are either just acquiring political attitudes or they possess ones only recently formed. The messages from the media need not penetrate the formidable psychological barriers formed by a long-standing set of reinforced beliefs, as is the case with adults. Moreover, the media communicate directly with the child, bypassing the filtering of parents, peers, or teachers. Nevertheless, it is difficult to identify the *independent* effects of media exposure over and above those of parents, peers, and teachers, each of whom may influence the media sources to which the child is exposed and interpret the content of the medium's message.

A recent literature review of the role of mass communications in political socialization presented four general conclusions.[74] First, the literature suggests that young people obtain most of their political information from the mass media, and that children who most use the media to obtain news also are more likely to talk about politics in their home. Dan Nimmo reports the results of several studies showing that "approximately one-third of younger children and two-thirds of older ones in elementary school watch nightly television newscasts; a majority of all children of all ages watch the Saturday morning 'In the News' formats sandwiched between televised cartoons."[75] Second, for young people the two most important sources of political information are television and the newspapers. Television dominates among younger children, but shares importance with newspapers among older children. Third, young people themselves say that the mass media provide them with political information and influence their political opinions. Fourth, apparently the use of television by children in recent years portends a long-term decline in the public's use of newspapers for political information. In recent years, as they have matured, children have not picked up the use of print media.

Steven H. Chaffee et al. found that among adolescents "political knowledge is clearly associated with heavy use of print media, but not with electronic media; indeed, among those who are high print users, the addition of high electronic media consumption is associated with *lower* knowledge scores."[76] In children, they found that media usage is unrelated to political trust, political efficacy, or strength of party identification. Yet the media have been important in children's acquiring information about Watergate and hence, the decline of children's trust in politics is attributed to that scandal. Robert Hawkins et al. concluded that,

> in short, it appears that exposure to information about Watergate was pervasive and relatively inescapable. Given the nature of much of that information, children's image of the president, and to some extent of the government, was severely tarnished. And, perhaps even more ominous, their faith in their own ability to have an effect on government decreased.[77]

Clearly, then, the mass media (and television in particular) now play a central role in the formation and change of children's political orientation, structuring their attitudes about politics and the information on which those attitudes are based. Nevertheless, much more work is needed in order to understand the permanence and dynamics of those changes, and the context in which they occur.

Other Sources

Both the family and the schools are readily identifiable sources of direct and indirect political cues. Both are separable social units in which the individual can be defined as member or nonmember, and both have the potential to "capture" the individual's political attitudes at a rather early stage in life. The potential impact of the media also is clear. Another set of sources of political attitudes cannot be ignored, but they are more difficult to isolate and they can affect the individual at any point during his or her life. This additional major source of socialization can be labeled political experiences. People come into contact with the political world throughout their lives. In part, at least, people may learn or change their political orientations as a consequence of those experiences. Although this learning may be interpreted for the individual by the family, schools, peers, or the mass media, it also may occur without that mediation.

Contact with the political world may occur in a number of situations — for example, when one attempts to influence political outcomes. The nature of the response may create certain attitudes. One study showed that black Americans with a low sense of political efficacy were more likely to have had difficulty in registering to vote than were people with high levels of efficacy.[78] During the civil rights and antiwar movements, many participants reported they were radicalized by their experiences with representatives of the political system.

One recent study has examined the impact of military service on political orientations.[79] It found that few general effects are associated with military service, although between 1965 and 1973 those men with military service lost faith in the national government at a slightly slower rate than did nonveterans. On the other hand, "those veterans who remained in the Southeast Asian theatre beyond the usual twelve-month tour are more cynical as a group than are nonservicemen."[80]

Major social or political events may generate or change political attitudes. The classic example is the impact of the Great Depression of the 1930s, which is given credit for restructuring the American party system and elevating the Democrats to a long-standing majority status. Recent analyses suggest that this partisan realignment generated by the Depression and the New Deal worked through the socialization process.[81] That is, the change in the number of Democrats and Republicans did not represent an even response across the entire electorate. Rather, it represented a disproportionate movement of young people to the Democratic party. The youngest generations, with recently formed and weakly held partisan orientations, were the most susceptible to socialization or resocialization by their political experiences.

Political figures also are central to political learning. Attractive personalities and officeholders may act as important sources of political socialization. In recent years, John Kennedy was thought to have a special appeal to young people,[82] stimulating in them a positive view of the president and the presidency. Kennedy has been given credit for creating in American youth an idealistic view of the political world and of the values that can be achieved through dedicated effort. The Peace Corps stood as a symbol both of those values and of the response of many Americans, particularly young Americans, to the call of Kennedy.

People also may change their attitudes and behavior when they enter new environments, even after maturation. One example is participation in political organizations. Political party organizations, legislatures, courts, and other political bodies have their own rules and norms,[83] and participants in these organizations have both explicit and implicit methods for communicating these norms to new members. Both the desire to be accepted, and the requirements for success in the organization exert pressure on the new member to acquire the appropriate attitudes and behavior. Also, entry into a new organization may affect the individual's ideological and policy orientations. The discussion of political questions, the attempts to reach political decisions, the provision of new information, the need for social adjustment—all can serve to modify existing beliefs or create new ones.[84]

Summary

It is clear that people may acquire their political orientations from a number of sources. These sources differ in the point in individual development at which they influence a person and in the conditions under which that influence occurs. While the family probably remains the single most important agent of socialization, it would be most unwise to dismiss the other sources. Under the appropriate conditions, and in times of political and social change, many different agents have the potential to create and to alter individual opinions.

VARIATIONS IN THE PROCESS

Political socialization is a process of interaction between individuals and sources of political learning. As the study of political socialization has matured, scholars have moved beyond a broad concern with the general attitudes and beliefs of children and the major sources of their learning, such as parents and schools. In recent years substantial attention has been given to potential variations in the process, to other factors that may intervene, mediate, or condition the beliefs articulated by children. In this section we review briefly the direction of some of the research into major variations in the socialization process. This discussion centers on two areas of variation: variations at the individual level, and variations associated with subcultures within the United States.

Individual Variations

What an individual learns about politics depends not only on what is taught, but also on the characteristics of the individual doing the learning. Jeanne Knutson stresses the importance of individual variation when she writes that "the emphasis . . . is on this process as one which is idiosyncratic to the person and begins with his prepolitical ideology."[85] Knutson argues that these variations can be explained in terms of the individual's personality, although "researchers have made little effort to include personality variables in their designs."[86] She reports, for example, that individuals who differ in their psychic needs also differ in their feelings of political efficacy. Children who think that participation will help in getting government to do something are more likely to be "high self-actualizers." That is, they are less likely to be motivated by physiological, safety, or esteem needs of their personality and more likely to seek fulfillment of aesthetic and intellectual needs. Thus, individual differences in personality development may cause variations in the orientations children acquire about the political world.

Another study has looked at the relationship between intelligence and political outlook in high school students. The rationale for assessing the impact of individual variations in intelligence in the study of political socialization is clear in the authors' minds:

> The findings enable us to think of individuals as organisms with certain different capacities, determined by hereditary or biological as well as social influences — not only for learning and internalizing knowledge, facts and patterns of action, but also for unraveling the sense of utility or perhaps truth of such political formulae as they do learn. Socialization from this perspective then, may be viewed as "organisms" determined as well as "agency" determined.[87]

The results of the study showed that the greater the intelligence of the student (as measured by a verbal reasoning inventory) the *less* likely he or she is to score high on anticommunism, militarism, and superpatriotism. The greater the intelligence the *more* likely the individual is to score high on the following: support for the Bill of Rights, knowledge of political facts, understanding of the political system, sense of relevance of government, and sense of citizen duty and sense of political efficacy. These effects of intelligence on adolescent political attitudes held even when controlling for such indicators of socioeconomic status as the educational level of parents and the family's wealth.

Thus, while one can think about political socialization as a general process in which dominant political orientations are transferred from agencies to individuals, it is necessary to recognize that the outcome of that transfer depends on the characteristics of the individual doing the learning. For that reason — that there are variations in individuals — there are variations in the outcome of political socialization.

Subcultural Variations

Many of the landmark studies of political socialization focused on white, middle-class children. However, researchers gradually realized that within the same political system political socialization may vary substantially among different subgroups. In recent years many studies have compared political socialization among black and white children. In some instances there is evidence that political socialization has similar consequences among both groups of children. Robert Weissberg summarizes a set of literature that shows that

> both *blacks and whites responded similarly to questions on whether the government cares for us, is helpful, knows a lot, is powerful, and can be trusted. Nor are young blacks very different from young whites when evaluating specific authority figures such as the president and the policeman. In both groups images are initially highly positive and then decline with age.*[88]

Yet such conclusions are not uniformly present in the literature. Previously in this chapter we noted several distinct characteristics of political socialization among blacks: civics courses in high school were found to have greater impact on the orientations of black students, and black children exhibited a loss of confidence in government and political figures earlier than the general decline in idealization that occurred among white children.

Moreover, there is some indication that even when black and white children articulate similar attitudes about government and politics there is a difference in the source of those attitudes. Richard Engstrom has reported the results of a study looking at the relationship between race and socialization of political compliance.[89] Engstrom examined black and white children's statements of the probability of their compliance with a figure of authority (doing what the authority asked), in this case a policeman. At the same time, he measured the children's perceptions of the policeman's benevolence, power to punish people, and the probability of that punishment if one does something wrong. Engstrom found equal levels of probability of compliance to authority figures among black and white children. Thus, on the face of it, it would appear that the system's ability to generate attitudes of compliance occurred equally in children of different subcultures. When probing the results further, however, one finds that the *sources* of that compliance differ. That is, among white children compliance is moderately related to perceptions of the policeman's benevolence and his power. But among black children compliance is unrelated to perceptions of benevolence, is moderately related to the probability of punishment, and is strongly related to the perceptions of the policeman's power.

Some recent research also has compared political socialization among Chicano and white children. F. Chris Garcia has made such a comparison in California.[90] Garcia wished to determine if the differing cultural backgrounds of the two groups of children result in different political attitudes. Of particular interest was whether the Chicano children, as members of an ethnic minority with less than equal political and economic status, exhibit less support for the political system than that shown by Anglo children. He concluded that "differences in the orientation of Mexican American and Anglo children with regard to support of the American political community are not large."[91] Moreover, disaffection with the political system increases among Chicano children at about the same rate as that for Anglo children. On the other hand, Garcia does find a somewhat greater personalization of government among Chicano children than among Anglo children.

In a different direction, Dean Jaros et al. have examined children's attitudes about political authority in a unique *white* subculture — Appalachia.[92] They begin with the finding in the dominant culture that children's positive feelings about familial authority (the father) becomes transformed into positive feelings toward political authority in general (see the quote earlier in this chapter). Jaros et al. suggest that in Appalachia there are negative feelings about family authority figures, and these may be generalized into negative feelings about political authorities. Indeed, this study finds that children in Appalachia possess attitudes "significantly less favorable" toward political authority.[93] Appalachian children also are significantly more cynical about government and politics than other children in the white culture. However, the explanation for their results differs from what had been expected. The source of these cynical attitudes was not in feelings generalized from negative attitudes about the children's fathers. Rather, the results stem from the direct transfer of attitudes from the parents to the children. The children have negative attitudes about political authority because those attitudes also are found in the parents. Thus, the *process* in the Appalachian subculture is fundamentally the same as processes elsewhere (the transfer of parental attitudes to children), but the *content* of that process differs.

These studies of political socialization in American subcultures suggest several things. First, one must be cautious in making generalizations about political socialization that extend across American society. While there are some shared aspects of socialization, there also are substantial variations among cultures. Within a single political system there may exist numerous subcultures. The status of the particular subculture may generate different content, structure, and outcomes in the socialization process.

Second, they suggest that there may be subcultural differences in changes in political socialization. Those differences are a consequence of the special relevance of changes in politics and society to those subcultures. The civil rights movement of the 1960s, the assassination of Martin Luther King, the movement of large numbers of southern blacks to northern urban areas undoubtedly held special meaning for blacks. They also undoubtedly had unique effects on the political orientations communicated to and adopted by black children.

POLITICAL SOCIALIZATION, CHANGE, AND DEMOCRACY

Change

A linkage between political socialization and change is a common theme in much of the recent work on socialization. Indeed, although the perspectives vary widely, it is a rare work that fails to contain at least passing consideration of the implications of political socialization for stability and change.[94] The postulated relationship of socialization to *stability* is clear, for in the eyes of many, political socialization contributes to the stability and persistence of existing systems, and change occurs only when socialization breaks down. This section reviews some of the major ways that political socialization has been linked to *change,* a relatively recent theme in the literature.

In varying degrees the content of political socialization can promote existing patterns or encourage an openness to change, a responsiveness to alterations in the political and social environment. Children may be taught to willingly accept change as a natural social process. Moreover, they may be provided the cognitive tools by which to integrate their current beliefs and orientations with changes in the world of politics. In a changing political world, changing patterns in individual beliefs are then a consequence of the normal socialization process, rather than a disruption of a process devoted to the persistence of the status quo. Similarly, part of the socialization process may deal with the methods of change that are acceptable in a political system.[95] The question here is this: If change in political and social patterns is acceptable, what methods are learned as legitimate for generating that change? Are children taught to accept only those changes brought about through peaceful processes, or do methods of protest and confrontation find favor in what children learn?

Political socialization also may be an overt vehicle for creating change in society, as when there is a conscious manipulation of the major institutions. Manipulative socialization can be viewed as the conscious and organized attempt to replace existing norms and allegiances with new ones, as when new nations are created out of groups and institutions with strikingly different norms and orientations, or in those nations where the ideology of the government undergoes substantial and rapid change. The use of the socialization agencies for such purposes, of course, depends on the extent to which they can be controlled. Educational systems may be easier to control than other agencies, for they usually are subject to varying amounts of government control. And they have regularized and systematic responsibility for the children during a period in which children acquire many of their political attitudes, or in which the attitudes they do hold are not strongly imbedded. As one author notes, "particularly among young people, attitudes can change to a remarkable degree in a remarkably short period of time under the proper stimulus."[96]

The content of the political socialization process itself responds to change in society, for important political and social events may disrupt normal patterns.[97] The revelation of corruption in high office may result in parents passing their own negative perceptions of political authority on to their children, although prior to the revelations they may have held and transmitted positive orientations. Thus, the family remains a dominant agency of socialization, but what it transmits may change. Moreover, parents, while emotionally attached to a prior system, may wish their children to fit in a new order, and hence may reinforce beliefs and behaviors with which they do not agree themselves.

Changes in society may alter the relative influence of socialization agencies. A new socialization agency may appear that communicates values that differ from those promoted by the existing agencies, as in the claims made for the impact of television in the socialization of American young people. Programs designed for children, both of the educational variety, a la "Sesame Street," and of the entertainment kind, such as the cartoons, are said to communicate to children certain social and political values.

It should be clear from the previous discussion that socialization can be both a medium of change in the system and a consequence of change. Traditional patterns of political orientations that are ordinarily transferred between generations or through the educational system can be disrupted and overwhelmed by changes over which those agents have no control. The assassination of a president, the revelation of corruption and illegalities in high political office, the development of new sources of information, widespread racial unrest and disorder, the nearly universal economic suffering of a prolonged depression, the development of unique social and cultural values expressed in the life-styles of peers — these all are changes in the environment over which the family and the schools may have little control. To be sure, such changes are subject to interpretation and, to some extent, filtering by traditional socialization agencies, but the interpretation and the filtering occur only within fairly defined limits.

In an open and democratic society, even the young cannot be completely screened from information that conflicts with the traditionally espoused political values held by relevant authorities of parents and teachers. And, in many cases, the authority figures, the agents of socialization, may not wish to screen out the contrary informaton; they, too, may respond to the same changes and deliver altered packages of acceptable or preferred beliefs to their charges.

Thus, even though the political socialization process is defined by some as the system's effort to perpetuate the status quo, few would argue that the process exists in a vacuum, that it is unresponsive to change in the system, that there are no substantial alterations both in the content and in the process that can stem from the major forces and events that shake and shift the structure of the society within which the socialization process occurs.

Changes in the content and the process of socialization also can have substantial consequences for the political system. Socialization and society exist in a reciprocal relationship. The values and orientations that emanate from an altered socialization process can become the dominant orientations of the succeeding generation, and themselves become the content of subsequent transmissions. One example should suffice to illustrate the consequence of changed socialization. In the United States, party identification has been transmitted through the family. We have noted that children traditionally acquired party identification rather early in life and that the party affiliation matched rather closely that of their parents. Moreover, large portions of the public expressed allegiance to one of the major parties. Yet, for some reason, that process began to break down during the late sixties. In 1972, 50 percent of the eighteen- to twenty-one-year-olds expressed allegiance with neither of the two major political parties. This absence of party allegiance among many of the country's young people may have long-run effects on electoral politics in the United States. Campaigns may attempt to attract voters with less emphasis on candidates' affiliation and greater emphasis on personalities.[98]

Finally, it should be noted that socialization is a developmental process. Once one acquires a political orientation it need not be forever cemented in the mind. Children acquire idealized views of political authority and government rather early, but with time become more discriminating. They become more cynical as they mature. People acquire additional information and may learn to separate ritual from reality and fantasy from fact. Personal experiences, both idiosyncratic and shared, provide the opportunity to compare what has been taught with what has been seen. This development occurs because of normal psychological processes, *and* because the individual moves from situations in which the sources of information may be rather rigidly controlled, as in the family, into situations in which less control is manifest. With the diminution of control the opportunity for conflicting information and images increases. And with those conflicts the opportunity for change also increases.

Thus, change related to socialization comes from within and from without the individual. From within, it is a consequence of the natural maturational processes the individual experiences and the normal processes of development in political learning in which knowledge builds on knowledge and is judged against subsequent experience. From without, it is a consequence of changes in the individual's learning environment, and in the political and social system, or the way those changes are interpreted for the individual by the agencies of political learning. Change may even result from alterations in the agencies themselves.

Democracy

Political socialization holds both promise and paradox for democracy. The promise lies in the potential of the socialization process for democratic attitudes and behavior. Political socialization can teach children to be mature democratic citizens when they enter adulthood. It can create support for democratic principles of governance and behavior and give children a push to participate in the nation's politics. Socialization can teach children to be tolerant and open, to revere democratic institutions, and to turn away from appeals that threaten the foundations of democratic politics. It can teach people to measure the reality of politics against the standards of democratic politics that they have learned.

How well do the current patterns of socialization foster these democratic orientations? The answer depends on the meaning of "democracy."[99] If democracy means developing the individual for full-scale involvement in a participatory politics, then the traditional answer has been that the socialization process is inadequate. Not only do many Americans hold values that apparently inhibit full-scale participation,[100] but serious questions have been raised about the degree to which Americans actually support democratic values.[101] On the other hand, Weissberg "suggests that we are indeed educating our children to be good democrats *provided one is willing to accept electoral competition* democracy as a valid concept of democracy,"[102] a system in which the individual participates in the selection of leaders who then make the important decisions with the support of the electorate. However, there is considerable evidence that Americans are not as willing as they once were to accept the electoral competition definition of democracy. Public support for party politics has declined precipitously in recent years.[103] Protest, civil disobedience, and conflict accompanied dissatisfaction with the behavior of public officials in the 1960s and 1970s. A number of policy areas have seen expanded opportunities for public involvement, but participation in electoral politics has been shrinking. At the same time, as subsequent chapters show, Americans seem to be moving toward meeting some standards of democratic citizenship. Americans are said to be more independent, more tolerant, more organized in their beliefs, and more concerned about public policy. These changes may not be directly linked to the socialization process, nor are they necessarily permanent; but the extent to which they are transmitted to succeeding generations may affect the long-term quality of American democracy.

Political socialization also provides a potential paradox for democracy, if democracy is defined in terms of the individual freely arriving at important opinions in the light of experience and information, including opinions about the most appropriate form of government. Yet political socialization suggests the presence of a process that systematically eliminates from serious consideration certain political orientations. Is it democratic to socialize the young to democratic attitudes and not give the child the choice of nondemocratic attitudes? On the other hand, is a democratic society and political system failing in its duty when it imperfectly prepares its citizens for participation in a democratic system? Do not the symbolism, ritual, civics texts, and generally positive signals about democracy and political authority smack of manipulation, either conscious or unconscious? As Tapper puts it,

> the socialization processes contain irreconcilable contradictions. This is neatly illustrated by the internal inconsistencies of formal education, which has to perform at least the following tasks: to dispense useful skills, to help in social training, to act as an instrument of political control and to stimulate personal enlightenment.[104]

CONCLUSION

Political socialization has been part and parcel of both the continuity and change in American public opinion. There also have been changes in the political socialization process and in the outcomes of that process. Parents apparently have declined in their influence on the political attitudes of their children, as evidenced by (among other things) the younger generation's greater reluctance to adopt a party affiliation. Peer groups seem to have a greater opportunity for influence in this time of "novel" issues particularly relevant to the younger generation. The mass media, especially television, play a much more important role in the child's acquisition of political information. Children are much less likely to idealize government and political authority. Each of these changes has prospects for long-term impact on American public opinion.

NOTES

1. Fred I. Greenstein, *Children and Politics* (New Haven, Conn.: Yale University Press, 1965), p. 73.
2. Angus Campbell et al., *The American Voter* (New York: John Wiley & Sons, 1960), p. 246.
3. Roberta Sigel, ed., *Learning About Politics: A Reader in Political Socialization* (New York: Random House, 1970), p. xii.
4. Robert Weissberg, *Political Learning, Political Choice and Democratic Citizenship* (Englewood Cliffs, N.J.: Prentice-Hall, 1974), p. 14.
5. Charles G. Bell, ed., *Growth and Change* (Belmont, Calif.: Dickenson, 1973), p. xi.
6. See the conceptualization in Greenstein, *Children and Politics,* pp. 12–15.
7. For a variety of conceptualizations and applications of developmental approaches see: Jean Piaget and Barbel Inhelder, *The Psychology of the Child* (New York: Basic Books, 1969); Charles F. Andrain, *Children and Civic Awareness* (Columbus, Ohio: Merrill, 1971); Jeanne N. Knutson, "Prepolitical Ideologies: The Basis of Political Learning," in *The Politics of Future Citizens,* Richard G. Niemi and Associates (San Francisco: Jossey-Bass, 1974), pp. 7–40; and Richard M. Merelman, "The Development of Political Ideology: A Framework for the Analysis of Political Socialization," *American Political Science Review* 63 (September 1969), pp. 750–67.
8. Richard E. Dawson and Kenneth Prewitt, *Political Socialization* (Boston: Little, Brown & Co., 1969), pp. 204–5. See also the examination of this contention in Donald A. Searing, Joel T. Schwartz, and Oldin E. Lind, "The Structuring Principle: Political Socialization and Belief Systems," *American Political Science Review* 67 (June 1973), pp. 415–32.
9. Campbell et al., *The American Voter,* p. 147.
10. Donald E. Stokes, "Party Loyalty and the Likelihood of Deviating Elections," in Angus Campbell et al., *Elections and the Political Order* (New York: John Wiley & Sons, 1966), p. 126. See also the examinations of party identification in a comparative context in Ian Budge, Ivor Crewe, and Dennis Fairlie, eds., *Party Identification and Beyond: Representations of Voting and Party Competition* (London: John Wiley & Sons, 1976).
11. David Easton and Jack Dennis, *Children in the Political System* (New York: McGraw-Hill, 1969).
12. Richard G. Niemi, "Political Socialization," in *Handbook of Political Psychology,* Jeanne N. Knutson, ed. (San Francisco: Jossey-Bass, 1973), pp. 121–22.
13. Ibid., p. 121.
14. Ibid., p. 122.
15. Greenstein, *Children and Politics,* p. 40.
16. Ibid., p. 45.
17. Ibid., p. 46.

18. Jack Dennis et al., "Political Socialization to Democratic Orientations in Four Western Systems," *Comparative Political Studies* 1 (April 1968), pp. 71–101.
19. David O. Sears, "Political Socialization," in *Handbook of Political Science,* Fred I. Greenstein and Nelson W. Polsby, eds. (Reading, Mass.: Addison-Wesley, 1975), vol. 1, p. 103.
20. Ibid.
21. Arthur Miller, "Political Issues and Trust in Government: 1964–1970," *American Political Science Review* 68 (September 1974), pp. 951–72.
22. Sears, "Political Socialization," pp. 108–11.
23. Jack Dennis and Carol Webster, "Children's Images of the President and of Government in 1962 and 1974," *American Politics Quarterly* 3 (October 1975), pp. 386–405.
24. F. Christopher Arterton, "The Impact of Watergate on Children's Attitudes Toward Political Authority," *Political Science Quarterly* 89 (June 1974), p. 273.
25. Ibid., p. 272.
26. Ibid., p. 287.
27. Dennis and Webster, "Children's Images of the President," p. 403.
28. Fred I. Greenstein, "The Benevolent Leader Revisited: Children's Images of Political Leaders in Three Democracies," *American Political Science Review* 69 (December 1975), p. 1385 (italics in the original).
29. As in most areas of public opinion, there are some studies of political socialization that challenge earlier conclusions on methodological grounds. In a study conducted in the early 1970s, Knutson employed different (projective) techniques. Rather than uniformly positive and benevolent pictures of politics and government, Knutson finds that children are quite capable of expressing a wide range of attitudes, a range much like one would find among adults, including hostile attitudes about government and politics. See Jeanne N. Knutson, "Prepolitical Ideologies: The Basis of Political Learning." Of course, since the study took place both at a later time period and with different techniques, it is difficult to identify the true source of the differences in conclusions.
30. James C. Davies, "The Family's Role in Political Socialization," *The Annals of the American Academy of Political and Social Science* 361 (September 1965), pp. 11–19.
31. Frank A. Pinner, "Parental Overprotection and Political Distrust," in *Cross-National Micro-Analysis,* John C. Pierce and Richard A. Pride, eds. (Beverly Hills: Sage Publications, 1972), pp. 97–109.
32. Andrew M. Greeley, "A Model for Ethnic Political Socialization," *American Journal of Political Science* 19 (May 1975), pp. 187–206.
33. M. Kent Jennings and Richard G. Niemi, *The Political Character of Adolescence* (Princeton, N.J.: Princeton University Press, 1974), pp. 39, 78.
34. Norman H. Nie, Sidney Verba, and John R. Petrocik, *The Changing American Voter* (Cambridge, Mass.: Harvard University Press, 1976), p. 63.
35. M. Kent Jennings and Richard G. Niemi, "Continuity and Change in Political Orientations: A Longitudinal Study of Two Generations," *American Political Science Review* 69 (December 1975), p. 1325.
36. M. Kent Jennings, personal communication, September 1978.
37. Warren E. Miller and Teresa E. Levitin, *Leadership and Change* (Cambridge, Mass.: Winthrop, 1976).
38. Kent Tedin, "The Influence of Parents on the Political Attitudes of Adolescents," *American Political Science Review* 68 (December 1974), pp. 1579–92.
39. Jennings and Niemi, "Continuity and Change in Political Orientations."

40. Ibid., p. 1335. Russell J. Dalton, however, recently has argued that Jennings and Niemi over-estimate the parent-child distance on political issues. See his "Reassessing Parental Socialization: Indicator Unreliability Versus Generational Transfer," *American Political Science Review* 74 (June 1980), pp. 421–31.

41. For examples, see Roald Dahl, *Charlie and the Great Glass Elevator* (New York: Bantam Books, 1977).

42. For examples, see: Norma Klein, *Girls Can Be Anything* (New York: E.P. Dutton, 1973); and Charlotte Zolotow, *William's Doll* (New York: Harper & Row, 1972).

43. Robert D. Hess and Judith V. Torney, *The Development of Political Attitudes in Children* (Chicago: Aldine, 1967), p. 219.

44. Ibid., p. 106.

45. Ibid., p. 105.

46. Reid Reading, "Political Socialization in Colombia and the United States: An Exploratory Study," *Midwest Journal of Political Science* (August 1968), pp. 352–81, Table 2.

47. Hess and Torney, *The Development of Political Attitudes in Children,* p. 218.

48. John J. Patrick, "Political Socialization and Political Education in Schools," in *Handbook of Political Socialization,* Stanley Allen Renshon, ed. (New York: Free Press, 1977), p. 203.

49. Dawson and Prewitt, *Political Socialization,* p. 155.

50. Edgar Litt, "Civic Education, Community Norms, and Political Indoctrination," *American Sociological Review* 28 (February 1963), pp. 69–75.

51. Patrick, "Political Socialization and Political Education," pp. 198–99.

52. Kenneth P. Langton and M. Kent Jennings, "Political Socialization and the High School Civics Curriculum in the United States," *American Political Science Review* 62 (September 1968), pp. 852–67.

53. Ibid., p. 858.

54. Judith A. Gillespie, "The American Government Course: Relationships Between High School and College Instruction," *Teaching Political Science* 2 (July 1975), p. 405.

55. Patrick, "Political Socialization and Political Education," p. 207.

56. Ibid., p. 210.

57. John J. Patrick, "The Impact of an Experimental Course, 'American Political Behavior,' on the Knowledge, Skills, and Attitudes of Secondary School Students," *Social Education* 36 (February 1972). See also, Judith A. Gillespie, "Comparing Political Experiences: A Final Report," NEWS for Teachers of Political Science No. 18 (Summer 1978), pp. 13–14.

58. M. Kent Jennings, Lee H. Ehman, and Richard G. Niemi, "Social Studies Teachers and Their Pupils," in *The Political Character of Adolescence,* p. 211.

59. Dawson and Prewitt, *Political Socialization,* pp. 158–59.

60. Ibid., p. 162.

61. Dean Jaros, *Socialization to Politics* (New York: Praeger, 1973), p. 107.

62. Hess and Torney, *The Development of Political Attitudes in Children,* p. 112.

63. Jennings, Ehman, and Niemi, "Social Studies Teachers and Their Pupils," p. 212.

64. Ibid.

65. Dawson and Prewitt, *Political Socialization,* p. 171.

66. David Ziblatt, "High School Extracurricular Activities and Political Socialization," *Annals of the American Academy of Political and Social Science* 361 (September 1965), pp. 21–31.

67. Sara L. Silbiger, "Peers and Political Socialization," in *Handbook of Political Socialization,* p. 172. Much of this discussion relies heavily on the excellent literature review in Silbiger's work.

68. Ibid., p. 174.
69. Suzanne Koprince Sebert, M. Kent Jennings, and Richard G. Niemi, "The Political Texture of Peer Groups," in *The Political Character of Adolescence,* p. 247.
70. Silbiger, "Peers and Political Socialization," p. 176.
71. Ibid., p. 179.
72. Andrain, *Children and Civic Awareness,* p. 86.
73. See the literature review of violence on television and children in *Young Children* (October 1976), and the literature review of the impact of television on pro-social behavior in *Young Children* (July 1977).
74. Steven H. Chafee et al., "Mass Communication in Political Socialization," in *Handbook of Political Socialization,* pp. 227–29. For other reviews of the role of media in political socialization, see: Lee B. Becker, Maxwell E. McCombs, and Jack M. McLeod, "The Development of Political Cognitions," in *Political Communication: Issues and Strategies for Research,* Steven H. Chafee, ed. (Beverly Hills: Sage Publications, 1975), pp. 21 – 63; Jack M. McLeod and Garrett J. O'Keefe, Jr., "The Socialization Perspective and Communication Behavior," in *Current Perspectives in Mass Communications Research,* F. Gerald Kline and Phillip J. Tichenor, eds. (Beverly Hills: Sage Publications, 1972) pp. 121–68; and Dan Nimmo, *Political Communication and Public Opinion in America* (Santa Monica, Calif.: Goodyear, 1977), pp. 322–24.
75. Nimmo, *Political Communication and Public Opinion,* p. 323.
76. Chafee et al., "Mass Communication in Political Socialization," p. 233.
77. Robert Parker Hawkins, Suzanne Pingree, and Donald F. Roberts, "Watergate and Political Socialization," *American Politics Quarterly* 3 (October 1975), p. 421.
78. John C. Pierce and Addison Carey, Jr., "Efficacy and Participation: A Study of Black Political Behavior," *Journal of Black Studies 2* (December 1971), pp. 201–23.
79. M. Kent Jennings and Gregory B. Markus, "The Effect of Military Service on Political Attitudes: A Panel Study," *American Political Science Review* 71 (March 1977), pp. 131–47.
80. Ibid., p. 137.
81. See Paul Allen Beck, "A Socialization Theory of Partisan Realignment," in *The Politics of Future Citizens,* pp. 199–219.
82. See the Sears quote earlier in the text of this chapter.
83. See Donald L. Matthews, *U.S. Senators and Their World* (New York: Vintage Books, 1960), pp. 92–117.
84. The reader is referred to the discussions of political organizations and public opinion in Chapter 13.
85. Knutson, "Prepolitical Ideologies," p. 80.
86. Ibid., p. 10.
87. Susan K. Harvey and Ted G. Harvey, "Adolescent Political Outlooks: The Effects of Intelligence as an Independent Variable," *Midwest Journal of Political Science* 14 (November 1970), p. 592.
88. Weissberg, *Political Learning,* p. 107.
89. Richard L. Engstrom, "Race and Compliance: Differential Political Socialization," *Polity* 3 (Fall 1970), pp. 101–11.
90. F. Chris Garcia, *Political Socialization of Chicano Children* (New York: Praeger, 1973).
91. Ibid., p. 49.
92. Dean Jaros, Herbert Hirsch, and Frederic J. Fleron, Jr., "The Malevolent Leader: Political Socialization in an American Subculture," *American Political Science Review* 62 (June 1968), pp. 564–75.

93. Ibid., p. 569.

94. Jennings and Niemi, *The Political Character of Adolescence,* Chapter 1; Weissberg, *Political Learning,* Chapter 10; Easton and Dennis, *Children in the Political System,* Chapters 2 and 3; and Ted Tapper, *Political Education and Stability* (New York: John Wiley & Sons, 1976), passim.

95. Easton and Dennis, *Children in the Political System,* Chapter 2.

96. Niemi, "Political Socialization," p. 137.

97. Weissberg, *Political Learning,* pp. 194–95.

98. See the analysis in Gerald M. Pomper, *The Voters' Choice* (New York: Dodd Mead & Co., 1975), pp. 186–209.

99. Weissberg, *Political Learning,* pp. 174–190.

100. See the figures on political participation contained in Sidney Verba and Norman Nie, *Participation in America: Political Democracy and Social Equality* (New York: Harper & Row, 1972).

101. See Samuel A. Stouffer, *Communism, Conformity and Civil Liberties* (New York: John Wiley & Sons, 1955); and Herbert McClosky. "Consensus and Ideology in American Politics," *American Political Science Review* 58 (June 1964), pp. 361–82. See Chapter 8.

102. Weissberg, *Political Learning,* p. 188 (italics ours).

103. See the evidence presented in Chapter 2.

104. Tapper, *Political Education and Stability,* p. 246. Merelman has also suggested that "the limitations of the transmission of democratic values in American schools are the price we pay for the strain between the school's demand for order and the egalitarian norms embedded in American political culture." Richard M. Merelman, "Democratic Politics and the Culture of American Education," *American Political Science Review* 74 (June 1980), p. 331.

CHAPTER 5

THE MASS MEDIA

Information acquisition precedes opinion formation. This does not mean that the information upon which an opinion is based must be anywhere near complete; rather, *some* perception of an opinion object must exist prior to the opinion.[1] Why this common-sense notion about information and opinions? If, as we have earlier stated, public opinion is a collection of individual opinions about a political object, then a discussion of the stability and change in public opinion must take into account the changes in the *sources* of political information that produce the individual opinions. If there occurs a change in the mass informational base, one would expect to see changes in public opinion.

Social science researchers have established the mass media as central purveyors of political information to the public. This is the case for all demographic groups.[2] Most of what people know about the political world is due to the media's coverage. This knowledge may be received *directly* from television viewing or reading of the newspaper, or it may be received *indirectly* from an acquaintance who received it directly. Given the media's preeminent position in information transmission, close examination of their institutional structures, transmission processes, and audience effects is vital in order to achieve a thorough understanding of the American public opinion process.

While this chapter focuses primarily on the media's role in the development of *political* opinions, the media are the most important sources of information for *all* areas of modern life. Some writers, such as Melvin DeFleur and Sandra Ball-Rokeach, argue that within advanced, urban-industrial societies, audiences are dependent upon the media for a number of personal needs.[3] First, they depend on the media for an *understanding* of the social world. Many theorists have argued that all individuals have a need to put the external world into some coherent order from which they can gain a better sense of their own role within that order.[4] This need has been termed *object appraisal*. In order to see why you are paying higher fuel bills, or why your favorite football team is in last place, you have to consult some source that provides the needed information. Ambiguity, especially in complex societies, is not a pleasurable state of mind for an individual, so he or she becomes dependent upon sources that serve to reduce this unpleasant state.

A second source of media dependency, according to DeFleur and Ball-Rokeach, is based upon the individual's need to *act* in a meaningful and effective way in the social world. Since most overt behavior takes place within a social context, the more information one has about that context, the greater will be the confidence about intended activity. Consulting a local weather forecast before departing from home in the morning is a simple demonstration of this dependency. The more complex the anticipated action, the greater is the need for information related to its possible outcome.

The third postulated source of dependency has been termed the need for *fantasy-escape* from the pressures and demands of daily life. The public is dependent upon the media for entertainment, and according to many observers this is the goal of the vast majority of media transmissions. While this is quite obvious in television programming, both private and public, it may not seem applicable to newspapers. Newspapers have the image of presenting more in-depth coverage of the news. While they do feature a smaller percentage of "pure entertainment" stories than does television, a quick check of the local newspapers will reveal that the space devoted to features such as sports, fashions, gardening, and the like equals or surpasses that devoted to public affairs. As David Altheide and Robert Snow argue, however, this emphasis upon entertainment is nothing new; it is simply that the media now provide entertainment that previously had been derived primarily at the interpersonal level.[5] While the entertainment function of the media seems, at first, remote from the subject of the formation of political opinions, the public's need for understanding and its need for entertainment play an important role in the type of information that most effectively influences political opinions.

This chapter first considers the institutional changes in the media over the past twenty years and how these changes influence the media's information transmissions, especially in the areas of news broadcasting and the coverage of political campaigns. The discussion then turns to how the media affect the public's political cognitions.

CHANGES IN MASS MEDIA

This chapter adopts the definition of a mass medium offered by Altheide and Snow. They identify a mass medium as "any social or technological procedure or device that is used for the selection, transmission and reception of information."[6] In addition to commonly accepted forms of mass media (television, newspapers, magazines, and radio), this definition can also include speeches, advertisements, billboards, motion pictures, handbills, and the like. *Mass media* implies communication intended for consumption by a collectivity rather than a specific individual. Personal conversations, therefore, are not instances of *mass* communication.[7]

This chapter is primarily concerned with the selection, transmission, and reception of *political* information to a *wide* audience, concentrating on the changes in, and effects of, television and newspapers as channels of information diffusion.[8] Changes in the *structural* characteristics of the media (i.e., technology, economics, and audience characteristics) have played a major role in changing the nature of information received by the public.

Technological Changes

Although it is simpler to think of the changes in mass media technology as resembling dramatic and rapid revolutions derived from the introduction of a new transmission channel (movable press, radio, and television), the real change induced by media technology was more gradual. For example, although television was technologically prepared for mass circulation as early as 1928 when the first regular broadcasts began in Schenectady, New York, commercial broadcasting did not begin until 1941. Between the decade of the fifties and that of the seventies, the number of regional broadcast licenses granted by the Federal Communications Commission (FCC) increased fivefold. However, this twenty-year increase occurred gradually rather than all at once. The same pattern holds for the increase in newspaper establishments and radio licenses. While there was a quick upsurge soon after the parent technology emerged, the following period was marked by a slow but ever-widening diffusion pattern.

The changing information technology has shown its greatest impact in two areas: the *speed* of the communication, and the audience's *access* to that message. Changes in each of these areas of *reception* have been accompanied by changes in the *content* of the communicated message itself.

The first area of technological change, the *speed* of the transmitted message, is the easiest to understand. Communication channels have undergone dramatic alterations in their ability to provide information quickly. At the time of the drafting of the Constitution, it took ten days for news originating in Boston to be printed in Philadelphia — a distance of 296 miles. At the beginning of the seventies, it took less than half a second for a message to travel from the moon to earth — a mean distance of 238,857 miles. The introduction and improvement of such technological carriers as wireless transmitters, radio signals, and microwave transmitters have reduced the time between an event and its mass reception.

At the same time, the economic stakes of the commercial information channels have also risen. The ensuing competition for the fastest provision of "new" information assures the audience of the most current information.[9] The most *current* information, however, is not the same as the most *complete* information. In fact, many media analysts, Ben Bagdikian in particular, have argued that the emphasis on speed of information transfer has been at the sacrifice of understanding.[10] Both electronic and print media operate under the general rule that some information is preferable to no information whatsoever. The assumption about public opinion that underlies this strategy is that, upon the receipt of additional information, people will "flesh out" their opinions on a particular subject. This assumption is, however, quite tenuous. Starting with Walter Lippmann, theorists have recognized the importance of "first impressions" in the formation of political opinions.[11] In order to bring the world into some order, argues Lippmann, people form generalized frames of reference — or, in his terms, stereotypes — which simplify the world. The consequence of rapid communication of incomplete information is that first impressions can form the basis of the individual's simplification of the communicated situation. Once this stereotypical picture has been formed, it becomes very resistant to modification.[12] Additional information that modifies the original communication may be evaluated in reference to the preformed stereotype, rather than as new and neutral facts.[13] It is in this way that the increased speed of communicated messages may work *against* the development of an informed public.[14]

The second impact of media technology is the increased *access* of the public to messages. The availability of media-provided information and entertainment has increased dramatically over the last 100 years. The growth in the diffusion of newspapers occurred during the period between 1870 and 1910. Since that time the number of newspapers in circulation has diminished slightly, but the degree of home consumption has remained fairly constant. While it is widely believed that newspapers are becoming less important in an electronic society, and that the economic basis of the print journalism enterprise is now unstable, circulation figures and business statuses argue against that assumption. As Bagdikian pointed out, the failure rates for daily papers is less than the national average for all commercial and industrial firms.[15]

It is clear, however, that the introduction of radio, and especially of television, has halted the further expansion of newspapers by providing alternate forms of access to information and entertainment. The characteristics of television diffusion and use over the past thirty-year period are quite striking. In 1952 there were 15 million television sets in American households; twenty years later there were over 100 million sets. It has been estimated that 97 percent of all households have at least one television receiver, and these sets are not there for ornamental purposes. Use has been estimated at three hours a day per individual, with the set in operation on an average of six hours per day per household.[16] What is evident, even from these cursory figures, is that the public's access to media channels is now quite broad, and the use of these channels is extensive.

Perhaps the most important result of the increased access to media is that they have come to be relied upon as sources of entertainment. The media are an easily accessible way of "escaping" from the pressures raised by living and working in a technologically advanced and complex society.[17] It is not without irony that technology serves as both the cause of and the release from tension. One indication of this entertainment emphasis is the content of the communications provided by the commercial television networks. It would indeed challenge credulity to believe that programs such as "Mork & Mindy," "Three's Company," and "Happy Days" exist for any other reason than for entertainment. Another interesting measure of the entertainment use of television is found in the patterns of motion picture attendance during the period in which television became a permanent fixture. In 1948, the dawn of the television age, weekly attendance at local movie houses averaged 2.22 per household. In 1971, the weekly attendance figure had dropped to .22.[18] Given that motion pictures traditionally have been viewed as exclusively providing mass entertainment, the mirror-image trends in television access and motion picture attendance strongly indicate that television is now being relied upon for entertainment purposes.

This increasing dependence of the public on television for entertainment has an important, yet not directly observable, impact on the nature of public opinion. The discussion of mass media effects will show that the provision of information on which to base opinions increasingly resembles other forms of media entertainment. A clear example of this is the program "Sesame Street." While the main purpose of the program is to provide basic educational foundations, the medium used is highly entertaining. The danger in programs such as this, some argue, is that children become accustomed to learning attached to brightly augmented entertainment devices, and that this impedes learning of more complex subjects.[19] In the area of political information, a similar argument is made. If political communications are most often accessed by individuals who want entertainment rather than information, the quality of public opinion may reflect the superficiality of the opinion source.

The change in media technology has allowed almost an entire population to see the world more fully than ever before in the history of mankind.[20] At the same time, the increased speed of information provision and the widening extent of information access can have an adverse effect upon the formation of public opinion. Both factors contribute to a greater *knowledge* of the outside world, but technological sophistication has also contributed to the *superficiality* of that knowledge. This last point will be of considerable importance once we consider the role of the media in political campaigns.[21]

Economic Changes

The most important thing to keep in mind when considering the structural effects of the mass media is that almost all media channels are privately owned businesses. The object of a business enterprise is to achieve a large enough profit to attract and satisfy investors. Although it may well be a cliché, both newspapers and television provide information and entertainment to the public in order to give the advertiser a large body of potential customers. In other words, the newspaper and television industry attempts to attract a readership (or viewership) that it can in turn "sell" to advertisers. This is apparent even to the most casual consumer of television. Programs live or die by their scores on the Nielsen ratings. Additionally, the cost of each advertising minute is set in accordance with the size and the demographic composition of the "delivered" audience. While it is commonly believed that the life thread of any given program is held by faceless network programmers, this is only half of the story. The other half is that the *programmers'* strings are operated by the advertisers themselves. As Les Brown points out, *when the advertiser's need is to set his fall budgets six or seven months ahead of the season, the networks adjust their fall schedules accordingly. When advertisers manifest an interest in sports, they proliferate on the home screen; an aversion to serious original plays, they evaporate. And when the advertisers spurn the viewers who are past the age of fifty and assert a preference for young married couples, the networks obediently disenfranchise the older audience and go full tilt in pursuit of the young.*[22]

For years, a large group of television critics has railed against the "lowbrow" orientation of television programming. However, their objections overlook the fact that what is programmed is there because it attracts a large audience. If more "cultural" programming could attract a large market, we would see a proliferation of such shows across all three commercial networks.[23] In this view, the networks' decision making is directed by only one value — that which can maximize the advertising dollar.[24]

Given this, it is all the more significant that, especially for television, the size of that advertising dollar has grown dramatically over the past twenty years. In 1950, only 3 percent of total advertising expenditures was devoted to television, while 32 percent was devoted to newspapers. In 1970, however, the percentage devoted to television had grown to 19 percent, while the newspaper allotment had remained stable. Given that over a fifty-year period advertisers have spent 10 percent more *per household* (holding dollar purchasing power constant), the money devoted to both television and newspaper advertising was considerable.[25]

Thus, there exists an intense competition for advertising dollars, both between the newspapers and television networks, and within each medium. The messages transmitted across the airways and across the pages of most daily newspapers are aimed at attracting an audience. Yet the influence of economic interest does not stop at the programming directly aimed at entertainment. The news organizations within the networks, wire services, and dailies are part and parcel of this financial effort. The major sources of political information are *not* motivated solely by a desire to better inform the public, but also to attract the largest possible number of viewers — two very different motivations. The result is that much information provision is never far removed from the realm of entertainment:

> *The news is dramatized for entertainment purposes. News organizations, such as local TV stations, are well aware that news is part of the entertainment fare of mass audiences, and must cater to those expectations or risk losing their audience. It is often said that news is not truth; perhaps it is more accurate to say that news is entertainment.*[26]

Ever since the days of "yellow journalism" and the muckrakers, the media establishment has realized that sensationalism sells. News coverage of crime provides a telling example of this bias toward the sensational.[27] In a 1978 study of how Chicago papers covered crime news, Sanford Sherizen found that sensational crimes such as murder and manslaughter accounted for less than 1 percent of the total number of reported crimes in 1975.[28] However, those crimes accounted for 45 percent of the dailies' crime reports during that year.

Fifty percent of all reported murders were covered by the press, but only 5 percent of all reported rapes and less than 1 percent of robberies and aggravated assaults were deemed newsworthy. This emphasis on the sensational aspect of crime extends into coverage of the judicial process as well. Sherizen found that 75 percent of all of the news coverage was devoted to pretrial matters such as capture, arrest, charging, and arraignment. Comparatively little attention was devoted to the lengthier and less spectacular adjudication process.[29]

The impact of the media crime reports on public opinion should be obvious. People who garner information about the crime level in Chicago will perceive it to be dominated by crimes of violence, and thus will derive a very incomplete picture of the criminal justice system. As Sherizen observed,

> the process of gathering crime news restricts the types of crime-related information which appears as crime news. Crime news is a constructed reality, selected from a series of events which occur and, from which, crime-newsworthy events are written as crime news.[30]

The selection of what is to be "news" and what shall go unreported is not based solely on its value as information. It is also based on its potential entertainment or sensationalist appeal to the viewer. What emerges from this selection process is information that is meant to be both exciting and entertaining, and that is often superficial. Political information is not only susceptible to this process, it has become its epitome.[31]

Changes in Audience Characteristics

In a sense, changes in the characteristics of those who consume media transmissions are due to changes in the technological and economic structures of the media establishments themselves. As improvements are made in delivery systems, they incur greater costs that make it imperative to attract wider audiences. The history of both the print and electronic media is marked by an expansionistic search for a wider readership and viewership.[32] For newspapers this was seen in the movement away from being primarily propaganda sheets for political parties to mass circulation pieces that attempted to appeal to as broad a spectrum of popular tastes as possible.[33] The mass acceptance of television, however, seems to have occurred at a much faster rate, especially in terms of information access. As early as 1952, 31 percent of a national sample selected television as the most important source of information as opposed to 22 percent favoring newspapers. In 1956 the margin had widened: 49 percent favored television as an information source, while 24 percent favored newspapers. The growth in information dependence during this four-year period had come mainly at the expense of radio, which dropped from 28 percent dependence in 1952 to 10 percent in 1956.[34] In the seventies, the gap between television and newspaper dependence continued to grow, the result of television attracting viewers from sources other than newspapers. In 1976, 64 percent of a national sample cited television as their major source of information, while 19 percent chose newspapers. Although television is growing in its contribution to the information needs of the mass public, this reliance is not based solely on the relative ease of accessing televised information. Opinion trends of the last twenty years have demonstrated that the public has developed a strong degree of trust in the medium as an information source.[35] Television clearly is the most important and most trusted source of political information for the mass public.

There are important differences in the socioeconomic composition of the audiences of each medium, as seen in Table 5–1. First, older people tend to rely less on television for political information and more on a combination of print and broadcast media. What must be noted, however, is that there is very little difference in sole newspaper reliance across age. None of the age groups differs in any great measure from the national average of newspaper dependency (19 percent). While older citizens were not reared on television, over a twenty-year period they have come to accept it as an information source.

TABLE 5 – 1 Medium That Is Most Relied Upon for Political Information Across Age, Education Level, Sex, and Race, 1976

	Newspapers	Television	Both
Age			
18– 25	17%	69%	14%
26– 40	20	67	13
41 – 60	21	62	17
61 and over	18	60	22
Education			
Less than High School	12%	74%	14%
High School	19	66	15
College	26	54	20
Sex			
Male	24%	58%	18%
Female	16	69	15
Race			
White	20%	64%	16%
Black	9	70	21

Source: Center for Political Studies. American National Election Study, 1976 [machine-readable data file].

More dramatic differences in audience characteristics are present in the area of education. Less-educated citizens tend to rely heavily on television for their political information. In sharp contrast, college-educated individuals have the lowest level of television dependence of all of the important socioeconomic groups studied. The most straightforward explanation of this pattern is that those individuals with higher education levels have developed through their studies a stronger "reading habit" than have those individuals with lower levels of education.

Differences in audience characteristics are also found across sexual and racial lines. Males tend to rely on newspapers for political information more than do females, while females are more likely than males to utilize television for the same information. Whites tend to have a heavier reliance upon the print medium than do blacks. One explanation of the male/female and black/white differences has been that news is made by and, in general terms, directed toward white males.[36]

TABLE 5-2 Most Relied Upon Medium for Political Information for Education Groups Across Age, Sex, and Race, 1976

	Low Education			Medium Education			High Education		
	Newspapers	Television	Both	Newspapers	Television	Both	Newspapers	Television	Both
Age									
18–25	10%	78%	12%	16%	71%	13%	21%	64%	15%
26–40	8	79	13	19	72	9	24	59	17
40–60	11	80	8	19	63	18	33	42	25
60 and over	14	68	18	22	50	28	27	46	26
Sex									
Male	17%	69%	14%	22%	59%	18%	31%	49%	21%
Female	9	76	13	17	69	14	22	59	19
Race									
White	13%	74%	13%	19%	66%	15%	27%	54%	19%
Black	7	77	16	12	70	19	11	59	30

Source: Center for Political Studies. American National Election Study, 1976 [machine-readable data file].

It has also been argued that the sexual and racial differences in each medium's audience are due to the differences in educational characteristics normally associated with age, sex, and race. There is a strong relationship between education and medium dependency. Could the differences in the other socioeconomic characteristics be due to the fact that each characteristic is also influenced by education level and that education, rather than medium choice, should be the major theoretic variable? The data presented in Table 5-2 argue against this theory. Even when education is taken into consideration, the differences observed earlier remain. For the age categories, there is a much larger difference in the dependence on television as a source of political information. When education is held constant (meaning that differences are examined *within* each education classification), older individuals are much more likely to rely on *both* newspapers and television and to avoid a sole reliance upon television than are younger individuals. This was not clear in Table 5-1. Because education level and medium choice are related, and younger individuals tend to have achieved higher education levels than have people who grew up in and around the depression and world war years, the true relationship between age and medium choice was obscured. When "correcting" for the generational effect of education, one can see the differences in medium choice across age.

Table 5-2 also shows that educational differences beween males and females do not account for differences in medium dependency. For each of the education groups there still exists a significant difference in the percentage of males and females favoring newspapers or television. Educational differences seem to account for the medium dependency of the two main racial groupings. When we look at white/black differences within each level of education, it is clear that the differences in television dependency are greatly reduced. While blacks still tend to rely less upon newspapers when education is controlled, their reliance upon *both* television and newspapers as equally important sources of political information is more pronounced.

This examination has shown that the audiences that rely on political information differ along age, educational, sexual, and racial characteristics. Different media attract different audiences. By itself, the fact that individuals with different social characteristics are attracted to different media for their information needs is neither alarming nor unexpected. The question of the differences between each medium's audience becomes more serious, however, when one looks at the levels of political involvement, political participation, and political information across each medium dependency classification.

Table 5-3 examines the relationship between choice of medium and questions relating to political interest, participation, and information. The data quite clearly point out that people who rely on television have lower levels of involvement with the political system than do those who either rely on newspapers or on a combination of the two media. Television-dependent people have less interest in the outcome of the campaign and in the campaign in general, and tend to devote less time to following public affairs. They also report lower levels of political activity (both voting and influencing others to vote). Finally, when asked a basic information question about which party controls the House of Representatives, television-dependent individuals clearly display a lower level of information.

TABLE 5–3 Medium That Is Relied Upon for Political Information and Interest, Participation, and Information Questions, 1976

	Newspapers	Television	Both
Care a good deal who wins elections	64%	55%	64%
High interest in political campaign	44	33	51
Follows public affairs most of the time	47	31	58
Voted in 1972	89	82	85
Voted in 1976	80	68	78
Tried to influence others to vote	46	33	43
Correct on House majority party before election	72	55	74
Correct on House majority party after election	72	54	64

Source: Center for Political Studies. American National Election Study, 1976 [machine-readable data file].

Again, it may be argued that these differences are not due to media effects but rather to the differences in the type of audience each medium attracts. Table 5–4 considers this question. It shows that across different educational levels, differences persist for political interest and information but disappear for political participation. Regardless of their education level, people who rely on television for political information tend to have lower levels of interest in the campaign. The differences are particularly large for higher-educated citizens. Medium choice also remains an important discriminator among correct responses to the party control question. While the higher-educated, television-dependent respondents show a higher proportion of correct answers than does the total sample (59 percent), the proportion is far less than that among their counterparts who rely upon newspapers or equally upon both media.

Participation differences remain within each education level, but they are reduced. It appears that while a dependency on different media is associated with an involvement in and understanding of the political system, it does not greatly affect the degree to which individuals interact with that system. But this could be taken another way. If political involvement and political information are important elements of sophisticated political decision making, then the participation of those who rely on television for political information is called into question. Research has shown that those who rely on television for political information have greater levels of distrust and political inefficacy.[37] This fact, coupled with lower levels of involvement and information, leads to the suspicion that the television-dependent individual will be more

TABLE 5–4 Most Relied Upon Medium for Political Information for Education Groups Across Interest, Participation, and Information Questions, 1976

	Low Education			Medium Education			High Education		
	News-papers	Tele-vision	Both	News-papers	Tele-vision	Both	News-papers	Tele-vision	Both
Care a good deal who wins election	60%	57%	63%	52%	52%	62%	74%	57%	66%
High interest in political campaign	36	34	44	35	26	46	54	40	59
Follow public affairs most of the time	30	25	47	38	25	53	59	46	67
Voted in 1972	75	72	74	94	85	87	92	90	90
Voted in 1976	58	59	70	77	67	80	91	82	83
Tried to influence others to vote	21	29	29	37	39	39	59	53	56
Correct on House majority party before election	51	41	58	63	54	70	87	72	86
Correct on House majority party after election	49	39	44	63	56	65	86	69	75

Source: Center for Political Studies. American National Election Study, 1976 [machine-readable data file].

affected by nonsubstantive political propaganda and the dramatic use of political symbols. Thus, while the frequency of political participation for television-dependent people may not be very different from that of other groups, the *quality* of that participation may be very different. This subject will be further pursued in the section dealing with media effects within political campaigns.

While research has not demonstrated that the choice of medium *causes* individuals to have certain political orientations, it has shown that certain media dependencies are strongly *associated* with certain political predispositions. Studies in this area repeatedly demonstrate that television dependence is associated with lower levels of involvement, information, and system affect.[38] While it cannot be proved that television causes such a situation, it can be argued that television allows such a situation to persist. In discussing television's capacity to inform, Walter Cronkite noted,

> we can introduce you to the people who make your news better than any other medium can possibly do it— in pictures, by taking a look at these people. We can background it in a very short fashion, but not in the depth that is necessary, probably, for a full understanding. Otherwise, we're an evening bulletin system.[39]

The primary problem is that a superficial understanding of the political world derived from this "evening bulletin system" may not be conducive to the development of attitudes necessary for an informed and attentive electorate. While political matters are sometimes cosmetic, in the general case they are complex and decidedly not superficial. Some observers argue that as the public becomes more dependent on television as an information source, assuming that the medium does not undergo significant structural changes in the way it delivers political information, there will result a greater disparity between the different media audiences. John Robinson pessimistically notes,

> the shocking ignorance of American citizens on issues of vital political and personal concern testifies to the limited fruitfulness of the interaction between the mass media and the public in the governmental process. One suspects that persons who claim to be getting most of their information from television may be euphemistically reporting that they are not receiving much information at all about what is happening.[40]

Mass Media Changes and Public Opinion

This section has examined changes in the mass media and their impact upon political information and mass public opinion. Technological, economic, and audience changes have all affected the nature of political information distributed to the American public. Technological changes have altered both the speed and the accuracy of transmitted information. People now know about political events much faster than before, but this knowledge, by the very speed of its delivery, is more superficial and may create stereotypic frameworks that are more difficult to alter upon receipt of new and more complete political information. Economic changes have raised the stakes of information diffusion so that it has become less and less fiscally feasible to offer in-depth public affairs programming. Political information, especially in the area of television programming, increasingly has been connected to entertainment formats in order to attract larger audiences for commercial sponsors. This information/entertainment overlap by necessity enhances the superficiality of the communicated information. Finally, over the past twenty years the American public has come more and more to depend on television as the primary source of political information. Partly as a result of the technological and economic changes in the medium, the television-dependent public differs from its newspaper-dependent counterpart in its interest and understanding of the political world. Although television has not convincingly demonstrated an ability to improve the public's understanding of important political matters, we cannot be sure that it has made things any worse.

Overall, then, the democratic ideal of an informed public may not square well with the view of a television-age public that is *aware* of political events but has less understanding of those events. To be sure, the educational *potential* of television has been well documented.[41] However, an apparent emphasis on entertainment, due mostly to the economic structure of the mass media, significantly affects the information diffusion network in America. As Altheide and Snow conclude,

> *we are not simply "vidiots" addicted to media, nor are we strictly victims of a conspiracy. Rather, we are cooperatives in a media comunications system in which we have come to accept a media culture as the real world. And to a large extent that media culture is entertainment.*[42]

THEORIES OF MASS MEDIA EFFECT

The preceding section dealt primarily with the general relationship between structural changes in the mass media and public opinion. However, it did not address the question of whether the mass media actually affect political opinion formation. While media-effect researchers have determined that the media do play a role in public opinion formation, the researchers differ as to the *nature* of this effect. Indeed, over the past decade there have emerged three theories of media effect. These theories are "media-central" effects (agenda-setting theory), "audience-central" effects (obstinate-audience theory), and "uses and gratifications." This section examines each theory of media effect.

The Agenda-setting Model

At the end of the continuum that stresses the dominant role of the media in the development of political cognitions, the most important explanation is the agenda-setting model. This model evolved from the summary work of Joseph Klapper.[43] One of the theories of media effect covered by Klapper was termed the "hypodermic effect." The hypodermic-effect theory, as its name implies, postulated that information transmitted via the media has a *direct* impact on how people view the world. The reasoning was that since all of our political information comes from the media, the media's coverages of political events becomes our basis for understanding those events. Personal differences in reception are minimized within this model.

Most researchers found the premises of the hypodermic model to be a bit too broad to describe the actual process of media effects. The agenda-setting model offered a somewhat less grandiose view of the media's power. Bernard Cohen summarized the model in the following manner:

> It [the news medium] may not be successful much of the time in telling people what to think, but it is stunningly successful in telling its readers what to think about. And it follows from this that the world looks different to different people, depending not only on their personal interests, but also on the map that is drawn for them by the writers, editors and publishers of the papers they read.[44]

The agenda-setting model of media effects argues that the media determine which events and issues are to receive attention, and that attention determines the degree to which the issues will be salient to the mass public. Put more formally, the media react to a stimulus in the environment that leads them to select and display certain information. The transmission of this information affects public cognitions, which then leads to mass behavioral responses.[45]

An example of this agenda-setting process can be seen in the rise of the environmental issue in the early seventies. Before 1970, media attention to the environment was quite sporadic, limited to isolated stories about pollution. In 1970, however, spurred by the growing articulation of environmentally related concerns on the part of small but well-organized environmental groups, stories dealing with the growing environmental problem began to appear with increasing regularity. Within a very short time public opinion pollsters began to find that environmental matters were listed among their respondents' answers to the question, "What do you feel is the greatest problem facing America today?" If we dismiss the possibility that during this short time period the environmental problem took a decided turn for the worse, the upsurge in mass concern for the environmental problem seems to have been the result of the media's decision to feature stories on that subject. The agenda of the mass public, which at that time was already quite crowded with the Vietnam War and mass protests, was expanded to include another issue, the salience of which was due in large part to the media's selection processes.

Empirical research investigating the agenda-setting model has provided some degree of confirmation. Studies show a high correlation between what voters thought was important during an election campaign and the frequency of the media's coverage of those issues.[46] Other studies, using public opinion polls as indicators of mass public opinion, also find high correlations between the frequency of media coverage and the salience of those issues most often covered.[47] Most of the studies involving the agenda-setting model encounter problems akin to the chicken/egg dilemma. Do the media cover stories because the public is interested in them? Or is the public interested in stories because the media have covered them? More recently, however, studies have been conducted across time assuming a time ordering — that media coverage precedes mass salience.[48] These studies provide some support to the agenda-setting hypothesis.

There also exists an adaptation of the agenda-setting model that allows for the impact of personal influence. This model has been termed the "two-step-flow" theory of information diffusion.[49] This adaptation argues that the media shape the cognitions of those who more often consume political information. These "opinion leaders" then pass on their interpretations of media communications to individuals who, having less of an inclination to attend to media-transmitted information, rely on the attentive individuals for political cues. This process allows for opinion leaders to "interpret" the political communication and to communicate the interpretation that coincides with their own political preferences.

The "Obstinate-Audience" Model

On the other extreme of the media-effect continuum is a model that has been termed by one writer the "obstinate-audience" model.[50] In contrast to the agenda-setting model, here people are seen to critically evaluate information, to reject that which does not coincide with their beliefs and to accept that which does. This model rests on twin principles of political cognition: selective exposure and selective perception.

Selective exposure means that individuals will avoid messages that conflict with their own values and beliefs and actively seek out those congruent with their own beliefs.[51] A person who has, for example, a particularly strong dislike for "fast" food will tend to avoid restaurants specializing in that cuisine. Similarly, a person who dislikes the Democratic party may avoid reading news stories on that party's candidates and ignore television broadcasts featuring Democratic party issues. The main problem with research in this area lies in the problem of differentiating *de facto* selectivity of exposure from *conscious* selective exposure.[52] That an individual avoids certain types of information does not prove that the avoidance is due to a conscious or subconscious attempt to defend against exposure. The hypothetical restaurant customer may avoid fast-food restaurants as a result of the service or food he or she has received in earlier encounters rather than as a result of a clear and distinct aversion to the food. Because actual selective exposure must involve psychological defense mechanisms, its empirical verification is much more difficult to achieve.

Selective perception differs from selective exposure in that people receive a communication but incorporate only those features of the communication that coincide with their own predispositions. In a study of the 1960 debate between Kennedy and Nixon, Elihu Katz and Jacob Feldman found that people with strong party and/or candidate preferences before the debate were much more likely to declare their candidate the debate "winner."[53] The selective-perception hypothesis, which is derived from the work on cognitive dissonance by Leon Festinger,[54] emphasizes the personal involvement of the individual in the assimilation of information. Rather than picturing the individual as an empty slate upon which the media write, the individual is seen as incorporating new evidence in a cumulative fashion — adding new information that strengthens previously held beliefs and values, and rejecting information that contradicts those beliefs and values. Empirical verification of this process has been far from conclusive.[55] Part of the problem lies in the difficulty of discerning the underlying *motivations* of the individual. Most of the research leads to the conclusion that individuals within the mass public act *as if* some selection process is occurring.

Uses-and-Gratifications Model

While the agenda-setting model stresses that media content produces media effect, the obstinate-audience model proposes that audience intention determines media effect.[56] In between these two extremes lies the uses-and-gratifications model. This model incorporates both the agenda-setting model's assumption that the media sets most of the issues and events before the national audience, and the obstinate-audience model's main assumption that the degree to which the media affect the individual is determined by the individual's own motivational hierarchy. As Walter Gantz describes the model, "the media are perceived as effective, although the type and amount of effect is seen as varying across viewers in relation to reasons for their exposure."[57] While the media set up the individual's information environment, the degree to which the information is assimilated by the individual depends on the reasons the individual has for assessing that information. As discussed earlier, the media serve three main functions for the individual: understanding, action, and entertainment. When the communicated message is aligned with the individual's purpose in receiving that message, according to this model, the message has the greatest chance of effect. Many people have had the urge at one time or another to attend a motion picture, thinking, "Any movie will do." And generally "any movie" is satisfactory if the primary purpose is the securing of movie entertainment. If, however, one is more specific about what would satisfy a need (say, a comedy), then only a selected set of motion pictures will have the desired impact. Similarly, if an individual consumes information from a particular medium with the goal of relaxation, political discussions and documentaries would be of little or no consequence. Indeed, research has shown that people who use television for recreational purposes have less information than people who use it for information purposes or who don't use it at all.[58]

The main attraction of the uses-and-gratifications approach to media effects is that it avoids the deterministic, stimulus-response posture of the agenda-setting model and the unrealistic view of the obstinate-audience model that people consciously weed out dissonant message transmissions. Simply put, the uses-and-gratifications model states that people get out of media what they want of it. If people approach the presidential debates with the goal of learning more about the two candidates, the probability is that the debates will have an effect upon their evaluations. If they view the debates to confirm their opinions of the two candidates, then the possibility of debate-induced attitude change is greatly reduced. If the approach to the debates is as a source of entertainment found in the clash of the personalities of two political celebrities, the substance of the debates will be overlooked. This model also helps put the data presented in the first section into a clearer perspective. People who rely on television for political information have lower levels of political involvement and information. This may result from individuals who are dependent upon television not having information access as their primary goal; their primary goal may be entertainment and relaxation. Then, according to the uses-and-gratifications model, television dependency should be associated with lower levels of political information and awareness.

While there exist other models of media effects,[59] the three models outlined above contain the most important elements of the ongoing debate within this area. The state of the art of media-effect research has not progressed far enough to enable social scientists to state with conviction that one model is superior to another. The uses-and-gratifications model seems the most fruitful because it contains important elements of the two polar models, and because it emphasizes the functions media transmissions perform for people. The final section of this chapter extends the discussion of this model to the arena where media transmissions and politics interact most strongly: the political campaign.

MEDIA EFFECTS WITHIN POLITICAL CAMPAIGNS

Symbiotic Relationships

Earlier sections of this chapter suggested that (1) individuals use the media for different purposes; (2) the structural characteristics of media communications have changed significantly over the past twenty years, and these changes have influenced the nature of the communicated message; and (3) media effects are most pronounced when the nature of the message coincides with the individual's purpose in receiving it. These themes come together most clearly during the political campaign. Ideally, media transmissions during campaigns enable people to arrive at an informed decision based on the issues and candidates. There exists an identifiable symbiotic relationship between the media organizations and the parties and candidates during the campaign. Since the campaign is highly newsworthy and arouses citizen interest, the media are strongly dependent on the candidates and political parties for news stories to provide to their audiences. On the other side, the candidates and parties must enlist the media in bringing their electoral crusade to the attention of the public. This use of the media goes beyond purchasing time for political advertisements; it extends to attempts to be covered by the media in order to get broadly based, not to mention free, mass exposure.

Thus, the media and the central characters in the campaign are heavily dependent upon each other. Newspapers and television networks invest heavily in their election coverage. All the major candidates have reporters assigned to them for varying amounts of time by each of the major networks. In addition, larger networks commission private polling agencies within most of the primary election states in order to provide their audiences with more accurate predictions of the winner. The political conventions of each party are now covered from start to finish by most networks.[60] As the general campaign draws to a close, greater time and exposure is directed toward the analysis and prediction of the final outcome. The presidential campaign represents a heavy investment of resources for the media, and thus there exists a great incentive on their part to maintain mass interest in the election, thereby providing a larger audience for political campaign coverage.

The candidates and parties also have an incentive to structure their campaigns to enhance media coverage. Media campaign coverage allows the candidates to reach a national audience without depending totally on advertising expenditures — a very salient point given the passage in 1971 of regulations limiting campaign contributions. To maximize media coverage of their activities, candidates arrange their schedules to coincide with newspaper and television evening news deadlines. In addition, candidates are now much more aware of how their personal appearances will look when covered by the media. This understanding of the way in which the media cover elections, especially in the case of the visual dimension of television, leads to devices such as renting halls for rallies that are too small for the expected crowds of supporters so that the newspapers can tell their readers that Candidate X spoke to "an overflowing crowd," and so that the televised record of the event will show the "standing-room-only" throng.[61]

The media are committed to covering the political campaign in as interesting a way as possible. On the other hand, the candidates attempt to posture themselves in order to be covered in as positive a light as possible. The result is that coverage of modern political campaigns tends to emphasize style over substance. In order to make the campaign attractive to viewers, the media emphasize the "horse-race" image of electoral politics rather than more substantive debates over vital political issues. Thomas Patterson and Robert McClure, in a content analysis of television's coverage of the 1972 election, estimated that close to 73 percent of the coverage was devoted to campaign activity (rallies, motorcades, polls, and electoral strategies). Only a quarter of the coverage was devoted to such things as the candidate's qualifications and stands on important issues.[62] The candidates also attempt to stylize their media coverage opportunities in order to communicate a sense of competence, honesty, and compassion to the mass public.[63]

Amidst the considerable effort exerted by media and candidates alike, the question must be asked: "Does it work? Are the viewers affected by these attempts to make politics more interesting and the candidates more appealing?" The answers to these questions must be delayed until we have examined the interaction of campaign messages and the uses to which the public puts them.

A Typology of Political Campaign Communications

Regardless of the temper of the electoral conflict, campaigns aim to structure and simplify political phenomena. Candidates seek to use the media's coverage of their campaign activities to advance their political fortunes. What remains fairly stable across election campaigns is the degree to which the campaigners can structure or control certain types of political stimuli. Robert Agranoff suggests there are two types of messages the campaigner uses to structure media communications: controlled and uncontrolled.[64] *Controlled messages* include activities such as "personal campaigning by the candidate and campaigner, party organization efforts, whether they be through mass media or delivered on a smaller scale."[65] The notion of control, then, comes from the ability of the campaigner to structure both the content of the message and the environment in which the message is communicated.[66] *Uncontrolled messages* are transmitted by an uncontrolled communications channel. The major broadcast networks' coverage of the campaign is an obvious example of an uncontrolled message.

The two classifications describe only the poles of a spectrum of message control by the candidates. As Agranoff points out,

> *It becomes readily clear that not all uncontrolled media are completely uncontrollable, when one stimulates or attempts to structure media. Some would say that these are semi-controlled media messages. However, all uncontrolled media messages are qualitatively different from messages produced and placed by the candidate, not only because what is said is not controlled, but because the format through which it is delivered is considered to be neutral and authoritative, and is regarded by the audience as information rather than propaganda.*[67]

But do these controlled and uncontrolled messages accomplish their purpose? The agenda-setting theorist would argue that the degree to which the candidate can control exposure to the public will determine the success of his or her political messages. The obstinate-audience theorist would argue that the candidate's success will be dependent on his or her ability to appeal to the values and beliefs of the majority of the voters. The closer the message comes to the predispositions of the electorate, the greater the chance of message impact. The uses-and-gratifications theorist, however, would want to have information about the *motivation* of the individual to consume the candidates' political messages before deciding on probable effect. This theorist would want to know if the individual voluntarily assessed the political message or if the exposure came about as the result of some purpose other than information seeking.

Using Agranoff's notion of controlled and uncontrolled transmissions and the uses-and-gratifications model's notion of voluntary and involuntary access as polar types of transmission and reception of political campaign information, we can illustrate the general *source* of information about political events and their probable impact. Table 5–5 presents a typology of information sources that predominate under different conditions of transmission and reception.

When the transmission is controlled and the access is involuntary, information usually is in the form of political advertising (cell A). Political advertisements are, of course, intended to present the subject in the best possible light; hence the transmission is strictly controlled. Also, since very few individuals seek out political advertising, access to them must be strategically plotted to be well nigh inescapable. "Novel" campaign events (cell B) are the main sources of political information when the transmission is uncontrolled, but the access is largely involuntary. Novel events are those covered outside of normal news channels. They may be interruptions of normal commercial broadcasts on the subject of personal communications. These events are usually highly dramatic and controversial. The absence of control indicates that they are unanticipated, and the involuntary access implies that they must utilize transmission channels usually unencumbered by political messages. Examples of such events are the riots during the 1968 Democratic convention, George McGovern's difficulties with his choices for vice-president in 1972, and the 1972 assassination attempt on George Wallace. Given the rather diffuse nature of these events, it would be difficult to gauge any systematic impact. Needless to say, parties and their candidates prefer to avoid such events because, given their dramatic and disruptive nature, they may affect even the most well-thought-out electoral strategy.

In cell C of Table 5–5 the source is uncontrolled and the access voluntary. Studies have shown that established channels of political news are attended by individuals who wish to learn more about the campaign and who distrust controlled transmissions.[68]

TABLE 5–5   Typology of Political Campaign Communications

Source Control	Access Form	
	Involuntary	Voluntary
Controlled	(A) Political Advertising	(D) "Pseudo events"
Uncontrolled	(B) "Novel" Campaign Events	(C) Campaign News Coverage

Not all of the information transmitted over established communications channels is uncontrollable. The candidates and their managers are well aware of the importance of reaching those most likely to vote and having that contact appear as "realistic" and spontaneous as possible. Many political events are "staged" to attract media coverage and at the same time to give the appearance of "news." Campaign strategists hope to combine the effectiveness of political advertising[69] with the drama of the novel event within a setting that appears to be an uncontrolled source of political information (but in reality is carefully orchestrated). In other words, the goal is to create media events, or "pseudo events,"[70] which are transmitted to the voters as straight political information or "news."

Pseudo events are the most effective means to transmit a message; they feature realism and drama but preserve the element of control. As Patterson and McClure have observed,

believability is the first requirement for effective media propaganda. The voters must accept what is being said about the candidates. . . . Television image making fails to make it past the believability barrier.[71]

If the communication is perceived to be an attempt at image making, voters tend to dismiss it. Television commercials that dwell on such elements tend to go unnoticed, especially by those who do not have high levels of political interest in politics.[72] When the message is interpreted as transmitting *factual* information, they communicate more effectively.[73] "Facts," or perceived "facts," voluntarily accessed are the most important ingredient of a successful message transmission.

The greatest media impact is found when exposure is motivated by a desire to acquire political information. From the point of view of the candidates, the greatest chance of effect lies in the controlled presentation of message forms to which there is voluntary attendance. This usually takes the form of a dramatic or exciting forum of candidate presentation. Politics is most salient to the American public when the capacity for drama and conflict is emphasized. When candidates use this capacity within a controlled setting, they aid the media channels in their attempt to attract an audience for the electoral contest. In this way the goals of both the candidate and the medium are served.

CONCLUSION

This chapter has covered two important dimensions of the American political media and their impact on public opinion. First, the structural changes in the media, especially with the advent of television, have influenced the form of the message that has been transmitted to the American public. The increased accessibility of information stemming from technological, economic, and audience changes has widened the *scope* of American public opinion but has done less to influence the substantive understanding of political affairs. It is important to understand that the primary function of most American media is entertainment. From both an economic and an audience expectation point of view, this function has assumed a position of prime importance. The provision of information, political and otherwise, takes a secondary place within the media transmission network in this society. But this secondary role is nothing new. Before television, Americans were no more a nation of informed and aware individuals than now. There existed other forms of diversion that took precedence over information acquisition. The advent of television has simply made access to entertainment and relaxation more direct. It would be a mistake to pin the blame for low levels of citizen information on television just because it is not being used to its fullest information potential. The situation exists because information access is not one of the overriding motivations of human interest and goal-directed behavior.

The second dimension of the political media involves theories of media impact. The day has not yet arrived for the precise identification of the specific circumstances that surround a successful media communication. The theory that best fits the political world states that people are affected by the media messages they seek out themselves. Media impact depends on the needs and expectations of the media consumer. This implies that the effectiveness of a media transmission will vary across individuals and perhaps across time periods. While this makes an integrated theory of media effects more difficult to achieve, it also presents a manner of evaluating the potential effects of the media more realistic than either one of its theoretical alternatives.

Understanding structural and audience characteristics in the American mass media information flow process allows a better grasp of the nature of the media's coverage of political phenomena and the public's reaction to that coverage. Political campaigns are perhaps the best area of study, for they feature intensified media attention and heightened public interest. The point that we have stressed throughout this chapter is that increased attention to the media does not necessarily mean that the public will gain a greater *understanding* of the central disputes of the political world. Because of structural changes, especially in its economic base, the media establishment features news stories that are, first and foremost, interesting to the attracted audience. While information is transmitted in this process, its scope is contingent upon the form of the message. If the form of the message is superficial, the information contained in that message is likely to be the same.

One of the most worrisome consequences of this "news-as-entertainment" phenomenon is that it may have a significant impact upon the type of person chosen to fill the highest positions of political power in this country. The increased attention to "style over substance" has led to an increased reliance on the personalities of the candidates as the final determination of vote choice:

> *Overall, three out of four answers people give when asked what they have learned about candidates and issues or why they would vote or refrain from voting for a certain candidate concern personality traits. People are interested in the human qualities of their elected leaders, particularly their trustworthiness, principled character, strength, and compassion.*[74]

There is no doubt that the personal characteristics of a candidate for a high office are an important consideration in determining support. In many cases, how a person handles stress is more important than his or her particular stand on a given issue. If campaign coverage by the media were able to provide an accurate examination of the personalities of the competing candidates, then its contribution would be worthwhile, even if issues were never covered in an in-depth manner.

The flaw in all of this is that the media establishment itself is subject to manipulation by candidate organizations, and this manipulation usually occurs in the area of candidate image making:

> *The skills of the campaign professionals are directed at producing a candidate who is informed of his constituents' views, beliefs, characteristics, and habits and who is able to adapt himself to that constituency during the course of the campaign. . . . But when a candidate uses opinion surveys and image advertising to give the appearance of being the leader of a popular movement, he is a captive not only of the movement but of the technicians as well. He becomes a manufactured, contrived "personality" contending with rival contrived "personalities" for public office.*[75]

Consequently, as it is now, the media's main political campaign usefulness may be to inform us about the personal qualifications of those who wish to lead us. As in many other areas of public opinion, however, there is much to learn about the role of the media.

NOTES

1. For a discussion arguing that people frequently give opinions with no information, see Philip E. Converse, "Attitudes and Non-Attitudes: The Continuation of a Dialogue," in *The Quantitative Study of Politics,* Edward Tufte, ed. (Reading, Mass: Addison-Wesley, 1971).
2. For an overview of the research relating to this area, see Lee B. Becker, Maxwell E. McCombs, and Jack M. McLeod, "The Development of Political Cognitions"; and Steven H. Chaffee, "The Diffusion of Political Information," in *Political Communication: Issues and Strategies for Research,* Steven H. Chaffee, ed. (Beverly Hills: Sage Publications, 1975).
3. Melvin DeFleur and Sandra Ball-Rokeach, *Theories of Mass Communication,* 3rd ed. (New York: David McKay, 1975).
4. See M. Brewster Smith, Jerome S. Bruner, and Robert W. White, *Opinions and Personality* (New York: John Wiley & Sons, 1956).
5. David L. Altheide and Robert P. Snow, *Media Logic* (Beverly Hills: Sage Publications, 1979).
6. Ibid., p. 11.
7. This does not imply, however, that personal communications are not a part of the information diffusion process.
8. At the local level, newspapers and radio are quite important. At the nonpolitical level, local media are the most important sources of all three dependency areas.
9. This emphasis on speed of message transmission has produced a format change in at least one television network's news programming. CBS News now runs a "West Coast Edition" of its nightly news broadcast in order to overcome the three-hour coastal time difference.
10. Ben Bagdikian, *The Information Machines* (New York: Harper & Row, 1971).
11. Walter Lippmann, *Public Opinion* (New York: Macmillan, 1922).
12. The social psychological literature has featured many discussions of this subject. Much of the research is found in the area of cognitive dissonance — the process by which individuals avoid or reject information that goes against their previously held beliefs. The basic work in this area is Leon Festinger, *A Theory of Cognitive Dissonance* (Stanford: Stanford University Press, 1957).
13. We deal more fully with the processes of selective perception and selective exposure later in this chapter.
14. One example of the informational costs incurred by speed was the coverage of the Attica Prison riots in 1971. The first reports that went out over the airways and into the newspapers on the following day stated that the captive guards' throats were cut by the rioting prisoners. When the true facts emerged later, it was found that the hostages had been killed by the National Guard troops. It is interesting to speculate whether the same process occurred during the coverage of the Watergate break-in. What was initially reported as a "third-rate" burglary in the Democratic National Committee offices turned out to be, again when the facts caught up with the coverage, something a bit more serious.
15. Ben Bagdikian, "Report of an Exaggerated Death," Newspaper Survival Study, Series Paper no. 1, Markle Foundation, 1976.

16. Edwin Diamond, *The Tin Kazoo* (Cambridge, Mass.: MIT Press, 1975).
17. Altheide and Snow, *Media Logic,* pp. 9–17.
18. DeFleur and Ball-Rokeach, *Theories of Mass Communication,* pp. 34–62.
19. A critique of the "Sesame Street" method of educating preschool children can be found in Frank Mankiewicz and James Swerdlow, *Remote Control* (New York: New York Times Books, 1978).
20. Indeed, as media technology spreads we are moving closer and closer to McLuhan's notion of a "global village." See Marshall McLuhan, *Understanding Media: The Extensions of Man* (New York: McGraw-Hill, 1966).
21. Two very good discussions of the relationship between the media's ability to provide information and their superficial presentation of that information are found in Edwin Diamond, *The Tin Kazoo;* and Tony Schwartz, *The Responsive Chord* (Garden City, N.J.: Anchor Press, 1973). For a recent examination of the amount of political knowledge transmitted by television, see Philip Palmgreen, "Mass Media Use and Political Knowledge," *Journalism Monographs* 61 (May 1979), pp. 20–33.
22. Les Brown, *Television: The Business Behind the Box* (New York: Harcourt Brace Jovanovich, 1971), p. 64.
23. The case of CBS's program "60 Minutes" is instructive. Soon after the program began to garner high Nielsen ratings, the other two networks introduced their own versions of television "newsmagazines." Thus, it is not always the case that commercial success works against public affairs programming.
24. Because the airways are owned by the public, private media enterprises must devote a certain percentage of their programming to public service content. The licensees, however, are the local media, not the national networks. The Public Broadcasting System (PBS), subsidized heavily by the federal government, is not as constrained by audience-attracting behaviors. It must be noted, however, that the entertainment content of PBS broadcasting has increased significantly over the past ten years in an attempt to draw the attention of potential contributors.
25. All reported figures are derived from Edwin Emery, *The Press and America* (Englewood Cliffs, N.J.: Prentice-Hall, 1972), pp. 618–20.
26. James E. Combs, *Dimensions of Political Drama* (Santa Monica, Calif.: Goodyear Publishing Co., 1980), p. 110.
27. Some sources on the media's coverage of crime are Paul Blake, "Race, Homicide and the News," *The Nation* (December 7, 1975), pp. 592–93; S. Chibinall, "The Crime Reporter: A Study on the Production of Commercial Knowledge," *Sociology* 9 (January 1975), pp. 49–66; P. Deeley and C. Walker, *Murder in the Fourth Estate* (New York: McGraw-Hill, 1973); and L. Sigelman, "Reporting the News: An Organizational Analysis," *American Journal of Sociology* 79 (February 1973), pp. 132–51.
28. Sanford Sherizen, "Social Creation of Crime News: All the News Fitted to Print," in *Deviance and the Mass Media,* Charles Winick, ed. (Beverly Hills: Sage Publications, 1978).
29. Ibid., p. 217.
30. Ibid., p. 272.
31. See Doris Graber, *Mass Media and American Politics* (Washington, D.C.: Congressional Quarterly Press, 1980), pp. 142–44.
32. Over the past twenty years, magazines have gone against this nationalizing trend and today are being directed more at specialized readerships.
33. See Emery, *The Press and America,* for a detailed history of the print medium's movement from a party press through penny-press and yellow journalism to the high-stakes economic situation of today.

34. Figures, derived from the 1952 and 1956 Michigan election studies, are cited in V. O. Key, Jr., *Public Opinion and American Democracy* (New York: Alfred A. Knopf, 1961), p. 346.

35. See Steven Chaffee, "Interpersonal Context of Mass Communication," in *Current Perspectives in Mass Communication Research,* F. Gerald Kline and Phillip J. Tichenor, eds. (Beverly Hills: Sage Publications, 1972).

36. Note that charges of cultural bias in the media are quite different from charges that the media are slanted toward one ideological stance.

37. See Garrett O'Keefe and Harold Mendelsohn, "Nonvoting: The Media's Role," in *Deviance and the Mass Media,* pp. 263 – 386; and Michael J. Robinson, "Public Affairs Television and the Growth of Political Malaise: The Case of the 'Selling of the Pentagon,'" *American Political Science Review* 70 (June 1976), pp. 409– 32.

38. See Arthur H. Miller, Edie N. Goldenberg, and Lutz Erbring, "Typeset Politics: Impact of Newspapers on Public Confidence," *American Political Science Review* 73 (March 1979), pp. 67 – 84; Robinson, "Public Affairs Television and the Growth of Political Malaise"; and Schwartz, *The Responsive Chord.*

39. Walter Cronkite quoted in "Talking Back to CBS," transcript of television broadcast, February 15, 1976.

40. John P. Robinson, "Mass Communication and Information Diffusion," in *Current Perspectives in Mass Communication Research,* p. 87.

41. See Chester M. Pierce, ed., *Television and Education* (Beverly Hills: Sage Publications, 1978).

42. Altheide and Snow, *Media Logic,* p. 60.

43. Joseph Klapper, *The Effects of Mass Communications* (New York: Free Press, 1960).

44. Bernard Cohen, *The Press and Foreign Policy* (Princeton, N.J.: Princeton University Press, 1963), p. 13.

45. This process is adapted from that presented in Becker et al., "The Development of Political Cognitions," p. 39.

46. Maxwell McCombs and Donald Shaw, "The Agenda-Setting Function of the Media," *Public Opinion Quarterly* 36 (Summer 1972), pp. 176– 87.

47. See G. Funkhouser, "The Issue of the Sixties: An Exploratory Study in the Dynamics of Public Opinion," *Public Opinion Quarterly* 37 (Spring 1973), pp. 533– 38; and Gerald Kline, "Sources and Impact of Political Information in the 1972 Elections." (Paper presented at the American Association for Public Opinion Research, 1973 Annual Meeting, Washington, D.C.)

48. See L. Tipton et al., "Media Agenda-Setting in City and State Campaigns," *Journalism Quarterly* 52 (Spring 1975), pp. 15– 22; D. Weaver et al., "Watergate and the Media: A Case Study of Agenda Setting," *American Politics Quarterly* 3 (October 1975); and R. McClure and T. Patterson, "Television News and Political Advertising," *Communication Research* 1 (January 1974), pp. 3– 31.

49. See E. Katz and P. Lazarsfeld, *Personal Influence* (New York: Free Press, 1955).

50. Raymond Bauer, "The Obstinate Audience: The Influence Process from the Point of View of Social Communication," *American Psychologist* 19 (May 1964), pp. 319– 28.

51. The basic works in the area of selective exposure are J. Klapper, *The Effects of Mass Communication;* L. Froman and J. Skipper, "Factors Related to Misperceiving Party Stands on Issues," *Public Opinion Quarterly* 26 (Summer 1962), pp. 265 – 71; and S. Star and H. Hughes, "Report on an Educational Campaign: The Cincinnati Plan for the United Nations," *American Journal of Sociology* 55 (November 1950), pp. 389– 400.

52. See Maxwell McCombs, "Mass Communication in Political Campaigns: Information, Gratification, and Persuasion," in *Current Perspectives in Mass Communication Research,* pp. 175–76.

53. E. Katz and J. Feldman, "The Debates in Light of Research," in *The Great Debates,* Sidney Kraus, ed. (Bloomington, Ind.: Indiana University Press, 1962); Paul R. Hagner and Leroy N. Rieselbach, "The Impact of the 1976 Presidential Debates: Conversion or Reinforcement?" in *The Presidential Debates,* G. F. Bishop, R. C. Meadow, and M. Jackson-Beeck, eds. (New York: Praeger, 1978).

54. Festinger, *A Theory of Cognitive Dissonance.*

55. See David Sears and J. Freedman, "Selective Exposure to Information: A Critical Review," *Public Opinion Quarterly* 31 (Summer 1967), pp. 194–213.

56. See Walter Gantz, "Uses Gratification and the Recall of Television News." (Paper presented to the Annual Convention of the Association for Education in Journalism, College Park, Maryland, July 25-27th, 1976.)

57. Ibid., p. 1.

58. Ibid.

59. See DeFleur and Ball-Rokeach, *Theories of Mass Communication,* and Klapper, *The Effects of Mass Communications,* for reviews of other media-effect models.

60. In 1976, however, ABC covered the conventions selectively and received the highest viewership ratings of the three networks.

61. Techniques of this sort are described by Joe McGinnis, *The Selling of the President 1968* (New York: Trident Press, 1969); and Timothy Crouse, *The Boys on the Bus* (New York: Random House, 1974).

62. Thomas Patterson and Robert McClure, *The Unseeing Eye: The Myth of Television Power in National Elections* (New York: G. P. Putnam, 1976), p. 41. See also Graber, *Mass Media and American Politics,* pp. 164–69.

63. Graber, *Mass Media and American Politics,* pp. 162–64.

64. Robert Agranoff, *The Management of Election Campaigns* (Boston: Holbrook Press, 1976), pp. 340–80.

65. Ibid., p. 379.

66. The distinction is not always clear cut. Sometimes "pure" political advertising is calculated to appear completely uncontrolled and spontaneous. Many elements of the 1968 Nixon campaign fit this description. See McGinnis, *The Selling of the President 1968.*

67. Agranoff, *The Management of Election Campaigns,* p. 341 (italics added).

68. See Kline, "Sources and Impact of Political Information." (Paper presented at the American Association for Public Opinion Research, 1973 Annual Meetings.)

69. Patterson and McClure, *The Unseeing Eye.*

70. The concept of the "pseudo event" was first introduced by Daniel Boorstin in *The Image* (New York: Harper & Row, 1961).

71. Patterson and McClure, *The Unseeing Eye,* p. 151.

72. Ibid., pp. 130–33.

73. Ibid., pp. 151–52.

74. Graber, *Mass Media and American Politics,* p. 184.

75. Dan Nimmo, *The Political Persuaders* (Englewood Cliffs, N.J.: Prentice-Hall, 1970), p. 197.

PART III

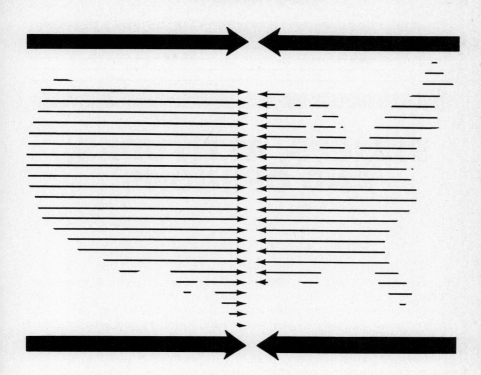

THE SUBSTANCE
OF PUBLIC OPINION

CHAPTER 6

BELIEFS, ATTITUDES, AND OPINIONS

The preceding two chapters concerned the *sources* of political beliefs, attitudes, and opinions. This chapter discusses both the *content* and the *dynamics* of the American public's political thinking. The first part of the chapter defines the basic elements of political cognition and examines their organization.

THE DEFINITIONS OF POLITICAL BELIEFS, ATTITUDES, AND OPINIONS

Much of the literature on American political thinking is downright confusing because writers tend to use interchangeably the terms *beliefs, attitudes,* and *opinions.* Such a blending of conceptual meanings can exact a serious toll in the student's understanding of important differences in the content and dynamics of the three concepts. This first section sets out firmly the differences among beliefs, attitudes, and opinions.

Beliefs

At a very basic level, people develop an understanding of how the external world is ordered. These understandings are termed *beliefs.* More formally, a belief can be thought of as "the probability or improbability that a particular relationship exists between the object of a belief, and some other object, concept or goal."[1] The sociologist Milton Rokeach identified three types of beliefs.[2]

Descriptive beliefs relate to the existence of conditions in the external world generally believed to be true or false on the basis of direct sensations, or of those by trustworthy or authoritative people. Adults take most descriptive beliefs for granted,[3] but children constantly incorporate new factual information into their belief networks. The learning theorist Jean Piaget called this process "assimilation."[4] While the process of assimilation continues throughout life, the *frequency* of encountering new information diminishes as the life cycle progresses. By adulthood, a person's interpretation of reality is fairly well fixed. Examples of descriptive political beliefs are statements such as the following: "Jimmy Carter is a Democrat," "Congress has two houses," and "The United States is a democracy." The second part of this chapter shows that while the American public has a vast array of descriptive political beliefs, the accuracy of these beliefs is widely varied.

Evaluative beliefs are when a statement is made about an object that involves a judgmental decision on the goodness or badness of that object. Osgood, Suci, and Tannenbaum have isolated four different modes of evaluating objects.[5] The first mode is termed "moral evaluation." This type of evaluation would include statements such as "Our criminal justice system is fair," or "The right to vote is sacred." The second mode is that of "aesthetic evaluation." Statements such as "Jimmy Carter has a pleasant personality" or "My town is a nice place to live" are examples. The third type, "social evaluation," can be seen in statements such as "Ronald Reagan is an honest man," or "Military service is a healthy experience." Finally, evaluations can be "emotional" in nature. "The economic situation is disturbing" or "Dwight Eisenhower had a calming influence on the nation" are examples. Each of these four modes of evaluation, whatever its factual basis, implies a predisposition of the holder. One cannot determine the general predisposition of the belief holder from a single evaluation, since it could be one of many. One may, for instance, believe that a candidate is honest (social evaluation), but also believe that he is wrong on important issues (moral evaluation) and abrasive (aesthetic evaluation).

Evaluative beliefs can be deeply rooted and form the basis for much of an individual's activity.[6] Allegiance to political symbols is one form of evaluative belief.[7] High degrees of affect for the flag, democracy, and the president could, analytically, take the form, "——— is good." The discussion of the content of American beliefs will examine the wealth of symbolic attachment present in the American public and the role it plays in the stability of the American political culture.

A related aspect of evaluative beliefs involves the extent to which they are generalized to a set of objects. Recall that beliefs are defined as the probability that two objects are related. If beliefs are based "upon too limited a set of experiences,"[8] and the evaluation of the object is overgeneralized, there is a danger that particularized evaluations could develop into *stereotypes*. If, based on limited negative experiences with members of a particular group, one extends the particularized negative evaluation to *all* members of that group, then the stereotyped response could preclude any further assimilation of new, and perhaps more complimentary, information pertaining to that group. Statements such as "All politicians are corrupt," if internalized, give the holder a simplistic and prejudicial view of reality.

Prescriptive beliefs center upon whether one believes that some end-state, or means of attaining a particular end-state, is or is not desirable. General prescriptive beliefs are also known as "values."[9] Prescriptive beliefs usually occupy central roles in a person's orientation to life, behavior, and the behavior of others. The things that people value govern their evaluations of almost all that they enconter. If a person values peaceful coexistence highly, then he or she might be expected to oppose military involvement abroad. Similarly, a person who feels that honesty is the most important characteristic to be found in an individual would be expected to have this quality utmost in his or her mind when deciding upon friends or even political candidates.

While there are as many different value systems as there are individuals, groups of people who share similar experiences and socialization tend to have similar values, especially in the area of politics. *Political culture* refers to this phenomenon and can be defined as "a set of patterned values which sum to a total way of life for a people."[10] The chapter on socialization emphasized the way in which values are transmitted from generation to generation. What makes people peculiarly American, aside from some differences in language, are the common values they believe to be important.[11]

The most important aspect of all three classifications of belief is that they occupy central positions within one's thinking. Belief in truth and falsity and right and wrong precede most people's behavior and general orientation toward themselves and the external world. Beliefs lie at the center of how people express themselves to the world through attitudes, opinions, and, ultimately, behavior.

Attitudes

The meaning of *attitude* is not universally agreed upon within the social sciences.[12] It is often used interchangeably with the concepts of *belief* or *values*.[13] To always equate attitudes and beliefs is to oversimplify what is, in reality, a complex process. Attitudes are more usefully thought of as the products of beliefs: after having considered his or her beliefs about a particular object, a person finally arrives at a *general orientation* toward that object. This general orientation, the composite of a variety of different types of beliefs and intensities of evaluation, can be termed an *attitude*. More formally, "an attitude refers to the amount of affect for or against a psychological object."[14] The key term in this definition is *amount,* for an attitude is the summation of all that one believes an object to be.

A simple example will help illustrate this usage of the term *attitude.* Suppose candidate Jones is running for president. Through the media and conversations with friends an individual comes to have the following set of ten *beliefs* about candidate Jones:

1. Candidate Jones is a Democrat.
2. Candidate Jones is a veteran.
3. Candidate Jones favors gun control.
4. Candidate Jones favors increased defense spending.
5. Candidate Jones opposes the draft.
6. Candidate Jones is honest.
7. Candidate Jones is not a dynamic speaker.
8. Candidate Jones is a good family man.
9. Candidate Jones believes in world peace.
10. Candidate Jones believes in economic prosperity for all.

Now suppose for the individual one has a measure of the *degree of affect* (pro or con feeling) he or she has for each one of these belief attributes. If this degree of affect were measured on a scale similar to the one below,

-7	-6	-5	-4	-3	-2	-1	0	$+1$	$+2$	$+3$	$+4$	$+5$	$+6$	$+7$

Very Bad   Neutral   Very Good

one would have an idea of the importance each belief attribute has to the individual. Suppose that when a hypothetical individual is asked to place each attribute on this scale, the following results are found:

1. Democrat: -4
2. Veteran: $+2$
3. Favoring gun control: -6
4. Increased defense spending: $+6$
5. Opposition to draft: -3
6. Honesty: $+7$
7. Not a dynamic speaker. -1
8. Good family man: $+5$
9. World peace: $+5$
10. Economic prosperity for all: $+7$

Further assume that the individual believes each of the ten statements about candidate Jones to be equally true. With all of this information, one would have a pretty good fix on the individual's overall assessment of candidate Jones. By weighing both the good and the bad points about Jones, the assessment produces a total of $+18$. Thus, for the ten beliefs, candidate Jones has an average evaluation of $+1.8$, or about $+2$. This would indicate that, while the individual is not a strong supporter of Jones because of his stand on gun control and the draft (not to mention the fact that he is a Democrat!), the overall balance tips in Jones's favor. If another candidate in the race had all of Jones's good qualities (according to the individual's beliefs) and had the "correct" party identification and issue stands, the overall assessment would be much more positive and make it unlikely that Jones would be the individual's choice for the presidency.

Attitude theory does not, of course, assert that anyone goes through such an exacting process to reach an overall assessment of a particular person or object. It does assert, however, that the measurement process outlined above *approximates* the type of decision making that takes place, whether consciously or unconsciously. People organize their beliefs about an object in such a way as to arrive at some general assessment of their feelings about that object.

Opinion

The first chapter argues that public opinion can play an important role in policy formation and system change or stability.[15] Opinions are based upon beliefs and attitudes. The difference between opinions and beliefs or attitudes is that, while beliefs and attitudes are internal orientations, opinions are articulated within some interpersonal forum. The concept of "keeping one's opinion to oneself" is dubious, for opinions are found in public expression.

When people respond to a survey poll, engage in a political discussion, or are just casually involved in conversation, their expression of positive or negative affect toward a particular object (or category of objects) is their *opinion* on that object. While the basis for the opinion may be found in the individual's own personal beliefs and attitudes, there are also other factors involved. One of the most important of these factors is the interpersonal context surrounding the articulation of the opinion.

An example of the importance of context was observed by Richard LaPiere in a 1934 study.[16] LaPiere and some Chinese friends took an extensive trip across the United States. Being an inquisitive social scientist, LaPiere was interested in seeing the degree of resistance on the part of motel and restaurant owners to having an Oriental stay in their establishments overnight or eat a meal there. Along the way the travelers stayed at 66 hotels, motels, or auto camps and ate in 184 restaurants. They were denied only once. After the trip was over, LaPiere wrote to all of the establishments they had visited asking them, "Will you accept members of the Chinese race as guests in your establishment?" Of the 128 replies, LaPiere was shocked to discover that all but one establishment said that they would *not* serve Orientals. The results of the questionnaire were a complete mirror image of what the establishments did in practice. LaPiere's conclusion based on this study is instructive:

> If social attitudes are to be conceptualized as partially integrated habit sets which will become operative under specific circumstances and lead to a particular pattern of adjustment they must, in the main, be derived from a study of humans behaving in actual social situations. They must not be imputed on the basis of questionnaire data.[17]

All of this recalls a famous line used by John Mitchell during the Nixon administration: "Watch what we do, not what we say." In other words, verbalizations or responses to questionnaires (opinions) may not always be trustworthy indicators of underlying beliefs and attitudes. Whenever an opinion is articulated, whether by means of a social survey or some other form of interpersonal communication, it is usually articulated for a purpose. The purpose may be to express one's real attitude or belief about an object, or it may be conditioned by the circumstances in which it is being expressed.[18] Thus, defining opinion as an *articulated* evaluation should warn the student of political behavior that the context of expression may be as important as the underlying belief that supports it.

This last point becomes particularly important in the discussion of opinion content. There has been a long-standing debate within the field of public opinion concerning the existence of what have come to be termed *nonattitudes*.[19] Nonattitudes have been defined as opinion articulations due solely to the context surrounding the articulation and not at all to an underlying belief or attitude. For instance, if someone were asked for an opinion on the current unrest in Northern Ireland, and the respondent really didn't know anything about the Irish situation, he or she still might volunteer an opinion on the subject. Far from being an attempt to subvert the intent of the survey, the respondent may be very interested in "helping out" the interviewer by saying *something* other than "I don't know." Another explanation might be

that the nonattitude opinion was given to avoid being thought of as uninformed. Or the opinion might be based in some general beliefs about Ireland
and political unrest that come together in responding to this particular question. Regardless of the motivation, the response of the individual is indistinguishable from that of the person who responded to the question on the basis
of his or her attitudes toward the specific of the Irish situation itself. This is
not to say, however, that the opinion grew out of no belief or attitude at all.
In a related example, a group of consumers was interviewed on their particular likes and dislikes for certain foods. A majority of the sample said that
they particularly disliked kippered herring. In a more in-depth follow-up
interview, it was discovered that fewer than 60 percent of those people who
said that they disliked kippered herring had ever tasted it before in their
lives![20]

THE STRUCTURES OF BELIEFS, ATTITUDES, AND OPINIONS

Figure 6–1 provides a summary of the preceding discussion. Beliefs occupy a
central position in political thinking. People's basic understanding of the
world and their values and evaluations of objects are derived from learning
experience patterns and socialization processes. In fact, much behavior is
based solely on these elemental understandings. For instance, consider the
basic act of voting. One may understand, descriptively, what this constitutes
as well as its function within the American political system. The act of voting
may have a high positive evaluation because of its connection to notions of
patriotism or citizen duty. Or, one may be motivated to vote on the basis of a
perception that voting has a role in the continuing stability of the American
system. Each of these beliefs may be sufficient to draw a citizen into the
voting booth.

As a potential behavior becomes more complex, many beliefs may have to
be combined to produce a disposition to act. The decision to vote may be based
on fairly simple, yet strongly held, beliefs that do not alter drastically from
election to election. However, the decision *for whom* to vote requires more
complex decision making if for no other reason than that the central attitude
objects, the candidates, change from election to election. Given this increased
complexity, many different types of beliefs may be combined to form attitudes
toward the different candidates. Then, based upon the comparison of these
attitudes, a behavioral decision is made *inside the voting booth*. It is not the
case, of course, that this attitudinal orientation must be derived from a complex synthesis of beliefs. An individual may believe quite strongly that all
Republicans are patriots and all Democrats are communists. If these are truly
that individual's beliefs, an attitude formation about the candidates within a
particular election will not be very difficult or complex. If, however, the underlying beliefs are not strongly stereotypic, and there is a variety of competing reasons to support or oppose particular candidates, the attitude formation
process will be more complex and will require greater time.

Finally, individuals may be asked to articulate their evaluations of particular candidates within an election. It is very possible that an opinion will
reflect the underlying belief/attitude network of the individual. However, one

can also envision a scene where an individual may be reluctant to divulge his or her "real" attitude toward a particular candidate because of to whom he or she is talking and the reasons behind the request for that information. Support for a socially unpopular candidate or issue is almost certainly underestimated in public opinion polling, for individuals may be reluctant to be publicly identified, even in an anonymous poll, with an "outlying" point of view.

FIGURE 6–1   Environmental, Cognitive, and Behavioral Elements of Political Thinking

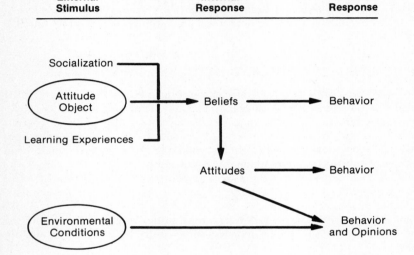

The most readily apparent ordering principle of the three elements (beliefs, attitudes, and opinions) of political thinking, then, is that of *centrality*.[21] Something is central to political thinking if other beliefs, attitudes, and opinions depend upon it. If a person believes that all war is morally wrong, he or she may logically have a negative attitude toward the resumption of the draft. The belief about war is more central than the attitude toward the draft. If a change occurs in the person's belief about war, one might also expect to see a shift in his or her attitude toward the draft. The reverse may not be true, however. Since one's attitude toward the draft could be composed of many different types of beliefs, additional beliefs may change the evaluative direction of the composite attitude but leave unaltered the other beliefs.

A useful way of thinking about the relative centrality of beliefs, attitudes, and values is to picture the construction of a spider's web.[23] If a person wished to bring about the greatest possible change in the shape of the web with the least effort, any one of the connecting strands in the middle of the web would be cut. Since the central strands form the basic support for the more peripheral areas, a change in the central structure of the web will produce great changes within the entire web itself. However, if one snipped an outlying strand, little change in the total web structure would occur. Analogously, changes in beliefs and values can have significant impact upon attitudinal and opinion structures that are based upon the changed belief. Changes in opinion may not force the general belief attitudinal system to undergo any great disruption. This is very much in line with our discussion of the sources of opinion. Since opinion is derived not only from beliefs and attitudes but also from the environment, environmental changes could influence opinion while leaving untouched more central beliefs and attitudes.

In addition to differences in centrality, there are two other ways to show the ordering and interrelationship of beliefs, attitudes, and values. The first of these is *content*. Beliefs and attitudes can be differentiated on the basis of the types of objects and the evaluations of those objects. Since beliefs are more central and are strongly influenced by cultural socialization patterns, there are fewer differences in belief-system content across individuals within a particular culture. As the cognitive process becomes more complex, with the formation of attitudes, there are greater differences in attitudinal orientations across subgroups within the population of a particular culture. The second ordering principle, *resistance to change,* is closely related to that of centrality. The more central the cognitive orientation, the greater will be the resistance to change. Thus, while opinions are open to variation across different situations and time periods, the more central orientations, such as beliefs, are much more resistant to variation over time. The next two sections of this chapter look at these two areas in greater depth.

THE CONTENT OF POLITICAL BELIEFS, ATTITUDES, AND OPINIONS

This section presents a picture of the content of American beliefs, attitudes, and opinions. Content means the general scope of objects, goals, and tactics that characterize the way Americans think about politics and society. While there exist as many unique combinations of beliefs, attitudes, and opinions as there are Americans, public opinion polls have demonstrated a surprising regularity in the way Americans conceptualize the social and political world.

Political Belief Content
Earlier, this chapter noted that beliefs are the most fundamental part of how people conceptualize the world. There are three different types of beliefs, each with an identifiable political content.

DESCRIPTIVE BELIEFS. Descriptive beliefs are the basic informational elements of political thinking. They define how the world is ordered. In the area of political opinion, beliefs are related to the amount of information the public has concerning the political world.

Some forms of classical democratic theory picture the citizens of a democracy as attentive and informed. Prior to the advent of mass public opinion polling, this mainstay of democratic theory was widely assumed to be correct. Once a means of actually measuring the amount of political information was achieved, however, researchers presented a very different picture of the information levels of the American public.[24] Consider the following findings, gleaned from over thirty years of survey research:

- In 1945, 21 percent of the American public could identify the Bill of Rights.[25]
- In 1954, 19 percent could identify the three branches of government.[26]
- In 1978, 52 percent knew that two senators represented their state.[27]
- In 1978, 30 percent knew that the term for representatives is two years.[28]
- In 1978, 23 percent knew which two nations were involved in the Strategic Arms Limitations Talks (SALT).[29]

The amount of survey evidence available to illustrate the very low levels of the public's political information is massive. Even a basic tenet of democratic theory, that the public knows how their representatives vote, is entirely suspect, if for no other reason than the fact that the majority of Americans cannot even *name* their representatives!

While such results are the mainstay of introductory texts in American politics and of arguments by proponents of elitism, they are quite understandable given the low levels of interest in politics in the American public. While it is not an overgeneralization to state that the mass public is uninformed politically, it is quite another thing to say that it is *not able* to be informed. For an illustration of this consider the following episode. Say that you are interested in buying a new stereo system. You like to come home and put on a little music, but your old system is pretty well shot. You are quite unprepared, however, when the stereo salesperson starts inquiring about such things as response limits, nominal impedance, crossover points, and suggested rms per channel. And that's just in connection with the speakers you need! Given all of the specialized information you lack, you could emerge from the store feeling like a complete fool. But this situation is not a reflection on your intelligence, but on your low informational level resulting from your peripheral interest in stereo equipment. Out of desperation you might say to the salesperson, "Don't tell me about woofers and tweeters! Just sell me something that sounds good!" Similarly, because the political world is not a top priority in people's lives, their lack of specific information about politics is not surprising. Yet even though they lack detailed information about Afghanistan, SALT, trade embargoes, and the like, they are nevertheless interested in the response of the political system to these problems. As with the harassed stereo buyer, the average American wants a political system that will provide certain services.

Therefore, it is too simplistic to dismiss the topic of descriptive political beliefs on the basis of low information levels. Americans are concerned about the external world, and they see different problems to be more important as the environment of the political world changes. Table 6–1 presents data from Gallup polls from 1937 to 1977. In these polls people were asked what problem they considered to be the most important facing the country. As Table 6–1 shows, there is a great deal of variation in the belief in the importance of problems facing the country and that variation is due to the nature of the political climate. During the Great Depression and World War II period, economic and foreign issues were of greatest importance. In the Korean War period, foreign affairs remained an important concern. In the fifties, with the economic boom and the growing fear of communism, foreign affairs became the dominant concern for Americans. This was the case in the sixties as well, with the Vietnam War as the catalyst. However, the rising urban unrest and the well-covered student demonstrations also were reflected in the growing concern over social and welfare issues. Finally, in the seventies, economic issues began to reassert themselves as the country began to recover from the agony of the Vietnam experience.

TABLE 6–1   Public Perception of Most Important Issues Areas, 1937–1976

Issue Area	1937–44	1945–52	1953–60	1961–68	1969–76
Economic Issues	60%	45%	30%	13%	35%
Foreign Affairs Issues	35	38	50	50	23
Social and Welfare Issues	5	17	20	37	42

Source: Compiled from poll data reported in *The Gallup Poll: Public Opinion 1935 – 1971* (New York: Random House, 1972); *Gallup Opinion Index* Report No. 149, 1977. Used by permission.

These figures point out that the most important concerns of the American public are, at least in part, a reflection of the political environment. Economic and threat-of-war issues have always been an important concern for Americans.[30] The degree of importance attached to these beliefs, however, shifts with the times. So while the information level of Americans concerning the nuts and bolts of how the system operates is low, their ability to direct attention and concern toward specific problem areas appears to be quite responsive.

EVALUATIVE BELIEFS. Evaluative beliefs are used in judgmental decisions about an object. They provide a useful shorthand method by which an individual's feelings can be expressed. The expression of evaluation is generally accomplished by means of connecting a particular object with a symbol. A *symbol* can be thought of as a part of language that has an agreed upon emotional charge. Terms like *democracy, communism, liberty* and *dictatorship* all carry identifiable emotional charges within different societies. While the exact definition of what a "democracy" is will vary considerably throughout the United States, the positive emotional charge of the term is not subject to the same degree of variability. Thus, labeling another country a "democracy" goes beyond a categorization of its political system and invests it with a favorable judgmental attitude. Social psychologists have termed the process by which a conditioned response is transmitted by language alone as *semantic generalization*.[32] It is quite obvious that the listener will develop widely different perceptions of a political actor, depending on whether he or she is described as a "freedom fighter" or as a "terrorist." Understanding a nation's political symbol system is, therefore, one way of comprehending the ways in which its citizens evaluate the external world.

In his book *The Political Culture of the United States,* political scientist Donald Devine argues that the political culture of the United States features a symbol system that supports and maintains a classical liberal value system:

> *The liberal tradition is offered as the core of the beliefs which comprise the American political culture. Its main representative is John Locke. It is maintained that Locke's republican principles have provided the basis for the behaviorally significant political beliefs of the United States from their founding to the present.*[33]

Devine supports his argument using public opinion poll data gathered between 1935 and 1970. The poll data, he argues, paints a picture of the American public as one in which symbols such as "liberty," "freedom," and "equality" have always received overwhelming mass support. An interesting content analysis of presidential inauguration addresses supports Devine's theory. John McDiarmond found that while the use of some symbols seems to be contingent on the particular time period involved, symbols such as "freedom" and "liberty" appear consistently throughout the addresses.[34]

Other studies have shown, however, that there is a large difference between generalized attachment to political symbols and a behavioral adherence to them. James Prothro and Charles Grigg[35] conducted a series of interviews in two American cities in 1959. They first asked respondents to evaluate such symbolic concepts as "freedom of speech" and "freedom of religion." Not surprisingly, they found near unanimous support for each of the Bill of Rights freedoms. When the respondents were then asked to react to specific applications of these rights, such as having a communist speak in one's town, the support ratings dropped dramatically. In 1972, CBS asked a random sample of 1,136 Americans to respond to specific applications of ten rights. The responses to these questions were not encouraging. CBS found that while five of the provisions of the Bill of Rights were supported by a majority of the respondents (confronting witnesses, public trial, avoidance of self-incrimination, protection against illegal search and seizure, and trial by a jury of one's peers), five of the rights were not supported by a majority of the sample (right of peaceful assembly, free press, free speech, protection against double jeopardy, and protection against preventive detention).

The implication of the above discussion is that while Americans share a general support for important political symbols, their behavior may not be inclined to follow the logical extensions of that support. Because certain political symbols occupy positions of respect and attachment within public attitudes, they are effective tools for political rhetoric. Such symbols can be used to gain adherents to one's cause and to denigrate the positions of an opponent.[36] During times of system stress, however, they may not be a significant factor in determining mass responses to controversial issues.

PRESCRIPTIVE BELIEFS. Prescriptive beliefs prescribe some desired situation toward which individuals would choose to direct themselves, or would choose to see government direct itself. Little direct empirical work assesses the American public's prescriptive belief content, although some studies raise interesting questions.

Lloyd Free and Hadley Cantril,[37] utilizing a series of surveys collected in the early sixties, operationalized a measure of prescriptive beliefs based upon the hopes and fears of the individual respondents.

> *The technique involves asking a person to describe in his own words, on the basis of his own assumptions, perceptions, goals and values, what he feels would be the best possible life for himself. At the other extreme, he is asked to define the worries and fears involved in his conception of the worst possible life.*[38]

Free and Cantril's findings are summarized in Table 6–2. In order of priority, the areas of future concern, either in terms of hopes or fears, are (1) personal economic or living conditions; (2) employment status; (3) welfare of children; (4) political subjects; and (5) international matters.[39] The results of the Free and Cantril research are not unexpected. Questions of politics are not first and foremost on the minds of individuals. Rather, people are more concerned with their individual life circumstances, especially in terms of health and economic security.

TABLE 6–2(a)   Personal Aspirations of the American Public (Specified by 5 Percent or More of the Sample)

Improved or decent standard of living	40%
Children — adequate opportunities for them (particularly education); children themselves do well, are happy, successful	35
Own health	29
Health of family	25
Happy family life	18
Peace — no war or threat of war	17
Have own house or get better one	12
Maintain status quo	12
Emotional stability and maturity — peace of mind	9
Good job, congenial work	9
Employment	8
Happy old age	8
Resolution of one's own religious, spiritual, or ethical problems	6
Recreation, travel, leisure time	5
Wealth	5

Source: From *The Political Beliefs of Americans* by Lloyd A. Free and Hadley Cantril. Copyright © 1967 by Rutgers, The State University. Reprinted by permission of Rutgers University Press.

TABLE 6–2(b)   Personal Fears of the American Publii (Specified by 5 Percent or More of the Sample)

War	29%
Health of family	27
Own health	25
Deterioration in or inadequate standard of living	19
Unemployment	14
Children — inadequate opportunities for them (particularly education); children themselves do poorly, are unhappy, unsuccessful	10
Can't think of any fears or worries	10
Relatives — separation from; not able to help or take care of them	8
Communism	8
To be dependent on others	6
Lack of freedom, including specifically freedom of speech, religion, etc.	6

Source: From *The Political Beliefs of Americans* by Lloyd A. Free and Hadley Cantril. Copyright © 1967 by Rutgers, The State University. Reprinted by permission of Rutgers University Press.

An important contributor to the research in this area is Milton Rokeach.[40] The concept of prescriptive belief is previously embodied in Rokeach's term *terminal values,*[41] which he refers to as "desirable end-states of existence."[42] Rokeach's research confirmed that values such as happiness and family security are extremely important to Americans. His later work has shown, however, that even though the American political culture emphasizes conformity in value positions, there are numerous and significant differences between the values of various subgroups within the society. Rokeach's work has revealed that the social position of the individual within the society is important to consider as a determinant of the prescriptive beliefs of that individual.

Rokeach used an eighteen-item inventory of terminal values (see Table 6–3), asking respondents to rank them by preference. He then compared the orderings of the respondents across levels of income, education, and race. Rokeach found that prescriptive beliefs relating to economic well-being ("a comfortable life" and "family security") were ranked significantly more important by lower-income respondents than by those with higher incomes. On the other hand, prescriptive beliefs relating to self-enlargement ("inner harmony," "mature love," and "wisdom") were ranked more highly by the upper-income-level respondents.[43] When the rankings of the respondents were broken down by level of education, the differences revealed were even more dramatic. The general trend established by these differences, presented in Table 6–4, is very clear. Those respondents with higher levels of education are much more interested in achieving end-states that maximize their own individuality. For instance, the highest education groups rated "wisdom" as the second most desirable goal, while those in the lowest education level rated it eleventh out of the eighteen. The value of "a comfortable life" declines in importance as the education level of the respondent increases.

TABLE 6–3   Rokeach Inventory of Terminal Values

A comfortable life
An exciting life
A sense of accomplishment
A world at peace
A world of beauty
Equality
Family security
Freedom
Happiness
Inner harmony
Mature love
National security
Pleasure
Salvation
Self-respect
Social recognition
True friendship
Wisdom

Source: Reprinted with permission of Macmillan Publishing Co., Inc. from *Understanding Human Values: Individual and Societal* by Milton Rokeach. Copyright © 1979 by The Free Press, a division of Macmillan Publishing Co., Inc.

When comparisons are made across the two main racial groups in society, few differences are observed in the ranking of prescriptive beliefs. However, the differences that were observed are of great interest. Whites rated the value of "a comfortable life" twelfth, while blacks rated it fifth. Most impor-

TABLE 6–4 Terminal Value Medians and Composite Rank Orders for Groups Varying in Education (N 1,404)

Value	0–4 Yr.	5–8 Yr.	Some High School	Completed High School	Some College	Completed College	Graduate School
N	64	263	320	426	180	90	61
A comfortable life	5.5 (3)	7.3 (6)	8.0 (7)	9.5 (12)	11.2 (13)	12.3 (13)	13.8 (15)
An exciting life	14.6 (18)	15.6 (18)	15.5 (18)	15.5 (18)	15.3 (18)	14.5 (16)	13.4 (14)
A sense of accomplishment	12.5 (13)	11.1 (12)	9.9 (11)	9.1 (9)	7.6 (6)	6.3 (5)	5.4 (4)
A world at peace	3.1 (1)	2.8 (1)	2.9 (1)	3.7 (2)	4.2 (2)	4.4 (2)	3.5 (1)
A world of beauty	13.6 (16)	13.2 (14)	13.5 (15)	14.0 (15)	13.6 (15)	13.3 (15)	11.3 (12)
Equality	10.8 (12)	8.6 (9)	8.5 (9)	8.3 (7)	8.4 (8)	9.2 (8)	8.0 (7)
Family security	4.2 (2)	4.6 (2)	3.7 (2)	3.3 (1)	3.5 (1)	3.6 (1)	6.6 (5)
Freedom	6.0 (4)	6.1 (3)	5.7 (3)	5.2 (3)	5.4 (3)	4.7 (3)	5.1 (3)
Happiness	7.0 (5)	7.2 (5)	7.4 (4)	7.2 (4)	7.8 (7)	10.3 (10)	9.7 (10)
Inner harmony	10.2 (9)	11.2 (13)	11.2 (13)	10.3 (13)	9.4 (9)	9.3 (9)	9.3 (9)
Mature love	13.9 (17)	13.4 (15)	13.1 (14)	12.1 (14)	12.2 (14)	10.5 (11)	10.1 (11)
National security	10.5 (10)	9.0 (10)	8.9 (10)	9.3 (10)	10.1 (10)	11.0 (12)	13.0 (13)
Pleasure	12.8 (14)	13.7 (16)	14.6 (17)	14.8 (17)	14.8 (16)	15.4 (18)	16.0 (18)
Salvation	9.5 (8)	6.7 (4)	7.9 (6)	8.6 (8)	10.3 (11)	12.5 (14)	15.1 (17)
Self-respect	8.9 (7)	8.3 (8)	7.7 (5)	7.8 (5)	6.9 (5)	6.8 (6)	6.8 (6)
Social recognition	13.5 (15)	13.8 (17)	14.1 (16)	14.8 (16)	15.1 (17)	15.2 (17)	14.3 (16)
True friendship	7.6 (6)	8.2 (7)	9.7 (12)	9.4 (11)	10.4 (12)	8.7 (7)	8.6 (8)
Wisdom	10.8 (11)	9.6 (11)	8.4 (8)	8.1 (6)	6.1 (4)	5.5 (4)	4.6 (2)

Figures shown are median rankings and, in parentheses, composite rank orderings (1 being the highest rank).

Source: Reprinted with permission of Macmillan Publishing Co., Inc. from *The Nature of Human Values* by Milton Rokeach. Copyright © 1973 by The Free Press, a division of Macmillan Publishing Co., Inc.

tant, the prescriptive belief in "equality" was ranked *eleventh* for whites and *second* for blacks.[44] Noting the general similarity between most of the prescriptive beliefs of whites and blacks, Rokeach wrote,

> given what is known at this point, it would be unfortunate if social policy were to be based on the assumption that there are substantial cultural differences between black and white Americans. The data described here show only one big and pervasive value difference between black and white Americans. Black Americans give equality high priority; white Americans place a far lower priority on equality. This one difference best summarizes the cultural difference observed in our national sample of black and white Americans, and this one cultural difference will undoubtedly decrease if equal opportunity genuinely increases.[45]

The differences in prescriptive beliefs observed by Rokeach across levels of education and income are interesting because they support the claims of theorists who argue that the beliefs, attitudes, and activities of an individual are formed on the basis of the particular *needs* they seek to have fulfilled. Much of the work of the "need theorists" is based on the writings of Abraham Maslow.[46] Maslow argues that individuals possess a hierarchical series of needs and that the individual's goal-directed behavior will depend upon the "need stage" within which he or she is located. Maslow hypothesized five need stages:

1. *Physiological needs* — physical survival of the organism.
2. *Need for safety and security* — fears relating to surviving within and controlling a hostile environment.
3. *Need for affection and a sense of belonging* — achievement of a sense of "mutuality in relationships with one's environment."[47]
4. *Need for esteem* — the need to be admired and respected for one's attributes or accomplishments.
5. *Need for self-actualization* — the need to expand and utilize one's abilities to their utmost extent.

Need theorists argue that beliefs and activities associated with higher-level needs cannot be secured until the demands associated with the lower-level needs are achieved to a minimal point. It is not possible, they argue, for an individual to be concerned with establishing meaningful relationships with another individual until the basic concerns of subsistence and fear of personal injury have been dealt with. Politically, this means that people will not be concerned about the problems of other citizens, the nation, or other nations until they have satisfied those personal demands based upon their own personal needs. Jeanne Knutson argued that the failure of U.S. policy in Vietnam can be traced to the fact that an alien value structure was imposed upon a society that could not support it:

> People who live at a starvation level are only peripherally concerned with the higher needs. The misunderstanding of this basic fact has again and again been the stumbling block of American foreign policy, as we have attempted without success to build democracy when the population is concerned with surviving physically.[48]

The evidence concerning differences in prescriptive beliefs across different educational and income levels fits well into the structure of need theory. The hierarchical ordering of needs can be thought of as a continuum going from an almost exclusive concern with the survival of "self" at one end to an outer directed concern for others and the enlargement of one's personal abilities at the other end. The literature featuring empirical verification of the connection between prescriptive values and the psychic state of the individual began with a concentration on political elites. As early as 1948, Harold Lasswell drew attention to the activities of political elites and their relationship to underlying psychic needs.[49] His now-famous theory is that elite political activity can be explained as the private motives of politicians being projected upon public objects and rationalized in the public interest.[50] The work of James David Barber in the area of personality and political office is an extension of Lasswell's need theory of elite behavior.[51]

At the level of the general public, the relationship between psychic needs and political beliefs and activity was first substantively treated at length in the book, *The Authoritarian Personality*.[52] In that study, the authors established a link between anti-Semitic attitudes and beliefs and the fixation on symbols of authority and providers of system security. In his book *The Open and Closed Mind*,[53] Milton Rokeach related the ability of individuals to receive and act upon new information to their own feelings of self-esteem and openness toward others. Paul Sniderman[54] uncovered a relationship between low feelings of self-esteem and antidemocratic beliefs and activities. Jeanne Knutson,[55] in a direct attempt to empirically demonstrate Maslow's theory using samples of three different types of employees, found some confirmation of the relationship between need level and prescriptive beliefs.[56] Most recently, Ronald Inglehart[57] has argued that post-industrial societies such as the United States are providing satisfaction of the lower needs of their citizens, thereby allowing greater expansion of "other-directed" or self-actualizing behaviors.

While a particular society may have the communications and material capacity to deal with the lower-level needs of its citizens, there still exists a wide dispersion of needs *within* a nation that creates different levels of political attentiveness, involvement, and activity. Since political attitudes are composed of political beliefs, this last point will provide a substantive beginning for the next section.

The Content of Political Attitudes

Political attitudes reflect a set of beliefs (which may be informational, evaluative, prescriptive, or a combination of all three) about a given political object. It follows that the most salient political attitudes involve objects about which people have the most intense beliefs. And, on the other hand, those areas that are not of great interest to an individual will produce less intense evaluations or no attitudes at all.

The last point is important in that, with the ever-increasing frequency of public opinion polling, we have come to expect everyone to have some sort of an attitude concerning every political object. This certainly is not possible if a person has no information about that object. The war in Vietnam is a good case in point. While the United States had initiated a military commitment to South Vietnam well before the election of 1964, the *issue* of Vietnam was not well known prior to that campaign. It was only as a result of the political rhetoric of both the Johnson and the Goldwater camps, and the subsequent military escalation after the election, that the Vietnam War became a salient issue. Once it became an important issue, people could marshal more enduring beliefs such as anticommunism and patriotism, and the percentage of people who had an attitude on the war increased dramatically. Figure 6–2 provides a graphic illustration of this pattern. In the spring of 1964, less than 40 percent of a national sample had a preferred method of resolving the dispute. This was because a large percentage of the American public had not heard enough about the situation to give a preference. As the involvement in Vietnam steadily increased its monopoly of the national agenda, the percentage of respondents who had no suggested resolution of the dispute dropped considerably. It is also interesting to note that the highest percentage of no-attitude responses in the post-1964 era came in 1967 and 1971 — years just prior to the presidential campaigns.[58] There is some evidence to suggest that the degree to which the environment gives cues influences the extent to which the mass public will form attitudes on a given political stimulus.[59]

FIGURE 6–2   Percentage of Respondents Answering "Don't Know" to Survey Questions of the Form, "What Should We Do in the War in Vietnam?"

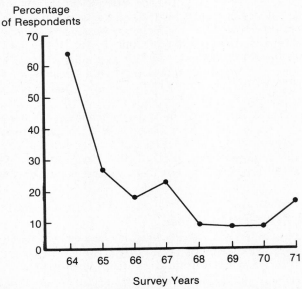

Source: John Mueller, *War, Presidents and Public Opinion* (New York: John Wiley & Sons, 1973), pp. 81–98. Used by permission.

The implication of the above discussion is this: the more *central* the beliefs involved in a political question, and the fewer the number of beliefs that must be called into play in developing an attitude, the greater the likelihood that an attitude will be developed. In other words, when the issue is salient and well drawn, there is a greater likelihood that the vast majority of Americans will have developed some sort of attitudinal position in relation to it.

How can one tell which issues are salient and also assess their degree of complexity? The first part of the question was examined in the discussion of the centrality of beliefs. A response to the second question can be generated by referring to Table 6–5. This table presents the percentage of "no-attitude" responses to eight questions. The questions relating to abortion, the speed of the civil rights movement, and federal spending all contained one central object of evaluation each. For each of the other questions, the respondent was asked to give his or her attitude on the preferred role of the federal government in relation to the given issue area. Thus, the respondent had to consider not only his or her beliefs on the issue, but also his or her beliefs concerning the involvement of the federal government in that issue. Given the increased complexity of two attitude stimuli, the percentage of "no-attitude" responses increased. In a related study conducted in Washington State in 1970,[60] Don Dillman and James Christenson found that there was a significant interaction between areas of policy concern and the degree of involvement of the federal government. Those policy areas that necessitated almost complete control by the federal government (national defense, assistance to agriculture, aid to foreign countries, and space exploration) were given the lowest priorities for increased governmental funding. As Dillman and Christenson note, "A cited preference to diminish the role of government in some activity areas might be compensation for a real wish to increase the role of the private sector."[61] The point being made here is that some single questions may be asking for evaluations of more than one belief object. When this occurs, attitude formation becomes more cumbersome.

TABLE 6–5   Percentage of "No-Attitude" Responses to Selected Issues in 1976

Issue	"No-Attitude" Responses
Abortion	2%
Speed of civil rights movement	5
Should federal spending be increased?	7
Busing	11
Legalization of marijuana	14
Federal support for jobs	19
Federal support for health care	21
Aid to other countries	32

Source: Center for Political Studies. American National Election Study, 1976 [machine-readable data file].

While we will save a discussion of the actual distribution of attitudes on different issue areas until the section on attitude stability, one final, substantive area of attitude content will be discussed: attitudes toward sitting presidents.

While different polling agencies adopt different ways of measuring the public's approval of the president, the general form for this question is,

Generally speaking, do you approve or disapprove of the way —— is handling his job as president?
 1. Approve
 2. Disapprove
 3. Don't know

Responses to this question are interesting because, while the president is known to be a salient belief object, and the question form requests a summarizing of beliefs directly relating to him alone, typically 14 percent of national samples profess to have no attitude toward the president. It is more remarkable that opinion polls since 1936 have shown that the 14 percent no-attitude rate persists through different presidents at different points during the time of their tenure. John Mueller commented on this pattern as follows:

> *This is a little surprising, since it might be expected that when opinion moves, say, from approval to disapproval of a president, the change would be revealed first in a decrease in the support figure with an increase in the no opinion percentage, followed in a later survey by an increase in the disapproval column with a decrease in the no opinion portion. There are a few occasions in which the no opinion percentage seems to rise and fall in this manner, one occurring in the early weeks of the Korean War, but by and large it seems that, if movements into the no opinion column do occur, they are compensated for by movements out of it.*[62]

Another explanation for the remarkable constancy of no attitudes toward the president across the years is that approximately 14 percent of the adult population do not consider presidential politics to be particularly salient; therefore, they have not stored away any set of beliefs upon which to base an attitudinal evaluation. What these surveys may well be saying is that the percentage of the population with low interest in presidential politics remains fairly constant over time.

Opinion Content
While it is important to stress the difference between attitudes and opinions, the similarity of the two concepts must also be kept in mind. Basically, an opinion is the same as an attitude: it is the expression of a synthesis of beliefs. The additional element contained in an opinion is that it may also contain influences that are separate from the belief object. For example, if one is asked one's opinion on the Equal Rights Amendment, the response, or at least the frankness of that response, might differ according to the sex of the person asking that question. Another problem might be the question itself. If one wished to know someone's attitude toward the proper response of United States foreign policy toward the Soviet Union and asked a question like, "Shall we forceably resist Soviet interventions or should we be cowards?" the question is not likely to get at that person's real attitude. Finally, as the first section of this chapter mentioned, people may wish to give some sort of response even if they have no belief structure upon which to base an attitude. Their response may sound like an attitude and be recorded as such. This is why special care must be given to the design and analysis of public opinion surveys.

It is useful to think of an opinion in the following way:

$$\text{OPINION} \quad = \quad \text{Attitude} \quad + \quad \begin{matrix} \text{Random} \\ \text{Circumstances} \end{matrix} \quad + \quad \begin{matrix} \text{Measurement} \\ \text{Error} \end{matrix}$$

Random circumstances are things that interfere with the true measurement of an attitude, the effects of which are going to be randomly distributed across all of the respondents in the survey. For instance, people may be a bit hesitant to have a surveyor conduct an interview in their homes, and this uncertainty may influence how a respondent will answer a question. But, because people are different in the ways that they react, it is expected that overall the distortion effects of home interviewing will cancel each other out. That is, there is no systematic harm done in the measurement of a given attitude; the effect is random. Thus, for public opinion surveys, if all that is present is a measure of an attitude and random circumstances, the aggregated opinion response to the question will be valid, and the interviewer will have a good idea of what the public's attitude is toward that issue.

The main problem in opinion measurement comes from *measurement error*. This means that something in the wording of the question causes people to react in a nonrandom fashion, so that the effects of asking the question *do not* cancel out across all people being interviewed. One form of measurement error could occur if the attitude object being investigated is controversial. As W. Phillips Shively noted,

> if we asked people whether they had a prison record, it is likely that there would be a good deal of nonrandom error in the measure, as people systematically tried to suppress their prison records. Even in the long run, on the average, this measure would not give an accurate estimate of the true value.[63]

There are some areas where people do have strong attitudinal structures but will not voice opinions that reflect these underlying attitudes, especially to strangers. While new, less obtrusive techniques have been developed to gain access to these attitudes,[64] they are only partially successful and rarely can be extended to large samples. Consequently, some areas, such as criminal and sexual activities and the like, are generally excluded from the realm of survey research, as many argue they should be.

Even if the attitude object is not controversial, measurement error could be introduced by poorly framed or misleading survey questons.[65] For example, in his study of public opinion and its relationship to presidential popularity, John Mueller noticed that polls taken at the same time by different polling agencies utilizing slightly different question forms produced different distributions of support for the president. Because the samples in these polls were randomly selected, we would expect the results to be quite close to each other. The fact that differences were observed was due to the differences in question format. Specifically, Mueller found that respondents were more willing to state that they "disapproved" of the president's actions than to associate themselves with a response category that stated that the president's actions were "wrong."[66]

There is an interesting connection between discussions of belief centrality and the problem of question wording. It appears that if the belief object is salient enough (and not so controversial as to create problems in response), the wording of the question diminishes in importance. Mueller noted that,

> in a 1941 study, it was found that even the most loaded questions about Hitler could not alter American opinion about him one way or the other; on other subjects, however, attitude was found to be highly sensitive to changes in wording. The sensitivity of opinion to changes in the wording of the stimulus, in fact, can be taken as a sort of index of uncertainty, indecision and lack of knowledge on the issue.[67]

Thus, there is an interaction between the degree to which a belief object is important to the individual and the ability of a question to measure the direction of interest on that object. As the individual's interest in the subject decreases, the way a question is posed becomes increasingly important.

One final area of question wording involves the changes in meaning of certain terms over time. While interviewers may ask the same question over a period of years, comparison of the responses to the repeated question requires an assumption of constancy of meaning of the central belief objects.[68] For example, in the fifties the term *liberalism* denoted matters of economic policy. In the sixties, however, liberalism was being extended to "social-issue" areas such as crime, drugs, and sexual permissiveness.[69] The problem this creates in studying opinion over time is summarized by Nie et al.:

> The point is that the person who was a liberal then and is conservative now may not have changed positions at all. He may have just changed his understanding of the issues to which the terms refer.[70]

What this should point out to the reader is that opinion poll results are not necessarily true indicators of underlying mass attitudes toward a given object. The student of public opinion should keep in mind that the interview situation will produce results that are only as good as the interviewer and the questionnaire allow. Careful design of questionnaires and proper training of interviewers can alleviate many of the factors that might differentiate an opinion from an attitude. While this book will, for the most part, equate articulated opinion with underlying attitudes, such equation will be done with care and an assumption of quality in the way the opinion was collected.

This section has shown that the centrality of a belief object plays an important role in both attitude formation and opinion articulation. The dimension of "content" has been viewed from the perspective of the importance of a particular question to an individual. As the importance grows, more beliefs are called into play and attitude formation becomes more complex. The next section will show that not only does the centrality of the belief object influence the content of opinion on that object, but also the stability of opinion over time.

STABILITY OF BELIEFS AND ATTITUDES

Belief Stability

Beliefs are the elemental part of an individual's thinking, and those that are system supportive are of extreme importance to a developed political culture.[71] Thus, those beliefs, both in their aggregated and individual forms, should not swing wildly across time but rather maintain a relatively stable pattern. While stability of beliefs over time is one indicator of a developed belief system, too strong an adherence to a set of beliefs — adherence that is contrary to environmental input — may actually be a sign of an unsophisticated belief network.[72] This pattern of refusing to accept new information or persuasion has been termed by Rokeach as *close-mindedness*.[73] Close-mindedness, he argues, is associated with high levels of personal anxiety[74] and the domination of the individual by primitive beliefs.[75] On the aggregate level, belief systems nourished by a developed political culture need to have elements of stability in order to pass on political and social traditions.[76] They also need the ability to adapt to environmental stress and incorporate change. As Devine noted,

> if all accept a framework within which conflict is to take place, and if all agree to settle conflict within this process and in general accord with certain beliefs, substantial stress can exist at the authority level without threatening the community or the regime. In the United States, consensual support for the liberal tradition has provided the framework within which serious conflict has been resolved. Even with substantial authority stress, the shaping strength of political culture has tended to maintain the regime.[77]

Accordingly, the analysis of beliefs over time, both at the individual and at the aggregate levels, should reveal a general trend of stability reacting to important trends within the environment.

AGGREGATE BELIEF STABILITY. Many theorists agree that a developed political culture must feature a consistent set of political symbols to which the mass public gives its allegiance. These symbols are then identified with national policies and goals in order to attract support. Table 6–6 shows that public support for the traditional symbols of a liberal democratic regime have remained very high over a thirty-five-year period. Additionally, the *order* of importance of these political symbols has remained fairly consistent across this time period of American history. It would appear that, at least in the era during which we have had public opinion polling, the American political culture has been remarkably successful in ensuring the recommitment of allegiance to important regime evaluative beliefs.

TABLE 6–6   Support for Political Symbols by Era, 1936–1971

Symbol	Mean Support Score		
	1936–1945	*1946–1955*	*1956–1970*
1. Popular Rule and Elections	—	86%	79%
2. Legislative Predominance	71%	62	78
3. Liberty	72	72	68
4. Equality	98	—	85
5. Property	60	66	66
6. Achievement	74	—	86
7. Belief in God	96	95	98
8. Religion	70	72	73
Average Support Score	74	75	77

Source: Adapted from Donald J. Devine, *The Political Culture of the United States* (Boston: Little, Brown & Co., 1972), p. 5. Used by permission.

While attachment to political symbols has remained fairly consistent, the most important concerns of the American public demonstrate an interesting interaction with environmental changes. Table 6–7 documents the areas that were the source of greatest concern for Americans in 1959, 1964, and 1971. Significantly, those concerns most directly related to the individual's family decreased in importance during this period. Of greater importance were issues of political relevance, with three issues (pollution, drugs, and crime) appearing in 1971 for the first time. Within this very turbulent time period of the nation's history there is evidence that the most important concerns of the American public are being defined increasingly in terms of political problems rather than personal or private ones.[78] There is an apparent growing interaction as the problems of the political world become more salient to the individual.

TABLE 6–7   Personal Fears of the American Public, 1959, 1964, and 1971

	Percent Mentions		
Fear	*1959*[a]	*1964*[a]	*1971*[a]
Ill health for self	40%	25%	28%
Lower standard of living	23	19	18
War	21	29	17
Ill health for family	25	27	16
Unemployment	10	14	13
Inflation	1	3	11
Unhappy children	12	10	8
Drugs a problem in the family	—	—	7
Pollution	—	—	7
Political instability	1	2	5
No fears at all	12	10	5
Crime	—	—	5

[a]Columns total more than 100 percent due to multiple answers
Source: Albert Cantril and Charles Roll, Jr., *Hopes and Fears of the American People* (New York: Universe Books, 1971), p. 19. Used by permission of Potomac Associates, Washington, D.C.

Another study by Milton Rokeach over a three-year period demonstrates both the stability of American beliefs and their ability to respond to changes in the political and social environment.[79] Table 6–8 presents the rankings for the eighteen prescriptive beliefs discussed earlier in this chapter for 1968 and 1971 random samples. The first impression one receives from these rankings is one of stability. Generally, those prescriptive beliefs that were highly ranked by the sample in 1968 also received a high ranking in 1971. There are some important differences, however. The most important shift came in the ranking of "equality." In 1968, the sample ranked equality seventh out of eighteen, with an average rating of 8.5. Just three years later, the prescriptive belief in equality had moved to a rank of fourth out of eighteen, with an average rating of 7.4. Also notable was the increased emphasis given to the goal of national security, going from a ranking of twelfth to eighth. Rokeach commented on this pattern in the following way:

Even within a short interval, we found that certain values underwent significant change. These changes seem to be a result of economic factors and the emergence of various issues concerning war and peace, racism, sexism, and ecology, all of which became more salient and thus a source of dissatisfaction for various subgroups of adult Americans.[80]

What these data suggest is that while the beliefs of Americans show demonstrable tendencies toward stability and constancy of importance, American public opinion is sensitive enough to changes in the environment that concerns are adjusted to deal with new problem areas.

TABLE 6–8   Change in Priorities of Prescriptive Beliefs, 1968–1971

Prescriptive Beliefs	Ranking of Beliefs (1 highest, 18 lowest)	
	In 1968	In 1971
A world at peace	1	1
Family security	2	2
Freedom	3	3
Happiness	4	6
Self-respect	5	5
Wisdom	6	7
Equality	7	4
Salvation	8	9
A comfortable life	9	13
A sense of accomplishment	10	11
True friendship	11	10
National security	12	8
Inner harmony	13	12
Mature love	14	14
A world of beauty	15	15
Social recognition	16	17
Pleasure	17	16
An exciting life	18	18

Source: Reprinted with permission of Macmillan Publishing Co., Inc. from *Understanding Human Values: Individual and Societal* by Milton Rokeach. Copyright © 1979 by The Free Press, a division of Macmillan Publishing Co., Inc.

INDIVIDUAL BELIEF STABILITY. Given the above evidence of continuity and change within the mass public's beliefs, we might automatically expect to see the same pattern at the individual level. This is not necessarily the case, for the change that occurred at the mass level might be due to the introduction of new political generations with different priorities of political beliefs. At the level of the individual, how open are belief systems to the incorporation of new information and value modification?

One interesting study by Doris Graber examined the ability of small samples of adults in three U.S. cities to recall information received through the media. Interviewing the respondents several weeks after they had watched or read about national events, Graber found patterns of recall that differed by both age and sex of the respondent. Table 6–9 summarizes Graber's findings. The recall ability of individuals within all four groups was quite low for the issue areas covered. Generally, younger respondents were able to recall more informational stories than older respondents, and males had higher recall percentages than females. Even given these differences, however, the total amount of informational recall is not impressive. It appears that, at least consciously, individuals are not aware of information assimilation, even in election periods.[81] These findings are in line with what political socialization literature has revealed about the learning and retention of political information after adolescence:[82] basic informational beliefs are fairly well set at the time of adolescence, and while we continue to learn throughout our lives, most information is stored and examined in light of earlier learned beliefs.

TABLE 6 – 9   Percent of Stories for Which Specific Details Were Recalled

	Women		Men	
Story Topic	Under 40	Over 40	Under 40	Over 40
Women's issues	0%	4%	8%	20%
Medical/health care	2	2	11	9
Education	6	2	11	6
Economy in general	3	3	2	0
Unemployment	13	5	9	15
Inflation	8	3	8	14
Celebrities	18	4	13	18
Entertainment	0	10	14	16
All news stories	5	4	14	13

Source: By permission of Doris Graber, from *Women and the News* (New York: Hastings House, 1978), p. 18. Copyright © 1978 by Laurily Keir Epstein.

While information acquisition remains fairly constant through the life cycle, some new studies in the area of individual prescriptive belief change indicate that individuals, given certain stimulation and motivational prerequisites, do alter their value positions, at least over a short time period. Using a technique termed *value confrontation,*[83] researchers have found that when individuals are advised of the comparison of their own value beliefs with those of other groups of varying social prominence, they tend to shift their values to fall more into line with those of group members with higher social status.[84] Other research has provided experimental evidence that suggests that persuasive media-provided information can alter, again in the short run, an individual's assessment of certain prescriptive belief objects.[85] Most of the empirical investigation into the area of individual belief change is still at the experimental stage, however, and has not yet convincingly demonstrated long-term value shifts. In the short term, the research indicates that beliefs are not so fixed and unchanging as earlier supposed and that, under certain conditions, belief change can be induced.[86]

There also is research in the area of the relationship between values and overt behavior. One study used a value confrontation technique that forced the respondent to compare his or her own prescriptive values with his or her smoking habit and produced dramatic changes in the smoking behavior of the participants. William Conroy compared the smoking behavior of two groups (an experimental group that had undergone value confrontation therapy and a control group without the therapy), the members of which had been instructed to keep track of their smoking habits after the initial contact.[87] The members of the experimental group showed significantly lower levels of smoking activities, even after a two-week period following the initial contact.[88] The results show, again only within the setting of an experiment, that value awareness does have significant behavioral effects.

While the studies involving belief stability are relatively few in the area of public opinion, there is an indication that upon proper environmental stimulation, belief modification does occur. The aggregate data reveals that the public at large is sensitive to changes in its environment and that their beliefs reflect those changes. The evidence at the individual level is more sketchy and still experimental. However, studies of individual level belief change indicate that people do not utilize their beliefs dogmatically, but are sensitive to change over time.

Attitude Stability

The previous section provided evidence that mass beliefs respond to changes in the environment. This section examines both aggregate and individual *attitude* stability. Given that attitudes are based on beliefs, fluctuations in attitude positionings should occur as well.[89]

AGGREGATE ATTITUDE STABILITY.   Attitudes on most political issues follow one of three change patterns over time: fixed, evolving, and cyclical. *Fixed patterns* are attitudinal patterns that do not vary across time. Perhaps the best example of a fixed pattern is provided by the nexus of beliefs that form a religious identification. The proportion of Americans who profess one of the three main faiths has remained remarkably constant over the past forty years (27 percent Catholic, 61 percent Protestant, 2 percent Jewish, 4 percent other, and 6 percent "no religious preference").[90] In keeping with the main theme of this chapter, one can clearly understand why this pattern occurs. Religious beliefs are very central to individuals, and there are very few, if any, environmental conditions that would change such well-ingrained attitudinal positions.

Issues with fixed attitudinal patterns all tend to be extremely central to individuals and quite resistant to external modification. One political issue that fits this description is abortion. While there appears to be a slight tendency for older respondents to be less in favor of abortion,[91] the aggregated response distributions concerning this issue show a remarkable stability. Figure 6-3 illustrates that the distribution of opinion across four different abortion options is essentially the same. The reason for this similarity is that one's attitude on the abortion issue calls into play many central moral and religious beliefs. Like the religious preference question, changes in the political environment will have very little impact on an individual's core beliefs in this area. Interestingly enough, although well over 50 percent of the population in 1976 was either totally against abortions or would allow them only when the life of the mother was in question, only 45 percent thought favorably about a constitutional amendment that would ensure this policy.[92] The drop-off occurs because the constitutional amendment question involves *two* attitude objects: abortion and amending the Constitution.

FIGURE 6–3   Mass Opinion on Abortion, 1972 and 1976

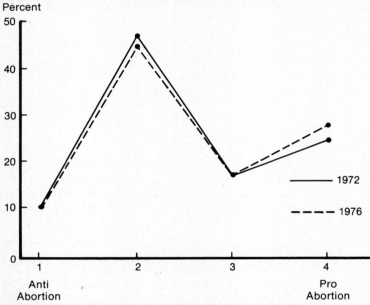

Source: Center for Political Studies. American National Election Study, 1976
[machine-readable data file].

Question: Which one of these opinions best agrees with your view on abortion?

1. Abortion should never be permitted.
2. Abortion should be permitted only if the life and health of the woman are in danger.
3. Abortion should be permitted for personal reasons, if the woman would have difficulty caring for the child.
4. Abortion should never be forbidden.

Evolving patterns describe most attitude changes when core beliefs are not strongly involved in an attitude formation. Evolving patterns are those that establish some recognizable trend. Because core beliefs are not utilized, mass opinion can be affected by the social and political environment and thus follow a slow or rapid pattern of shifting. One example of this evolution can be seen in the twelve-year pattern of responses to the question, "Do you think that the civil rights people have been trying to push too fast, too slow, or just about right?" As Figure 6–4 demonstrates, there has been a significant change in mass attitudes toward this issue over the period 1964 to 1976. The clear trend is for Americans to accept more and more the activities of the civil rights movement. In 1964 the vast majority believed that the process of integration was moving much too rapidly. But by 1976 the majority of opinion holders believed that the progress of integration was proceeding at an acceptable speed. The trends also demonstrate that the proportion of those who believed the process of integration to be moving too slowly was disassociated from the general trend of acceptance noted above. This would indicate that a persistent minority of Americans has strong negative feelings toward what

FIGURE 6–4   Mass Attitudes toward the Speed of the Civil Rights Movement, 1964–1976

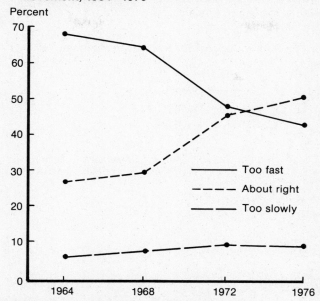

Source: Center for Political Studies. American National Election Study, 1976 [machine-readable data file].

Question: Some say that the civil rights people have been trying to push too fast. Others feel that they haven't pushed fast enough. How about you? Do you think that civil rights leaders are trying to push too fast, are going too slowly, or are they moving at about the right speed?

they see to be the slow pace of integration. That a majority of those who feel the progress is too slow are black suggests that the question taps obvious core beliefs for those individuals. Overall, the trend of this attitude squares very nicely with the changes in how Americans evaluate the prescriptive belief of "equality" described earlier. It does appear that in this area the trend is one of assimilation and an acceptance of the speed of that assimilation.

Another illustration of an evolving attitudinal pattern was presented by John Mueller in his excellent analysis of public opinion on the war in Vietnam.[93] Figure 6–5 documents the pattern of public support for the war from 1965 to 1971. Again we see evidence of the crossing pattern observed in the civil rights question. As the war progressed and opposition to it grew, there was a gradual decline in support for the war effort. As Mueller notes, support for the war remained fairly constant until the Tet Offensive in early 1968. From that point on, attitudes toward the war effort kept turning in a negative direction. Again this pattern can be explained by the fact that as more information was received about problems with the war effort, and as reports of domestic instability grew, the attitude object was no longer merely involvement in Vietnam; it expanded to include beliefs about the domestic, international, and economic ramifications of the war. Thus, central beliefs involving patriotism and support for United States war efforts began to be offset by other salient core beliefs. The result was a weakening of commitment to the Vietnam War effort.

FIGURE 6–5   Public Support for the War in Vietnam, 1965–1971

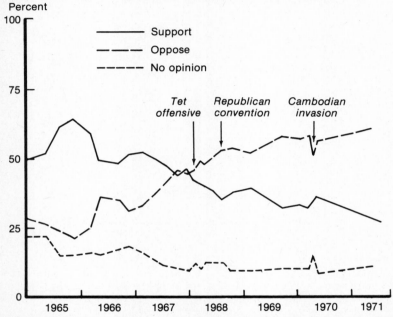

Source: John Mueller, *War, Presidents and Public Opionion* (New York: John Wiley & Sons, 1973), p. 56. Used by permission.

An understanding of the general trends of mass attitude change, brought about by either changing beliefs or the incorporation of new beliefs, can assist the student of public opinion in forecasting the probable direction of opinion on current issues. The legalization of marijuana is one area where this might be applied. Figure 6–6 presents attitudes toward the legalization question for 1972 and 1976. While the distributions of opinion on this issue are similar for both years, a trend toward acceptance begins to emerge, even though a majority of Americans still had negative attitudes toward the issue in 1976. While, of course, nothing in public opinion forecasting is certain, we may be witnessing the beginning of a change in mass belief orientation toward the acceptance of marijuana legalization — a trend that can only be accelerated as younger political generations mature and incorporate their experience into mainstream public opinion.

Cyclical patterns of public opinion recall the old dictum, "History repeats itself." Some attitudinal patterns tend to repeat themselves at different time periods in the nation's history. The repetition of attitudinal patterns is primarily due to the fact that some environmental circumstances occur at regu-

lar intervals, and public opinion reacts to these repeating stimuli. Undoubtedly, the best documented case of cyclical attitudinal patterning is again provided by John Mueller in his analysis of public evaluations of presidents.[94]

**FIGURE 6 – 6   Public Opinion on Legalization of Marijuana Issue,
1972 and 1976**

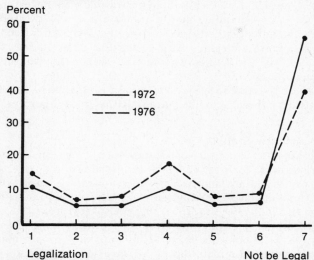

Source: Center for Political Studies. American National Election Study, 1972, 1976
[machine-readable data file].

Question: Some people think that the use of marijuana should be made legal. Others think
that the penalties for using marijuana should be higher than they are now. Where would you
place yourself on this scale, or haven't you thought much about it?

Looking at the patterns of support for presidents from Franklin Roosevelt
(last whole term) to Richard Nixon (last whole term), Mueller found a pattern
of support that fit each president's popularity curve for each term he was in
office.[95] Mueller's main thesis was that regardless of who occupies the office,
regularly occurring environmental conditions will affect the way he is
evaluated. The general trend for a president's term is to start off with his
largest degree of public support at the time he enters office, to receive his
lowest support ratings about midterm, and then to receive a general upsurge
of approval as the end of his term approaches. While novel events will influence popularity evaluations in a given president's term, Mueller argues that
even these can be categorized:

> *In summary, the expected behavior of presidential popularity is as follows.
> It is anticipated (1) that each president will experience in each term a gen-
> eral decline in popularity; (2) that this decline will be interrupted from time
> to time with temporary upsurges associated with international crises and
> similar events; (3) that the decline will be accelerated in direct relation to
> increases in unemployment rates over those prevailing when the president*

began his term, but that improvement *in unemployment rates will not affect his popularity one way or another; and (4) that the president will experience an additional loss of popularity if a war is on.*[96]

The trends in presidential popularity fluctuate because the *environment* surrounding the president changes. As other salient belief objects are connected to the president, the attitudinal portrait of his support shifts accordingly. Rather than remaining blindly attached to one or two central beliefs upon which an evaluation is based (such as the party affiliation of the president), public opinion displays a cognizance of different factors affecting the evaluation of a sitting president and responds with corresponding attitude fluctuations.

Thus, unless the attitude object involves a central mass belief, trends in political attitudes reveal a public quite sensitive to environmental changes.

Individual Attitude Stability

Along with the question of the consistency of the American public's political beliefs (discussed in the next chapter), the issue of the degree to which an individual can give the same response to the same question over time has captured a great deal of research attention.[97] Utilizing a panel of respondents interviewed in 1956, 1958, and 1960, Philip Converse looked at responses to the same issue in each of the three years.[98] Operating under the assumption that responses to the same questions administered in the same manner over a four-year period should remain constant, Converse found that the majority of individuals were not stable in their responses. His conclusion was that the majority were responding in a random fashion to the questions, that their "nonattitudes" were the result of having no discernible beliefs concerning the attitude objects.

The debate opened by Converse has hit the distinction between attitude and opinion squarely. Converse argued that opinions are not the same as attitudes, *and* that the majority of respondents in the panel had opinions lacking any foundation in political beliefs.

Such analysis assumes that the questions used to tap these attitudes do not themselves contribute to the response instability. Recall that measurement error is one of the factors that might influence the articulation of an attitude. One writer, Christopher Achen, has argued that the instability of the responses to these issues was not due to respondent error, but due to the poor construction of the questions.[99]

Another assumption is that true *attitude change* did not occur over the period covered by the panel. This assumption has been called into question by Paul Hagner and John McIver.[100] Using a panel sample collected over the period of the 1976 campaign, Hagner and McIver tested a model of attitude stability that provided for the possibility of campaign-induced attitude change. Thus, while the stability correlations for contiguous time periods were low — in fact, about the same level as Converse had found in the late fifties — when attitude change is accounted for, the proportion of respondents with sophisticated attitudinal positionings increased dramatically.

Once again, such a finding is in line with previous discussions. American public opinion has been shown to be quite sensitive to environmental factors. When new information is assimilated, or other long-standing beliefs are connected to an attitude object, the attitude toward that object may also change. We would expect, however, that if the attitude object incorporated core beliefs, individual attitudinal stability would increase. It comes as no surprise, then, that this is exactly what Converse and Gregory Markus found in their analysis of a 1972–1976 three-wave panel. They found that attitudinal stability on moral issues (abortion, women's role, and the like) is significantly higher than that found on more purely political issues. On issues that do not involve core beliefs, many Americans change their attitudes when the issue is shown to them in a new light. Measurement *and* respondent error both occur, but their presence is not as dominant as many would suppose.

CONCLUSION

This chapter has presented a portrait of American public opinion by examining its constituent parts and their interrelationships. The following points have been stressed:

1. Beliefs, attitudes, and opinions are interrelated, and to understand the dynamics of public opinion one must first understand its foundations.
2. The content of political beliefs, attitudes, and opinion is influenced by the degree to which the object under evaluation is regarded as central to either the individual or the political culture, or both.
3. Changes in the public's beliefs, attitudes, and opinions are also related to the centrality of the source object, with highly central objects being much less likely to exhibit great variations in belief or attitudinal stability.

The portrait of American public opinion that begins to emerge from this discussion is one in which politics takes a back seat to other social and private matters. However, even when an issue is not very central to the public, evidence suggests that the opinion reaction to that object is not simplistic, that it is a function of a complex interaction of the individual with his or her environment.

NOTES

1. Martin Fishbein and Fred S. Coombs, "Basis for Decision: An Attitudinal Approach toward an Understanding of Voting Behavior" (Paper presented at the 67th Annual Meeting of the American Political Science Association, Washington, D.C., September 2–4, 1971), p. 6.
2. Milton Rokeach, *Beliefs, Attitudes and Values* (San Francisco: Jossey-Bass, 1968).
3. Daryl Bem, *Beliefs, Attitudes and Human Affairs* (Belmont, Calif.: Brooks/Cole, 1970), p. 5.
4. Ruth M. Beard, *An Outline of Piaget's Developmental Psychology for Students and Teachers* (New York: Basic Books, 1969), p. 3.
5. Charles Osgood, George Suci, and Percy Tannenbaum, *The Measurement of Meaning* (Urbana, Ill.: University of Illinois Press, 1957), p. 70.

6. David Easton and Robert D. Hess, "The Child's Political World," in *The Learning of Political Behavior,* Norman Adler and Charles Harrington, eds. (Glenview, Ill.: Scott, Foresman, 1970), pp. 40–44.
7. Two excellent introductions to the area of political symbols are Raymond Firth, *Symbols: Public and Private* (Ithaca, N.Y.: Cornell University Press, 1973); and Murray Edelman, *Political Language: Words that Succeed and Policies that Fail* (New York: Academic Press, 1977).
8. Bem, *Attitudes and Human Affairs,* p. 10.
9. Three basic works on human values are the best compilation of source material in this area: Milton Rokeach, *Beliefs, Attitudes and Values;* Milton Rokeach, *The Nature of Human Values* (New York: Free Press, 1973); and Milton Rokeach, *Understanding Human Values: Individual and Societal* (New York: Free Press, 1979). For a perspective somewhat different from the Rokeach model, see Gene Vickers, *Value Systems and Social Process* (New York: Basic Books, 1968).
10. Donald J. Devine, *The Political Culture of the United States* (Boston: Little, Brown & Co., 1972), p. 5. See also the discussions of political culture in Chapters 8 and 9.
11. One of the reasons Americans who had gone to Canada to avoid the draft returned was that they couldn't get used to the "strange customs" in Canada.
12. For a discussion of the many different ways the term *attitude* has been used, see Gordon W. Allport, "Attitudes," in *Readings in Attitude Theory and Measurement,* Martin Fishbein, ed. (New York: John Wiley & Sons, 1967), pp. 3–13.
13. Theodore Newcomb, John Turner, and Philip Converse, *Social Psychology* (New York: Holt, Reinhart & Winston, 1965).
14. Fishbein and Coombs, "An Understanding of Voting Behavior," p. 5.
15. Robert E. Lane and David O. Sears, *Public Opinion* (Englewood Cliffs, N.J.: Prentice-Hall, 1964), p. 2.
16. Richard T. LaPiere, "Attitudes Versus Actions," *Social Forces* 13 (December 1934), pp. 230–37.
17. Ibid., p. 237.
18. See Robert Abelson "Simulation of Social Behavior" in *The Handbook of Social Psychology,* vol. 2, Gardner Lindzey and Elliot Aronson, eds. (Reading, Mass.: Addison-Wesley, 1968); Nicholas Caplan and Samuel Nelson, "On Being Useful: The Nature and Consequence of Psychological Research on Social Problems," *American Psychologist* 28 (March 1973); pp. 199–211; and Martin Orne, "On the Social Psychology of the Psychology Experiment: With Particular Reference to Demand Characteristics and Their Implications," *American Psychologist* 17 (November 1962), pp. 776–83.
19. The term *nonattitudes* is a bit of a misnomer as shall be noted later in this chapter.
20. Vance Packard, *The Hidden Persuaders* (New York: David McKay, 1957), pp. 15–16.
21. We also will use the term *salience* in reference to this concept.
22. Bem, *Attitudes and Human Affairs,* p. 17.
23. Rokeach, *Beliefs, Attitudes, and Values,* Chapter 1.
24. For two overviews of poll data in this area see Hazel G. Erskine, "The Polls: The Informed Public," *Public Opinion Quarterly* 26 (Winter 1962), pp. 669–77; and Hazel G. Erskine, "The Polls: Textbook Knowledge," *Public Opinion Quarterly* 27 (Spring 1963), pp. 133–41.
25. NORC, poll conducted November 1945.
26. AIPO, March 1954. Reported in *Gallup Opinion Index,* p. 52.
27. NORC, General Social Survey, Spring 1978.

159

28. NORC, General Social Survey, April 1978, news release, p. 10.
29. CBS/NIT Poll.
30. See Lloyd A. Free and Hadley Cantril, *The Political Beliefs of Americans: A Study of Public Opinion* (New Brunswick, N.J.: Rutgers University Press, 1967).
31. For the most recent source of literature on symbolic politics see James Combs, *Dimensions of Political Drama* (Santa Monica, Calif.: Goodyear Publishing Co., 1980).
32. Bem, *Attitudes and Human Affairs,* p. 44.
33. Devine, *The Political Culture of the United States,* p. 58.
34. John McDiarmond, "Presidential Inaugural Addresses—A Study in Verbal Symbols," *Public Opinion Quarterly* 1 (July 1937), pp. 79–82.
35. James W. Prothro and Charles M. Grigg, "Fundamental Principles of Democracy," *Journal of Politics* 22 (Spring 1960), pp. 276–94.
36. See Murray Edelman, *The Symbolic Uses of Politics* (Urbana, Ill.: University of Illinois Press, 1964); and Doris Graber, *Verbal Behavior and Politics* (Urbana, Ill.: University of Illinois Press, 1976).
37. Free and Cantril, *The Political Beliefs of Americans.*
38. Ibid., p. 94.
39. Ibid., p. 99.
40. Three works by Rokeach are essential reading for students interested in this area: *Beliefs, Values and Attitudes; The Nature of Human Values;* and *Understanding Human Values: Individual and Societal.*
41. Rokeach, *The Nature of Human Values,* p. 7.
42. Ibid.
43. Ibid., p. 60.
44. Ibid., p. 67.
45. Ibid., p. 72.
46. The basic work by Abraham Maslow is *Motivation and Personality* (New York: Harper & Row, 1954). See also C. S. Hall and G. Lindzey, *Theories of Personality* (New York: John Wiley & Sons, 1957), for a useful overview of this perspective.
47. Jeanne N. Knutson, *The Human Basis of the Polity: A Psychological Study of Political Men* (Chicago: Aldine, 1972), p. 36.
48. Ibid., p. 26.
49. See Harold Lasswell, *Power and Personality* (New York: Viking Press, 1948); and Harold Lasswell, *Psychopathology and Politics* (New York: Viking Press, 1960).
50. Lasswell, *Power and Personality,* p. 38.
51. See James D. Barber, *The Lawmakers* (New Haven, Conn.: Yale University Press, 1965); and James D. Barber, *The Presidential Character: Predicting Performance in the White House,* 2nd ed. (Englewood Cliffs, N.J.: Prentice-Hall, 1972).
52. T. W. Adorno et al., *The Authoritarian Personality* (New York: John Wiley & Sons, 1950).
53. Milton Rokeach, *The Open and Closed Mind* (New York: Basic Books, 1960).
54. See Paul M. Sniderman, *Personality and Democratic Politics* (Berkeley: University of California Press, 1975).
55. See Jeanne N. Knutson, *Human Basis of the Polity.*
56. Knutson's analysis suffers some from an extremely low return rate for her questionnaires and a tendency to give low correlations more import than they are due.
57. See Ronald Inglehart, *The Silent Revolution* (Princeton, N.J.: Princeton University Press, 1977).
58. See John Mueller, *War, Presidents and Public Opinion* (New York: John Wiley & Sons, 1973).

59. This is the argument of Benjamin Page and Richard A. Brody, "Policy Voting and the Electoral Process," *American Political Science Review* 66 (September 1972), pp. 979–95.
60. Don A. Dillman and James A. Christenson, "Toward the Assessment of Public Values," *Public Opinion Quarterly* 38 (June 1974), pp. 206–21.
61. Ibid., p. 220.
62. Mueller, *War, Presidents and Public Opinion,* p. 203.
63. W. Phillips Shively, *The Craft of Political Research,* 2nd ed. (Englewood Cliffs, N.J.: Prentice-Hall, 1980), p. 55.
64. Eugene J. Webb et al., *Unobtrusive Measures: Nonreactive Research in the Social Sciences* (Chicago: Rand McNally, 1966).
65. For discussions of question wording and its effects, see George Bishop, Robert Oldendick, and Alfred Tuchfarber, "Effects of Question Wording and Format on Political Attitude Consistency," *Public Opinion Quarterly* 42 (Spring 1978), pp. 81 – 92; and George Bishop, Alfred Tuchfarber, and Robert Oldendick, "Change in the Structure of American Political Attitudes: The Nagging Question of Question Wording," *American Journal of Political Science* 22 (May 1978), pp. 250–65.
66. Mueller, *War, Presidents and Public Opinion,* p. 230.
67. Ibid., pp. 18–19.
68. This is, of course, not the case for questions relating to presidential performance since the belief object will change over time.
69. See Richard Scammon and Ben Wattenberg, *The Real Majority* (New York: Coward, McCann & Geoghegan, 1970).
70. Norman H. Nie, Sidney Verba, and John R. Petrocik, *The Changing American Voter* (Cambridge, Mass.: Harvard University Press, 1976), p. 11.
71. See David Easton, *A Systems Analysis of Political Life* (New York: John Wiley & Sons, 1965), p. 109.
72. See W. Lance Bennett, *The Political Mind and The Political Environment* (Lexington, Ky.: Lexington Books, 1976).
73. See Rokeach, *The Open and Closed Mind.*
74. Rokeach, *Understanding Human Values,* p. 211.
75. Ibid., p. 40.
76. See Chapter 4 for a discussion of political socialization.
77. Devine, *The Political Culture of the United States,* p. 365.
78. See Nie et al., *The Changing American Voter,* pp. 106–7, for a discussion of this phenomenon.
79. Rokeach, *Understanding Human Values,* pp. 129–47.
80. Ibid., p. 146.
81. For an overview of this area, see John P. Robinson, "Mass Communication and Information Diffusion," in *Current Perspectives in Mass Communication Research,* F. Gerald Kline and Phillip Tichenor, eds. (Beverly Hills: Sage Publications, 1972), pp. 71–94.
82. See M. Kent Jennings and Richard Niemi, *The Political Character of Adolescence: The Influence of Families and Schools* (Princeton, N.J.: Princeton University Press, 1974).
83. For an interesting discussion of the ethical considerations of this technique, see Milton Rokeach and Joel Grube, "Can Values Be Manipulated Arbitrarily?" in *Understanding Human Values,* pp. 241–56.
84. Rokeach, *Understanding Human Values,* pp. 210–25.
85. Keith R. Sanders and L. Erwin Atwood, "Value Change Initiated by the Mass Media," in *Understanding Human Values,* pp. 226–40.

86. For the interaction between human values and the commercial sphere, the best source is still Vance Packard, *The Hidden Persuaders.*
87. William Conroy, "Human Values, Smoking Behavior and Public Health Progress," in *Understanding Human Values,* pp. 199–209.
88. K. L. DeSeve, "An Examination of the Relationship between Values and Smoking Behavior" (Ph.D. diss., Washington State University, 1975).
89. Opinions will not be treated separately in this section. All trend questions used have identical wording.
90. Gallup Opinion Index, "Religion in America, 1976," Report No. 130.
91. Gerald M. Pomper, *The Voters' Choice: Varieties of American Electoral Behavior* (New York: Dodd Mead & Co., 1975), p. 106.
92. NORC, General Social Survey, 1976.
93. Mueller, *War, Presidents and Public Opinion.*
94. Ibid.
95. The only exception to this pattern was Eisenhower's first term as president.
96. Mueller, *War, Presidents and Public Opinion,* pp. 219–20. Samuel Kernell takes issue with Mueller's thesis, arguing that the "president does not simply become less popular." See his "Explaining Presidential Popularity," *American Political Science Review* 72 (June 1978), p. 520.
97. See also Stephen Bennett, "Consistency among the Public's Social Welfare Policy Attitudes in the 1960s," *American Journal of Political Science* 17 (August, 1973), pp. 544–70; Philip E. Converse, "The Nature of Belief Systems in Mass Publics," in *Ideology and Discontent,* David Apter, ed. (New York: Free Press, 1964); Philip E. Converse, "Attitudes and Non-Attitudes: Continuation of a Dialogue," in *The Quantitative Analysis of Social Problems,* R. R. Tufte, ed. (Reading, Mass.: Addison-Wesley, 1970), pp. 168–89; Philip E. Converse, "Public Opinion and Voting Behavior," in *Handbook of Political Science,* vol. 4, F. Greenstein and N. Polsby, eds. (Reading, Mass.: Addison-Wesley, 1975), pp. 75–165; Philip E. Converse and Gregory Markus, "Plus ça Change . . .: The New CPS Election Study Panel," *American Political Science Review* 73 (March 1979), pp. 32–49; Robert Erikson, "The SRC Panel Data and Mass Political Attitudes," *British Journal of Political Science* 9 (January 1979), pp. 89–114; John C. Pierce and Douglas Rose, "Nonattitudes and American Public Opinion: The Examination of a Thesis," *American Political Science Review* 68 (June 1974), pp. 626–66; and Paul Hagner and John McIver, "Attitude Stability and Change in the 1976 Election: A Panel Study," in *The Electorate Reconsidered,* John Pierce and John Sullivan, eds. (Beverly Hills: Sage Publications, 1980), pp. 31–48.
98. See Converse, "Attitudes and Non-Attitudes"; and Converse and Markus, "Plus ça Change . . ."
99. Christopher Achen, "Mass Political Attitudes and the Survey Response," *American Political Science Review* 69 (December 1975), pp. 1218–31.
100. Hagner and McIver, "Attitude Stability and Change."

CHAPTER 7

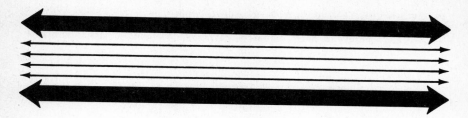

THE POLITICAL THINKING OF THE AMERICAN PUBLIC

The quality of the American electorate's political thinking is one of the most frequently addressed questions in recent studies of public opinion. The answers to that question are often used to evaluate the rationality of the American public and its ability to meet the demands of a democratic citizenry. This chapter examines three primary characteristics of the public's political thinking: the level of conceptualization with which the public confronts political objects; the consistency of the public's beliefs about political issues; and the public's self-identification with major ideological positions (i.e., liberalism and conservatism).

LEVELS OF CONCEPTUALIZATION

What standards do Americans employ to evaluate political objects, such as political parties and presidential candidates? This question intrigued the authors of *The American Voter*.[1] Campbell et al. thought an examination of those standards and their use would provide important clues as to the character of the public's political thinking. In order to find the answer, they developed a measure called the "levels of conceptualization." That measure has become a widely used standard for describing the quality of the American electorate.[2]

In the 1956 survey of the American electorate, on which much of *The American Voter* is based, respondents were asked a series of questions about what they liked and disliked about the two major political parties (the Democrats and the Republicans) and the candidates for president (Eisenhower and Stevenson). Respondents were given a chance to provide whatever reasons they might wish, instead of being forced to choose among alternatives provided by interviewers. The resulting evaluations differed in length, in substance, and in complexity and abstractness. At the same time, certain common themes occurred, suggesting that a systematic analysis of the evaluations might provide a good way to classify people's political thinking.

After a careful reading of the public's evaluations of political parties and presidential candidates, each respondent in the survey was placed into one of four broad levels of conceptualization: ideological, group benefit, nature of the times, and no issue content. People in these levels of conceptualization differ in the abstractness and in the substance of the criterion they use to judge the parties and the candidates.

The *ideological* level of conceptualization is the most abstract and "embraces all respondents whose evaluations of the candidates and the parties have any suggestion of the abstract conceptualization one would associate with ideology."[3] An example of such an ideological evaluation is drawn from one of the 1956 interview protocols:

(What do you like about the Democrats?) Well, that depends on what you are thinking of—historically or here lately. I think they are supposed to be more interested in the small businessman and low tariffs. (Is there anything in particular that you like about the Democratic party?) Nothing except it being a more liberal party, and I think of the Republicans as being more conservative and interested in big business.[4]

Also included in the ideological level of conceptualization are three kinds of "near-ideologues." Near-ideologues use ideological concepts and categories, but with little "dynamic or highly relativistic quality"; use the ideological concepts, but with little specific issue-related material buttressing the use; or use a number of specific comments, all of which appear to be closely related to each other.

The second level of conceptualization is labeled *group benefit*. People at this level differ from ideologues both in the abstractness of their evaluations and in the substantive content of the criteria they employ. Group benefit respondents evaluate candidates and parties in terms of their sympathy and hostility toward "visible groupings" in the society. In a simple form, this may be a person describing how one party or candidate helps or harms a group with which that person is associated. With greater elaboration, the parties and the candidates may be evaluated in terms of their relative positions on some dimension or conflict splitting two groups, such as labor or business. Campbell et al. refer to the use of this level as "ideology by proxy" and note that these people have the potential to become ideologues under certain circumstances.

The third level of conceptualization is the *nature of the times*. Comments and evaluations at this level are of two kinds. First, some people provide a general reference to the usual state of the economy or the historical presence or absence of a state of war under a particular party. An example would be that one likes the Democrats because "the times are better when the Democrats are in power." The second category at this level contains those people whose evaluations are all in terms of a narrow, isolated, and specific issue concern such as a particular piece of social legislation.

The fourth level of conceptualization is labeled *no issue content*. Here, evaluations are made in terms of the personal characteristics of the candidates, family tradition of party allegiance ("I was just raised a Democrat, and I guess no matter what I'll always be a Democrat. It's like being born to a religion and always staying with it."), or simply general expressions of like or dislike.

It is possible for someone to make evaluations that would fall into more than one level of conceptualization. In such cases, the respondent was assigned to the highest possible level of conceptualization. Thus, if someone gives both ideological and group-benefit evaluations of the Republicans, he or she would be placed into the ideological level. At the same time, it should be recognized that there are some limitations in the measure's ability to reflect the individual's *inherent* capacity for sophisticated thought. People may be able to conceptualize at higher levels than they reveal in their evaluations of political parties and candidates. First, an interview situation does not promote considered and thoughtful reflection; people may be more likely to respond superficially in terms of party and candidate attributes, when in fact they are capable of more abstract thinking. Second, the terms and concepts revealing more abstract thinking (e.g., ideological or group-benefit terms) may be inappropriate bases for evaluating parties and candidates at a particular time. It may be that the parties and candidates differ very little in their ideological positions or that the candidates are mirror images of each other. In such cases people may refrain from ideological evaluations even when they are capable of making them. Thus, the available personal resources may set some upper limit on the abstractness of the evaluations, but they do not preclude evaluations at a level lower than that possible for a person. On the other hand, some people may give responses that result in their being placed at a level higher than they might ordinarily be placed. A period of politics may be so intensely ideological that the terms and concepts become part of the ordinary political discourse. Consequently, some people may use them with no deep understanding of their meaning.

Thus, the public's distribution among levels of conceptualization will result from two forces. One is the distribution of personal resources helpful for abstract conceptualization. These resources may be relatively stable through time, and hence would contribute to stability in the distribution of the public on the levels of conceptualization. At the same time, other gradual changes, such as increases in the public's level of education, might slowly change the distribution of cognitive resources in the public and hence the distribution of the levels of conceptualization.

The second force is the nature of politics. In times of political crisis, the nature of the political rhetoric and disputes might shift people between levels. In a time of war or of severe economic crisis one might find a movement of individuals from "no issue content" to the "nature of the times" level.[5]

> In general, then, we would expect some shifts over time in the distribution of the electorate across levels, particularly in the lower ranges and in periods of crisis. However, we would never expect this change to be of sweeping magnitude.[6]

Just what is the distribution of the public among the levels of conceptualization, and how stable has this distribution been? That is the question to which we now turn.

Changes in the Levels of Conceptualization

The distribution of the American public across the levels of conceptualization is available for presidential election years starting in 1956. Figure 7–1 shows the percentage of the public that has been classified at the ideological level (both full and near-ideologues) for that time period. Table 7–1 presents the distribution of the public across the full conceptualization measure for the years 1956 to 1976. The data in Figure 7–1 are obtained from two different ways of measuring levels of conceptualization. One set of measures retains the original *American Voter* method. These are classifications from an actual reading of the recorded interview responses. The results of this original measure also are employed in Table 7–1. The second set of measures employs a surrogate method. Rather than reading the set of evaluations recorded during the interview, this surrogate method employs coding categories used to reduce the responses to computer readable form. As Figure 7–1 shows, the differences in the methods assume some importance because there are rather major departures in the amount of change revealed by the two.[7]

TABLE 7–1   Distribution of Levels of Conceptualization 1956–1976

Levels of Conceptualization	1956	1960	1964	1968	1972	1976
Ideologues	12%	19%	27%	26%	22%	21%
Group Benefit	42	31	27	24	27	26
Nature of Times	24	26	20	29	34	30
No Issue Content	22	23	26	21	17	24
Total	100%	99%	100%	100%	100%	101%
N	(1740)	(1741)	(1431)	(1319)	(1372)	(2870)

Source: 1956, Center for Political Studies; 1960–1976, coded from Center for Political Studies interview protocols for the respective CPS election year studies.

In 1956, only 11.5 percent of the public could be classified at the highest level of conceptualization — as ideologues or near-ideologues. Another 42 percent rested at the group benefits level. This led to the following description of the 1956 electorate by the authors of a later work:

> *The American public had a remarkably unsophisticated view of political matters characterized by an inability to consider such matters in broad abstract terms.*[8]

Indeed, many observers saw inherent limitations in the resources of the public to intelligently evaluate politics — to employ abstractions, to conceptualize and compare political objects along dimensions.

Yet, in the years following 1956 there was an increase in the percentage of the public at the ideological level of conceptualization. To be sure, the size of that increase depends on which measure of conceptualization is used. The original Survey Research Center (SRC) method applied again in 1964 produced twice as many ideologues as in 1956 (27 percent compared to 11.5 percent), but also a similarly sized drop in the percentage at the group benefits level (42 percent to 27 percent). The percentage of ideologues stayed at about the same level from 1964 to 1968 and then declined some from 1968 to 1976.

The surrogate measure of conceptualization (the one using the precoded computer categories) produces much larger changes. While beginning in 1956 at only a slightly higher level than the SRC measure, a substantial gap occurs in 1964 and widens even more in 1968. According to the latter measure, by 1972 half of the American public conceptualized politics in ideological terms.

Nie et al. recently reported the partial results of the application of the surrogate method to 1976. They found a substantial *drop* in the proportion of the public evaluating *candidates* in ideological terms. On the other hand, there was a big increase in the proportion providing an ideological evaluation of the *political parties*.[9] In any case, it is clear that by 1964 the traditional picture of the American public's political thinking had changed: many more people appeared at the highest level of conceptualization.

FIGURE 7–1　Percentage Ideologues and Near-Ideologues, 1956–1972

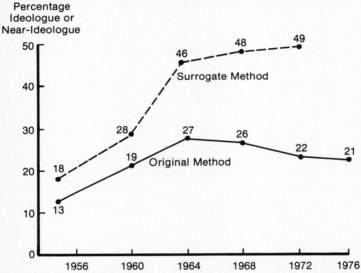

Source: Original method, see Table 7–1. Surrogate method from Norman H. Nie, Sidney Verba and John R. Petrocik, *The Changing American Voter,* enl. ed. (Cambridge, Mass.: Harvard University Press, 1979), p. 115. Copyright © 1976, 1979 by the Twentieth Century Fund. Reprinted by permission.

Interpreting and Explaining the Changes

There are two major interpretations of the changes in conceptualization. In the first case, Nie, Verba, and Petrocik argue that the changes in conceptualization have been substantial and that they indicate a "real" increase in the sophistication of the public:

> If answers to the open-ended questions on why a respondent likes or dislikes a candidate or party provide some good indications of his political reasoning — and we think they do — there has been substantial change in the quality of that reasoning since the analysis of level of conceptualization was first presented in The American Voter. The proportion of citizens who think

in ideologically structured ways about parties and candidates and, perhaps more important, who link those general characteristics to specific issue positions has grown substantially.[10]

Similarly, Inglehart uses this change in conceptualizing as one piece of evidence reflecting "rising levels of political skills" in Western publics.[11]

On the other hand, while admitting that "a definite increase in ideological thinking has occurred," Niemi and Weisberg reason that much of that increase reflects no real upgrading of the public's sophistication.[12] They share the concerns expressed by Phillip Converse, who developed the measure for *The American Voter* and has employed it in subsequent discussions. Converse comments that in the face of other rather sizable changes in the public, the increases in ideological conceptualization are rather limited.[13] Indeed, he suspects that beyond a marginal increase accounted for by rises in education, there have been only minor changes in the sophistication of the public's political conceptualization. As partial evidence, Converse points to the distributions in 1956, 1964, and 1968 (see Table 7 – 1). Those figures show the increases in the number of ideologues to be closely mirrored by comparable decreases in the number at the group benefit level. While one cannot be certain when using only aggregate distributions,[14] there may have been no change at all in the members of the public populating the two lower levels of conceptualization.

With this disagreement about the nature of the changes in conceptualization, what can be said about resolving the differences? Part of the difference results from the two different methods used to measure the same variable. The biggest increase in the proportion of ideologues is shown by the measure that strays from the original. Nevertheless, the changes seem substantial whatever measure is used. At a minimum, the number of ideologues and near-ideologues doubled — to over a quarter of the public. And it is possible that some people expressing ideological evaluations in the 1950s dropped to lower levels in the 1960s. If so, that would mean that the proportion of the public with the resources for evaluating politics ideologically is even greater than that reflected in the distributions for the late 1960s and early 1970s. Given only aggregate data, we do not know whether the people appearing as ideologues in different years are the same people with some additions, or whether some people have advanced to ideological evaluation while others have retreated from it.

It is clear that even if the resources for ideological conceptualization may be relatively stable both for individuals and across the public, the *articulation* of that conceptualization is quite elastic. It is responsive to other forces — either in the individual or in the political system. Indeed, these two sets of variables — those at the individual level and those at the political level — comprise the major explanations for the changes in conceptualization.

At the individual level, attention has focused on the contribution of increasing levels of education to increases in ideological conceptualization. This is based in two findings. First, in 1956 the authors of *The American Voter* found a strong relationship between education and conceptualization: those

with higher levels of education were more likely to employ ideological conceptualization.[15] Second, there was a simultaneous increase in the proportion of
the public with higher levels of education and the proportion of the public
with higher levels of conceptualization. Hence, it was natural to hypothesize
a link between the two — that the increase in education had contributed to
the increase in conceptualization. Bruce Campbell, for example, has recently
suggested that "since the average level of education is rising continuously in
the United States, this should mean that more and more people will qualify
as ideologues as time passes."[16] Miller and Levitin argue that "the increase
in average education level and the enhanced interest in politics that had
occurred during the intervening years were reflected in the new results."[17]
And, as noted above, Converse attributes much of the increase (albeit, playing down the total size of the increase) to changing educational levels.

The relevant data, however, suggest that education accounts for very little
of the increase in conceptualization. As Figure 7–2 shows, during the 1956–
1968 period, increases in ideological conceptualization took place at all educational levels. The same educational differences in conceptualization continued
because of the upward conceptualization movement all across the education
dimension. If the increases were due solely to changes in education, the proportion of ideologues would have remained the same in all educational
categories, but more people would have appeared in the high education
categories, increasing its total contribution to the percentage of ideologues in
the public. However, given the data, it seems clear that as Asher puts it, "the
increase in the number of ideologues between 1956 and 1968 is not due to the
rise in education levels in that time period."[18] Nie et al. reached the same
conclusion employing their surrogate measure of conceptualization.[19]

**FIGURE 7–2   The Percentage of Ideologues at Three Educational Levels,
1956, 1964, and 1968**

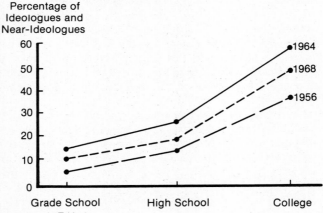

Source: See sources in Table 1.

If education is related to conceptualization at some point in time, but changes in education are not the sources of increased ideological conceptualization, then some additional explanation is needed. One possibility is that the sophisticated conceptualization of politics — at least as reflected in the measure under discussion — may be the product of two different forces. Part of the presence of ideological conceptualization may be education driven. For people whose conceptualization is based in education, we would expect their evaluations of politics to remain relatively consistent through time. Other people's conceptualizations may be driven by some other force, such as the nature of the politics at the time, where they respond to the content of the political discourse rather than imposing their own conceptualization on it.[20]

Indeed, the most prevalent explanation for the increase in conceptualization relates to changes in the nature of the times. The increase in conceptualization occurred during the same period as the nature of the conflict between and among political leaders became more ideological. Not only did Goldwater emphasize his conservatism in the 1964 presidential campaign, but the entire politics of the 1960s and the early 1970s were argued and couched in ideological terms. As Niemi and Weisberg conclude,

> an important ingredient in the level of voter sophistication appears to be elite behavior.... Elites, then, play a role not only in determining which particular issues attract attention at a given time, but in determining the way in which voters organize and structure their political thinking.[21]

Thus, if the candidates and parties distinguish themselves ideologically, the voters will make their choices among them on those bases — or, at least, greater numbers will use those bases for making their choices. Such a response becomes a reasonable way for the citizen to adapt to changes in politics. And, of course, having been offered ideological alternatives provides the voters with greater opportunity to express and exhibit their highest levels of conceptualization.

Yet the process may be a little more complicated than simply a straightforward and uniform response on the part of the public to changes in the political leaders' actions. We know that large portions of the public did not respond to the increased ideological content of politics by increasing their conceptualization. We also know that the increases in educational level do not account for the changes in conceptualization. What else might account for the changes? One possible answer is a change in political interest.[22] Political interest increased in the public in the early 1960s, and this forced some people to increase their attentiveness to the content of political conflict. With the ideological content of politics, the newly attentive portion of the public responded to those distinctions in their evaluations of parties and candidates, perhaps discarding the group-benefit or nature-of-the-times evaluations based in the old politics of the New Deal, World War II, and the Eisenhower-dominated 1950s. It may be, then, that the elasticity of the public's ideological conceptualization is a function of the public's conceptual resources, modified by the variable character of the public's interest in politics and the ideological content of the political arena.

These patterns also suggest that the public may *learn* from changes in the environment. That is, the ideological foci of the sixties and seventies campaigns were candidates. Many in the public responded to them with ideological evaluations. When less ideological candidates appeared in 1976, ideological evaluations of candidates declined, but the ideological evaluations of the parties increased. The stimulus of the candidates in earlier years may have taught many in the public the usefulness of ideological evaluations.[23] Thus, this mode of thinking was transferred by many in application to the parties when the candidate qualities seemed inappropriate. The result is an electorate more ideological and more abstract in its conceptualization of parties and candidates.

POLITICAL BELIEF SYSTEMS

Many Americans will offer opinions about all kinds of political issues, parties, groups, and politicians. But how well do those beliefs fit together? Are the beliefs consistently related to each other in a coherent or well-organized way? By knowing people's beliefs on one issue can we accurately predict their beliefs on another issue? Although this consistency among the public's beliefs has been a fundamental question confronted in the study of political thinking, the answers have oscillated radically in recent years.

The consistency among the public's beliefs is important for several reasons. First, that consistency is one more indication of the quality of the electorate's political thinking. Consistency is said to reflect the ability of the public to understand and fit together the common content of different issues. There is an assumption that there is something desirable about people holding a variety of beliefs that all seem to point in the same direction, usually defined as liberal or conservative. Second, consistency among the public's beliefs may enhance political communication. If people agree on what issues go together, as well as what positions on those issues go together, then there can be developed symbols that stand for those sets of issues. If we know that beliefs on a set of social-welfare issues tend to go together, and that these sets of beliefs can be labeled as liberal or conservative, then it becomes easier in the communication process to talk about a general liberal or conservative position than a position on each of the many social-welfare issues.

The Meaning of Belief Systems

A political belief system is a set of political opinions that are interrelated, that go together. Converse puts it more formally, defining a belief system as "a configuration of ideas and attitudes in which the elements are bound together by some form of constraint or functional interdependence."[24] The definition of a belief system, however, requires some elaboration.

The *elements* of a belief system comprise any orientation of an individual toward politics, including opinions about issues of public policy; beliefs about government and its responsibilities; evaluations of and attitudes toward political figures, such as candidates for public office; attitudes and evaluations of political groups; and general ideological orientations. One important characteristic on which these elements of a belief system differ is their *generality*. The greater the number of the other elements in a system that can be subsumed under a belief, the greater is that belief's generality. Thus, ideological orientations (e.g., liberal, conservative) are usually considered to be quite general elements of a belief system. Being a liberal, or being of liberal orientation, would imply certain beliefs about issues of public policy, about groups in society, and about political individuals, all of which may be identified in some position relative to "liberal."

The beliefs in a belief system also can be grouped into *domains* or sets of belief objects that share common content. Thus, foreign policy beliefs would constitute one domain, and domestic policy beliefs might constitute another domain. It is generally expected that beliefs about issues within a domain will be more consistent than will beliefs across different domains. Thus, beliefs about medicare should be more consistently related to beliefs about social security than they should be linked to beliefs about the stationing of U.S. troops in Europe.

The consistency among beliefs is called *constraint*. Constraint is the degree to which the beliefs are bound together into a consistent unit — the belief system. Constraint among political beliefs takes two directions — vertical and horizontal.[25] *Vertical* constraint is when general beliefs are consistent with specific ones — as when people who are pro-liberal (a general belief) take liberal positions on specific issues. *Horizontal* constraint is when the public's positions on issues within each level of generality are consistent. Horizontal constraint is present when the public's beliefs on different issues of social-welfare policy are consistent with each other — people who are in the liberal direction on one issue tend to lean in the liberal direction on the other issues.

Why is it that certain beliefs go together in the mind of the public? Why do people who share one belief (e.g., support medicare) also share another belief (e.g., support food stamps)? One possibility, of course, is that there is a logical relationship among the issues. The public may see that logic. In order to preserve the logical relationship, people may hold certain beliefs.[26]

Another source of consistency is political learning. This may operate in several ways. First, as people acquire their beliefs through socialization they may learn that certain beliefs go together. To the extent that people experience a common learning process they will share in the sets of beliefs they acquire. Second, people learn consistency from the content of current political rhetoric. People listen to and respond to political leaders. The leaders articulate and disseminate sets of issue positions to the public, positions that go together.[27] The public adopts the set of issue positions because their favored cue-givers provided them.

There also are psychological sources of constraint. One results from people feeling discomfort from inconsistent opinions.[28] To avoid the discomfort produced by inconsistency, people will alter their beliefs. Second, a person's existing belief system may screen or filter new information and the formation of new political beliefs. The individual may accept only those positions on new issues that are consistent with existing beliefs. The existing beliefs about related issues or general orientations (e.g., liberal or conservative) will provide a cue for the appropriate response to new but related issues.

One further distinction is important. There is a difference between *shared* or collective belief systems and *idiosyncratic* belief systems.[29] In *shared* belief systems large portions of the public agree in the connections among their beliefs. Thus, one may take two issues — medicare and food stamps — and find that across the public people who tend to support one tend to support the other, and people who oppose one tend to oppose the other. In this sense, the consistency results from people *sharing* perspectives on the relationships among the two issues, seeing them to possess some common thread, and thereby linking the two in their beliefs. On the other hand, *idiosyncratic* belief systems are unique to the individual. That is, the person's particular pattern of political beliefs may be shared with no one else. That person may see some unusual or unique relationships among the issues. Most political issues have several characteristics in terms of which they can be interpreted. The issue of the busing of children for the purpose of school integration may be responded to by some people in terms of their opinions about racial equality, by others in terms of their beliefs about the role of government in social issues, and by others in terms of their feelings about government spending. People who differ in their interpretation of the issue may link their opinion about busing to different issues or to different positions on other issues. Thus, that a person's opinions do not share the *conventional* perspective on the linkages among political issues does not mean necessarily that the person has *no* consistency among those opinions.

Observed Patterns of Belief System Consistency

The consistency of belief systems usually is measured through a correlational technique.[30] That is, measures have been used that depict the degree to which people's opinions on one issue go with or can predict their opinions on another issue. The greater that prediction level (the more often beliefs on different issues tend to go together) the greater the level of *shared* belief system consistency. The measures reflecting the level of consistency usually have scores ranging from -1.0 to $+1.0$. A zero (0.0) relationship means that there is absolutely no relationship between the two. A perfect positive relationship ($+1.0$) means that support for one issue always goes with support for another,[31] and that opposition to one issue goes with opposition to the other. A negative relationship indicates that support for one issue goes with opposition to the other. The absolute size of the relationship, regardless of whether positive or negative, is the important result. With a series of issues, the level of constraint or consistency is reflected in the *average* size of the relationship between the pairs of issues.

Philip Converse assessed the level of belief system constraint in the American public in 1956 and compared it to that exhibited by an elite sample.[32] On issues of domestic policy the public's average level of constraint was less than half that found among the elite sample. The conclusion was drawn that across the public there was little consistency in opinions on issues that in principle held *in common* some relationship to the liberal-conservative dimension.

As in a number of the public's characteristics, the apparent low level of belief system consistency was challenged by data on the public of the middle and late 1960s.[33] Between 1960 and 1964 there apparently occurred a large increase in the consistency of the American public's beliefs about political issues (see Figure 7–3). Indeed, the index of attitude consistency (constraint) doubled. Moreover, that higher level of consistency persisted into the early and mid-1970s, although results from 1976 clearly suggest some drawing back to levels lower than 1964.

FIGURE 7–3 Average Gamma Coefficient Among Five Issue Domains, 1956–1976

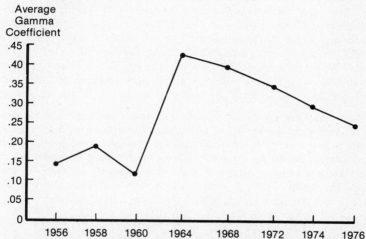

Source: This figure adapted from "Contextual Sources of Voting Behavior" by John R. Petrocik is reprinted from *The Electorate Reconsidered: The Changeable American Voter* (SAGE FOCUS EDITION Volume 20) John C. Pierce, John L. Sullivan, Editors, copyright © 1980, p. 262 by permission of the Publisher, Sage Publications, Inc. (Beverly Hills/London).

Explanations of Changes in Belief System Consistency

What might account for the patterns in the consistency of the public's beliefs about issues of public policy? Again, a variety of explanations have been suggested.

POLITICAL LEADERS. Perhaps in no place has the role of political leaders been more underscored than in explanations of the increase in the consistency of political belief systems. There are two fundamental positions.

One position argues that the increase in belief system constraint resulted from public dependence on political leaders for the answers as to what issues go together.[34] Political leaders articulate issue positions in their public debate. In that debate they also define the nature of the relationships among the issues. The members of the public — although, to be sure, not all of the public — turn to their preferred leaders for answers as to how to respond to issues and for clues as to the implications of issues for each other. The use of political leaders as these cue-givers substantially reduces the effort required of people. They do not need to determine for themselves all of the responses to issues and the relationships among them.

However, the behavior of the political leaders is variable. There will be fluctuation in the extent to which elite rhetoric clearly defines the issues and their relationships to each other, and in the extent to which the leaders clearly communicate those positions to the public. In the mid-1950s, it is argued, the leaders provided fuzzy or ambiguous cues as to the appropriate response to issues. They did not make clear to their followers the alternative positions on issues and the relationships among those issues. It was not that the leaders themselves necessarily differed little on the issues,[35] but rather that they failed to communicate this difference to the public and that they failed to use the difference as the basis for the electoral campaigns. However, in 1964 the party leaders revealed wide differences in their political positions, and they apparently communicated clear and distinct packages of beliefs to the voters. This distinctiveness and clarity of the cues provided to the public continued through the early 1970s, all the while without any necessary growth in the *ability* of the public to put the issues together consistently for themselves. Converse summarizes this position in the following passage:

> *Various reference group cues and other social mechanisms could help to create ideological patterning of political attitudes and behaviors on the part of individuals, even though these patterns might not be accompanied by much explicit understanding of the more overarching and abstract reasons why these patterns go together in the conventional "ideological" sense. . . . (Thus, the public) fell into positions of heightened ideological clarity without any clear recognition of the fact that they were doing so.*[36]

Yet the ideological, issue-based conflict of the early 1970s evolved into the more diffuse, nonissue electoral campaign of the post-Watergate 1976 election.[37] The level of belief system consistency also declined. The constraint did not recede to its 1950s level, but then neither did the issueless nature of the leaders' cues.

Converse notes that this cue-giving process is not dependent solely on the actions of political leaders. It also depends on the public's possession of some "elastic motivational characteristics such as interest and attentiveness." They are elastic in the sense that they can expand and contract. The expansion of the public's interest and attentiveness at the same time as the increase in the distinctiveness and clarity of the leaders' positions can combine to create greater levels of belief system organization. Increased interest and attentiveness will increase the public's exposure and receptivity to changes in the leaders' cues.

A second position agrees that the increase in belief system organization is linked to the voters' responsiveness to changes in politics. As Gerald Pomper writes, "As politics has become more pressing and more relevant, Americans have developed a more coherent, constrained belief system." Indeed, "These changes must be seen as a remarkable development of popular political consciousness."[38] The response of the electorate is not *simply* a rather superficial parroting of the cues provided by political leaders. Rather, the voters are able to comprehend, absorb, and take coherent positions on a variety of issues — if that coherence is available in the world of politics so that it makes sense to do the necessary labor:

For their part, voters have shown themselves ready to respond, to realign their loyalties, to comprehend abstract belief systems, and to fit their votes to their ideology. Their response depends on the stimuli they receive from the political environment. If these stimuli are issueless and static, as they largely were in the 1950s, the citizenry is likely to react in like manner. If these stimuli are seen as irrelevant, the link drawn to the parties will be weak, as in 1972. If the stimuli are more ideological and dynamic, on the other hand, we are likely to see different perceptions and behavior, such as that evidenced in the 1964 and 1968 elections. Confused voters reflect confused parties; clarity among the voters follows from clearheaded parties.[39]

The voter is seen as responsive to the nature of politics, capable of confronting and processing coherent issue and ideological content when it is available and withdrawing to other concerns when it is not.

Thus, both positions agree that the level of consistency in public belief systems is largely a function of the alternatives and cues provided by political leaders. Where they differ, however, is in the assessment of the foundation of the public's response. The first school argues that the public's response is fundamentally shallow, mirroring the stimuli provided by leaders. On the other hand, the second school contends that the response is the result of an able public *processing* changes in political stimuli and altering belief systems when such a change is rational and relevant to what is going on in politics.

INDIVIDUAL CHARACTERISTICS. We have noted often that the level of education increased substantially in the public during the same period as a number of changes took place in the character of the public's political thinking. Indeed, many of those changes in public opinion seem directly related to education. The level of belief system consistency or constraint is another example. It makes sense that people with more education would be better able to connect different political issues and therefore to be more consistent in their beliefs about those issues. Likewise, it seems to make sense that when the levels of education increase while the levels of belief system constraint also swing upward, that the latter might stem from the former. Table 7–2 presents some data that reflect on those expectations — the relationship of education and belief system consistency from 1956 to 1976.

In 1956 there was a very weak relationship between education and belief system consistency; the beliefs of the college graduate were only slightly more consistent than were those of the person with only a grade-school education. However, by the standards of the political elites, the level of consistency is rather low at all educational levels. The figures through 1968 show that belief system consistency increased substantially in all educational categories. Indeed, the increase was somewhat greater among those with the least amount of education. By 1968, there was a curvilinear relationship — the highest levels of consistency appeared at both ends of the education continuum. Then, in 1972 a large drop in consistency occurs among the lesser educated, but no drop takes place among the college graduates. The drop in consistency shows up among the college educated four years later, in 1976.

What does this say about the role of education? First, except for the 1972 study, there are few educational differences in consistency. Second, increases in consistency occur in all educational categories. Consequently, the overall increase in consistency could not be accounted for solely by the movement of people up through the educational levels. If so, the figures at the lower level would have remained low, and the figures at the higher level would have remained high, but there would have been many more people at the higher educational levels.

TABLE 7–2   The Relationship of Belief System Consistency to Levels of Education, 1956–1976[a]

	Education				
Year	0–8 Grades	Some High School	High School Graduates	Some College	College Graduates
1956	.13	.18	.19	.22	.24
1960	.35	.30	.35	.30	.31
1964	.46	.46	.36	.44	.51
1968	.51	.41	.41	.47	.49
1972	.27	.21	.29	.33	.46
1976	.31	.28	.23	.34	.38

[a]The entry in each cell is the average gamma among beliefs about issues of domestic policy.
Source: Stephen Earl Bennett and Robert Oldendick, "The Effect of Education on Mass Belief Systems: The Case of Issue Constraint Among Domestic Policy Opinions, 1956–1976" (Paper prepared for delivery at the 1978 Annual Meeting of the Midwest Political Science Association, Table 1). Reprinted by permission.

What might explain these patterns? One possibility, of course, is that people at all educational levels are simply responding to some other phenomenon (e.g., political leaders), and that educational level (or the cognitive abilities and the information it allegedly represents) is simply irrelevant to belief system consistency. That is, the entire public may be capable of evaluating and rationally incorporating the increased clarity in American issue politics. Or, the entire public may simply be "falling into heightened ideological clarity" without its knowing, or it may be that several forces are working simultaneously. For some, in this case the more highly educated, the increase in belief system consistency may be a result of a more consistent world of politics to which they are rationally and reasonably responding. For others, namely the lesser educated, the increase in belief system consistency may be a result of their responding to the cues provided by their political referents with no conscious evaluation and sensitivity to the actual relationships among the issues.

Nie and Andersen have suggested that the increase in belief system consistency is the result of changing levels of political interest in the public.[40] The 1964 presidential election is said to have generated greater political interest among the public. Belief consistency increased the most among those with the greatest levels of political interest; with the greater numbers of people with high levels of political interest, the overall magnitude of constraint increased.

As Nie and Andersen conclude,

the combined impact of the rise in attitude consistency among those inter-ested in politics and the increase in the numbers of such citizens accounts for a major proportion of the observed growth of ideological constraint in the population as a whole.[41]

On the other hand, Sullivan et al. re-examine the Nie interest data and apply the hypothesis to differences in some new data and conclude that it is "doubt-ful that they are large enough to sustain the 'interest' explanation put forth by Nie and associates."[42] The alternative explanation for the increase in con-sistency put forward is methodological, the argument to which we now turn.

QUESTION FORMAT.   As we have noted, the major increases in belief sys-tem consistency occurred between 1960 and 1964, a pattern generally attri-buted to the actions of political leaders in clarifying political issues and stimulating public interest in those issues. However, a number of recent scholars have noted that in the major set of data used to make these conclu-sions (the SRC-CPS National Election Studies) some substantial changes in question wording took place at precisely the point at which the correlations among the question responses increased.[43] Given the nature of those changes in question format, these authors have suggested that the changes them-selves account for most of the increases in consistency. The earlier question format is said to have been biased, in that the question itself contained only one alternative rather than offsetting alternatives, both making it harder to disagree and producing response set — the tendency to answer questions in an agree or disagree direction regardless of their content. Similarly, the content of the questions used in 1964 and in the following years is said to deal more directly with the liberal-conservative dimension. Without that common con-tent there would be little substantive reason for the responses on pairs of issues to go together.

In order to test the effect of question format on belief system consistency, Sullivan and his colleagues administered a survey to a sample of the public of the Minneapolis/St. Paul area. Half of the sample answered questions pre-sented in the pre-1964 format, while the other half responded to 1964-format questions.[44] The results showed that "the differences in the correlations be-tween [the] two samples are quite similar in size to the differences found in the SRC data before and after 1964."[45] In both cases, the higher correlations (constraint or consistency) appear in those questions believed to be the more reliable. Thus, they argue, "constraint in the mass public probably did not increase very much between 1956 and 1972; rather, reported changes were due to modifications in the survey items used to measure constraint."[46]

The implications of the methodological criticisms are twofold. First, the levels of belief system constraint identified in the 1950s public may have been *under*estimated; the public's belief system consistency may have been much higher than previously thought. Second, the increases in belief system con-straint attributed to the 1964 election and the following era of tumultuous politics may have been illusory. That is, the politics of the 1960s may have had no impact on the organization of the public's political beliefs. If the latter is true, then the question becomes even more intriguing: How could the public's political beliefs remain insulated from the changes in the behavior and cues of the political leaders? Or, on the other hand, was there first observed a false change in the public's beliefs, followed by a groping for an answer founded in the structure of the leadership behavior, when perhaps the leadership behavior itself changed much less than we had thought — or at least in ways irrelevant to the structure of the public's political beliefs?

As one might expect, the methodological critiques have not gone uncontested.[47] The rebuttals point to other sets of issues in which there has been no change in question format but which exhibit the same patterns of change as in those cases where the format was altered. Similarly, variations in constraint patterns are different in different subgroups in the public, a pattern that should not appear with only question format at issue.[48] They also note that a substantial decline in constraint appeared between 1972 and 1976 with the continued use of the new questions (see Figure 7 – 3). If question format were the only variable involved in the increases in constraint, then there should not have been the decline in constraint with no change in format. Thus, at worst, they feel the format alterations account for only a portion of the changes in constraint — the remainder is a true change in belief system consistency, responsive to the varying nature of the political conflict among political leaders.

IDEOLOGICAL IDENTIFICATION

Conceptualization and constraint are important parts of the public's political thinking, but both fail to capture how people place *themselves* with respect to the major ideological divisions of the day. People have an ideological identification when they position themselves on some dimension of ideological conflict — such as liberalism and conservatism. The ends of the dimension are defined by some general concept (e.g., liberal or conservative) that subsumes a set of more specific political beliefs. Major changes in the public's concern with political issues or in the public's position on important questions often are interpreted in broad sweeping ideological terms — e.g., general movements of the public to the "right" or to the "left" or swings to liberalism or conservatism. Indeed, the major changes in the past two decades have often been described in just such terms — Goldwater's "conservatism," the radicalism of the sixties and the seventies, and the apparent returning conservatism of the late 1970s and early 1980s. Ideological identification provides a shorthand way of determining how to respond to a public policy, to an individual, or to a political group. If people call themselves liberals or conservatives, and political issues are labeled liberal or conservative, then those people need only relate to the symbol rather than engage in a detailed analysis of every issue that appears.

This section examines the public's identification with the ideological positions of liberalism and conservatism. Liberalism and conservatism have dominated the American political agenda and are foremost in the public's mind when ideological terms are used to evaluate politics. Nevertheless, it should be kept in mind that there are a number of dimensions along which people may place themselves and organize their beliefs.

Changes in the Distribution of Ideological Orientations

The politics of the last three decades have been characterized by rising and falling ideological tides.[49] The quiescent years of the Eisenhower presidency stimulated the widespread prediction of "the end of ideology." No sooner had this become a dominant theme than ideology seemed to bust out all over in American politics. The electoral arena, in the 1964 presidential campaign, provided clear-cut ideological distinctions between Goldwater and Johnson. The 1972 contest between the liberal "populism" of George McGovern and the traditional Republican conservatism of Richard Nixon again highlighted certain ideological dimensions in politics. Yet, in the eyes of many, the American political scene since has at least partially turned away from ideological politics.

Have the changing emphases on ideological politics been reflected in changes in the orientations of the American public to the liberal-conservative dimension? The available data are presented in Table 7–3

TABLE 7–3   The Distribution of Ideological Self-Identification on the Liberal-Conservative Dimension, 1964–1978[a]

Ideological Position	1964	1972	1974	1976	1978
Liberal	29%	26%	28%	24%	25%
Middle of Road	38	37	36	38	29
Conservative	33	37	36	38	46
	100%	100%	100%	100%	100%

[a]All calculations are based in the number of the public willing to express an identification or self-positioning on the liberal-conservative dimension.

Source: The 1964 data are recalculated from Lloyd A. Free and Hadley Cantril, *The Political Beliefs of Americans* (New York: Simon & Schuster, 1968), p. 41; 1974, 1976, and 1978 distributions are based in the results of the Center for Political Studies National Election Studies.

Throughout most of the period there appears to have been a slow growth in the percentage of self-identified conservatives in the American public. The differences in the 1964 and the 1976 distributions are rather small — only 5 percentage points, but a substantial increase appears in 1978. In 1964, self-identified conservatives outnumbered liberals by only four percentage points (33 percent to 29 percent). However, that gap had widened to 14 percent (38 percent to 24 percent) in 1976 and 21 percent in 1978. The aggregate distribution of the American public is more conservative than liberal. Indeed, Levitin and Miller used a more complex measure of ideological self-positioning and concluded that "conservatives outnumbered liberals by a margin of almost 2 to 1" in both 1972 and 1976.[50] Through that period, then, the distribution of ideological positions is fairly stable. On the other hand, stability in the aggregate distribution of opinions is not necessarily the product of great stability at the individual level. Large amounts of symmetrical change at the individual level could produce aggregate stability. The only panel data available for ideological self-positioning come from the 1972–1976 national studies of the Center for Political Studies. In those data, the individual stability of ideological self-location has been calculated and compared to the stability for party identification and a series of issue positions. Ideological identification was more stable than were the issue positions, but somewhat less stable than party identification for the same four-year period.[51] In total, then, through 1976 at least, the aggregate and individual-level data provide similar pictures.

Ideological Identification and Political Issue Position

The foundations for a systematic connection between the public's ideological orientations and political issue positions are explicit. One important function of an ideological orientation, such as self-identification, is to serve as a capsule or summarizing device for a series of interrelated positions about political issues. People's liberal/conservative orientations also allow them to interpret and screen information about political issues and political figures. If a person identifies as a liberal and a policy is widely labeled "liberal," then that policy can be supported prior to the development of any detailed understanding of it.

The systematic relationship of ideological identification to issues of public policy will result from two conditions. One is the presence of ideological orientations in the public and their willingness to use them to interpret politics. The second is the structure of politics itself. Liberals and conservatives will differ on particular political issues only to the extent that those issues are central to the liberal/conservative dimension, the alternatives to the issues coincide with different positions on that dimension, and the public relates the two (issue and ideology).

Liberal and conservative positions are defined on almost any important issue that comes before the American people: civil rights, civil liberties, the size of government, the role of government in social-welfare activities, the Vietnam War, the environment, women's liberation, and many others. Thus, we would expect some differences between liberals and conservatives across a wide variety of issues. At the same time, however, when a number of policy areas are linked to liberal and conservative orientations, the strength of the relationship in any one policy area may be diminished. Some people may call themselves liberals because of their views on civil rights while others are liberals because of their feelings about civil liberties. Consequently, people who share a liberal designation may share few policy positions. We also would expect some change through time in the relationships of public opinion to the liberal/conservative dimension. Some policy areas may come to the political forefront, crystallizing their ideological relevance. Moreover, people's general political orientations may remain relatively stable, but the political meaning of political issues may change. Issues that divided liberals and conservatives, for example, may become consensual — the same opinion shared by everyone regardless of ideology.

Recent studies suggest only moderate relationships between ideological identification and positions on issues of public policy.[52] Table 7 – 4 presents the relationships between the public's issue preferences and their liberal/conservative self location. None of the relationships are of great magnitude, but the moderate level of association extends across a rather wide variety of issues.

TABLE 7 – 4   Ideological Identification and Political Issue Position, 1976

	Ideological Identification		
Political Issue Position	Liberal	Moderate	Conservative
Government Should Guarantee School Integration	59%	35%	28%
Civil Rights Being Pushed Too Fast	27	43	45
Government Should Guarantee Jobs	42	27	14
Protect Rights of the Accused	52	33	27
Government Health Insurance	65	40	25
Cut Military Spending	38	18	12
Government Limit Gas Use	74	65	71
Equal Role for Women	74	60	50

Source: Center for Political Studies. American National Election Study, 1976 [machine-readable data file].

One issue has undergone some interesting changes in recent years. Traditionally, many liberals have been aligned on the side of increasing the size of the government in order to deal with pressing economic and social problems, while conservatives have opposed that government activity, arguing that it interferes with individual initiative and free enterprise. For a number of years, the American public has been asked their opinions about the size of the government: Is it about right, is it too big, or is it not big enough? In the 1960s, liberals and conservatives differed in the traditional and expected ways on the question of the size of government.[53] The self-defined conservatism of the 1964 Republican presidential candidate and his constant criticism of the size of government is clearly reflected in the conservative portion of the American public. Indeed, in the 1964 – 1968 period about twice as many conservatives as liberals said that government is too big. By 1972, however, there was a dramatic change. Liberals became much more likely to agree that government is too big, while the same sentiment became less frequent among the conservatives. The result of those changes was that in 1972, self-defined liberals were actually a little *more* likely to be critical of the size of government. Then, in 1976 the previous and more traditional order was restored. In 1976 *both* the liberals and the conservatives were more critical of the size of government than they were in the sixties, although the liberals had retreated somewhat from their 1972 high level.

How can we explain changing patterns of relationships between ideological identification and positions on the size of government issue? One answer is that positions on the issue of size of government are liberal or conservative only in the *context* of the political environment. Over the period of modern American politics, dating, perhaps, from the inception of the New Deal, the size-of-government issue has been argued in terms of the use of government to solve domestic social and economic problems — e.g., unemployment, civil rights, health care, education. Thus, liberals quite regularly supported extensions of government activity, while conservatives opposed them. Yet, in the late 1960s and on into the early 1970s the political context of the size of government underwent change. As Petrocik argues, *liberals began to see the question as a probe about government spying and the erosion of civil liberties, a change that coincided with the rise of the "social issue" . . . and a heightened concern with domestic disorder. As a result, the proportion of liberals agreeing that the government was "too big for the good of the country and the individual citizen" exceed the proportion of conservatives making this response in 1972.*[54]

The political context had again changed by 1976. The overriding concern with civil liberties fell away, perhaps as the substantive issues that stimulated them (protest, civil rights) also became less visible.

In summary, liberals and conservatives differ in rather predictable directions on a number of political issues, although the size of the relationship usually is not large. The magnitude of the relationship of any particular issue position to ideological identification probably is attenuated by the wide range of issues that at one time or another have been parked under the shelter of liberalism and conservatism. Moreover, the degree to which liberals and conservatives differ in their issue positions seems to be changeable through time, depending on the political context within which conflict over the issue takes place.

Ideological Identification and Party Identification

Ideology also has a clear implication for the public's choice among political parties. Parties may promote contrasting ideologies so that members of the public who differ in their ideological orientations also may differ in their party choices. That is, liberals in the public should choose the liberal party, and conservatives should choose the conservative party. Basing the choice of political parties on ideological grounds acts as a short-cut for the individual. Choosing the party with the closest ideological fit to the individual's own ideology eliminates the necessity of constantly evaluating and comparing the parties on a great number of specific political issues.

The American public of the 1950s was described as nonideological in the choice of their political parties. Herbert McClosky, for example, found the relationship between party and ideology in the public to be much weaker than among the members of an elite stratum.[55] The 1964 election, however, increased the concern with the relationship between party and ideology, as did the ideological politics of subsequent years.

TABLE 7 – 5   Ideological Identification and Party Identification, 1976

	Ideological Identification		
Party Identification	*Liberal*	*Moderate*	*Conservative*
Democrat	54%	38%	24%
Independent	38	42	32
Republican	8	19	44
Total	100%	99%	100%
N	(460)	(720)	(728)

Source: Center for Political Studies. American National Election Study, 1976 [machine-readable data file].

In 1964, two-thirds of the liberals also called themselves Democrats, and only 12 percent were Republican.[56] However, conservatives were almost as likely to identify with the Democrats as with the Republicans (37 percent versus 41 percent). By 1972, however, the Democratic proportion of both the liberal and the conservative categories dropped considerably. Among liberals and conservatives the percentage calling themselves Independent increased. In 1976 the Democrats recovered some of the liberals' allegiances, moving back to over half of that ideological category (see Table 7–5). Clearly, in 1972 many liberals were disenchanted with the Democratic party and its legacy of discord both in that year and in 1968. From 1964 to 1976 a gradual but consistent decline occurred in the percentage of the conservatives identifying with the Democratic party. Even with all of this movement, however, ideological identification remains connected to partisan choice. Over half of the liberals identify with the more liberal party and only 8 percent identify with the more conservative party. Nearly half of the conservatives identify with the more conservative party and only a quarter identify with the more liberal party (and the latter figure is a substantial drop from a decade earlier).

Ideological Identification and Vote for President

Most analyses of the opinion sources of the American public's vote for president concentrate on candidate images, party identification and political issue position. Historically, party identification has been the most important and most stable clue to how the individual will vote. The role of political issues has been of varying importance, apparently increasing in the mid-sixties, continuing on for the next several elections, and then receding again in the 1976 election. In these analyses the ideological orientation of the voter has been minimized. Yet there has been an increasing awareness of the potential impact of ideological identification, with several studies indicating that ideology may rival party identification in explaining the voter.

John Holm and John Robinson have recently examined the role of ideological identification in the 1972 election.[57] They found that party identification and ideological identification were both related to presidential vote choice at about the same level (r=.51 for party; r=.47 for ideology), and that both "show a strong independent effect relative to each other."[58] Moreover, ideology was a strong voting force among Independents (who do not have party as an explicit cue as to how to vote) and among people who are more aware ideologically.

Holm and Robinson did not have the ideological-identification question available for a long period of time. Consequently, they constructed an alternative measure of ideological orientation that could be employed from 1964 through 1972. In three election years (1964, 1968, and 1972) they examined the relative impact of party and ideology on individual vote choice. They concluded that "the impact of ideology . . . varies greatly over elections," and that the independent effect of ideology was much greater in 1972 than in prior elections.[59] Not only did the relative impact of party identification decline in 1972 (to .51 from .68 and .62), but the association of ideology and the vote increased (to .48 from .40 and .29). Thus, while 1964 clearly had ideological content, considerable party content also was involved in people's voting behavior. On the other hand, the McGovern-Nixon race of 1972 appeared to have defined ideological alternatives even more clearly and reduced the partisan implications of the alternatives.

Levitin and Miller have examined the role of ideology in the 1976 election. One might expect that the role of ideology would have diminished, given the less ideological nature of the campaign. However,

> *party voting may have been more important to the election outcome in 1976 than in 1972, and issue voting may have been less important in 1976 than in 1972, but voting in accord with self-placement on an ideological continuum was virtually as prevalent — independent of party voting — in 1976 as in 1972.*[60]

This suggests that the nature of the election campaign cannot be the sole source of ideological response to the voting situation. If it were, then the importance of ideology would have declined in 1976. Individual concern with ideology also must be crucial. The ideological concerns reflected in the voting of 1976 (see Table 7 – 6) may stem from the ideological candidates of earlier years. That is, Barry Goldwater in 1964, George Wallace in 1968, and George McGovern in 1972 may have stimulated a particular sensitivity to ideological concerns in the public that could not be easily erased in a single election.

TABLE 7 – 6   Ideological Identification and the Vote for President, 1976

	Ideological Identification		
Vote	Liberal	Moderate	Conservative
Carter	78%	52%	22%
Ford	22	48	78
Total	100%	100%	100%
N	(295)	(434)	(503)

Source: Center for Political Studies. American National Election Study, 1976 [machine-readable data file].

CONCLUSION

This chapter has focused on three key elements in the public's political thinking: conceptualization, belief system consistency, and ideological identification. The patterns of political thinking in the past two decades suggest a continuing interaction between the content of the political environment and individual characteristics. In particular, the presence of ideologically distinct candidates appears to have stimulated greater incidence of ideological conceptualization, greater belief system consistency along a liberal/conservative dimension, and greater consistency between ideological identification and party identification and presidential vote choice. Yet personal factors clearly enter into the equation. Many Americans did not respond to changes in the political environment, perhaps for reasons of education, political interest, or age. Moreover, the newly acquired cognitive characteristics frequently persist beyond the termination of the politics that stimulated them. Thus, just as we cannot discount the role of the public in a democratic political system, we likewise cannot ignore the role of democratic politics in structuring the public's political thinking.

NOTES

1. Angus Campbell et al., *The American Voter* (New York: John Wiley & Sons, 1960), pp. 216–65.
2. See William H. Flanigan and Nancy H. Zingale, *Political Behavior of the American Electorate,* 4th ed. (Boston: Allyn & Bacon, 1979), pp. 118–19; Bruce A. Campbell, *The American Electorate* (New York: Holt, Rinehart & Winston, 1979), pp. 150–52; and Richard G. Niemi and Herbert F. Weisberg, eds., *Controversies in American Voting Behavior* (San Francisco: W.H. Freeman & Co., 1976), pp. 68–83.
3. Campbell et al., *The American Voter,* p. 222.
4. Ibid., p. 229.
5. Ibid., p. 255.
6. Ibid., p. 256.
7. The surrogate measure apparently was first developed in John Osgood Field and Ronald E. Anderson, "Ideology in the Public's Conceptualization of the 1964 Presidential Election," *Public Opinion Quarterly* 33 (Fall, 1969), pp. 380–98. The surrogate measure's reliability and validity recently have been criticized. Because of the substantial differences in the distributions of the original and the surrogate measure's results, the challenge to the surrogate measure seems to have limited implications for the original measure. See Eric R. A. N. Smith, "The Levels of Conceptualization: False Measures of Ideological Sophistication," *American Political Science Review* 74 (September 1980), pp. 685–96.
8. Norman H. Nie, Sidney Verba, and John R. Petrocik, *The Changing American Voter* (Cambridge, Mass.: Harvard University Press, 1976), p. 18.
9. Norman H. Nie, Sidney Verba, and John R. Petrocik, *The Changing American Voter,* enl. ed. (Cambridge, Mass.: Harvard University Press, 1979), p. 366.
10. Ibid., p. 116.
11. Ronald Inglehart, *The Silent Revolution* (Princeton, N.J.: Princeton University Press, 1977), p. 310.
12. Niemi and Weisberg, eds., *Controversies in American Voting Behavior,* pp. 76 ff.
13. Philip E. Converse, "Public Opinion and Voting Behavior" in *Handbook of Political Science,* vol. 4, *Nongovernmental Politics,* Fred I. Greenstein and Nelson W. Polsby, eds. (Reading, Mass.: Addison-Wesley, 1975), p. 103.
14. Recall the discussions in earlier chapters about the problems in estimating individual change from aggregate distributions.
15. Campbell et al., *The American Voter,* pp. 250–51.
16. Ibid., p. 152.
17. Warren E. Miller and Teresa E. Levitin, *Leadership and Change: The New Politics and the American Electorate* (Cambridge, Mass.: Winthrop Publishers, 1976), p. 14.
18. Herbert A. Asher, *Presidential Elections and American Politics* (Homewood, Ill.: Dorsey Press, 1976), p. 113.
19. Nie et al., *The Changing American Voter,* pp. 119–21.
20. This explanation is similar to Converse's explanation for changes in political efficacy as expressed in his "Change in the American Electorate," in *The Human Meaning of Social Change,* Angus Campbell and Philip E. Converse, eds. (New York: Russell Sage Foundation, 1972), pp. 263–337.

21. Niemi and Weisberg, eds., *Controversies in American Voting Behavior,* p. 83.
22. Miller and Levitin, *Leadership and Change,* p. 14.
23. For an analysis of the usefulness of ideological evaluations in the electoral setting, see Anthony Dawns, *An Economic Theory of Democracy* (New York: Harper & Row, 1957).
24. Philip E. Converse, "The Nature of Belief Systems in Mass Publics," in *Ideology and Discontent,* David E. Apter, ed. (New York: Free Press, 1964), pp. 206–61.
25. Pamela Johnston Conover and Stanley Feldman, "Belief System Organization in the American Electorate: An Alternative Approach," in *The Electorate Reconsidered,* John C. Pierce and John L. Sullivan, eds. (Beverly Hills: Sage Publications, 1980).
26. Converse, "The Nature of Belief Systems in Mass Publics."
27. Sartori calls this "hetero-constraint." See Giovanni Sartori, "Politics, Ideology and Belief Systems," *American Political Science Review* 63 (June 1969), pp. 398–411.
28. For an example of this approach, see Stephen E. Bennett, "Consistency Among the Public's Social Welfare Policy Attitudes in the 1960s," *American Journal of Political Science* 17 (August 1973), pp. 544–70.
29. Allen H. Barton and R. Wayne Parsons, "Measuring Belief System Structure," *Public Opinion Quarterly* 41 (Summer 1977), pp. 159–80.
30. See George Balch, "Statistical Manipulation in the Study of Issue Consistency: The Gamma Coefficient," *Political Behavior* 1 (Fall 1979), pp. 217–42.
31. Some statistics (e.g., gamma) used in belief system measurement will indicate high levels of constraint with curvilinear or "scalar" relationships. For problems with these measures, see Balch, "Statistical Manipulation."
32. Converse, "The Nature of Belief Systems in Mass Publics."
33. Bennett, "Consistency Among the Public's Social Welfare Policy Attitudes in the 1960s"; and Nie et al., *The Changing American Voter,* pp. 123–44.
34. Converse, "Public Opinion and Voting Behavior."
35. McClosky presented evidence that in the 1950s the leaders of the two political parties differed widely on a number of issues while their followers in the mass public were rather close to each other. See Herbert McClosky, Paul J. Hoffman, and Rosemary O'Hara, "Issue Conflict and Consensus Among Party Leaders and Followers," *American Political Science Review* 54 (June 1960), pp. 406–29.
36. Converse, "Public Opinion and Voting Behavior," p. 107.
37. John R. Petrocik, "Contextual Sources of Voting Behavior," in *The Electorate Reconsidered,* pp. 257–77.
38. Gerald M. Pomper, *The Voters' Choice: Varieties of American Electoral Behavior* (New York: Dodd, Mead & Co., 1975), p. 180.
39. Ibid., p. 184.
40. Norman H. Nie with Kristi Andersen, "Mass Belief Systems Revisited: Political Change and Attitude Structure," *Journal of Politics* 36 (August 1974), pp. 540–87.
41. Ibid., p. 574.
42. John L. Sullivan, James E. Piereson, and George E. Marcus, "Ideological Constraint in the Mass Public: A Methodological Critique and Some New Findings," *American Journal of Political Science* 22 (May 1978), p. 244.
43. See Sullivan et al., "Ideological Constraint in the Mass Public"; George F. Bishop, Robert W. Oldendick, and Alfred J. Tuchfarber, "Effects of Question Wording and Format on Political Attitude Consistency," *Public Opinion Quarterly* 42 (Spring 1978), pp. 81–92; and Gregory B. Brunk, "The 1964 Attitude Consistency Leap Reconsidered," *Political Methodology* 5 (Summer 1978), pp. 347–60.
44. Sullivan et al., "Ideological Constraint in the Mass Public."
45. Ibid., p. 240.

46. Ibid., p. 247.
47. Norman H. Nie and James N. Rabjohn, "Revisiting Mass Belief Systems Revisited," *American Journal of Political Science* 23 (February 1979), pp. 139–75.
48. John C. Pierce and Paul R. Hagner, "Stability and Change in the Public's Political Thinking: Personal and Political Sources of Belief System Constraint" (Paper presented at the annual meeting of the Southern Political Science Association, November 1–3, 1979, Gatlinburg, Tennessee).
49. Paul Allen Beck and M. Kent Jennings, "Political Periods and Political Participation," *American Political Science Review* 73 (September 1979), pp. 737–50.
50. Teresa E. Levitin and Warren E. Miller, "Ideological Interpretations of National Elections," *American Political Science Review* 73 (September 1979), p. 753.
51. Ibid., p. 756.
52. Flanigan and Zingale, *Political Behavior of the American Electorate,* p. 125.
53. Petrocik, "Contextual Sources of Voting Behavior."
54. Ibid.
55. McClosky, "Issue Conflict and Consensus Among Party Leaders and Followers."
56. Recalculated from Lloyd A. Free and Hadley Cantril, *The Political Beliefs of Americans* (New York: Simon & Schuster, 1968), p. 235.
57. John D. Holm and John P. Robinson, "Ideological Identification and the American Voter," *Public Opinion Quarterly* 42 (Summer 1978), pp. 235–46.
58. Ibid., p. 239.
59. Ibid., p. 243.
60. Levitin and Miller, "Ideological Interpretations of National Elections," p. 758.

CHAPTER 8

POLITICAL CULTURE AND POLITICAL TOLERANCE

A country's *political culture* is that set of political beliefs upon which there is a high level of agreement among the public. Political culture is

> *a set of common attitudes and beliefs about common objects, where the primary belief is that these objects bear a relationship to the political system. . . . A political culture is a fundamental consensus of interest and evaluation with regard to a given set of attitude objects.*[1]

Similarly, political culture "must be a patterned value system which tends to be widely supported,"[2] or "the particular distribution of patterns or orientation toward political objects among the members of the nation."[3]

Not all opinions of a country's public are candidates for inclusion in political culture. Walter A. Rosenbaum, for example, identifies three sets of core orientations that constitute political culture.[4] These include a public's "orientations toward governmental structures," their attitudes about "others in the political system," and their feelings about their "own political activity." Within each of these sets of orientations there are several subsets, making the overall mapping of political culture a difficult task. The number of possible combinations of these relevant orientations provides substantial opportunity for countries to develop *unique* political cultures, to possess distinct combinations of orientations about government, others, and self.

The content of a country's political culture is important because it is said to structure the nature of the country's political life.[5] Politics — the processes, patterns, and criteria for political decisions and the legitimacy of those decisions — may reflect the beliefs about politics held by the public. Thus (other things being equal, and they rarely are), countries that share certain kinds of politics (e.g., democratic) should share certain characteristics in their political culture. The publics should share certain orientations about government, about others, and about their own roles in politics. And, where these political systems differ, there also should be some corresponding variations in the supporting opinions of their publics.

The beliefs constituting a country's political culture also have an historical element to them.[6] That is, they are passed more or less intact from generation to generation. The primary vehicle for this historical transmission is the political socialization process. Parents, schools, and other institutions attempt to inculcate in new generations support and affection for the existing political arrangements (see Chapter 4). This historical continuity in political culture contributes to long-term stability in the ways political decisions are made.

There is considerable evidence that in recent years important elements of the American political culture have experienced substantial alteration. This and the following chapter present information describing those changes in two critical areas. From the set of orientations toward others in the political system, this chapter examines public support for "the rules of the game," focusing on the American public's tolerance for political dissent; from the set of orientations toward governmental structures, the following chapter looks at the decline in political trust in the American public. Each of these is central to the conception of the United States as possessing a democratic political culture — one in which people have confidence in the integrity, responsiveness, and abilities of people in government, and one in which people are tolerant of the views and activity of others with differing political orientations.

The changes in these key elements of the American political culture are important in several respects. First, they may reflect or be responses to major changes in the country's politics. Indeed, one measure by which to assess the impact of political events is the degree to which they upset the fundamental patterns of political culture. Second, changes in political culture may portend long-range changes in the political process. If political systems tend to reflect the content of the political culture, then changes in political culture may generate evolutions in the structure and processes of the political system. Thus, political culture stands in a reciprocal relationship to politics and society. At the same time that it may govern much of what takes place in the political system, political culture also is a mirror, informing us of the public's response to political currents and revealing the consequences of that response for the kind of system in which Americans live.

POLITICAL TOLERANCE

Political tolerance is the willingness of the individual to extend certain fundamental procedural rights and civil liberties to others, even to those groups and individuals with whom one disagrees or that stand outside of the mainstream of political and social life. A widely tolerant citizenry, one with procedural norms exhibiting tolerance, is central to the major conceptions of a democratic political culture. As David Lawrence has written, "procedural norms are basic to our understanding of what democracy is. Democracy is often defined in purely procedural terms."[7] Indeed, certain procedural norms, such as freedom of speech, are called the democratic "rules of the game."[8] Moreover, political tolerance means not only an agreement with the abstractions of such principles as freedom of speech, but also with their *application* to specific circumstances and to identifiable and even unpopular groups and individuals. Political tolerance means that the rules of the game are applicable even to the nonconformists of society, the people who promote social and political positions at variance with the majority of the public.

Public attitudes toward the role of others in society make up one aspect of a political culture. A democratic political culture is one in which the public's beliefs and behaviors both exhibit and foster an openness to others in the society. Yet it has been noted by some scholars that it is possible for the democratic rules of the game to be applied widely even in the absence of widespread support for them in the public.[9] That is, rules of the game may be applied to the nonconformists of society even though support for that application is absent from the political culture (when the latter is defined as *consensual* public support). How might this occur? Those people with the greatest impact on how the system operates may hold opinions that differ from those held by the general public. Political "elites" by definition have the most to do with the operation of the political system. Their opinions have a greater impact on the opportunities and actions of others. Thus, the intolerant opinions held by the general public may be diffused or deflected from impact on how the system actually operates. At the same time, to be sure, it is also possible for the general public to hold tolerant political attitudes and for the elite to prevent their implementation, for the content of the political culture of a society to be inconsistent with the actual operation of the political process.

Discontinuity between the political culture (widespread agreement on relevant political questions) and the political process has important implications for a system. First, of course, such an inconsistency would suggest a lack of responsiveness to the public's political preferences, itself one conception of a democratic system (see Chapter 1). Second, it would call into question the immutability of the application of the rules of the game. To be sure, all operating rules for political systems are subject to change. However, if the practices are supported only by the elite but not by the public, threats to their application may be more difficult to fight off. Elites or "counterelites," those challenging the people presently in power, that oppose the existing rules of the game will have a potential reservoir of support in the public. There will not be the weight of the political culture against which the antidemocratic challenges must push.

The Established View of Political Tolerance among Americans

Historically, the United States has been said to possess a democratic political system and a democratic political culture. Therefore, it was assumed by many that the American public held opinions favorable to the fundamental principles of a democratic process and to the application of those principles to specific political situations.[10] Indeed, 1938 and 1940 surveys of the American public showed that 96 percent professed belief in freedom of speech.[11] However, in 1940, 76 percent opposed "allowing radicals to hold meetings and express their views in this community," and in 1941, 53 percent opposed allowing anybody to speak on anything "any time he wants to."[12]

These indications of some lack of depth in public support for fundamental democratic procedural norms received little systematic scholarly attention until after World War II. The anti-Semitism of Nazi Germany spawned a series of studies into the psychological bases of intolerant political beliefs.[13] Closer to home, the "McCarthy era" of the early 1950s, named for the then Wisconsin Senator Joseph R. McCarthy, contained numerous examples of disregard for traditional democratic procedural norms in the attempts to identify and penalize people *suspected* of disloyalty to the country and its government. McCarthy, for example, leveled charges that a number of communists worked in the U.S. State Department. In 1950, the public was polled about its beliefs about the impact of those charges. Thirty-nine percent said the charges did more good than harm, while only 29 percent said they resulted in more harm than good. Moreover, "61 percent compared to 30 percent approved (with some qualifications) of the Senator's charges about Communists in the State Department."[14] The activities of McCarthy and the apparent public support for him led some scholars to seriously consider the proposition that many Americans did not hold beliefs supportive of the fundamental rules of the game, that they were not tolerant, and that political tolerance may not really be a significant part of the political culture of the United States. If this were the case, how could one account for the nature of the political system, taken to be generally democratic (even in the face of McCarthy-like aberrations)? Several major studies addressed this question, and out of these studies came the traditional view of American tolerance.

Samuel A. Stouffer's work, *Communism, Conformity and Civil Liberties,* is perhaps the most significant contributor to the "traditional" view of the American public's tolerance for nonconformity.[15] Stouffer examined data from interviews with 4,933 members of the public and 1,500 local community leaders conducted in 1954. He searched for the respondents' willingness to tolerate four groups of nonconformists: socialists, atheists, accused communists, and admitted communists. Overall, Stouffer found the community leaders to be more tolerant than the cross section of the general public. Thus, in response to the question, "If a person wanted to make a speech in your community favoring government ownership of all the railroads and big industries, should he be allowed to speak, or not?," 84 percent of the leaders said yes, but only 58 percent of the public assented. Similarly, 64 percent of the leaders would allow atheists to speak against "churches and religion," but such conduct would be allowed by only 37 percent of the national public sample. And, while a bare majority of the leaders (51 percent) would allow an admitted communist to make a speech, only 27 percent of the public would do so.[16] Thus, in general, Stouffer concluded that the country's political elite were more tolerant of nonconformists than was the general public. Indeed, on a summary scale of tolerance, 66 percent of the elite were "more tolerant" compared to only 31 percent of the public.[17]

Stouffer also examined those individual characteristics that would distinguish among different levels of tolerance in the public. Thus, the "younger generation" was more tolerant than the older generation, and the better educated were more tolerant than the less educated. He found 47 percent of those in the twenty-one to twenty-nine age group to be "more tolerant" compared to only 18 percent in the sixty-and-over age group.[18] Sixty-six percent of the college graduates were "more tolerant," while only 16 percent of those with a grade-school education were so classified. Among people with the same level of schooling (e.g., college graduates), the younger respondents were more tolerant; and among each age group (e.g., the twenty-one- to twenty-nine-year-olds), those with more education were the more tolerant.[19] Combining youth with education, of course, resulted in the highest levels of tolerance: 77 percent of the college graduates in the twenty-one to twenty-nine group were "more tolerant" compared to only 13 percent of those with a grade-school education in the sixty-and-over group.

Stouffer's study also revealed tolerance to vary by region and by residential location (rural versus urban). He concluded that "the West seems to have the largest proportion of relatively tolerant people on the scale of willingness to tolerate nonconformists, and the South the smallest proportion. The East and the Middle West are in-between."[20] People who live in cities and metropolitan areas are more tolerant than rural dwellers. Southerners remain less tolerant within type of community and within levels of education. And "rural people in every region are less likely to be tolerant of nonconformists than city people, even when we compare urban and rural people with the same amount of schooling."[21]

Stouffer's results can be briefly summarized: they revealed rather low levels of tolerance for nonconformity in the American public; they showed greater tolerance for nonconformity among local community leaders; and they demonstrated variations in public tolerance among people differing in age, education, region, and the size of the local community. These findings can be taken to imply several things. First, the American public is not particularly tolerant of nonconformists, and such tolerance, if it is to operate in politics and society, must come primarily from the elite, the community leaders. Second, Stouffer took the results on variations among the public to suggest that the country would see some increase in public tolerance. His primary emphasis was on the relationship of education to tolerance. With greater levels of education appearing in the public, and with education apparently contributing to tolerance, then long-term increases in education should increase the overall level of tolerance in the country.

In 1960, James Prothro and Charles Grigg published a study of public attitudes about "fundamental principles of democracy" in Ann Arbor, Michigan, and Tallahassee, Florida.[22] They looked at the extent to which a consensus existed on both the abstract principles of democracy and on the application of the norms. They found substantial evidence of consensus on the abstract principles: from 94.7 to 98.0 percent of their sample agreed that democracy is the best form of government and supported the principle of majority rule and the principle of minority rights. However, "when these broad principles are translated into more specific propositions ... consensus breaks down completely."[23] Thus, only 63 percent would allow an antireligious speech, and only 44 percent would allow a communist to speak in public.[24]

Since a consensus on the application of democratic principles did not exist in the general public, Prothro and Grigg sought to determine whether such a consensus could be found in particular elements of the public, a group that could be identified as the "carriers of the creed." They compared the beliefs of people of high and low education and high and low income. As one might expect, people of higher education and income were more likely to support democratic principles. However, even among their high-education group (twelve or more years of education) they failed to find the consensus for which they were searching. Sixty-three percent of the high-education group but only 24 percent of the low-education group would allow a communist to speak; 77 percent of the high-education group but only 47 percent of the low-education group would allow an antireligious speech. Education holds up as an important source of tolerant beliefs even when controlling for income and for the community in which the individual lives.

Prothro and Grigg conclude that support for the application of democratic principles does not reach a consensus in the American public. Moreover, "while the highly educated . . . come closest to qualifying as the carriers of the democratic creed, the data do not support our hypothesis; consensus in a meaningful sense . . . is not found even among those with high education."[25] Finally, they conclude with some reservations about the relationship between political culture and the character of a country's politics. Assuming that the country is democratic, then in light of their findings there apparently is no need for that democracy to spring out of some consensus among the public. That is, a democratic political culture, in the sense of public consensus on the application of democratic principles, does not appear necessary for the presence of democratic political practice.

The "established" view of tolerance in the American public was cemented by the appearance of a major study by Herbert McClosky in 1964.[26] In 1957–58, McClosky surveyed national samples of the public and of political leaders, the latter being the delegates and alternates to the 1956 national conventions of the Democratic and Republican parties. He found that the political elite sample was more likely than the general public sample to support "fair play, respect for legal procedures and consideration for the rights of others."[27] Although a majority of the public supports these rules of the game, support is substantially greater among the political influentials.

A different pattern emerges when looking at the two samples' support for the ideas of freedom of speech and freedom of opinion. Support for these two general principles is very high in both groups: "Both groups, in fact, respond so overwhelmingly to abstract statements about freedom that one is tempted to conclude that for these values, at least, a far-reaching consensus has been achieved."[28] However, the consensus breaks down in the application of those principles to specific cases. For example, in response to the statement that "a book that contains wrong political views cannot be a good book and does not deserve to be published," 50 percent of the public agreed, but only 18 percent of the political influentials did so.[29] McClosky also found the public to be less favorable toward the idea of political equality. Forty-eight percent of the public but only 28 percent of leaders agreed that "most people don't have enough sense to pick their own leaders wisely"; 58 percent of the public and 41 percent of the leaders agreed that "the main trouble with democracy is that most people don't really know what's best for them"; and 62 percent of the public and 38 percent of the leaders agreed that "issues and arguments are beyond the understanding of most voters."[30] Interestingly, consensus fails to materialize even among the leaders on the democratic concept of equality. McClosky hypothesizes that this is because, unlike freedom, "the egalitarian aspects of democratic theory have been less adequately thought through than other aspects, and partly in the complications connected with the concept itself."[31] McClosky's findings receive support in a later time period from the work of Milton Rokeach, who found freedom to be a more highly ranked value than equality among Americans.[32]

The importance and weight attached to McClosky's findings can be found in the following summary from his study:

> If American ideology is defined as that cluster of axioms, values and beliefs which have given form and substance to American democracy and the Constitution, the political influentials manifest by comparison with ordinary voters a more developed sense of ideology and a firmer grasp of its essentials. This is evidenced in their stronger approval of democratic ideas, their greater tolerance and regard for proper procedures and citizen rights, their superior understanding and acceptance of the "rules of the game" and their more affirmative attitudes toward the political system in general. The electorate displays a substantial measure of unity chiefly in its support of freedom in the abstract; on most other features of democratic belief and practice it is sharply divided.[33]

The Stouffer, Prothro and Grigg, and McClosky studies (along with some others) generated the "traditional view" containing the following elements:

1. Consensus on democratic principles, particularly freedom of speech for nonconformists, while present on abstractions, is absent in the American public when it comes to the application of those principles to unpopular groups.
2. Certain segments of the public (the well educated, the young, the urban) are more tolerant, are more likely to be the source of support for the application of democratic principles.
3. Community leaders/political influentials are substantially more tolerant of nonconformists than are members of the general public.
4. If the democratic nature of a political system reflects democratic attitudes in the society, it is the attitudes of the elite that have the greatest impact on the system and, in effect, are the most supportive of the principles that would maintain the influence of those not enjoying elite status.[34]

A New Picture of Tolerance

In recent years there has emerged a new picture of tolerance in the American public. This new picture has several sources, one of which is methodological. There have been challenges to measures employed to assess the level of tolerance and to the methods used for identifying the distinct character of elite and public attitudes. The second source is apparent change in the actual content of the public's beliefs; there is substantial, though not unanimous, agreement that the American public is becoming more tolerant, that it is more willing to extend civil liberties to nonconformists.

METHODOLOGICAL CRITIQUES.   One of the most significant consequences of the traditional picture of public tolerance has been the contrasting
outlines of those beliefs in the public as opposed to those held by political
leaders. Some years subsequent to the appearance of the initial studies there
emerged others arguing that there was nothing about being a political leader
per se that predisposed one to be more tolerant. Yet, in the aggregate, political leaders indeed articulated greater tolerance than did the public. In the
public, greater tolerance was found among people living outside of the South,
with higher education, greater exposure to the mass media, and higher status
occupations. However, these variables associated with tolerance in the public
are precisely the variables that distinguish leaders from the public: leaders
tend to be better educated, come from urban areas, and are exposed to more
mass media. Thus, the question was confronted: Is there anything about political leaders, over and above their individual characteristics, that leads to
greater levels of tolerance?

Robert Jackman, based on the above background, investigated the proposition that the elites, "through their participation in the political process, . . .
support democratic principles such as minority rights even when the majority
of the polity may not."[35] He cites interpretations of the McClosky and Stouffer studies that "within categories of education, elite groups still appeared to
be more tolerant than the mass public."[36] This distinction was said to be due
to a "resocialization" effect consequent to the entry of the individual into the
elite stratum: people become more tolerant upon becoming part of the elite.
Jackman reanalyzed the Stouffer data and found that,

> *after introducing controls which make the samples more comparable (that
> is, controls for region, sex, and — for the mass sample only — city size), we
> see that there is no substantial difference between the tolerance scores of the
> two samples within educational categories . . . As a result, theories that
> attempt to account for the differential rates of support for minority rights
> among elites and the mass public by invoking the notion that elites undergo
> some unique resocialization process are basically superfluous.*[37]

Although Jackman subsequently was criticized himself on methodological
grounds,[38] Nunn et al. examined the same question in a 1973 replication of
the Stouffer study. After controlling for a series of variables related to tolerance in the public, they compared the elites and the public and found that
"the difference was reduced to nonsignificance."[39] Thus, one important
change in the picture of the public's tolerance is a challenge to the position
that there is something about being elite per se, perhaps as the result of
socialization into such status, that makes the elite more tolerant. Instead,
if the elite are more tolerant it is because they possess the attributes
of those people in the public that are the most tolerant, and not because of
their elite position.

A second methodological challenge to the proposition that elites are more
tolerant than the public is based in objections to the belief *objects.* That is,
several studies argue that the reason the elites or leaders appear more tolerant is because the earlier studies included as belief objects those groups that
would be particularly objectionable to those in the public generally, or at

least to those in the public not sharing demographic characteristics of the elite. The early studies of tolerance, particularly that of Stouffer, focused on the public's tolerance for such groups as socialists, communists, and atheists. It may be that the elite appear more tolerant because they are more tolerant of *these* groups, rather than because they are more tolerant per se. Perhaps there are groups that are less acceptable to the elites, and to which they would be unwilling to extend fundamental principles of democracy. Perhaps the public appears intolerant because the objects of intolerance are left-wing groups; the public might be more tolerant of right-wing groups, and the elite less tolerant. Thus, several studies have appeared that attempt to assess tolerance, controlling for the individual's attitudes about the particular group involved.

David Lawrence examined the "issue-relatedness" of tolerance using 1971 data.[40] That is, he looked at whether people's tolerance of political acts depended on their attitudes about the issues toward which they were directed. He placed his work within the context of six issues and found that

> in the population as a whole there is considerable *issue-relatedness* of tolerance. Large consensual majorities of those favoring the goals of demonstrators or petitioners will allow the acts for all six issues. As issue orientation becomes increasingly negative, however, the population becomes increasingly intolerant.[41]

This issue-relatedness holds even when controlling for education. That is, "while the educated are regularly more tolerant, their tolerance is not less issue-related."[42] Lawrence also looked at the extent to which people applied general norms of tolerance to specific instances, particularly in those cases where a person has a negative issue-orientation. In these cases, "the overall pattern is clearly one of permissive general norms dominating intolerant issue-orientations."[43] Indeed, "inconsistency is more likely to lead to tolerance than to intolerance."[44]

John Sullivan agrees with the direction of Lawrence's argument, namely that tolerance is likely to be issue- or group-related.[45] He argues that "one is tolerant to the extent he is prepared to extend freedoms to those whose ideas he rejects."[46] The problem, according to Sullivan, is that researchers have defined for the public the groups employed as objects of the tolerant beliefs, usually of the "radical left bent." The trouble with this approach is that one might be tolerant of the provided groups but intolerant of other groups, namely those of a right-wing orientation. "What is needed, therefore, is a measurement procedure which allows respondents themselves to specify the groups they most strongly oppose."[47] Thus, Sullivan provided respondents with an entire range of groups, from the far left to the far right, and asked them to identify the groups they *least* liked. Respondents then were asked to indicate their willingness to allow those least-liked groups to engage in certain political activities, such as making speeches, holding public rallies, or teaching in the public schools. To a different sample, he also presented the same questions as those employed in the Stouffer study.

Sullivan found that the items employing the respondent-defined groups "generate[d] more intolerant responses than the Stouffer items . . . no doubt because the content-controlled items allowed respondents to select from a much wider range of groups."[48] Thus, Sullivan argues, the public has not become more tolerant. Rather, the targets of intolerance have multiplied, so that even though the public is more tolerant of groups of the left (communists and socialists), it remains intolerant to other groups that have replaced left-wing groups as objects of dislike. Sullivan also shows that there are educational differences in the choice of the least-liked group. In particular, the lesser educated are more likely to pick left groups while the better educated are more likely to pick right groups. Thus, it should be no surprise that studies that focus on left groups show the lesser-educated members of the public to be less tolerant.

These studies have attacked the question of tolerance in the public from a variety of methodological approaches. The net result is to generate a different picture of tolerance in the public, although the picture remains blurred. Another group of studies urges that the public is more tolerant than previously pictured. It is to these that we now turn.

CHANGES IN THE LEVEL OF TOLERANCE. Several studies suggest that the American public now is more tolerant of nonconformists than it was during the period of the Stouffer and McClosky studies. This greater tolerance usually is documented by comparing 1970s responses to those obtained in the 1950s, such as the willingness to allow socialists or communists the right to make public speeches. Unfortunately, there is very little panel data on political tolerance, so it is difficult to trace the stability of individual levels of tolerance. There are studies at widely separated points in time (fifteen to twenty years apart) based in independently drawn samples. However, these provide only the changes in the aggregate distributions of tolerance in the public or in subpublics and may underestimate the nature and amount of individual change (see Chapter 2). Moreover, they make it difficult to identify the pattern of change during the elapsed time period. That is, a study taken twenty years after Stouffer may show an increase of 20 percent in the proportion of the public that can be identified as "more tolerant," but it cannot show when that increase took place. It may have occurred abruptly at any particular point in time during the twenty years (e.g., at either year one or year nineteen); it may have been a uniform increase appearing gradually across the entire time period; or the level of tolerance at the time of the second study actually may be lower than during some other point in the interim. With these caveats in mind, we turn to a brief review of changing patterns of tolerance.

Nunn, Crockett, and Williams have recently published a major replication of Stouffer's original work based in a 1973 national survey of the American public and of community leaders.[49] They report a variety of findings suggesting increases in tolerance among both the public and community leaders. Some of their findings are summarized in Table 8–1.

TABLE 8–1   Changes in Public and Community Leaders' Tolerance of Nonconformists, 1954–1973

		Public		Leaders	
		1954	1973	1954	1973
Is it more important to find out all the communists, even if some innocent people should be hurt or to protect the rights of innocent people, even if some communists are not found out?	Find Out Communists	58%	23%	42%	11%
	Protect Innocent	32	70	52	87
If a person wanted to make a speech in your community favoring government ownership of all the railroads and big industries, should he be allowed to speak?	No	31	21	14	8
	Yes	58	72	84	91
Overall Tolerance Scale	More Tolerant	31%	55%	66%	83%
	In Between	50	25	29	13
	Less Tolerant	19	16	5	4

Source: Clyde Z. Nunn, Harry J. Crockett, Jr., and J. Allen Williams, Jr., *Tolerance for Nonconformity* (San Francisco: Jossey-Bass, 1976). Adapted from Tables 4, 5, and 10. Used by permission.

Between 1954 and 1973 there were substantial increases in the American public's preference for protecting innocent people, even if it meant not pinpointing some communists — a change from 32 percent to 70 percent; a change of similar magnitude occurred for the community leaders, although they were more tolerant at both time periods. Similarly, a smaller but still significant increase occurred in the percentage of the public willing to allow someone to make speeches favoring governmental ownership of industries and railroads (from 58 percent to 72 percent). On the overall tolerance scale the percentage of the public scoring "more tolerant" nearly doubled, from 31 percent to 55 percent. The community leaders started out more tolerant than the public and likewise increased in tolerance, but at a less striking rate (inhibited, of course, by the absolute limits on increases because of the percentage already "more tolerant"). Thus, it is clear that, *at least on the questions and issues measured in the original Stouffer study,* there has been a substantial increase in the American public's willingness to tolerate nonconformity.

Table 8–2 provides some even more recent information on the public's tolerance, with data from 1972 through 1977. In general, in that five-year period there was substantial stability in the public's tolerance of communists, atheists, socialists, and homosexuals. There was some increase in tolerance for communists, with most of that occurring during 1973 and 1974, and some marginal retreat since then. While the willingness to tolerate homosexuals' books in libraries or to allow them to speak in the community increased somewhat, there was some decline in the willingness to allow a homosexual to be a college teacher. Nevertheless, unless the slight drops in tolerance evidenced in the 1977 survey (all of which could be due to sampling error) portend a new trend downward, it appears that the increase in tolerance toward these targets exhibited through 1973 continues.

When did this increase in tolerance occur? Without precise longitudinal studies replicating the initial questions it is difficult to say. However, there are some other pieces of information that may provide some help in answering the question. Jennings and Niemi conducted a panel study of high school seniors and their parents from 1965 to 1973. Several of the questions they asked dealt with opinions on civil liberties issues. Their data suggest the presence of change at both the individual and the aggregate levels.[50] On the question of whether a communist should be allowed to hold public office, 37 percent of the youth and 30 percent of the parents held opinions in 1973 that differed from those they held in 1965. This change is predominately asymmetrical. That is, only 19 percent of the youth that were tolerant in 1965 were intolerant in 1973, while 47 percent of the intolerant youth in 1965 changed to tolerant in 1973. The comparable figures for the parents are somewhat different: 29 percent of the tolerant parents changed to intolerant, and 30 percent of the intolerant changed to tolerant. Yet the overall distribution of tolerant attitudes changed in the direction of greater tolerance for both groups. Among the youth, 37 percent were tolerant in 1965 and 59 percent in 1973; among the parents, 30 percent were tolerant in 1965 and 42 percent in 1973 — a substantially greater change among the youth.[51]

TABLE 8–2 Changes in Public Tolerance of Communists, Atheists, Socialists, and Homosexuals, 1972–1977

| | Percent Tolerant In: | | | | |
Type of Nonconformist	1972	1973	1974	1976	1977
Communist					
College teacher	32%	39%	42%	41%	39%
Books in library	53	58	59	56	55
Speaker in community	52	60	58	55	55
Atheist					
College teacher	40	41	42	41	39
Books in library	61	61	60	60	59
Speaker in community	65	65	62	64	62
Socialist					
College teacher	56	58	57	—	—
Books in library	68	71	69	—	—
Speaker in community	77	77	76	—	—
Homosexual					
College teacher	—	61	62	52	49
Books in library	—	47	50	55	55
Speaker in community	—	54	55	62	62

Source: Clyde Z. Nunn, Harry J. Crockett, Jr., and J. Allen Williams, Jr., *Tolerance for Nonconformity* (San Francisco: Jossey-Bass, 1976), p. 55. Used by permission.

While somewhat limited for our purposes, the Jennings and Niemi data provide some insight into the time during which change in tolerance occurred. If the issue contained in their data is representative, then much of the increase in tolerance took place in the late 1960s and early 1970s, the same period during which so much social and political upheaval shook the system. There is, however, some indication that intolerance on other issues may have actually increased during the same period. Rita Simon reports poll results showing an increase in opposition to demonstrations against the Vietnam War in the period of 1965–1970.[52] While in 1965 only slightly more than 30 percent opposed the demonstrations, that increased to slightly more than 50 percent in 1969 and reached a high of 75 percent in 1970. This departure from the overwhelmingly positive beliefs about the exercise of free speech may be due to the increase in the actual exercise of that freedom by "nonconformists." When confronted with a perceived threat the public may withdraw its application of the general principles of tolerance. These contrasting figures return us to some of the methodological critiques of the early studies, namely that the level of tolerance is a function of the object of the tolerance, the particular group to which the public is asked to extend procedural norms. Thus, apparent increases in tolerance toward a single object (e.g., communists) may reflect a decrease in the political salience and perceived danger of the group, rather than an increase in tolerance per se, particularly when at the same time increases appear in intolerance toward new and potentially threatening objects.

There clearly are major changes in the American public's responses to questions of political tolerance in the 1970s when compared to the 1950s. However, some things are not so clear. Do these changes reflect real change in levels of tolerance? If so, are those changes permanent? If not, are they artifacts of methodological techniques, or the consequences of the changing dynamics of the political process and the participants at work in it?

Change and the Sources of Political Tolerance

What might account for the alleged changes in the American public's political tolerance? The explanations are found in the hypothesized personal sources of that tolerance. There apparently has been some change in the distribution of individual characteristics that generate tolerance or intolerance. In this section we address separately the dominant explanations of that change.

THE TARGETS OF INTOLERANCE HAVE CHANGED.   This explanation is based in the methodological critiques noted above and suggests that the absolute level of tolerance in the public has not changed. To be sure, Americans are more willing than before to allow communists, atheists, and socialists to exercise fundamental procedural rights. However, the political salience of these groups has diminished significantly since the Stouffer and McClosky studies; communists, atheists, and socialists are not considered as threatening as earlier perceived. Thus, the public becomes more tolerant of *those* groups. However, as the political environment changes and the constellation of political objects changes, new nonconformist groups may become the object of intolerance as they become threatening or at least come into the political mind's eye. Unless one is sufficiently sensitive to this possibility, that the targets of intolerance may have changed rather than the level of tolerance increasing, strict adherence to over-time comparability in questions may provide an inaccurate picture of change in tolerance.

AGE AND COHORT REPLACEMENT. In *Communism, Conformity and Civil Liberties,* Samuel Stouffer posed the question of whether tolerance is related to age, whether those classified as "more tolerant" are "likelier to be the young people or the older people?" According to Stouffer, "the answer is clear. It is the younger people."[53] Indeed, among those twenty-one to twenty-nine years of age, 47 percent were "more tolerant." Comparable figures for those in other age groups declines until for those sixty and over only eighteen percent were "more tolerant." Even more substantial differences are found in the 1973 replication reported by Nunn et al.: 76 percent of the twenty-one- to twenty-nine-year-olds are "more tolerant" while only 29 percent of those sixty and older are so classified.[54]

The resulting question, of course, is this: What accounts for the age differences in tolerance? Several alternative explanations exist, one of which is that as people grow older they become less tolerant; there is a natural conservatism that comes with aging, a rigidity of thinking and categorizing that, perhaps, coupled with physiological changes, leads to closed-mindedness. A second possibility is cohort or generational, that it is not the age of the individual per se that leads to tolerance or intolerance, but rather that age reflects the content of shared political learning when the individuals acquired their beliefs. That is, people retain the beliefs they acquire during their formative years. Age groups differ because they differed in the beliefs that were acquired. Thus, older people are less tolerant not because they are older, but because they always have been less tolerant, even when youthful. Members of the current younger generation, then, will retain their present level of tolerance (more or less) throughout their life cycle, and succeeding generations may be more *or* less tolerant, depending on the content of political learning for them. And, as they age, the overall tolerance of the public will increase as the younger cohorts replace the less tolerant older generations.

Cohort differences reflected in age differences in tolerance may be linked to the targets of tolerance employed in research. That is, age cohorts may appear to differ in tolerance because the targets of intolerance are cohort specific. People socialized at different time periods may differ in the particular groups that are the least liked but not necessarily in the absolute level of intolerance. If the research procedure includes target groups relevant only to the intolerance of a particular age cohort, that cohort will appear less tolerant. Older people may be less tolerant of communists than are young people because of the focus on communists when they (the older people) first acquired their political attitudes. Younger people, however, may be intolerant of right-wing groups because of the politics of their generation. If the research procedures ask only for tolerance of communists it will appear that there are age differences in tolerance. Age differences *may* disappear if the measurement strategy includes as potential objects of intolerance groups relevant to each cohort.

A third possible explanation is that the different age groups differ in tolerance because they also differ in the extent to which they possess some other characteristic that leads to tolerance. Again, it would not be age that affects tolerance, but rather another attribute, differences in which happen to correspond to age differences. One strong candidate for this latter pattern is education. People with more years of formal schooling are more likely to express tolerance toward the nonconformists measured in the Stouffer study. Due to increasing educational opportunity in recent years, younger people are more likely to have the higher levels of education associated with tolerance. Thus, the substantial age differences in tolerance that contribute to the overall increase in tolerance may be a consequence of changes in educational levels, rather than a consequence of age differences (either generational or life-cycle).

Recent investigations shed light on the alternative explanations of the age/tolerance relationship. These studies reject the aging or life-cycle explanation. Rather, they point to an overall increase in tolerance resulting from interaction among the following: cohort or generational differences; increased levels of education among the younger cohorts; and increases in tolerance in all age and educational categories (what is known as a "period" effect). A study by James A. Davis has examined each of those patterns,[55] identifying the average proportion of "more tolerant" responses on six questions for four age cohorts, in three educational categories, for 1954 and 1972 – 1973. Since Davis did not have access to a twenty-year panel study of the same respondents, he employed cohort analysis. That is, for example, he compared a sample of twenty- to twenty-nine-year-olds in 1954 with a sample of forty- to forty-nine-year-olds twenty years later. Thus, he has a sample of the same cohort, but not the same people, at two points in time. Davis summarizes the findings:

> In each year and educational level, the older cohorts are less tolerant . . . within cohort and year, the better educated are more tolerant. Finally, . . . each cohort and educational group was more tolerant 18.5 years later.[56]

Thus, the aging explanation is rejected. The impact of generational or cohort factors is accepted, as is the impact of educational factors. That is, the general level of tolerance in the American public has increased because more tolerant generations have entered the public, replacing less tolerant generations, and because the overall level of education in the public has increased. At the same time, there is an increase in tolerance over and above the impact of generation and education. What might account for this additional increase in tolerance? One explanation, of course, is that the objects of intolerance have changed, that asking Stouffer's questions again twenty years later ignores the possibility that other objects of intolerance have replaced those important in the early 1950s. A second possible explanation is that there have been some other changes in society that have altered the character of other possible sources of intolerance. One of the most important of those other changes deals with the potential psychological bases of tolerance and intolerance. It is to this possibility that we now turn.

PERSONALITY AND POLITICAL TOLERANCE. Several studies link individual personality characteristics to levels of political tolerance. Indeed, as one author has noted, "tolerance is a dimension of political learning that is particularly likely to be mediated by personality needs."[57] Thus, while political tolerance can be directly learned, as is the case with many political orientations, it also can be an outgrowth of the individual's personality needs, in the way those needs structure learning. We noted in Chapter 2 how political opinions can serve "functions" for one's personality needs. That is, personalities have certain requirements or needs that must be satisfied, such as the need for resolving internal conflicts or for resolving low levels of self-esteem. It has been argued that appropriate political attitudes can help meet those needs. Thus, attitudes about nonconformists or other groups in society may grow out of the personality's drive to satisfy the needs or at least to reach some adjustment between the personality and the environment.

In a recent work, Paul Sniderman has examined the relationship between self-esteem and political tolerance.[58] In particular, he focused on the degree to which low levels of self-esteem lead to political intolerance. His data base was several samples of the public and political leaders conducted in the mid-1950s. Sniderman found that "high self-esteem promotes a tolerant outlook; low self-esteem inhibits it."[59] This relationship prevails both in the leaders and in the general public. People with low self-esteem face certain "impediments to social learning";[60] moreover,

> insofar as low self-esteem inclines an individual to feel insecure and in some danger, it strengthens his desire to strike out against others. Because his sense of vulnerability is diffuse, he is overready to mistrust others and to believe they pose a danger to the community, perhaps only because their views are unconventional or their appearance unfamiliar.[61]

Thus, there is a translation between the individual's personality characteristics (in this case, self-esteem) and that person's willingness to tolerate people with different political and social views.

Political tolerance also has been connected to personality needs through the structure of the need hierarchy developed by Abraham Maslow.[62] Fundamentally, this approach argues that all people share a hierarchy of needs, with some needs more basic than others. The individual will concentrate on the basic needs and until they are satisfied will not move on to the higher-level needs. The lower-level needs are physiological and safety needs. Higher-level needs include the desire for self-esteem and a sense of belonging. The highest needs relate to intellectual and aesthetic concerns and are labeled self-actualization. How is this related to political tolerance? Inglehart, for example, suggests that freedom of speech is one of those values most important for people at the highest personality levels, the levels of self-esteem and self-actualization.[63] Thus, people who can be placed at those levels should be more tolerant of nonconformity. John Sullivan has examined this relationship in a sample of the Twin Cities (Minneapolis/St. Paul) public.[64] His results are shown in Figure 8–1. That figure clearly shows a steep rise in the level of political tolerance as one progresses up the Maslow need hierarchy. Few people at the physical- and security-needs levels are classified as "more tolerant," while 50 percent of those at the self-actualization level are more tolerant. The major breaking point is between levels two (security needs) and three (affiliation needs).[65]

How can these views of the relationship between personality and tolerance explain recent *increases* in that tolerance? The most obvious answer would be that the distribution of personality types in the United States has changed, either in the form of fewer people with low levels of self-esteem or more people at the higher levels of the Maslow need hierarchy. These changes in personality distributions could come about either from changes in individual personalities (i.e., people changing their personality structures) or from replacement (people with tolerance-producing personalities entering the public, replacing people with intolerance-producing personalities). Inglehart suggests that there indeed has been an increase in the percentage of the population at the higher levels of the Maslow need hierarchy, due to relative economic and physical security in recent years.[66] This aggregate increase in higher-level personalities would result in an aggregate increase in the level of political tolerance. Unfortunately, no information is available that details whether individuals who have changed in their personality structures also have changed in their tolerance for nonconformity.

FIGURE 8–1   Tolerance and Self-Actualization

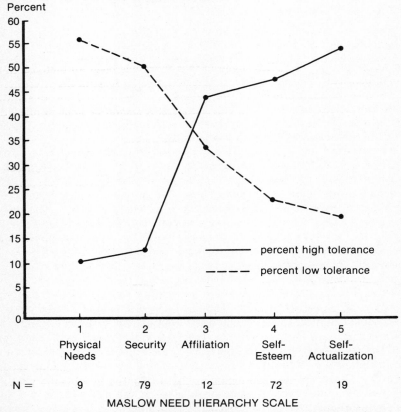

Source: John L. Sullivan, "The Development of Political Tolerance: The Impact of Social Class, Personality and Cognition" (paper prepared for the International Conference on Political Socialization and Political Education in Tutzing, West Germany, 1977), p. 43. Used by permission.

Changes in political tolerance, although not uniformly seen in the literature, have been linked to generational differences, changes in education, and changes in the distribution of personality characteristics. These changes have been traced to environmental forces (particularly as they impact changes in personality distributions) and to changes in individual characteristics, as in increasing levels of education. Oddly, there is little analysis that attributes the change to changes in leadership behavior. We say "oddly" for two reasons. First, the earlier literature emphasized the role of political leadership as the "repositories of the democratic creed" and one would expect some speculation as to their role as educators of the general public. Second, many other changes in the public's attributes have been linked to altered leadership behavior, and it is strange that tolerance should be divorced causally from those same forces. If leadership were to be the source of that change, how would it occur? One might argue that the increased clarity in the leaderships' cues to the public evidenced in other opinion characteristics also took place on tolerance. In other words, the leaders may have been able to communicate tolerant attitudes more effectively than in previous years. Or, if the change in tolerance is a methodological artifact (function of changes in the targets of tolerance), the new targets of intolerance may have been defined for the public by the political leaders.

CONCLUSION

The weight of recent studies suggests that there has been an increase in the level of political tolerance in the American public, at least in the tolerance for those nonconformists who were the targets of intolerance in the 1950s (communists, atheists, and the like). Nevertheless, it should be kept in mind that there are those scholars who argue that the apparent changes in tolerance are merely a facade produced by the methods employed in the studies.

The early findings on democratic tolerance in the public were widely employed to justify a particular form of democracy, "democratic elitism."[67] Democratic elitism viewed the public as less than satisfactorily prepared for participation in a democratic system and, in some cases, as a threat to that democracy. Similarly, it was the elite that best approximated the normative demands for democratic citizenship; indeed, the elite acted to preserve democracy for the public even though the public did not exhibit wholesale support for it themselves. The more recent analyses of public tolerance provide the basis for challenge to this particular aspect of democratic elitism. That challenge comes both from the methodological critiques and from the estimates of real change. The methodological critiques, of course, deny any real difference in the level of tolerance of elites and publics. The apparent differences were the function of (1) inadequate controls for the demographic sources of tolerance and their presence in the public and the leader samples; and (2) a failure to investigate the possibility that the elite simply were intolerant of different groups than were the public. The estimates of real change, of course, suggest that public tolerance now approximates that evidenced by the elite in previous years. If so, then, whatever rationale the prior studies provided for democratic elitism must disappear. The changes have made the public more democratic, in this view, and therefore better prepared for active participation in a democratic process.

NOTES

1. Jarol B. Manheim, *The Politics Within* (Englewood Cliffs, N.J.: Prentice-Hall, 1975), p. 8.
2. Donald J. Devine, *The Political Culture of the United States* (Boston: Little, Brown & Co., 1972), p. 15.
3. Gabriel Almond and Sidney Verba, *The Civic Culture* (Princeton, N.J.: Princeton University Press, 1963), pp. 14–15.
4. Walter A. Rosenbaum, *Political Culture* (New York: Praeger, 1975), pp. 6–7.
5. See Almond and Verba, *The Civic Culture,* pp. 473–505.
6. Devine, *The Political Culture of the United States,* pp. 16–17.
7. David G. Lawrence, "Procedural Norms and Tolerance: A Reassessment," *American Political Science Review* 70 (March 1976), p. 80.
8. Herbert McClosky, "Consensus and Ideology in American Politics," *American Political Science Review* 58 (June 1964), p. 362.
9. Robert A. Dahl, *Who Governs? Democracy and Power in an American City* (New Haven, Conn.: Yale University Press, 1961), p. 314.
10. Ibid., p. 311.
11. Rita James Simon, *Public Opinion in America: 1936–1970* (Chicago: Markham, 1974), p. 105.
12. Ibid., p. 106.
13. Theodore W. Adorno et al., *The Authoritarian Personality* (New York: Harper & Row, 1950).
14. Simon, *Public Opinion in America,* p. 109.
15. Samuel A. Stouffer, *Communism, Conformity and Civil Liberties* (New York: John Wiley & Sons, 1966).
16. Ibid., Chapter 2, passim.
17. Ibid., p. 51.
18. Ibid., p. 89.
19. Ibid., p. 93.
20. Ibid., pp. 129–30.
21. Ibid., p. 130.
22. James W. Prothro and Charles M. Grigg, "Fundamental Principles of Democracy: Bases of Agreement and Disagreement," *Journal of Politics* 22 (May 1960), pp. 276–94.
23. Ibid., p. 286.
24. Ibid., p. 285.
25. Ibid., p. 288.
26. McClosky, "Consensus and Ideology in American Politics."
27. Ibid., p. 364.
28. Ibid., p. 365.
29. Ibid., p. 367.
30. Ibid., p. 369.
31. Ibid., p. 368.
32. Milton Rokeach, *The Nature of Human Values* (New York: Free Press, 1973), passim.
33. McClosky, "Consensus and Ideology in American Politics," p. 373.
34. Thomas R. Dye and L. Harmon Zeigler, *The Irony of Democracy,* 2nd ed. (Belmont, Calif.: Duxbury Press, 1972), p. 4.
35. Robert Jackman, "Political Elites, Mass Publics, and Support for Democratic Principles," *Journal of Politics* 34 (August, 1972), p. 753.
36. Ibid., p. 756.
37. Ibid., p. 766.

38. David R. Johnson, Louis St. Peter, and J. Allen Williams, Jr., "Comments on Jackman's 'Political Elites, Mass Publics, and Support for Democratic Principles,'" *Journal of Politics* 39 (February, 1977), pp. 176–84.
39. Clyde Z. Nunn, Harry J. Crockett, Jr., and J. Allen Williams, Jr., *Tolerance for Nonconformity* (San Francisco: Jossey-Bass, 1976), p. 152.
40. Lawrence, "Procedural Norms and Tolerance."
41. Ibid., p. 89.
42. Ibid., p. 90.
43. Ibid., p. 96.
44. Ibid., p. 96.
45. John L. Sullivan, "The Development of Political Tolerance: The Impact of Social Class, Personality and Cognition" (Paper prepared for the International Conference on Political Socialization and Political Education in Tutzing, West Germany, October 10–14, 1977). See also John L. Sullivan, James Piereson, and George E. Marcus, "An Alternative Conceptualization of Tolerance: Illusory Increases 1950s–1970s," *American Political Science Review* 73 (September 1979), pp. 781–94; and James E. Piereson, John Sullivan, and George Marcus, "Political Tolerance: An Overview and Some New Findings," in *The Electorate Reconsidered*, John C. Pierce and John L. Sullivan, eds. (Beverly Hills: Sage Publications, 1980).
46. Sullivan, "The Development of Political Tolerance," p. 20.
47. Ibid.
48. Ibid., p. 23.
49. Nunn, Crockett, and Williams, *Tolerance for Nonconformity*.
50. M. Kent Jennings and Richard G. Niemi, "The Persistence of Political Orientations: An Overtime Analysis of Two Generations," *British Journal of Political Science* 8 (July 1978), p. 353.
51. The parental patterns may seem incongruent in that the overall distribution changed, but the percentage shifts from tolerant to intolerant and vice versa were equal. This pattern occurred because of the greater numbers in the intolerant category in 1965; thus, 30 percent of the 1965 intolerant group is a greater percentage of the total parental group than is 30 percent of the tolerant group.
52. Simon, *Public Opinion in America*, p. 117.
53. Stouffer, *Communism, Conformity and Civil Liberties*, p. 89.
54. Nunn, Crockett, and Williams, *Tolerance for Nonconformity*, p. 78.
55. James A. Davis, "Communism, Conformity, Cohorts, and Categories: American Tolerance in 1954 and 1972–73," *American Journal of Sociology* 81 (November 1975), p. 507.
56. Ibid.
57. Jeanne N. Knutson, "Prepolitical Ideologies: The Basis of Political Learning," in *The Politics of Future Citizens*, Richard G. Niemi, ed. (San Francisco: Jossey-Bass, 1974), p. 13.
58. Paul M. Sniderman, *Personality and Democratic Politics* (Berkeley: University of California Press, 1975).
59. Ibid., p. 197.
60. Ibid., p. 187.
61. Ibid., p. 189.
62. See the discussion in Chapter 2 of this book.
63. Ronald Inglehart, *The Silent Revolution* (Princeton, N.J.: Princeton University Press, 1977), p. 42.
64. John L. Sullivan, "The Development of Political Tolerance."
65. Ibid., p. 43.
66. Inglehart, *The Silent Revolution*.
67. See the discussion in Peter Bachrach, *The Theory of Democratic Elitism* (Boston: Little, Brown & Co., 1967).

CHAPTER 9

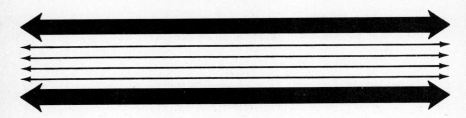

POLITICAL CULTURE AND POLITICAL TRUST

Political trust, like political tolerance, is part of a country's political culture; trust is the public's positive "evaluative or affective orientation toward the government."[1] Political cynicism, the other side of the same coin, is the critical or negative evaluation of government and politics. Yet, as simple as they may sound, political trust and political cynicism turn out to be rather complex concepts.

First, political trust is a differentiated evaluation of government and politics. Following David Easton,[2] many scholars distinguish three or more separate *objects* of trust:[3] the political *authorities* (those people in important formal positions, such as the presidency); the political *regime* (the institutions of government and the formal and informal rules by which they operate and through which access to them is gained);[4] and the political *community* (the group of people with a shared identity and set of goals, such as "Americans"). Political trust or cynicism may be directed at all of the objects or at one of the objects and not at the others. For instance, members of the public may be cynical about the political authorities but still exhibit high levels of trust toward the regime and the political community. At the same time, the public may manifest continued distrust of the political authorities but still display high levels of trust toward the regime and the political community. Continued distrust of the political authorities may become "generalized" into distrust of the regime or the political community.[5]

Second, the concepts of political trust and political cynicism are related closely to several other terms widely used to describe public evaluations of government and politics. To some scholars, political trust/political cynicism is but one of several components of political *alienation,* a somewhat broader orientation to politics and society.[6] Political alienation is said to subsume the individual's feelings of political *efficacy* — the belief that one's participation in politics has some impact on political outcomes — and his or her general "estrangement" from politics.[7]

The multiplicity of concepts describing the public's evaluations of government may differ according to which particular term is used and how that term is measured. Similarly, the identification of the sources and locations of any changes also depends considerably on the particular concept and its measurement. This chapter's contents are derived from studies of political trust, political cynicism, political efficacy, and political alienation. For the most part this chapter uses the terms of *trust, cynicism,* and *alienation* interchangeably. Nevertheless, it is important to remain sensitive to variations in use, definitions, and measurement, and to the impact those variations may have on conclusions about the amounts and sources of political trust.

Third, political trust and political cynicism also summarize more specific evaluations — feelings about in whose interest the government acts, perceptions of the efficiency of government, judgments as to the abilities of the people in government, and evaluations of the honesty in government.[8] These specific feelings may have a "generalization" effect on political trust. That is, revelations of corruption in government may cause the public to change its evaluations of other governmental attributes, such as its efficiency. On the other hand, the presence of positive views of governmental efficiency may temper the impact of perceptions of corruption on more general feelings about government.

THE IMPORTANCE OF POLITICAL TRUST

The amount of political trust exhibited by the public is important for several reasons. First, the level of political trust may be one indication of the extent to which political authorities and government are meeting the expectations of the public.[9] Increasing cynicism or alienation may reflect a decline in the responsiveness of government to the demands of the American public. These demands may concern questions of public policy as well as preferences for particular modes of ethical behavior and political style. The level of political trust thus becomes particularly important to those conceptions of a democracy that emphasize the responsiveness of government.

Second, political trust may affect the level of public support for the proposals and actions of government. If the public lacks trust, if it is cynical, it may be less likely to find acceptable and comply with the policies of government, particularly where discretionary compliance may be involved (e.g., energy conservation). A cynical public may question the motives of government in promoting a policy and may doubt the efficacy of the policy in reaching its stated objectives. Such lack of trust may cause particular problems for government in times of crisis, when a rapid mobilization of public support is needed. An alienated public may be slow to respond to the government's call. Indeed, some have speculated that the absence of trust would threaten the stability of democratic political systems, for the public would have little confidence in the processes through which leaders are chosen (e.g., elections).

Third, political cynicism may stimulate different kinds of political behavior.[10] Conceptions of "traditional" political behavior center on the electoral process, including voting, campaigning, and running for office. Traditional behavior also involves attempts to influence public officials through personal contacts or formal communication and participation in political organizations. On the other hand, political cynics — the alienated — have been said to be more likely to engage in "nontraditional behavior." Cynics may view the political process as unresponsive or meaningless and withdraw from it into apathy, or they may engage in different kinds of behavior, such as civil disobedience, political protest, or political violence. Thus, the growth of political cynicism and alienation in recent years has been linked to both increased political apathy and to increased political protest and violence.

Fourth, shifts in public trust may act as a barometer of the impact of important issues and political events. It may help answer such questions as "How important was Watergate to the political behavior of the American public?" Or, "Did the domestic conflict over civil rights and the Vietnam War have a long-term impact on the American public?" Political trust is a fundamental orientation to politics and hence is part of a country's political culture. A political culture is rooted firmly in the institutions and processes of a society. If an event is of sufficient force to alter the structure of the political culture then there can be little doubt as to its importance.

CHANGES IN THE LEVEL OF POLITICAL TRUST

There is little disagreement that in recent years the public's evaluations of governmental institutions and authorities have become increasingly critical and cynical. Relatively high levels of political trust existed during the 1950s and the early 1960s, but, beginning sometime in the middle 1960s, all indicators now suggest a long-term decline in support for the political system.

The Trustful Public

One picture of the supportive character of the American public in the 1950s and early 1960s appears in Almond and Verba's classic work, *The Civic Culture.*[11] Almond and Verba conducted interviews with national samples of the publics in the United States, Germany, Great Britain, Mexico, and Italy. They determined the percentage of the public that could be classified as "alienated or parochial" in each of those countries, distinguishing between the public's orientations to governmental outputs and governmental inputs. In 1960, only 12 percent of the American public was alienated or parochial in regard to governmental outputs, only 20 percent in terms of governmental inputs, and only 7 percent in terms of both outputs and inputs. William Gamson suggests that political trust refers specifically to public beliefs "about the outputs of the political system."[12] Thus, with only 12 percent of the American sample alienated or parochial about the outputs of the system, one has a picture of a public that is indeed trustful.

The Almond and Verba picture of the trustful American public of the early 1960s is reinforced by other work. The chapter on political socialization showed that American children in the early 1960s held benevolent or trusting attitudes about government, politics, and leaders. Similarly, a 1964 survey of the American public found that only 28 percent of the public believed that "leaders don't know what they are doing."[13] Philip Converse has shown that in 1960 over 70 percent of the American public believed that public officials do care and that people have some say about what government does.[14] To be sure, these findings are only one part of a larger picture that also contains elements of a "healthy mixture of trust and skepticism."[15] Nevertheless, in the 1960s the general thrust was an electorate satisfied with government and with the public's role in it.

The Decline in Political Trust

After 1964, public support for government began a long decline. Figure 9–1 presents the changes in the distributions for five questions widely used to measure political trust.

As Figure 9–1 shows, the percentage saying that government can be trusted to do what is right "most of the time" or "all of the time" dropped from 71 percent in 1958 to only 29 percent in 1978. In 1978, only 40 percent believed that the people in government are "smart people and know what they are doing," compared to 56 percent in 1958 and 69 percent in 1964. And in 1958, 51 percent thought that government wastes "not much or only some" of taxes; that figure is only 20 percent in 1978.

The pattern of decline in political trust shown in Figure 9–1 is mirrored in a number of other sets of information. One series of polls taken between 1966 and 1978 asked the public how much confidence they have in people running key institutions.[16] The results are shown in Table 9–1. It is clear that the public lacks confidence in all branches of government. By 1978, only 29 percent of the public had a great deal of confidence in the Supreme Court, and there is a drop to only 14 percent with great confidence in the executive branch of government. Each segment of government experienced a decline in public confidence from 1966 to 1978. Moreover, by 1978 other major institutions began to share the low level of confidence attached to the government (i.e., the press, large corporations, and organized labor). Still other institutions experienced similar declines in public confidence (i.e., medicine and higher education), although television news actually experienced some increase. The latter is ironic given the concerted attacks on the integrity of the television news operation.

In a 1972 study by William Watts and Lloyd Free, on a scale from 0 to 100, the public gave the governmental system "as a whole" ratings of only 46 for honesty, fairness, and justice, 44 for efficiency, and 41 for responsiveness.[17] The Harris poll found "rising alienation" in the American public from 1966 to 1977: in 1966, only 26 percent agreed that "people running the country don't really care what happens to you," but the 1977 figure is 60 percent; similarly, the percentage agreeing that "what you think doesn't count anymore" rose from 37 percent in 1966 to 61 percent in 1977.[18]

Information also is available on changes in the public's feelings of political efficacy.[19] Political efficacy, as we have defined it, is the individual's belief that his or her political behavior has some impact on government outcomes. Political efficacy usually is distinguished from political trust, although, as we have noted, both have been considered components of political alienation. As shown in Table 9–2, the changes in the indicators of the public's political

FIGURE 9–1   Indicators of Public Trust in Government: 1958–1978

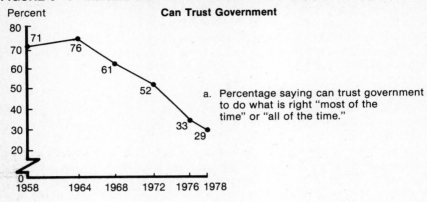

a. Percentage saying can trust government to do what is right "most of the time" or "all of the time."

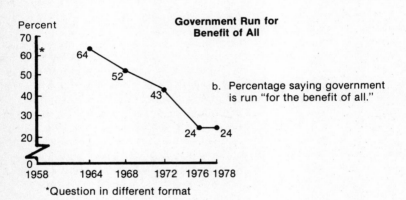

b. Percentage saying government is run "for the benefit of all."

*Question in different format

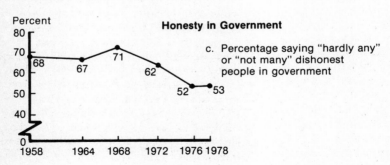

c. Percentage saying "hardly any" or "not many" dishonest people in government

FIGURE 9–1   Continued

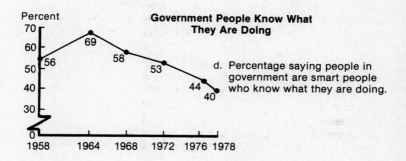

Government People Know What They Are Doing

d. Percentage saying people in government are smart people who know what they are doing.

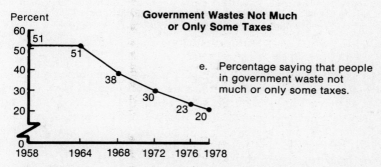

Government Wastes Not Much or Only Some Taxes

e. Percentage saying that people in government waste not much or only some taxes.

Source: Center for Political Studies 1958, 1964, 1968, 1972, 1976, and 1978 Election Studies.

TABLE 9–1   Percentage with Great Deal of Confidence in People Running Key American Institutions: 1966–1978[a]

Institution	1978	1973	1972	1966	Change
Medicine	42%	57%	48%	72%	−30
Higher Education	41	44	33	61	−20
Television News	35	41	17	25	+10
Organized Religion	34	36	30	41	− 7
Press	23	30	18	29	− 6
Major Companies	22	29	27	55	−33
Organized Labor	15	20	27	22	− 7
Military	29	40	35	62	−33
U.S. Supreme Court	29	33	28	51	−22
U.S. Senate	10	30	21	42	−32
U.S. House of Representatives	10	29	21	42	−32
Executive Branch of Government	14	19	27	41	−27

[a]The entry in each cell is the percentage of the public having a "great deal of confidence" in the people running each of the key institutions.
Source: Harris poll data, 1966, 1972, 1973, adapted from Subcommittee on Intergovernmental Relations of the Committee on Government Operations of the U.S. Senate, *Confidence and Concern: Citizens View American Government* (Washington, D.C.: U.S. Government Printing Office, 1973), p. 33. 1978 data reproduced by permission of the publisher, F. E. Peacock Publishers, Inc., Itasca, Illinois, from David B. Hill and Norman R. Luttbeg, *Trends in American Electoral Behavior*, 1980 copyright, p. 122.

efficacy parallel those of political trust. The percentage of the public believing public officials care "what people like me think" dropped from 71 percent in 1960 to 44 percent in 1978; the percentage believing that "people like me have some say in what government does" dropped from 71 percent in 1960 to 41 percent in 1974 and rose again to 53 percent in 1978; and the percentage believing that politics and government is not "too complicated to understand" dropped from 40 percent in 1960 to 26 percent in 1978.

TABLE 9–2   Political Efficacy in the American Public: 1960–1978

	1960	1964	1968	1972	1974	1976	1978
Public officials care what people like me think	71%	61%	56%	49%	46%	44%	44%
People like me have some say in what government does	71	69	59	59	41	56	53
Politics and government not too complicated to understand	40	31	29	26	27	27	26

Source: Center for Political Studies. American National Election Study.

The studies cited above are directed at the public's evaluations of government in general, the federal government, or the "government in Washington, D.C." There is some evidence that the decline in trust in government is focused on the federal government, or at least that it is the target of the greatest cynicism. A 1978 poll of the American public showed that in response to the question, "Which level of government do you think wastes the biggest part of its budget — the federal government, the state government, or local governments?," 62 percent said the federal government, while only 12 percent pointed at the state government, and just 5 percent named local governments.[20] Yet tax-limitation initiatives at the state level may signal a generalization of dissatisfaction and distrust from its original object, the federal government, to all levels of government.

In summary, there is little doubt that government, especially the federal government, is the object of considerable distrust and cynicism on the part of the contemporary American public. Similarly, there is little question that the present state of distrust is the consequence of a rapid decline during the past decade. The agreement on the presence of the decline does not extend to reasons given for it. It is to the alternative explanations that we now turn.

EXPLANATIONS OF THE DECLINE IN POLITICAL TRUST

As with most changes in American public opinion, explanations of the decline in political trust range from far-reaching global conceptualizations to methodological ones. This section reviews the major explanations of the growth in cynicism.

The New Politics Environment

The major changes in political trust occurred during the same period that witnessed the rise of the "new politics." It is said that the new politics emphasized different kinds of issues, issues that cut across traditional patterns of political (e.g., partisan) allegiances in American politics. These issues concerned social and political priorities (race, sexual equality, war, the environment), matters of life-style (the development of a "counterculture"), and the relative emphasis to be given to social control and social change and the methods to promote them.[21] It was widely speculated in the media that the proponents of new politics issue positions comprised a segment of the public particularly alienated from politics and government; the social-protest movements that employed mass demonstrations, civil disobedience, and in some cases political violence were thought to be comprised of these alienated new politics partisans. Thus, one might expect levels of political trust to be associated with positions on the new politics issues, and that those in support of the new politics positions or those particularly threatened by its demands might become more alienated from the system.

Miller and Levitin have classified members of the American public into three groups: the New Liberals, the Center, and the Silent Minority.[22] The new liberals and the silent minority comprise the new politics groups, those consistently in support of or in opposition to the new politics issues. Miller and Levitin compared the system-support scores of those three groups in 1972 and in 1976.[23]

The new politics groups were compared on four dimensions: political cynicism (trust in government as reflected in the items in Figure 9–1); political responsiveness (perceptions of how much various institutions, including government, pay attention to the public); internal efficacy (how much the individual thinks he or she understands or influences what government does); and external efficacy (how much public officials, Congress, and political parties are interested in people's opinions). The New Liberals were somewhat "less trusting than the Silent Minority, but on this scale and on the other familiar scales of support for the political system differences among the three New Politics groups were negligible."[24] Thus, Miller and Levitin conclude that the new politics divisions are unrelated to the decline in political trust in the American public. As they note,

> these results correct conclusions that the protest and dissent of the 1960s reflected enduring alienation from the political system, and that such alienation was especially characteristic of those who supported the new politics. ... Alienation from the political system, whatever the reasons and consequences, is simply not associated with response to the new politics.[25]

Clearly, the Miller and Levitin conclusions serve to minimize any *direct* contribution of the new politics to the decline in political trust.

Yet the impact of the new politics may have been somewhat more complex than would be reflected in simple aggregate variations among groups that differ in their positions on the relevant issues. That is, the forces that led to the rise of the new politics may have generated issues or politics that cause a *general* decline or alienation rather than among specific policy subgroups. Such an explanation might be found within the framework of the movement to postindustrial politics. It will be recalled that some scholars contend that relative prosperity and peace in the post-World War II period created an environment in which large groups of young people acquired values different from those of preceding generations. These new values, ones of political freedom and equality and of aesthetics, have been labeled postmaterialist.[26] Greater numbers of people with postmaterialist values may have placed new demands on government resulting in conflict over such issues as civil rights and the Vietnam War effort. These issues, it is said, "reflect a shift in public expectations of government and an inadequate effort of governments to adjust to new demands," which in turn might lead to a decline in trust and confidence in government across the *entire* public.[27]

Thus, according to Inglehart, the *immediate* cause of the decline in political trust is apparent:

> Reasons for this decline are not hard to find. The most obvious ones include: the civil rights struggles of the 1960s during which the government seemed unresponsive to some because it moved too swiftly in bringing about racial integration and lost the confidence of others because it moved too slowly; the deceptions and disillusionment of the Vietnam era almost certainly added to this process, when again the government frustrated some because it failed to win, and others because it failed to withdraw; and, finally the scandals that brought the resignations of Vice President Agnew and President Nixon.[28]

However, the *long-term* sources of this decline may be found in far-reaching environmental changes that created new values and from those new values

stimulated new kinds of issues and political forces with which government
had to contend, and in the eyes of many, did so unsuccessfully.

Political Issues and Political Leadership

The issues of the later 1960s and early 1970s had a special intensity and
divisiveness about them. One scholar argues that the decline in political trust
can be accounted for by the particular nature of the response of the government and the political parties to those issues.[29] This explanation differs
slightly from the new politics explanations in two regards. First, it does not
explicitly trace the importance of the issues to fundamental value changes in
society stemming from broad-scale alterations in the political and economic
climate. Second, it claims that the issue positions of the public are the source
of political cynicism: "by 1970, Americans to a considerable degree had with-
drawn some of their trust from the government because they had become
widely divided on a variety of issues. . . ."[30] Miller argues that the rejection of
the system comes from those members of the public on the extremes of the
issues. Political trust is lower among those on the left and the right because
they perceive the policies of the government and of the opposition party to be
in the middle. This perception of issue distance is the source of the development of two groups of distrustful Americans, the "cynics of the left" and the
"cynics of the right." It is the absence of responsiveness to the extreme positions that produces the cynicism, a theme also found in Richard Dawson's
comment that "it is not strange that concern with political responsiveness
should be significant. In a time of considerable conflict over new issues and
the absence of stable issue and group coalitions it is not strange that government and political leaders find it difficult to respond."[32]

Miller's issue-responsiveness thesis has been subjected to criticism from
several locations. Jack Citrin argues that Miller mistakenly confuses dissatisfaction with the policies of the incumbent and dissatisfaction with government generally.[33] Moreover, Miller is said to overlook parts of his own
data that "reveal several deviations from the reported tendency of both the
'leftist' and 'rightist' camps to contain relatively more political cynics than
the group at the center of the political spectrum."[34]

Nie, Verba, and Petrocik also examine Miller's argument. They argue that
the "cynics of the left" and "cynics of the right" pattern is time-bound. That
is, Miller's result is based in 1970 data, "but that apparently is the only year
in which that happens."[35] Nie et al. have traced the level of political cynicism
among leftists, centrists, and rightists from 1958 through 1972.[36] The authors
summarize their results as follows:

> *Between 1958 and 1964 distrust rises most among the rightists. The in-*
> *crease in distrust from 1964 to 1972, in contrast, comes from the leftists and*
> *the centrists, but especially from the former. The rightists remain the most*
> *distrustful through 1968. Between 1968 and 1972 distrust goes up for all*
> *groups, but for leftists the most and rightists the least. The result is that by*
> *1972 the left is the most distrustful (although all three groups are more*
> *distrustful in 1972 than they were in 1958).*[37]

Nie et al. instead forward a long-term explanation of the rise of political cynicism that concentrates on the impact of presidential politics.[38] The election
and incumbency of John Kennedy stimulated an increase in the public's political interest. This more-interested public had its political issue positions
"crystallized" and made more consistent by the candidacy of Barry Goldwater. These high levels of interest and attitudinal consistency were carried into
the political traumas of the late 1960s, with the consequence that "such a
populace was ripe for the disillusionment associated with Vietnam, the racial
crisis and the multitude of shocks that began in the mid-Sixties."[39]

FIGURE 9–2   Ideological Identification and Political Trust in 1976

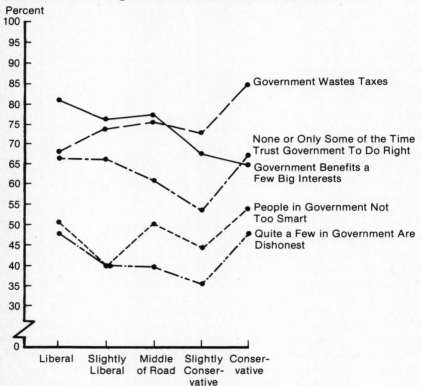

Source: Center for Political Studies. American National Election Study, 1976
[machine-readable data file].

The response to five political trust items in ideological groupings is shown
in Figure 9–2. People place themselves in the groupings (self-identification).
In 1976, at least, it is important to examine the specific indicator of trust
rather than a more general index combining responses across different questions. Liberals are more likely than any other group to say government benefits only a few big interests. On the other hand, conservatives are more
likely to distrust government because they think it wastes taxes. With some

reservations, on the other three questions the people in the middle are more trustful, and those on the extremes the least trustful. While these data are not strictly comparable to those of Miller or Nie et al., where conclusions are based on issue beliefs, they do suggest an important point. In assessing the ideological basis of distrust one must be sensitive to the interaction of the indicator of distrust and the ideological position. People at each position seem to have their own particular reason for being cynical, as well as sharing with each other some rather negative perceptions of government.

Thus, for many scholars the decline in political trust is rooted in issues of public policy. While the precise route by which issue discontent feeds cynicism varies from analysis to analysis, political leaders play a crucial role in defining the issues for the public. Political leaders also played a key part in another issue — Watergate.

The Watergate revelations and the resignation of President Nixon clearly possessed the potential for damaging political trust. After all, the president of the United States exhibited great disregard for the system's norms and legal processes, and in the eyes of many displayed contempt toward the American public. Scholars quite naturally have examined the impact of Watergate on the public's political trust and confidence.

The studies of the impact of Watergate on political trust argue against any *large-scale* and *abrupt* turn in the public's confidence in government as a result of the scandal's revelations. One analysis concluded that "evaluative attitudes toward the national government tended to be stable" during the period of summer 1972 to summer 1973; it found "no disproportionate change toward increased alienation."[40] Nie et al. go a little farther by contending that Watergate gave an added push to the public's increasing alienation. As they put it, Watergate resulted in "an acceleration — in some cases a sharp acceleration — of changes that had begun much earlier."[41] Miller et al. assert that their "data clearly indicate that the Watergate crisis had no substantial *direct* effect on trust in government."[42] Indeed, they present data (shown in Table 9–3) suggesting that attitudes about the nature of the domestic economy had a greater direct impact on feelings of political cynicism than did feelings about Watergate. As that table shows, in 1974, 42 percent of those with negative feelings about Watergate but not about the economy held distrusting attitudes, while 54 percent of those negative about the economy but not about Watergate were distrusting. These figures compare to only 34 percent of those positive toward both that were identified as distrusting. However, through the process of generalization Watergate had an *indirect* effect on cynicism:

> *Watergate obviously had a profound and direct effect on the rating of incumbents; these in turn spilled over to affect the prestige of the presidency; and, this undermining of respect fot the institution brought about a reduction in trust.*[43]

Thus, Watergate may have affected political trust in three ways. First, it may have accelerated a preexisting decline in political trust. Second, it may have had an indirect impact on political trust, operating through its impact on perceptions of the incumbent president, through the institutions of the presidency, and then to the regime in general. Third, it is possible that Watergate was seen as confirming evidence of previous perceptions held by the public, cementing attitudes of cynicism and working against the recovery of feelings of trust once the issue-oriented sources of civil rights and the Vietnam War retreated from prominence.

TABLE 9 – 3   The Impact of Public Perceptions of Watergate and the Economy on Feelings of Political Trust: 1974[a]

	Negative Toward Watergate and the Economy	Negative Toward Watergate, but Not Economy	Negative Toward Economy, but Not Watergate	Positive Toward Both
% Distrusting	66%	42%	54%	34%
% Trusting	11	34	21	40
(N)	(737)	(559)	(336)	(459)

[a]The table presents only the two end categories, omitting the middle category of trust.

Source: Arthur H. Miller, Jeffrey Brudney, and Peter Joftis, "Presidential Crises and Political Support: The Impact of Watergate on Attitudes Toward Institutions" (Paper prepared for delivery at the 1975 Midwest Political Science Association Convention, Chicago, May 1 – 3). Used by permission.

Individual Characteristics

The decline in political trust has been general across the American public. However, there has been considerable evidence that for individuals with certain characteristics that decline was more severe, reached lower absolute levels, or had an unusual shape. Four of those characteristics — age, race, education, and personality — have received special attention.

AGE.   Examinations of the decline in political trust have focused on age for several reasons. Young people historically have been less cynical than have older people, beginning in childhood with benevolent attitudes toward government and political authorities and only gradually acquiring the less positive attitudes of their parents (see Chapter 4). Yet much of the visible political activity suggesting political alienation and opposition to government policies was found among young people, both in their political behavior and in their life-style.[44] However, no consistent patterns prevail in the results of studies examining the relationship between age and political trust.

Watts and Free report only very minor differences between the eighteen- to twenty-nine-year-olds and older groups in their evaluation of the honesty, fairness, justice, and efficiency of the governmental system, and only a slightly larger difference in the evaluation of the responsiveness of the governmental system.[45] Nie et al. "considered the possibility that distrust was a function of the entrance of the more disenchanted cohorts of the late 1960s, but found them quite similar to the electorate as a whole in terms of their distrust level."[46] And Miller writes that

it should be noted that a model based upon the replacement of older, less cynical individuals in the population (who have presumably died) with more cynical, newly eligible voters does not explain the general increase in cynicism for the population.[47]

Less directly, we have noted that there is no significant relationship between political alienation and support of new politics issue positions, the latter of which is substantially more likely to appear among young people.

On the other hand, a substantial body of literature suggests an especially cynical response on the part of young people to the events and issues of the 1960s and the early 1970s. Citrin et al. report "a relatively strong negative relationship between age and political alienation."[48] Most studies, however, argue that the unique characteristic of the young was their more rapid *increase* in political cynicism, rather than greater absolute levels of distrust. Although Robert Gilmour and Robert Lamb contend that "in sheer numbers . . . the quiet alienation of the aged is a more impressive story," they also show that the youngest age group (eighteen to thirty-four years old) exhibited the greatest increase in extreme alienation between 1968 and 1972.[49]

Jennings and Niemi compared the levels of political cynicism among high school seniors and their parents in 1965 and in 1973. They found substantial changes among the young people and their parents, with both groups becoming more cynical. However, they also found that the cynicism of the young people grew much more rapidly than it did among their parents.[50] Part of the change among young people might be attributed to "political aging," increasing cynicism that has traditionally accompanied entry into adulthood. However, when compared to their parents, "the young have changed more, drawing closer to, and in two cases overtaking, parental levels. . . . In 1973 the young adults [were] consistently more cynical than were their parents in 1965."[51] In addition to life-cycle effects (becoming more cynical with aging) and period effects (increasing cynicism across the entire population in a particular political period), this also points to the possibility of generational effects — the events of a particular period having a distinct impact on a particular age cohort over and above that associated with period and life-cycle effects.

Pomper suggests that the increasing cynicism of the young is more precisely located among the college-educated members of that cohort. Between 1964 and 1972, college-educated young people increased in their political cynicism at a rate much greater than did older cohorts and their non-college-educated fellow cohort members. "Those who had not attended college . . . came to resemble the older generation, . . . [but] the experiences of the period pushed a significant group [college-educated] in the opposite direction."[52] Pomper argues that the cynicism of the young results from a combination of the fact that "young people are particularly impressionable" and the particular events of the period. "It is the character of politics at the time they reach political maturity that is critical in determining whether new voters will support or reject that politics."[53]

While the results are mixed, the general weight of the research on age and political trust suggests the following: younger people are somewhat (with the exception of the oldest citizens) more cynical than other age groups, and they appear to have changed levels of trust more rapidly than expected and more rapidly than other age groups. This pattern *may* stem from a normal increase in cynicism among the young, a special sensitivity of young people to the impact of the content of contemporary politics, and the presence of political issues of special relevance to the younger generation.

RACE.   In the early and mid-sixties, black Americans were as trustful or more trustful than were whites, even in the face of the historical patterns of racism and discrimination. The pattern of greater political trust was true for both black adults and black children. Various commentators have linked this surprisingly high level of political trust to the promises and policies of the federal government. The Civil Rights Act, the 1965 Voting Rights Act, and the Great Society programs were both symbolic and tangible evidence of an apparent commitment to the goals of racial equality.

Yet the national commitment to civil rights waned and the promises of the Great Society were slow in being fulfilled. In many cases the 1964 and 1965 rights acts wrought only marginal short-term changes in American life. Martin Luther King was assassinated. Many cities erupted in protest and riot. Law-and-order politicians surged to prominence. Attention turned to the U.S. involvement in Southeast Asia. The federal government adopted a policy of less vigorous pursuit of the goal of racial equality ("benign neglect").

After 1966, black Americans' trust in government began a period of rapid decline, and it continued at a rate much steeper than that found among whites.[4] The more rapid *rate* of decline for blacks did not continue after 1972. Between 1972 and 1976, trust among whites dropped off more than it did among blacks. However, "the higher absolute levels of black cynicism in 1972 and their continued increase in 1974 mean that blacks remain notably more cynical than whites in the 1970s."[55]

Other studies confirm the current state of greater political cynicism among blacks. Chapter 4 noted that black children apparently developed critical evaluations of political figures and government before similar attitudes were found among white children. Watts and Free report the results of a 1972 national survey showing that blacks gave lower ratings than whites to the governmental system for honesty, fairness, justice, efficiency, and responsiveness.[56] Although focusing on the more general concept of alienation, rather than political trust, Citrin et al. found that "in virtually every demographic subgroup racial differences in the level of political alienation were substantial."[57]

Thus, blacks exhibited an earlier decline in political trust and an overall lower absolute level of political trust in the mid-1970s. However, Pomper argues that "race does not predetermine political alienation; such feelings develop in response to political events."[58] Special and relevant events precipitated the earlier decline among blacks:

> *Trust in the government may have thus declined sharply among blacks after 1966 because of frustration arising out of the unfulfilled expectation of more active government involvement in the area of integration.*[59]

The events generating cynicism among whites came later, pushing them down some of the same roads traveled by black Americans. And the sources of white cynicism served only to compound and deepen the already growing alienation of blacks.

EDUCATION. The relationship of the individual's level of formal education to his or her political trust is somewhat of an anomaly. Studies of political trust and political efficacy conducted in the 1950s and 1960s found a rather strong relationship between education and attitudes toward government. That is, people with more education were more likely to feel politically efficacious and were more likely to exhibit trust in government. Education would make one better able to understand the political system and hence "objectively" more competent or efficacious.[60] And, for the period between 1952 and 1960, as the level of education rose so did political efficacy and political trust at a comparable rate.[61] Yet, during the 1960s and the 1970s, education continued to rise while the feelings of efficacy and trust began their steep decline. Although the better-educated Americans remain more trustful than Americans with less education, they also experienced a substantial growth in alienation.[62]

How can one explain the decline in efficacy and trust during the same period as the rise in education when education is supposed to make one objectively more competent? Philip Converse provides one answer.[63] He decomposes both the measure of political efficacy and the time period under observation. He believes that political efficacy has two components: the personal competence of the individual, and the responsiveness of the political system and government. The perceived competence of the individual should be most sensitive to changes in education. Converse found the personal-competence component to be "education-driven" (increasing with increases in education) and the system-responsiveness component to be responsive to political events (declining in response to politics of the late sixties). In short, then, the relationship between education and trust is not a simple one. It depends on the particular component of trust, other characteristics of the individual (e.g., age), and the content of the political arena.

PERSONALITY. In the study of public opinion there is a strong tradition linking individual personality characteristics to views about government and politics. The nature of that link has been that one's opinions serve to satisfy some need of the individual's personality. Knutson notes that "personality theorists have long noted a relationship between personal anxieties and generalized hostility," and "such generalized insecurity has a definite political dimension."[64] People who are insecure, who exhibit greater levels of personal anxieties, may be more cynical about the political world and about the nature of government in particular.

Several recent studies investigate the relationship between personal psychological characteristics and political cynicism. Sniderman has concluded that "whether a person's overall orientation to politics emphasizes trust or cynicism strongly depends on his level of self-esteem."[65] People with low self-esteem are more likely to come out high on a political-cynicism scale than are people with high self-esteem (43 percent compared to 12 percent).[66] Stanley Renshon has looked at the impact of people's feelings of personal control on their faith in government. He found that

> the political system is evaluated differently by citizens with high and low personal control. The government is evaluated as much more effective by respondents with high personal control, while citizens with external feelings of control are not only more likely to give a negative evaluation, but are also less likely than respondents with high personal control to view the government as having limited (mild) effectiveness.[67]

Moreover, "respondents with high personal control were much more likely than those with low personal control to hold favorable evaluations of government."[68]

If personality characteristics are related to alienation, then one must confront the possibility that changes in the level of alienation also are somehow rooted in the psyche. This linkage might take several forms. First, there may have been an increase in the number of people possessing those personality characteristics that lead directly to alienation. If the politically alienated are more likely to view themselves as incompetent, to lack trust in other people, or to have low self-esteem, perhaps there are now greater numbers of people with those personality characteristics and hence more politically alienated Americans. Yet, noting that the distribution of these relevant personality characteristics has remained relatively stable in recent years, Jack Citrin argues that "we cannot conclude that the recent erosion of public confidence in the political process reflects change in these psychological dispositions."[69] If present at all, the relationship between alienation and personality may be more subtle.

A second possibility is that the impact of personality on political cynicism depends on the nature of the politics at the particular time. In certain times, politics may possess little relevance for the personality needs of large portions of the public. At other times (say, periods of strife or instability), the nature of the politics may "engage" certain personality characteristics. Uncertainty or challenge to established ways may tap a *latent* cynicism or alienation, bringing to the surface feelings about government and politics that were previously unmined. That is, psychological sources of the response of political alienation may depend on the presence of the appropriate political stimulus.

A third personality-based explanation of the increase in political alienation returns us to the concept of the postindustrial society. Changes in the distribution of personal values (themselves based in changes in personality needs linked to political/economic conditions during personality formation) may lead to new demands on government and politics. Failure of government to meet these demands, or the political conflict in the process of expressing and responding to these demands, may in turn lead to increasing political cynicism.

CONCLUSION

In the face of considerable conflict over conceptualization, measurement, and explanation, there remains general agreement that Americans have become more estranged from government and politics. To be sure, it may be unclear whether that estrangement reflects a temporary reaction to the political authorities or a more fundamental rejection of basic elements in the political community. In either case, however, there is considerable speculation that the decline in political trust has implications both for individual political behavior and for the future of the political system.

Political cynicism and alienation have been traced to two rather distinct patterns of behavior: apathy or withdrawal from politics, and support for or entry into unconventional or radical patterns of political behavior. At the aggregate level, at least, there is considerable support for both hypotheses. During the same period as the recent decline in political trust there also has been a gradual decline in electoral participation and an apparent increase in the incidence of political protest and violence.[70] That the aggregate patterns moved together, of course, does not necessarily mean that those people who became less trusting are the same people who withdrew from politics or who participated in political protest. Political alienation has been linked to the urban, civil rights, and antiwar protests of the late sixties and early seventies. However, the weight of the available evidence suggests that *among the general public* political alienation contributes to political apathy but not to political protest. Alienated or cynical Americans are less likely to participate in politics. As James Wright has found, "in 39 tests of the hypothesis, covering 4 elections and 10 measures of participation, the basic relationship does not suffer a single reversal: However measured, the alienated participate less."[71] Moreover, the alienated do not appear to be "mobilized" by candidates whose appeals seem designed to draw them into the electoral arena. Thus, despite the explicit nature of their appeals, the 1964 candidacy of Goldwater and the 1968 candidacy of Wallace failed to draw into the electorate great numbers of disenchanted Americans.

Alienated and "allegiant" members of the public do differ in their approval of legal protest meetings and mass marches.[72] However, some of those differences are in an unexpected direction. For example, in 1968 the allegiant were substantially *more* likely than the alienated to approve of protest and mass marches, but by 1972 the differences between the two groups were much smaller. Thus, between 1968 and 1972 the *increases* in support for protest and marches were greater among the alienated. On the other hand, in both 1968 and 1972 the alienated were more likely to approve of civil disobedience, although less so in 1972. And, between 1968 and 1972, the alienated increased their support for disruptive protest more than did the allegiant. Moreover, although in 1968 the allegiant were more likely to approve of disruptive protest, only very slight differences existed in 1972. In summary, the relationship of political alienation to support for protest in the general public remains clouded.

At the start of this chapter we noted that some scholars believe alienation to have two components: political trust and political efficacy. Lester Milbrath and M.L. Goel have suggested that different kinds of political behavior result from different combinations of levels of trust and efficacy.[73] People who have high levels of *both* trust and efficacy seem more likely to be active and allegiant and to engage in conventional participation above and beyond simply voting. However, people who are high in political trust but low in political efficacy are more likely to engage in supportive and "ritualistic" participation, primarily voting. Radical or unconventional participation is most likely to occur among people with low levels of trust but with high levels of efficacy — they feel they can have some impact on a system in which they have little confidence. Finally, those low in both efficacy and trust — the alienated — are the most likely to withdraw from politics completely, to retreat to political apathy. Thus, political behavior appears to depend on how a person feels about the political system (trust) and about his or her ability to influence the system (efficacy). The absence of both trust and efficacy — what some call "alienation" — does not lead to striking out against the system; rather, in the presence of inefficacy, cynicism leads to apathy and withdrawal.

Turning in a different direction, a second concern is the extent to which the presence of widespread alienation threatens the stability and the persistence of a democratic political system. Can a democratic political system, one which among other things is supposed to respond to and enhance the preferences of the general public, continue long in the absence of support and trust from that public? Or, on the other hand, will the alienation lead to a deterioration of or challenges to democratic processes and traditions because the public feels estranged from the institutions and authorities produced by those processes?

It has been argued by some that there is little evidence to suggest that the American political system has disintegrated in the face of public cynicism. According to this view, in recent years the fundamental political processes have remained essentially unaltered.[74] Moreover, political alienation is not consistently related to support for *antidemocratic* behavior. To be sure, recent years have seen episodes of widespread protest and, in some cases, political violence. Yet, as noted above, support for antidemocratic behavior in the general public is not *systematically* related to political alienation. To the contrary, political alienation — or the absence of both trust and efficacy — is related to *withdrawal* from politics. In the absence of other forces, withdrawal does not represent a *direct* pressure to alter current ways of doing things, although it certainly will alter the composition of those to whom the system responds. Even so, any decline in popular involvement in politics fails to match in magnitude the decline in political trust. Many Americans continue their present levels of involvement even while expressing political cynicism. Thus, if political cynicism is to threaten democratic politics it may be by default, rather than by revolution. Democratic institutions and processes may lose their symbolic legitimacy as people's cynicism erases feelings of citizen duty to participate in electoral processes.

NOTES

1. Arthur H. Miller, "Political Issues and Trust in Government: 1964–1970," *American Political Science Review* 68 (September 1974), p. 952.
2. See David Easton, *A Systems Analysis of Political Life* (New York: John Wiley & Sons, 1965).
3. See William A. Gamson, *Power and Discontent* (Homewood, Ill.: Dorsey Press, 1968); and Donald J. Devine, *The Political Culture of the United States* (Boston: Little, Brown & Co., 1972).
4. Gamson distinguishes betwen the institutions and the regime's "public philosophy," which may or may not be congruent with the institutions. See *Power and Discontent*, p. 50.
5. Gamson, *Power and Discontent*, pp. 50–52.
6. Ada W. Finifter, "Dimensions of Political Alienation," *American Political Science Review* 64 (June 1970), pp. 389–410; and Melvin Seeman, "On the Meaning of Alienation," *American Sociological Review* 24 (December 1959), pp. 783–91.
7. See the discussions of the conceptualization of alienation in J. Milton Yinger, "Anomie, Alienation and Political Behavior," in *Handbook of Political Psychology*, Jeanne N. Knutson, ed. (San Francisco: Jossey-Bass, 1973), pp. 176–86; Jack Citrin et al., "Personal and Political Sources of Political Alienation," *British Journal of Political Science* (January 1975), p. 3; and James D. Wright, *The Dissent of the Governed* (New York: Academic Press, 1976), pp. 3–4.
8. Miller, "Political Issues and Trust in Government."
9. Wright, *The Dissent of the Governed*, p. 200.
10. David C. Schwartz, *Political Alienation and Political Behavior* (Chicago: Aldine, 1973).
11. Gabriel A. Almond and Sidney Verba, *The Civic Culture* (Princeton, N.J.: Princeton University Press, 1963).
12. Gamson, *Power and Discontent*, p. 42.
13. *Public Opinion* (March/April 1978), p. 23.
14. Philip E. Converse, "Change in the American Electorate," in *The Human Meaning of Social Change*, Angus Campbell and Philip E. Converse, eds. (New York: Russell Sage Foundation, 1972), p. 328.
15. Norman H. Nie, Sidney Verba, and John R. Petrocik, *The Changing American Voter* (Cambridge, Mass.: Harvard University Press, 1976), p. 35.
16. See sources in Table 9–1.
17. William Watts and Lloyd A. Free, *State of the Nation* (New York: Universe Books, 1973), p. 326.
18. Reported in *Public Opinion* (May/June 1978), p. 23.
19. Political efficacy questions have been a staple of Center for Political Studies National Election Studies for many years.
20. June 19–23, 1978, CBS–New York Times Poll, reported in *Changing Public Attitudes on Government and Taxes* (Washington, D.C.: Advisory Commission on Intergovernmental Relations, 1978), p. 5.
21. Warren E. Miller and Teresa E. Levitin, *Leadership and Change: The New Politics and the American Electorate* (Cambridge, Mass.: Winthrop Publishers, 1976).
22. Ibid., chap. 3.
23. Ibid., pp. 174–75.
24. Ibid., p. 175.
25. Ibid., pp. 176–77.

26. Ronald Inglehart, *The Silent Revolution* (Princeton, N.J.: Princeton University Press, 1977), p. 42.
27. Ibid., p. 107.
28. Ibid., p. 305.
29. Miller, "Political Issues and Trust in Government."
30. Ibid., p. 963.
31. Ibid., p. 962.
32. Richard E. Dawson, *Public Opinion and Political Disarray* (New York: Harper & Row, 1973), pp. 46–47.
33. Jack Citrin, "Comment: The Political Relevance of Trust in Government," *American Political Science Review* 68 (September 1979), pp. 973–88.
34. Ibid., p. 986.
35. Nie et al., *The Changing American Voter,* p. 285.
36. It should be noted that their measurement and placement of these groups differs from that employed by Miller.
37. Nie et al., *The Changing American Voter,* p. 285.
38. Ibid., pp. 283–84.
39. Ibid., p. 284.
40. Paul M. Sniderman et al., "Stability of Support for the Political System," *American Politics Quarterly* 3 (October 1975), p. 443.
41. Nie et al., *The Changing American Voter,* p. 227.
42. Arthur H. Miller, Jeffrey Brudney, and Peter Joftes, "Presidential Crises and Political Support: The Impact of Watergate on Attitudes Toward Institutions" (Paper prepared for delivery at the 1975 Midwest Political Science Association Convention, Chicago, Illinois, May 1–3), p. 15.
43. Miller et al., "Presidential Crises and Political Support," p. 38.
44. See, for example, Kenneth Keniston, *The Uncommitted: Alienated Youth in American Society* (New York: Dell, 1965).
45. Watts and Free, *State of the Nation,* p. 326.
46. Nie et al., *The Changing American Voter,* p. 280.
47. Miller, "Political Issues and Trust in Government," p. 957.
48. Citrin et al., "Personal and Political Sources," p. 18.
49. Robert S. Gilmour and Robert B. Lamb, *Political Alienation in Contemporary America* (New York: St. Martin's Press, 1975), pp. 63–65. See also David B. Hill and Norman R. Luttbeg, *Trends in American Electoral Behavior* (Itasca, Ill.: Peacock, 1980), pp. 126–30.
50. M. Kent Jennings and Richard G. Niemi, "The Persistence of Political Orientations: An Overtime Analysis of Two Generations," *British Journal of Political Science* 8 (July 1978), p. 356.
51. M. Kent Jennings and Richard G. Niemi, "Continuity and Change in Political Orientations: A Longitudinal Study of Two Generations," *American Political Science Review* 69 (December 1975), p. 1331.
52. Gerald M. Pomper, *The Voters' Choice: Varieties of American Electoral Behavior* (New York: Dodd, Mead & Co. 1975), p. 105. Wright, however, reaches a contrary conclusion in *The Dissent of the Governed,* p. 147.
53. Pomper, *The Voters' Choice,* p. 105.
54. Arthur Miller, Thad Brown, and Alden Raine, "Social Conflict and Political Estrangement" (Paper presented at the Annual Meetings of the Midwest Political Science Association, Chicago, Ill., 1973), p. 13. Wright, *The Dissent of the Governed,* pp. 176–81.
55. Miller et al., "Social Conflict," p. 8.

56. Watts and Free, *State of the Nation,* p. 327.
57. Citrin et al., "Personal and Political Sources," p. 16.
58. Pomper, *The Voters' Choice,* p. 124.
59. Miller, "Political Issues and Trust in Government," p. 958.
60. Inglehart, *The Silent Revolution,* p. 305.
61. Converse, "Change in the American Electorate."
62. Gilmour and Lamb, *Political Alienation,* p. 48.
63. Converse, "Change in the American Electorate."
64. Jeanne N. Knutson, *The Human Basis of the Polity* (New York: Aldine, 1972), p. 72.
65. Paul M. Sniderman, *Personality and Democratic Politics* (Berkeley: University of California Press, 1975), p. 191.
66. Ibid., p. 193.
67. Stanley Allen Renshon, *Psychological Needs and Political Behavior* (New York: Free Press, 1974), pp. 163–64.
68. Ibid., pp. 156–57.
69. Citrin, "Comment," p. 974.
70. For data on recent declines in presidential and congressional elections, see William H. Flanigan and Nancy H. Zingale, *Political Behavior of the American Electorate,* 4th ed. (Boston: Allyn & Bacon, 1979), p. 20. Whether the turmoil of the late sixties and early seventies represented an unusual amount of protest and violence is less clear. Flanigan and Zingale note, for example, that "recent decades are probably the least violent period in our history, at least in terms of mass participation" (p. 195).
71. Wright, *The Dissent of the Governed,* p. 227.
72. Gilmour and Lamb, *Political Alienation,* pp. 116–17.
73. Lester W. Milbrath and M.L. Goel, *Political Participation* (Chicago: Rand McNally, 1979), p. 69. See also Gamson, *Power and Discontent.*
74. "Even during the worst of times, things persisted more or less as they always had." Wright, *The Dissent of the Governed,* p. 262.

CHAPTER 10

PARTY SUPPORT

The American public's attachment to political parties has long been recognized as a key element in public opinion and political behavior. Further, strong party loyalties have been labeled a major source of stable democratic politics. But the events of recent years raise serious questions about these roles of the American political parties. Commentators see widespread malaise in the party system. Not only is the public more reluctant to identify with a party and to vote along party lines, but party organizations have suffered as well. There is much concern about the implications of such change both for individuals and for the electoral system. Many agree with E.E. Schattschneider that "the political parties created democracy . . . and democracy is unthinkable save in terms of the parties."[1]

WHAT IS PARTY SUPPORT?

Party support refers to the public's attitudes about and behavior toward political parties. When we move beyond this general definition, however, party support takes on several forms.

The best-known aspect of party support is *party identification*. The importance credited to party identification stems largely from the development of the concept in *The American Voter* in 1960.[2] To Campbell et al. the essence of party support is neither formal party membership nor voting behavior. Rather, the connection between individual and party is "a psychological identification, which can persist without legal recognition or evidence of formal membership and even without a consistent record of party support."[3] People's identifications are classified as strong or weak Republican or Democrat, or as Independent or leaning Independent, depending upon their responses to the following set of questions:

*"Generally speaking, do you think of yourself as a Republican, a Democrat,
an Independent, or what?" Those who classified themselves as Republicans
or Democrats were also asked, "Would you call yourself a strong (Republican, Democrat) or a not very strong (Republican or Democrat)?" Those who
classified themselves as Independents were asked this additional question:
"Do you think of yourself as closer to the Republican or Democratic Party?"*[4]

According to Campbell et al., party identification is among the most important political orientations of the American public. They note that most individuals describe themselves as party identifiers (around 75 percent during
the 1950s), and that party divisions establish the cleavages that define election battles.[5] Further, party identification is normally adopted early in life
and, "once established, is an attachment which is not easily changed."[6] Not
only are party attachments relatively stable for individuals, but there is also
a great deal of intergenerational continuity. Children quite frequently adopt
the party affiliation of their parents.[7]

Party identification is a popular indicator of party support because it
"can profitably be treated as having two highly distinct components."[8]
Converse notes that the measure tells us the *direction* of party choice —
whether a person is a Democrat, an Independent, or a Republican — and the
strength of attachment to either party — whether one is a "strong" or a
"weak" Democrat.[9]

Party identification is the most common indicator of party support, but it
is not the only one. Jack Dennis focuses attention on *diffuse support*. Diffuse
support includes "endorsement of the party system as a whole and of the
general norm that partisan spirit and activity is allowable in political life."[10]
Diffuse support reflects disagreement with statements like the following: "It
would be better if, in all elections, we put no party labels on the ballot."[11]
Diffuse support specifically defines public reactions toward the "party system"
or toward parties as institutions rather than affections for *one* party.

Related to diffuse support are the concepts of party evaluation or party
image used by Nie et al. and by Richard Trilling.[12] Trilling argues for replacement of the identification concept with one called party image, which
represents net positive or negative feelings about the parties. To measure the
concept, Trilling uses survey respondents' answers to a query about what
they like and dislike about each of the parties. Levels of party support can
then be determined by simply counting the number of positive and negative
comments made by each respondent.[13] The assumption is that people who
support parties should demonstrate on overall positive stance (i.e., make
more positive observations than negative ones).

Other types of party support, which are also similar to diffuse support,
include several notions of "party-system support." Party-system support relates to the parties' abilities to act as linkage mechanisms. Questions address
"the efficacy of parties in making government pay attention to the demands
of the public" and perceptions of "party concern for people's opinions."[14] Comparison of parties with other institutions and the public's perceptions of their
capacities to influence parties also indicate party-system support. People who

view parties as ineffective and unconcerned or evaluate them as worse than other governmental institutions are nonsupporters.

Party-related behavior is a final type of support. For example, Walter De-Vries and Lance Tarrance argue that reported attitudes toward parties may be less instructive than the public's behavior toward parties, the latter being more central to electoral outcomes.[15] Whereas psychological independence (identification with neither of the parties) has traditionally been considered the primary evidence of nonsupport, it can also be defined as "actual ticket-splitting, since this is what ultimately counts on the campaign level."[16] Ticket-splitting is casting votes for candidates of competing parties in the same election. A ticket-splitter, in other words, does not vote a straight party line. Still another behavioral indication of nonsupport is the practice of switching parties. A party "switcher" votes for the presidential candidate of one party in one election and for the candidate of another party in a subsequent election.[17]

The preceding paragraphs show that party support has been defined in many ways. But most recent treatments of the subject reach similar conclusions, regardless of the measurement strategy chosen. During the past two decades, more and more Americans have claimed independence from political parties. A majority of the youngest voters now call themselves Independents, and even party identifiers are increasingly likely to withhold their votes or other types of support from political parties.

In considering alternative conceptualizations of party support, it is important to note a methodological difficulty. Several survey items used to solicit attitudes and behavior toward parties fail to distinguish among the national, state, and local organizations. In particular, the party identification measure does not direct a respondent's attention to a specific level of party organization. Since the hallmark of American political parties is decentralization, this omission may cause considerable confusion in the minds of the public. Respondents may feel strongly attached to the state Democratic party, for example, but alienated from the national party. Similarly, individuals may buck the party in presidential elections while voting a straight party ticket in congressional and state races. In noting the recent decline in party identification, it is difficult to distinguish among the targets: Is the public disaffected from national parties or state organizations or both? To some extent this problem is alleviated by the use of two behavioral measures of party support. Measures of ticket-splitting often reflect behavior in state and local elections, while measures of vote-switching refer explicitly to presidential elections. Both of those measures show similar trends, suggesting that party support has declined at all levels of party organization. Nevertheless, parties are diverse organizations, and that diversity warns against oversimplification in the analysis of both party support and party choice.

THE IMPORTANCE OF PARTY LOYALTIES

Why are the public's feelings about political parties important? The answers to this question comprise a long list. Party loyalties are thought to be primary components of political attitudes and behavior. Parties, and the loyalties they generate, provide the primary organizing mechanisms for electoral politics. In fact, elections are often characterized by the continuity (or discontinuity) of party loyalties. Parties serve as vehicles through which public opinion can be effectively articulated, and it has been argued that they help enforce democratic ground rules in American politics. At both the individual and the system levels, then, parties are thought by many to be *central* to democratic government.

Since the publication of *The American Voter*, party identification has been viewed as the most stable and effective cue for the American electorate. Campbell et al. argued in 1960 that,

> apparently, party has a profound influence across the full range of objects to which the individual responds. . . . Responses to each element of national politics are deeply affected by the individual's enduring party attachments.[18]

Researchers in the early 1960s reported that the public's party loyalties were much more stable than were its issue positions; they concluded that the likelihood was high that issue positions were more often dictated by party positions than the opposite.[19] In other words, people were not basing their party choices on their issue preferences; rather, party affiliation helped identifiers formulate issue opinions. Moreover, those whose electoral decision making was not tied to party loyalty (Independents) exhibited numerous undesirable characteristics:

> Far from being more attentive, interested, and informed, Independents tend as a group to be somewhat less involved in politics. They have somewhat poorer knowledge of the issues, their image of the candidate is fainter, their interest in the campaign is less, their concern over the outcome is relatively slight, and their choice between competing candidates, although it is indeed made later in the campaign, seems much less to spring from discoverable evaluations of the elements of national politics.[20]

Thus not only is party viewed as a primary cue-giver for the American public, but party loyalists are described as higher quality participators.

Extensions of these arguments contributed to the establishment of the distribution of party loyalties as a basis for the prediction of electoral outcomes (against which deviations of a short-term nature could be evaluated). Converse called party identification the "long-term" component of electoral behavior.[21] Although short-term forces, in the form of issues and candidates, cause temporary movement away from the behavior suggested by party alignment, voters are expected to return to their anchored party loyalties. Miller and Levitin metaphorically compare the long-term partisan commitment to an elastic cord.[22] For strong partisan identifiers, "there is little elasticity in the cord"; short-term forces will cause only slight movement from the individual's original position. Less strongly attached citizens will be more likely to defect from regular party commitment. But, the authors note, such defections are normally temporary:

> Actual partisan conversion occurs only when the anchors themselves are dislodged, not when the cords holding those anchors are temporarily

stretched. Election events rarely have enduring impact on the party loyalties of most voters.[23]

Not only were partisan identifications seen as long-term attachments, but they were also thought to intensify over time. The result was "the progressive binding in of popular loyalties to one or another of the traditionally competing parties."[24] In the long run, this "binding in" would lead to very high aggregate levels of partisan loyalty and finally to democratic stability. Converse believed that parties would suffer numerous threats to their survival during their formative periods. But the mature party would have a firm basis of support among the electorate; it would become "sanctified and protected by 'the weight of historical tradition.'"[25] This sanctification of the party would in turn lend stability and continuity to the governmental process.

This emphasis on the permanence and intensity of party attachments also led to the development of a typology that classified elections according to the stability or instability of party choice. Elections in which "the pattern of party attachments prevailing in the preceding period persists and is the primary influence on forces governing the vote" are called "maintaining elections"; such elections are determined by long-term forces or party identifications.[26] In maintaining elections (most American ones), the majority party remains in power. But occasionally short-term forces are strong enough to temporarily bring the minority party to power. A temporary dislodgement of the majority party is a "deviating election." In this case, the political situation should normalize after short-term forces responsible for temporary alterations in the party balance have disappeared. The more serious case of party reversal is one in which a more permanent *realignment* of party loyalties occurs.[27] As some observers perceive the 1980 election (see Chapter 15), realignments can represent slow processes of party change (called "secular realignments"),[28] but they can also occur abruptly, perhaps precipitated by the circumstances surrounding a single election.[29] Such a realignment is called a "critical realignment" and occurs in a "critical election," a time of great crisis.[30] Critical elections are usually accompanied by changes in the political rules of the game, in political behavior, and in the very nature of the party system.[31] Perhaps the best example of a critical realignment in American politics was the rise of the Democratic party during the early 1930s.

The arguments made above are largely empirical ones. The findings presented in *The American Voter* and in subsequent work by its authors stress the dependence of political decision making on party cues. Without the party, they imply, political participation is low in quality and fails to meet the standards set by democratic theorists. But political parties and the loyalties they inspire lend meaning to democratic processes and stability to democratic governments; they provide a basis for the evaluation of American elections.

Other arguments stressing the importance of parties and party loyalties to a democratic polity spring from more normative sources. They argue not that party *is* the central cue for American voters, but that party organizations both *should* and do serve democracy in various ways. Frank Sorauf notes that parties reaffirm the basic values of democracy by encouraging "the political activity and participation that a democracy depends on. And they reinforce the basic democratic rules of the game."[32] In addition, parties aggregate the demands of a diverse electorate. David Broder writes of a need parties should fill in American politics:

> That need is for some institution that will sort out, weigh, and to the extent possible, reconcile the myriad conflicting needs and demands of individual groups, interests, communities, and regions in this diverse continental Republic; organize them for the contest for public office; then serve as a link between the constituencies and the men chosen to govern. When the parties fill their mission well, they tend to serve both a unifying and a clarifying function for the country.[33]

In the absence of strong parties to organize elections, Gerald Pomper has argued that American politics would degenerate into a "national politics of fits and starts" characterized by irresponsibility in the political system and "alienation" of the American public.[34] Parties, then, are thought to lend continuity and accountability to the political system.

Each role played by political parties (and thus the importance attributed to the parties) depends directly on public support. Unless the American public relies upon, takes cues from, and supports the parties in other ways, the parties cannot reinforce the rules of the game, unify American politics, or lend continuity to the electoral agenda. Hence, the normative importance of parties as democratic institutions is directly tied to their success as linkage mechanisms between public opinion and government policy, which is in turn immutably tied to the public's willingness or unwillingness to support political parties.

The remainder of this chapter is devoted to what appears to be substantial erosion of the public's party loyalties during the past two decades. First, we turn to the general patterns of support for parties — declines in support for both parties across a variety of indicators. Second, we assess the changing bases of party choice — changes in the sources of support commanded by the Democratic and Republican parties.

CHANGE IN PARTY SUPPORT

Few changes in American public opinion have received as much attention as the recent decline in affection for political parties. As Dennis notes,

> the assessment that the party system's store of legitimacy is being rapidly depleted has become a recurrent contemporary theme. Indeed, a number of recent observers have been predicting that the party system will soon disappear as a major institution of American politics.[35]

Those observations, coupled with the preceding discussion of the importance of political parties, should provide a backdrop for the alarm expressed over the decline of party. In almost every way, public support for parties is decreasing.

The Evidence of Declining Support

First, and most noted, are the data on party identification. Even though party identification is thought to be the most constant of all political orientations, aggregate indicators show substantial drop-offs since the 1950s. Figure 10–1 shows that since 1972, more than one-third of the electorate call themselves Independents. This represents substantial change from the 1950s, when the percentage of Independents hovered around 20 percent.[36] This trend toward Independence is even more dramatic among new voters; there, a *majority* (50 percent in 1974, 51 percent by 1976) disclaim party affiliation.[37]

FIGURE 10–1   The Increase of Political Independence: 1952–1978

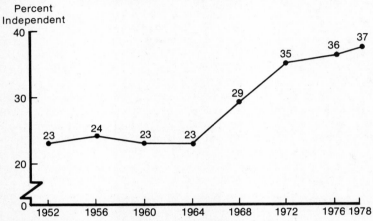

Source: Center for Political Studies. American National Election Studies.

Other measures of party support, including diffuse support,[38] party evaluations,[39] and measures of party-system support,[40] also demonstrate notable drops since the 1950s. The public has proven increasingly likely to agree with statements like the following: "It would be better if, in all elections, we put no party labels on the ballot."[41] They are also increasingly negative in expressing their likes and dislikes about the parties,[42] and they are decreasingly likely to agree that "parties help a good deal to make the government pay attention to what the people think."[43]

Growing discontent is also evident in the public's behavior toward political parties. Split-ticket voting below the presidential level more than doubled between 1960 and 1972 (increasing from 32 to 65 percent).[44] The proportion of "floating" voters or party "switchers" has also increased in recent years, although the changes have not been so dramatic. Figure 10 – 2 shows one indicator of the decline in behavioral party support since 1952. The percentage of voters always voting for the same party for president has declined substantially.

The evidence is strong that public support for parties has declined across a variety of indicators. Over the past two decades the electorate has become less likely to identify with, positively evaluate, and vote consistently with the political parties. We now turn to a very difficult question: Why?

FIGURE 10–2 **The Percentage Always Voting for the Same Party for President: 1952–1976**

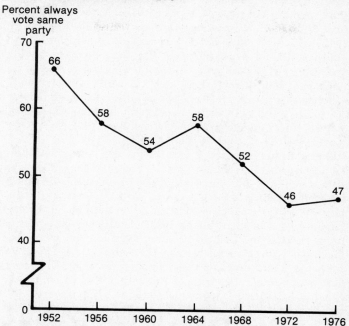

Source: Center for Political Studies. American National Election Studies.

Explanations for Changing Party Support

Although there has been no definite explanation for the drop-off in party support, many hypotheses have been developed. Three explanations are prominent. The first links party support to age. A second explanation ties waning party support to public dissatisfaction with the issue positions taken by the parties or their candidates. A third hypothesis focuses on leadership: a new breed of political leader may have loosened party loyalties.

AGE AND PARTY SUPPORT. It is common knowledge that older persons are more strongly tied to political parties than are their younger counterparts. In the 1950s, the youngest voters were twice as likely to call themselves Independents as were voters over the age of sixty-five. *The American Voter* reports that between 1952 and 1957, 31 percent of the twenty-one- to twenty-four-year-olds were Independents whereas only about 15 percent of those over sixty-five were Independents.[45]

There is widespread agreement that recent declines in party identification can be traced, at least in part, to "the entry into the electorate of . . . those most apt to be Independents and least apt to have strong party ties—that is, the young."[46] But one must continue to ask *why* young people are less likely to exhibit strong party loyalties. There is considerable disagreement among scholars on the answer. First, the *aging* (or life-cycle or maturational) hypothesis of partisan change argues that strength of partisanship tends to increase as voters grow older.[47] If true, recent declines in party loyalty may be temporary and present little cause for concern. A second explanation is the *generational* thesis, which contends that partisanship does not appreciate notably with increasing age. Rather, succeeding generations, for whatever reasons, may be less (or more) partisan than their predecessors.[48] The long-term consequences of generational change for political parties is much more serious. Scholars who have investigated the aging/generational question have, in the absence of the preferred panel data, relied on cohort analysis to study age groups' stability in party support over time. As Chapter 3 explains, cohort analysis traces an age group's (say, eighteen- to twenty-four-year-olds) attitudes over several time points.[49]

The authors of *The American Voter* develop the "aging" or "life-cycle" explanation of partisanship, arguing that it is not age per se but length of attachment that is really the important factor in partisan identification. The longer a person is associated with a group — in this case a political party — the stronger becomes that person's identification with and attachment to the group.[50] Age serves as a surrogate for length of attachment and helps predict strength of party identification. In other words, young voters can be expected to have weak party attachments because their attachment to political parties is new and weakly anchored. As those voters grow older, their party affiliations should gain strength by virtue of long-term association with the parties.

If the aging hypothesis adequately explained recent party declines, we could simply attribute those party problems to the post–World War II baby boom and the lowering of the voting age. A large influx of young voters, expected to be less tied to parties, would naturally lower aggregate distributions of party identification.[51] But those new members of the electorate could be expected to *develop* firmer party ties as their length of association with the parties increased.

Many, however, have challenged the aging explanation. In fact, recent commentary tends to side with the generational thesis. For example, the use of cohort analysis has supported the conclusion that the stability of party identification *within* age cohorts between 1945 and 1965 "apparently resulted from a general lack of strong influences for change."[52] Even though older cohorts displayed stronger aggregate levels of party identification, groups of persons in the same age group did not show a tendency to become stronger partisans with the passage of time. During a later time period (1965 to 1969), when forces for change were strong, party identification within age cohorts shifted considerably. In other words, forces for change (leading to lower levels of partisanship in successive generations), and not the process of aging, may have caused the depletion of party support.[53]

Criticism of the life-cycle explanation comes from other sources as well.[4] In fact, as Converse notes, the generational "answer seems well on its way to a scholarly consensus."[55] Increasingly, scholars are concluding that the evidence speaks against the aging hypothesis; rather, younger voters with weak party loyalties have replaced older voters with more firmly anchored party attachments.[56]

The recent popularity of the generational explanation underscores the rising concerns of party enthusiasts. If declines in party strength are best explained by this thesis, the consequences for parties and for the public are likely to be long-term, even if current trends are soon reversed.

The controversy between proponents of the aging and generational theses continues. But some recent commentators note that party disaffection is probably more complex than either explanation, taken alone, suggests. For example, Gerald Pomper argues that historical events affect the partisanship of different age groups differently. He stresses "the distinctive importance of issues to youth" and notes the emphasis younger voters place on policy matters.[57] According to Pomper, the young are more aware of candidate issue positions than are other age groups, and those policy positions play a major role in young voters' electoral decision making. Moreover, the young are more ideological: "we would expect new voters to be more concerned with issues than older generations and to evidence that concern more in their ballot choices."[58]

The issues that have pulled younger voters away from the parties have also affected the sentiments of older voters. But Nie, Verba, and Petrocik explain that older cohorts demonstrate greater resistance to those forces:

> *Those who have been in the electorate a shorter time before being exposed to the events of the middle and late sixties have been more easily moved into the Independent category. The length of affiliation has a delaying effect on party erosion.*[59]

Younger voters are clearly less partisan than their elders, but the reasons for this are complex. At this point it appears likely that the young, socialized during an antiparty period, have come into the electorate without strong party loyalties and are failing to adopt them after entering the electoral system. Older persons — probably for reasons stressed in the aging thesis — have been slower to move away from parties. But move they have, probably because of historical events, political issues, and the leaders who articulate those issues. We now turn to a closer examination of the relationship between partisanship and issues — how the issue positions taken by the parties may have affected party support.

ISSUES AND PARTY SUPPORT. The political parties have come under fire in recent years; many believe they are failing in their primary function — representing the people. Commentators have hypothesized that party support has decreased because the voters judge the parties' issue positions to be dissimilar from their own. The charge has become a familiar one, but it has several variations. The first is perhaps most familiar. David Broder, in his book *The Party's Over,* claims that the parties are and have been too moderate and similar to one another; in fact, they are virtually indistinguishable.[60] A second hypothesis is that the parties' leadership became too ideologically extreme, thus alienating a largely moderate electorate.[61] A third critique is also grounded in the issue theme, but it is more directly tied to issues new to the political agenda.[62] New "social" issues — crime, race, drugs, Vietnam, pollution, and others — may have caused party disaffection.

The notion that American political parties should be more readily distinguishable along policy lines is not a new one. Numerous commentators in the 1940s and 1950s espoused "responsible party government," in which parties would offer distinct policy alternatives.[63] More recently, David Broder laments the American parties' failure to perform as responsible parties.[64] To Broder, the parties have failed to offer clearly distinct alternatives and to provide the means of pursuing those alternatives in government; the result has been rising popular dissatisfaction with the two-party system.

Broder is pessimistic about the future of the party system. He predicts "the further fracturing of the already enfeebled party structure in this decade";[65] and he places the blame squarely on the parties themselves. They have failed in their primary missions: building and maintaining party programs, rallying public support, and pursuing those programs in the policy arena. The first failure is primary — the failure to build and present to the public clear policy programs, to present "real choices" in elections. Consequently, the public's "perception of party differences is growing visibly weaker."[66]

A second variation of the hypothesized issue–party support connection is found in the work of Everett Carll Ladd and Charles Hadley.[67] Like Broder, they tie the decline in support for parties to the rising importance of issues in American politics. But their analysis hypothesizes a completely different relationship between the two trends. They submit that it is not the absence of differences between the parties but rather the extreme polarization of the parties that caused the decline in support. Party "politicians" (primarily concerned with the maintenance and success of the party organization) are being replaced by a new breed of "party activists" (primarily concerned with the advancement of an ideological program). These party activists are ideologically more extreme than most party members. Aided by recent changes in election rules, they have "overwhelm[ed] the party regulars and temporarily take[n] over the party, imposing their preferred nominees."[68] As control of the parties has shifted to the activists, party platforms have tended to become more polarized and national politics more divisive. Simultaneously many among the public find the major party nominees too extreme for their tastes, and that distaste is manifested in declining party support.[69]

Note that Ladd and Hadley, like Broder, hypothesize that declining party support is based in public perceptions that the parties' preferred issue positions are distant from their own. But while Broder fears that the parties have become overly moderate and thus indistinguishable to the public, Ladd and Hadley find the parties' policy stances too extreme for the preferences of the average voter. Most voters, they claim, have more moderate policy preferences than those expressed by the parties' candidates in elections, and therein lies their disaffection.

Still a third variation of the political party support/issue connection is based in the growth of new politics issues. New types of issues hit close to home for voters, and yet the parties seem to fail to respond to these issues in satisfactory ways. Nie, Verba, and Petrocik note that some of the new issues — race, in particular — cut across party lines.[70] For example, the Democratic party is deeply divided on that question. Another set of issues — including

Vietnam, crime, drugs, and inflation — also cuts across party ties, generating substantial discontent with government and with the parties. Nie, Verba, and Petrocik note that

> *issues of this sort are likely to generate unhappiness with the government. And they are likely to weaken party ties — simply because neither party is seen as responsive to the issue. They do not generate clear group conflict, but they do help create a climate of discontent in which other conflicts can become more intense.*[71]

Miller and Levitin develop a similar argument linking the decline of party to new politics issues.[72] But instead of emphasizing generalized discontent with party performance on new issues, they note the growth of two new ideologically extreme groups, the "Silent Minority" and the "New Liberals," which have formed with the advent of the new politics. These new politics "extremists" hold issue positions inconsistent with those of most Democrats and Republicans, who comprise the mass center. The extremists have not been convinced that their policy demands will be met. Thus, they feel dissatisfied with the parties, and they are distrustful of government. The presence of these groups creates a clear dilemma for the parties: how does a candidate or an incumbent president persuade the cynics that their demands will be met without alienating the "mass center?"[73]

Table 10–1 makes two important points about the new politics hypothesis. First, even in 1976, an election in which both candidates made concerted efforts to deemphasize social issues, new politics issues deeply divided the affiliates of both parties, particularly the Democrats. Second, it is interesting that on most new politics issues the Independents show the highest propensity to take liberal positions, lending some support to the claim that these issues have pushed people away from party affiliations.

Obviously, the connection between political issues and party support is complex. A great deal of analysis remains before we can hope to fully understand the relationship. It seems probable that the relationship between issues and party loyalties is not a static one; rather, the two interact differently for different people at different times. Nevertheless, we can probably feel safe in drawing several general conclusions. First, as the public continues to develop the tools with which to critically evaluate the parties' policy positions, those evaluations promise to remain linked to the public's attitudes about and behavior toward political parties. Thus, support for parties will not be automatic; rather, it will depend at least partially on policy stances taken by the parties and by the public's reactions to those positions. Second, as the political agenda grows more complex (and it promises to continue to do just that) American political parties will find it increasingly difficult to develop consistent policy positions across the full range of salient issues. This was a recurring problem to the parties during the 1960s and 1970s. And even if the new politics issues fall from prominence, other issues may pull the public from their traditional party loyalties. We can, in the future, expect party support to be conditioned at least partially on the policy stances of the parties and the public's reactions to those positions.

TABLES 10–1 (a–d)   The Relationships between "New Politics" Issue Positions and Party Identification, 1976

	Party					Party		
	DEM	IND	REP			DEM	IND	REP
Liberal	30%	27%	19%		Liberal	37%	49%	41%
Moderate	38	39	42		Moderate	34	37	41
Conservative	33	34	38		Conservative	18	13	18
Total	101% (904)	100% (851)	99% (512)		Total	99% (818)	99% (792)	100% (527)
	a. Rights of Accused					**b. Women Equal Role**		

	Party					Party		
	DEM	IND	REP			DEM	IND	REP
Liberal	23%	32%	26%		Liberal	20%	24%	14%
Moderate	62	60	65		Moderate	29	35	33
Conservative	15	8	9		Conservative	51	41	53
Total	100% (879)	100% (827)	100% (548)		Total	100% (790)	100% (756)	100% (489)
	c. Legal Abortion					**d. Legal Marijuana**		

Source: Center for Political Studies. American National Election Study, 1976 [machine-readable data file].

LEADERS AND PARTY SUPPORT. To some extent the public's heightened interest in political issues springs from changes in political leadership. In particular, presidential candidates since 1964 usually have emphasized issues (rather than party), have sometimes contradicted the issue positions of fellow party members, and have often torn party supporters from their traditional voting patterns.[74]

There are several reasons for the leadership changes. The rules and regulations governing the conduct of elections and party behavior have changed, and those changes in the electoral environment have fostered the growth (and success) of new types of political leadership — often to the detriment of the political parties. It would be impossible and repetitive to detail those environmental changes here. But certainly prominent among them are the growing popularity of the direct primary and federal campaign financial aid in presidential elections. Both have been touted as practices that help to remove control of presidential nominations from the traditional party leadership, emphasizing the importance of individual candidates rather than their party sponsors.[75] Thus, the institutional environment for American elections increasingly encourages the public to "vote for the person, not for the party."

The growing importance of leadership to party support is also directly tied to political issues. But here the relative importance of issues and leaders becomes tangled. The problem is one of the cart and the horse: which comes first, the issues or the leaders? The answers to those questions are unclear, and they are likely to remain so. Miller and Levitin opt for an interpretation stressing the importance of political leadership in bringing issues to the forefront during the 1960s. In other words, they suggest that issues and events grew in importance (and later contributed to party declines) because "political leaders publicly and vigorously argued about policies to resolve newly urgent national problems."[76] Perhaps an equally tenable argument, however, views the public as cue-giver rather than cue-receiver. Perhaps the public, aided by a new institutional environment and discouraged with party alternatives, has chosen leaders who articulate different types of issues and who threaten party loyalty.

Both the rising importance of issues and the increased role of leadership are tied to the altered use of the mass media in political campaigns. Television in particular has revolutionized political campaigning — and in doing so has dealt a serious blow to political parties. Candidates no longer rely as heavily on party workers and party backing. Instead, new styles of campaigning have developed. As Agranoff points out, "Party organization no longer has a near monopoly on campaign communication."[77] Television now fills the role of party worker, "conveying candidate style, image, and issues."[78]

The result is a campaign that is candidate-centered. Sorauf stresses that television has fostered an emphasis on the candidate, not on the party, and it has reinforced "the development of personalism in politics":

> The campaign techniques, therefore, foster a tie between candidate and voter — a new personalism in politics — in which the role of party loyalty is less important. The new campaign technicians threaten to displace the party "within" the voter as well as the party organization in the campaign.[79]

Certainly, television increases citizen potential for following news and forming opinions on issues, in part because of the articulation of issues by candidates via the medium. But the media may actually "set the agenda" for political campaigns, defining the important issues for the public and for the candidates.[80]

Thus, television has the potential to alter party support in several ways. First, it has personalized political campaigns, emphasizing candidates over parties. Second, it has increased the information flow about political issues (and candidates' stands on those issues), perhaps even setting the issue agenda. In doing so, television encourages the voter to rely on issue and candidate cues in elections — again, to the detriment of the political party.

PARTY CHOICE

The upheaval within the party system during the past two decades has not been limited to the growth of antiparty feelings. Substantial change has been noted in the underpinnings of party loyalty. Since the early days of survey research observers have expected certain types of people to become attached to the Democratic and Republican parties. Certainly, the post–New Deal years have created expectations that, for example, high-income white Protestants will choose the Republican party, while blacks, Catholics, Jews, blue-collar whites, and southerners will develop Democratic loyalties. But recent years have seen the erosion of those patterns. Not only have all of these groups' members grown less loyal to parties, but group membership has also become less reliable as a clue to party choice.

We have already noted the substantial rise in political independence. That rise, although it certainly has had the potential for altering the balance of electoral strength between the two parties, has failed to do so. But even though aggregate change in party loyalties has not affected the *relative* strength of the two parties, individual or group change need not inevitably flow toward the Independent category. Indeed, symmetrical changes in party affiliation can be completely obscured by aggregate statistics (see Chapter 2). Such hidden changes have occurred in recent years, altering not the relative distributions of party loyalties, but certainly the bases of party choice. Nie, Verba, and Petrocik call the change a "realignment" — not in the usual sense of a changed balance of party strength, but a change in the sources or correlates of party choice.[81]

Social Groups and Political Parties: An Historical View

Regional, racial, religious, and economic affiliations have historically exhibited strong connections to an individual's party choices. Americans have tended to adopt the party preferences of the groups of which they are a part. As David Knoke notes, "The viability of party loyalty derives largely from the penetration of the political world into the life of nonpolitical primary and secondary social groups."[82] As a result, southerners have, since the Civil War, exhibited an overwhelming tendency to be Democrats. Likewise, blacks and the working class turned to the Democratic party during the New Deal. Members of the three largest religious groups also show partisan tendencies along group lines.

THE SOUTH, RACE, AND PARTY CHOICE.   At least until very recently, certainly the characteristic most strongly linked to party choice was residence in the southern states. Although southerners sometimes defected from the Democratic party in their presidential votes, Democrats claimed a substantial majority (78 percent of white Protestants in 1952[83]) of southerners until the mid-1960s. But more recently, southerners have become far more like their northern counterparts in their party choices. In other words, region has come to have lessened impact on party choice.[84]

The influence of Reconstruction on the party preferences of southerners, both black and white, is well known. Southern whites, in reaction to the Republican-led Civil War and Reconstruction, became solidly Democratic.

Southern Democratic loyalties were reinforced and strengthened during the New Deal. In fact, the New Deal received greater support in the South than in other areas of the country.[85]

Southern blacks, due to numerous tactics by southern whites (including the poll tax, literacy test, grandfather clause, white primary, and others) were almost totally disenfranchised and therefore, in most cases, exhibited *no* party preference.[87] Northern blacks, on the other hand, unhampered by many of the legal restrictions imposed on black voting in the South, developed loyalties to the Democratic party in the aftermath of the Great Depression. Prior to the 1930s, those blacks with party loyalties were, of course, largely Republican. During the 1920s, blacks began migrating in large numbers to northern industrial centers, where the avenues to political participation were more open. Not until after 1932 did blacks move into the Democratic camp.[88]

The impact of Reconstruction and the New Deal on the party choice of southern whites was destined to erode. The Democratic stronghold on the region loosened during the 1948 presidential campaign and continued to decline in strength as the civil rights movement gained momentum. The southern Democratic vote dwindled to 52 percent in 1948 and has exceeded that level only once since — in the 1976 presidential race.[89]

To attribute changing party choice among southern whites solely to the rising importance of civil rights issues would certainly be misleading. Several sources suggest that party change in the South can, in large measure, be traced to in-migration of Republicans and out-migration of southern Democrats.[90] In other words, the composition of the southern electorate has changed, and with it the distribution of party preferences. Other scholars, however, point out that change in the South is more complex. For example, Nie, Verba, and Petrocik believe that change away from the Democrats is attributable to migration *prior to* but *not* after 1964:

> *Clearly, there have been two stages in the transformation of the South. From the early fifties to the 1964 election, the majority of the change came from the migration of citizens into the South. After 1964, the native Southerners changed.*[91]

If Nie, Verba, and Petrocik are correct, a change in the composition of the electorate and not changes in individual's party choices led to changes in party followings through 1964. But what accounts for the continuation of the trend away from the Democrats *after* 1964?

Several sources point to attitudinal change among southerners as the impetus for later changes in party choice. For example, there has been a trend of rising conservatism in the South. White southerners, who supported Roosevelt's New Deal and foreign politics, have made a dramatic swing in their opinions. Even those who have remained nominal Democrats have demonstrated considerable erosion of support for their party's issue positions.[92] Further, southerners have become, in some ways, more like their northern counterparts in their choice of parties. With the growth of the Republican party in the South, social class and economic differences have found expression in party choice.[93]

It should be noted that change in the South *did not* precipitate wholesale conversion to Republicanism. In fact, change has primarily benefited the Independent category to the detriment of the Democrats. But even Democratic southerners are now more likely than other Democrats to abandon their party for the Republican candidates in presidential elections, and have been since 1948.[94]

Like southern whites, southern blacks have changed party preferences but not in similar directions. As for southern whites, 1964 also seems a critical turning point for black political loyalties. Although northern blacks, drawn by policy attractions of the Roosevelt administration, flocked into the Democratic party during and after the New Deal, southern blacks remained largely outside of the electoral process, since the doors to political participation were closed to them (and, in 1940, 70 percent of all American blacks still resided in the South).[95] But those barriers were slowly lifted during the 1940s and 1950s, and by 1960 southern blacks were both voting and identifying with the Democratic party. The 1964 election saw the new mobilization of southern blacks and the nearly complete migration of blacks from the Republican party's ranks.[96]

Thus, a realignment of the nation's black population (both southern and northern) was complete. By 1968, 92 percent of southern blacks were Democrats; 76 percent of northern blacks were Democrats.[97] The realignment of black party choice was complete by the late 1960s, and it has changed little since. Both black party identifications and black votes are now heavily Democratic.[98]

Perhaps the best description of changing party choice among southerners emphasizes the declining uniqueness of the region. Southerners, black and white, have become more like their northern counterparts in their party preferences. Region appears to have lost its edge in dictating party choice.

SOCIAL CLASS AND PARTY CHOICE.   The party realignment of the 1930s was based in large measure on social class. The depression pitted the "haves" (Republicans) against the "have-nots" (Democrats). Although Democratic successes during this period were probably less due to conversion from Republicanism than to the entry of previously apolitical persons into the electorate, the Democrat successfully accentuated class differences:

> *By stigmatizing the Republican party as responsible for the collapse and by championing legislation on behalf of the socioeconomic have-nots, the Democratic party sharpened the class differences in the mass bases of the two parties.*[99]

After the depression, there was a clear tendency for white-collar workers to opt for the Republican party, while the blue-collar workers or the working class sided with the Democrats.[100]

But the decades since the 1930s have seen a gradual lessening of class distinctiveness in party affiliations, at least in the North. There, postwar differences in the party preferences of manual and nonmanual workers, while still present, have hovered around 10 percent.[101] Norval Glenn, in his analysis of long-term class alliances, cites a "trend outside of the South away from the traditional class pattern of voting."[102] He notes that by 1968, class voting had declined markedly, particularly among young adults, while party identification continued to show higher class differences.[103] Although Glenn's study demonstrates that southerners — slow to move to class-based partisan loyalties — failed to show the erosion of those distinctions through 1968, a later study confirms a similar trend in the South by 1972.[104] Glenn even notes "an apparent reversal of the traditional difference,"[105] particularly among young southerners. Not only did class differences begin disappearing by 1972, but blue-collar workers actually became *more* likely to support the Republicans than the Democrats by 1972.

The 1976 presidential election revealed an abrupt reversal of the trend to minimal class differences in voting. In 1976, class voting returned to pre-1972 levels and, in fact, surpassed every year since 1952.[106] Class voting in 1976 increased in both the North and the South.[107] Why the return to higher levels of class voting in 1976? Class voting does not necessarily reflect a conscious assessment of the relevance of candidates and parties for the individual's class self-interest. Rather, it may reflect traditional allegiances to the parties, historical in origin, returning to the fore in an election noticeably absent in major issues and powerfully attractive or repugnant candidate personalities.

Why the decline in class-related party allegiances through 1972? The explanations for the change are varied. One view cites the "impact of 'good times' and the abating stigmatization of the Republican party" as primary deterrents to class polarization.[108] Related to that thesis is another that ties declining class-specific party choice to new noneconomic issues — civil rights, criminal rights, the environment, and others. On these new issues blue-collar workers may prove more conservative than white-collar workers; the result is considerable ambivalence on the part of both classes toward both political parties.[109]

A third explanation for receding class distinctions ties together and extends the first two. Ladd and Hadley describe a "class inversion," in which the upper class demonstrates considerably more commitment to liberalism (in the new sense) than do the lower classes.[110] Their argument is largely founded in the two explanations mentioned above. First, "good times" have changed the makeup of the middle class; more persons now claim membership in that class, and they exhibit different political leanings than did the middle class of the 1930s. Second, since different issues now dominate the political agenda, the *meaning* of "liberalism" and "conservatism" has changed.[111] Whereas liberal and conservative traditionally referred to New Deal economic positions, they now also include positions on social issues such as equal rights for women or the general need for social and political change. These latter positions do not necessarily parallel those on the New Deal issue. The result has been "a shift of considerable magnitude":

> *In most policy areas, whites in the higher socioeconomic status categories have become decisively more liberal than the middle and lower cohorts. There are exceptions in economic policy, but even these are being reduced or removed.*[112]

The affluent are now more liberal and more Democratic — and the result is the blurring of class lines in party affiliation.

Class distinctiveness, like southern distinctiveness, has dwindled markedly and perhaps is even in the process of reversal. Aside from race — blacks remain overwhelmingly Democratic — are there still demographic characteristics that guide the public's party choice?

RELIGION AND PARTY CHOICE. Religious differences in party choice have always existed in American politics, but they were underscored in 1928 and again in 1960, election years in which one of the two major party candidates for the presidency was Catholic.

Religious differences in party choice have been traced to several sources. Initially, the political divisions between Protestants and Catholics were probably attributable to cultural differences, party positions on immigration restrictions in the early 1800s, and differing views about the proper relationship between government and religion.[113] Those divisions were then reemphasized during the New Deal era, when Catholic immigrants suffered grave economic difficulties. The majority of American Jews, on the other hand, supported the Republican party *until* the New Deal, when they began a rapid transition to Democratic loyalty.[114] Again, the appeal of the New Deal Democrats for Jews must have sprung partly from their deprivation as relatively recent arrivals in the United States during the depression. But several other causes can be noted as well. American Jews clearly supported the foreign policy (anti-Nazi) stance of the Roosevelt administration. Further, the group's leanings toward the political left (resulting in large measure from discrimination inflicted by Protestants) made the Roosevelt Democrats a natural home for its members.[115]

Thus, Catholics and Jews have aligned themselves more distinctly with the Democrats than have Protestants.[116] In part, their partisan preferences stem from deprived immigrant status during the depression and the ensuing party realignment. In part, the differences may be theological ones, for both Jews and Catholics viewed the Democratic party as a protector against the legislation of Protestant morality.

The question at issue here is whether these long-standing patterns of religious cleavage in party choice have eroded in recent years — and the answer is a qualified yes. Although change has been substantial, it consists in large part of growing independence among all religious groups.[117] The *relative* support for Democrats and Republicans *within* religious groups has changed very little. That is, although Jews are increasingly likely to be Independents, they are still more drawn to the Democrats than to the Republicans; the same is true of Catholics.[119] For Protestants, change has been more complex, largely because of varying patterns in the southern and northern sections of the country. Northern white Protestants have become less Republican (and much more Independent).[119] Southern Protestants, on the other hand, have become *more* Republican (and much more Independent).[120]

Although they have become less prominent, religious distinctions in the selection of party affiliations persist. Moreover, several investigations have uncovered a relationship between church *attendance* and party choice; that is,

Catholics who attend church regularly are *more likely* to be Democrats than are nonregular Catholic attenders.[121] Church attendance, then, intensifies the relationship between religion and partisanship. But why? Knoke points out that the answer to that question is far from clear. Three possibilities are present: (1) theology or church doctrine may form the basis of a common political philosophy; (2) association with groups of persons with common interests may lead to political alliances with parties; or (3) religious and political values and choices may be transmitted from parents to children. Also, political socialization may occur after childhood, as adults learn and reinforce attitudes within religious groups.[122]

To disentangle these explanations for the linkage between party and religion — and for the impact of church attendance on that linkage — is at least difficult and perhaps impossible. In fact, all three explanations may hold true:

> *High rates of church attendance may expose one to greater theological instruction, to greater insight into the interests of one's religious group, and to greater interaction with one's fellow attenders. Which set of factors has the most important influence, if any, on reinforcing and preserving the distinctive political patterns of the religious groups is a matter not resolvable by an investigation focused primarily on determining the impact of church attendance on political orientation.*[123]

In summary, demographic characteristics — region, race, social class, and religion — seem less pertinent to political party choice than they once were. Even among Jews and blacks, we find fewer Democrats and more Independents. And some groups — southern whites, for example — have shown a tendency toward shifting their party loyalties from one party to another. The result is that we are much less able to predict party choice from knowledge of a person's social-demographic characteristics than we were in the early 1960s. Furthermore, this trend seems even more serious in light of the fact that it has accelerated among younger voters.[124]

Explanations for Changing Party Choice

Since the primary product of shifting bases of party choice has been rising political independence, explanations for change substantially overlap those offered for the declines in party support. In other words, if political issues and the new leadership that represents them are responsible for changing public attitudes and behavior toward political parties, then they are also, by definition, connected to the primary change in party choice, increasing political independence. The real question is, then, why do social-demographic groups no longer emit strong party cues? Or, if they still give such cues, why are they not heeded? The answer is not a simple one. In fact, the changing role of demographics in party choice probably results from the interaction of several forces. Included in the list are the diminished role of the family in transmitting party identification, the increased role of the mass media as political cue-giver (even for the very young), new issues on the political agenda, and increased issue awareness among the public. Each explanation is discussed in prior sections of this text in some depth and will only be mentioned briefly here.

As Chapter 4 notes, the role of the family in transmitting party identification has declined notably in recent years. But why? Probably because (1) family cues are weakened since parents view party as less important; and (2) children are now exposed to more information about politics, particularly from television, which does *not* emphasize party choice. Thus, the socialization process may have changed, and the new configuration of the process does not encourage party loyalty. If that is true, party declines among most social groups come as no surprise.

But in some social groups, the trend away from parties has also included a shifting balance *between* the parties. For example, southern white Protestants are becoming more Republican, northern white Protestants more Democratic. It seems that change must be more complex than simple negative feelings about parties. Perhaps a more viable explanation is one that incorporates change in socialization and in media influence but also stresses changes in the issue agenda and in the public's reactions to it. We have noted many times the presence of new types of issues on the political agenda of the past two decades. Those new issues, in a time of increased issue awareness and ideological fervor, have often created new lines of battle in American politics.

The issue agenda can affect the party affiliations of social groups in several ways. First, new issues may provide party cues that conflict with those emitted by traditional social groups. Blue-collar reactions to the environmental movement are a case in point. Certainly, the changing issue agenda has created some ambivalence toward parties — and some confusion about which party is more closely aligned with a social group's political goals. A second possibility is that new issues, because they often divide social-group members, make demographic categories *less relevant* to party choice. People whose primary policy concerns are crime and pollution may be unlikely to base party choices on their religious affiliation or region of residence. Finally, of course, issues can alter the bases of party choice simply because both individuals and groups have become disenchanted with parties thought to be indistinguishable.

In any case, the waning distinctiveness of social-group party preferences is not irreversible, particularly if its source is issue-based. If political issues now pull voters away from established party loyalties, issues certainly have the potential to realign or reestablish those loyalties. Depending on the issues that dominate the political agenda and the candidates who articulate those issues, social-demographic distinctions can return to prominence as significant determinants of party choice.

The Issue Preferences of Party Identifiers

Political issues are central to recent declines in party support and to the weakening of demographics as explanations of party choice; this has been a theme of this chapter. Similarly, the choice between parties seems to exhibit a stronger issue connection than it once did. Traditional demographic lines of party choice have faded. In part, the blurring lines represent abandonment of the parties by all categories in the public — racial, regional, religious, and class. But in part, declining demographic distinctiveness of party choice represents increased issue content in the public's political decision making.

Individuals no longer need to rely on cues dictated by demographic group attachments. Instead, they rely on their own issue opinions, and the connections between demographic characteristics and party choice may fade in the process.

In addition, Nie, Verba, and Petrocik argue that the electorate has become more polarized on issues by moving away from middle-of-the-road positions and toward leftist and rightist positions.[125] Figure 10–3 (a–d) helps to illustrate this blurring of lines in the case of party choice. Note that in 1976 black Democrats tend to align fairly solidly on the liberal side of the four issues displayed — government-guaranteed jobs and living standards, minority group aid, government medical insurance, and tax rates. In other words, blacks in 1976 were in agreement on policy preferences and probably experienced little issue conflict with their party affiliation. Southern Democrats, on the other hand, experienced a great deal of dissonance. There is no majority position on any issue among this group. Although traditionally a very Democratic group, issue preferences vary enormously, and that variation must cause dissonance among those whose issue preference and party preference are at variance.

FIGURE 10–3   Positions on Four Issues among Black Democrats and Southern Democrats, 1976

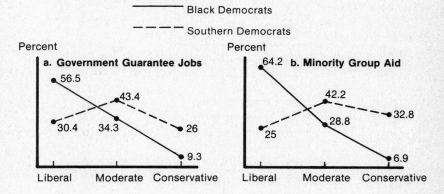

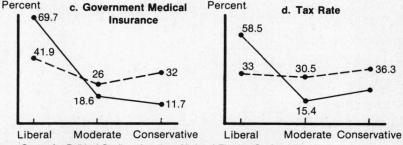

Source: Center for Political Studies. American National Election Study, 1976 [machine-readable data file].

It is not that issue positions have taken over political decision making, or that the public has become so informed and opinionated that it has thrown parties to the wind. Instead, issues have had a much more subtle effect on party choice. The public is now better equipped to base choices in issue positions—and when that option is exercised, party support suffers and the traditional lines of party division may be altered. This does not mean that the public has waged war on the parties, or that the parties cannot retrieve the higher levels of support they once enjoyed.

A PROFILE OF THE POLITICAL INDEPENDENT

The primary changes noted in this chapter boil down to disaffection from the political parties. Individuals, especially the young, are increasingly hesitant to identify with a party. That fact obtains great significance if the political participation of Independents is of lower overall quality than is that of party identifiers. Indeed, one traditional picture of the Independent voter is of a

FIGURE 10–4   Voting Participation, Interest, and Efficacy by Party Identification, 1976

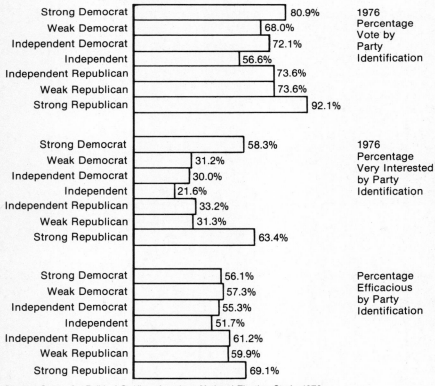

Source: Center for Political Studies. American National Election Study, 1976 [machine-readable data file].

disinterested, uninformed, inattentive, and unthinking participant in politics.[126] If this view holds true, the increase in Independents noted above holds grim implications for the American political system.

Recently, as the ranks of Independents have continued to swell, the traditional view of the Independents has been challenged. In the first place, the Independent category does not comprise an homogeneous group. Some Independents are probably guilty as charged — an apathetic group whose members may change their minds many times over the course of a campaign. On the other hand, as V. O. Key, Jr., pointed out years ago, many Independents are rational, interested participants who are more informed than many party identifiers.[127] More recent comparisons of Independents and party identifiers show that perhaps "the case against the Independents has been overstated."[128] Independents are not strikingly different from partisans in political interest and involvement, in ideological thinking, or in political efficacy.[129] And leaning Independents (Independents who lean toward the Republican or Democratic parties) are more interested, concerned, and attentive to politics than are weak party identifiers.[130] Figure 10–4 compares Independents to party identifiers across three characteristics. Note that the leaning Independents were just as likely to vote in 1976, to be "very interested" in the campaign, and to disagree that "people like me have no say" in government as were weak party identifiers. This new picture of the Independent is far brighter than the traditional view. While the rising numbers of Independents may cause concern in many quarters, new trends do not mean that the electorate is being reduced to an uncaring, unqualified lot.

CONCLUSION

What, then, are the implications of changes in party support and party choice for the broader political system? Clearly, the changes threaten the perpetuation of the party system as we now know it. But what consequences does an altered or weakened party system hold for democracy?

Certainly, the opinion of many scholars supports profound consequences for the political system if support for the political parties continues to weaken. At the heart of that argument is the view that the party organizations play a critical part in representative government. That role, in large measure, consists of aggregating the electorate's preferences for leadership and assuring that those preferences are central to election choices. The parties thus put together bodies of diffuse and sometimes poorly articulated political preferences and produce political candidates. Walter Dean Burnham stresses the sentiments of many — that parties

> are the only devices thus far invented by the wit of Western man which with some effectiveness can generate countervailing collective power on behalf of the many individually powerless against the relatively few who are individually — or organizationally — powerful.[131]

In other words, very few members of the public possess the resources necessary to wield political power individually. The political parties, according to many, provide the best avenue through which individuals can be heard in the political process. Another party scholar, Gerald Pomper, stresses the same consequences of party decline, noting that the underprivileged, without parties, will lose their voice in policymaking.[132] Further, he claims that the result will be "a fundamental conservatism" in the making of public policy.[133]

Still another cost to the public can be noted. It can be argued that the parties play an important educational and cue-giving role for members of the American public. Reliance on the parties for voting cues can be a rational strategy for many voters, who simply do not have the time or other resources to gather great quantities of political information. As Benjamin Page notes, the average citizen "has better things to do than to pore over the *New York Times* or *Congressional Quarterly* to see what the candidates are saying and doing."[134] Strong parties can help the individual economize by sorting through great quantities of information and providing voting cues to the general public.

Even though parties can make political participation less costly, many observers point to the increased access of the electorate to education and to political information. The voters are now better able to base their electoral decisions on issues and candidate characteristics. As a consequence, it is argued, "it is a simple fact that Americans need parties much less now than in the past as intermediaries in shaping their electoral decisions."[135]

Perhaps the public's need for parties has declined. Certainly all indicators point to a growing trend of individualism in American politics. In one sense, the trends may seem encouraging. The growing antiparty feelings of the electorate seems to be based, at least in part, in increased capabilities to perform some functions previously delegated to the party system. The movement away from political parties comprises, in part, a public comment on their failure to perform well.

Clearly, it also is possible that the public's disaffection from parties could, in the long run, have positive ramifications for the party system. Some onlookers speculate that the Democratic and Republican parties will be forced to reevaluate their policy stances and to realign their positions with the changing configuration of the public preferences. What are the possibilities that a realignment of party preferences will occur, once again creating strong partisan loyalties? In some ways, the American voters seem "ripe for realignment."[136] Large numbers of young voters with nonexistent or weak party loyalties could perhaps be pulled in new directions by parties that have reformed around a "catalyzing traumatic event" or an issue of great importance.[137] But conditions have encouraged a realignment for some years now, and the change has not been forthcoming. Absent a realignment, the decline of party is likely to continue. And unless other institutions arise to coordinate policy and aggregate public opinion, the consequences may be severe.

NOTES

1. E. E. Schnattschneider, *Party Government* (New York: Holt, Rinehart & Winston, 1942), p. 1.
2. Angus Campbell et al., *The American Voter* (New York: John Wiley & Sons, 1960), chap. 6.

3. Ibid., p. 121.

4. Ibid., p. 122.

5. Ibid.

6. Ibid., p. 149.

7. See the extended discussion in Chapter 4.

8. Philip E. Converse, *The Dynamics of Party Support: Cohort Analyzing Party Iden-tification* (Beverly Hills: Sage Publications, 1976), p. 10.

9. Ibid. In recent years many scholars have begun to challenge the traditional mea-surement and conceptualization of party identification. See the review and discus-sion in W. Phillips Shively, "The Nature of Party Identification: A Review of Recent Developments," in *The Electorate Reconsidered,* John C. Pierce and John L. Sullivan, eds. (Beverly Hills: Sage Publications, 1980), pp. 219–36.

10. Jack Dennis, "Support for the Party System by the Mass Public," *American Political Science Review* 60 (September 1966), p. 601. See also a second article by Dennis entitled "Trends in Public Support for the American Party System," *British Journal of Political Science* 5 (April 1975), pp. 187–230.

11. Dennis, "Support for the Party System," p. 603.

12. Norman H. Nie, Sidney Verba, and John R. Petrocik, *The Changing American Voter,* enl. ed. (Cambridge, Mass.: Harvard University Press, 1979), pp. 57–58; and Richard J. Trilling, "Party Image and Electoral Behavior," *American Politics Quarterly* 3 (July 1975), pp. 284–314.

13. Trilling, "Party Image and Electoral Behavior," pp. 288–89.

14. Dennis, "Trends in Public Support," pp. 203–8.

15. See Walter DeVries and Lance Tarrance, *The Ticket Splitter* (Grand Rapids, Mich.: Eerdmans, 1972), Chapters 1 and 2.

16. Ibid., p. 23.

17. See V.O. Key, Jr., *The Responsible Electorate: Rationality in Presidential Voting, 1936–1960* (Cambridge, Mass.: Harvard University Press, 1966), Chapter 4.

18. Campbell et al., *The American Voter,* p. 128.

19. Ibid., p. 133.

20. Ibid., p. 143.

21. Philip E. Converse, "The Concept of a Normal Vote," in *Elections and the Poli-tical Order,* Angus Campbell et al., eds. (New York: John Wiley & Sons, 1966), pp. 9–18.

22. Warren E. Miller and Teresa E. Levitin, *Leadership and Change: The New Poli-tics and the American Electorate* (Cambridge, Mass.: Harvard University Press, 1976), p. 34.

23. Ibid.

24. Philip E. Converse, "Of Time and Partisan Stability," *Comparative Political Studies* 2 (June 1969), p. 141.

25. Ibid., p. 139.

26. Campbell et al., *The American Voter,* pp. 531–35. These authors develop the classification discussed here from earlier work by V. O. Key, Jr., including "A Theory of Critical Elections," *Journal of Politics* 17 (February 1955), pp. 3–18; and "Secular Realignment and the Party System," *Journal of Politics* 21 (May 1959), pp. 198–210.

27. Campbell et al., *The American Voter,* p. 534.

28. See Key, "Secular Realignment," pp. 198–210.

29. Gerald M. Pomper, *Elections in America* (New York: Dodd, Mead & Co., 1970), pp. 101–4.

30. Ibid. See also Walter Dean Burnham, *Critical Elections and the Mainsprings of American Politics* (New York: Norton, 1970), chap. 1.

31. Burnham, *Critical Elections,* pp. 2–3.

32. Frank J. Sorauf, *Party Politics in America,* 3rd ed. (Boston: Little, Brown & Co., 1976), p. 54.
33. David S. Broder, *The Party's Over: The Failure of Party Politics in America* (New York: Harper & Row, 1972), p. xx.
34. Gerald M. Pomper, *The Voters' Choice: Varieties of American Electoral Behavior* (New York: Harper & Row, 1975), p. 350.
35. Dennis, "Trends in Public Support," p. 189.
36. Campbell et al., *The American Voter,* p. 124.
37. Nie et al., *The Changing American Voter,* p. 365.
38. Dennis, "Trends in Public Support."
39. Nie et al., *The Changing American Voter,* pp. 57–59.
40. Dennis, "Trends in Public Support," pp. 203–8.
41. Ibid., pp. 199–200.
42. Nie et al., *The Changing American Voter,* p. 58.
43. Dennis, "Trends in Public Support," pp. 204–5.
44. Nie et al., *The Changing American Voter,* p. 53.
45. Campbell et al., *The American Voter,* p. 162.
46. Miller and Levitin, *Leadership and Change,* p. 193.
47. Campbell et al., *The American Voter,* pp. 161–65.
48. For example, Campbell et al. present evidence that "the Great Depression swung a heavy proportion of the young electors toward the Democratic Party and gave that party a hold on that generation, which it has never relinquished" (p. 155). This type of change has been labeled generational change.
49. Chapter 3 also discusses a third explanation for the decline of party loyalties. That explanation, called the period-effects model, ties declining party loyalties to historical events and issues affecting the partisanship of *all* age groups. Cohort analysis is also used to separate period effects from the effects of aging or generation. A discussion of period effects is found in the following section of this chapter.
50. Campbell et al., *The American Voter,* p. 161–65.
51. Converse, *The Dynamics of Party Support,* pp. 72–73.
52. Norval D. Glenn and Tedd Hefner, "Further Evidence on Aging and Party Identification," *Public Opinion Quarterly* 36 (Spring 1972), p. 47.
53. Ibid.
54. See, for example, Paul R. Abramson, "Generational Change and the Decline of Party Identification in America: 1952–1974, *American Political Science Review* 70 (June 1976), pp. 469–78; and David Knoke, *Change and Continuity in American Politics: The Social Bases of Political Parties* (Baltimore: Johns Hopkins University Press, 1976), p. 136.
55. Converse, *The Dynamics of Party Support,* p. 15.
56. Knoke, *Change and Continuity,* p. 136.
57. Pomper, *The Voters' Choice,* p. 111.
58. Ibid., p. 95.
59. Nie et al., *The Changing American Voter,* p. 64.
60. Broder, *The Party's Over,* intro. and Chapter 11.
61. Carll Everett Ladd, Jr., with Charles D. Hadley, *Transformations of the American Party System: Political Coalitions from the New Deal to the 1970s* (New York: Norton, 1978), pp. 333–42.
62. See, for example, Miller and Levitin, *Leadership and Change,* especially pp. 83–90.
63. Cf. Committee on Political Parties of the American Political Science Association, *Toward a More Responsible Two-Party System* (New York: Holt, Rinehart & Winston, 1950).

64. Broder, *The Party's Over,* p. xx–xxv.
65. Ibid., p. 251.
66. Ibid.
67. Ladd with Hadley, *Transformations,* Chapter 11.
68. Ibid., p. 319.
69. Ibid., Chapter 11.
70. Nie et al., *The Changing American Voter,* p. 105.
71. Ibid.
72. Miller and Levitin, *Leadership and Change,* Chapter 3 and pp. 212–19.
73. Ibid.
74. The 1976 presidential contest may have been an exception to that trend, at least partially in response to the post-Watergate public search for a candidate both "competent" and "trustworthy."
75. For an excellent discussion of the effects of election rules and rule changes on political parties, see Sorauf, *Party Politics,* chaps. 9–11, 13.
76. Miller and Levitin, *Leadership and Change,* p. 19.
77. Robert Agranoff, *The New Style in Election Campaigns,* 2nd ed. (Boston: Holbrook Press, 1976), p. 6.
78. Ibid.
79. Sorauf, *Party Politics,* p. 264.
80. Maxwell E. McCombs and Donald R. Shaw, "The Agenda-Setting Function of the Mass Media," *Public Opinion Quarterly* 36 (Summer 1972), pp. 176–87.
81. Nie et al., *The Changing American Voter,* p. 213.
82. Knoke, *Change and Continuity,* p. 11.
83. Nie et al., *The Changing American Voter,* p. 218.
84. Cf. Knoke, *Change and Continuity,* Chapter 3; and Nie et al., *The Changing American Voter,* pp. 217–23.
85. Ladd with Hadley, *Transformations,* pp. 131–34.
86. Ladd and Hadley note that only 250,000 blacks were even registered to vote by 1940 (p. 131).
87. Knoke, *Change and Continuity,* p. 41.
88. Blacks who developed party loyalties between the Civil War and the Great Depression were, of course, usually Republicans. During that period, most blacks (about 90 percent in the late 1800s) lived in the South and were virtually disenfranchised. Not until the 1920s did blacks migrate in large numbers to northern industrial centers, and not until after 1932 did blacks move into the Democratic camp. See Ladd with Hadley, *Transformations,* pp. 57–60. See also, the classic by V.O. Key, Jr., *Southern Politics* (New York: Alfred A. Knopf, 1949), pp. 286–91.
89. Ibid. p. 135.
90. Converse, *The Dynamics of Party Support,* p. 315; and Knoke, *Change and Continuity,* pp. 51–54.
91. Nie et al., *The Changing American Voter,* p. 221.
92. Knoke, *Change and Continuity,* pp. 46–50.
93. Nie et al., *The Changing American Voter,* pp. 221–23.
94. Ibid., p. 223.
95. Ladd with Hadley, *Transformations,* pp. 112–14.
96. Knoke, *Change and Continuity,* p. 42.
97. Ibid., p. 41.
98. Nie et al., *The Changing American Voter,* pp. 227–28; Ladd with Hadley, *Transformations,* p. 291.
99. Knoke, *Change and Continuity,* p. 63.

100. Norval D. Glenn, "Class and Party Support in the United States: Recent and Emerging Trends," *Public Opinion Quarterly* 37 (Spring 1973), p. 1.
101. Knoke, *Change and Continuity,* p. 88.
102. Glenn, "Class and Party Support," p. 16.
103. Ibid., p. 7.
104. Norval D. Glenn, "Class and Party Support in 1972," *Public Opinion Quarterly* 39 (Spring 1975), p. 118.
105. Ibid., p. 120.
106. James Clotfelter and Charles L. Prysby, *Political Choices* (New York: Holt, Rinehart & Winston, 1980), p. 66.
107. William H. Flanigan and Nancy H. Zingale, *Political Behavior of the American Electorate,* 4th ed. (Boston: Allyn & Bacon, 1979), p. 90.
108. Knoke, *Change and Continuity,* p. 88.
109. Glenn, "Class and Party Support," p. 19; and Glenn, "Class and Party Support in 1972," p. 121.
110. Ladd with Hadley, *Transformations,* Chapter 4.
111. Ibid., p. 217.
112. Ibid., p. 213.
113. See Knoke, *Change and Continuity,* pp. 19–20; and Ladd with Hadley, *Transformations,* pp. 46–53.
114. Ladd with Hadley, *Transformations,* p. 61.
115. Ibid., pp. 61–64.
116. The reader should not assume that all Protestants (or even most Protestants) are Republican. Between 1952 and 1972, Republicans had plurality support from northern Protestants. This pattern did not, of course, hold in the South, where a majority of Protestants were Democrats through 1964. Even today the Republican party does not enjoy the following of a majority of Protestants. In fact, Jews were the only religious group lending *majority* support to either party by 1972 (Knoke, *Change and Continuity,* p. 23).
117. Knoke, *Change and Continuity,* p. 25.
118. In *The Changing American Voter,* Nie et al. suggest that Catholics have become even more Democratic over time (p. 229).
119. Nie et al., *The Changing American Voter,* p. 224.
120. Ibid., p. 210.
121. Knoke, *Change and Continuity,* pp. 29–36. See also Converse, *Elections and the Political Order,* for an analysis of the effects of Catholicism in 1960.
122. Knoke, *Change and Continuity,* p. 35.
123. Ibid., pp. 35–36.
124. In *The Changing American Voter,* Nie et al. note that much of the change in every demographic group is explained by the entry into the electorate of new cohorts, or the young (pp. 234–38).
125. On a five-point scale ranging from left to moderate left, center, moderate right, and right, 43 percent of the Democrats were either left or right in 1972 compared to 26 percent in 1956; 44 percent of the Republicans were in the extreme categories compared to 27 percent in 1956. See Nie et al., *The Changing American Voter,* p. 199.
126. Campbell et al., *The American Voter,* p. 143.
127. Key, *The Responsible Electorate.*
128. Flanigan and Zingale, *Political Behavior of the American Electorate,* p. 60.
129. Ibid., p. 62.
130. John R. Petrocik, "An Analysis of Intransitivities in the Index of Party Identification," *Political Methodology* 1 (Summer 1974), pp. 31–47.

131. Walter Dean Burnham, *Critical Elections,* p. 133.
132. Gerald M. Pomper, "The Decline of the Party in American Elections," *Political Science Quarterly* 92 (Spring 1977), p. 41.
133. Ibid.
134. Benjamin I. Page, *Choices and Echoes* (Chicago: University of Chicago Press, 1978), p. 104.
135. Ladd with Hadley, *Transformations,* p. 332.
136. Paul Allen Beck, "A Socialization Theory of Partisan Realignment," in *Controversies in American Voting Behavior,* Richard G. Niemi and Herbert F. Weisberg, eds. (San Francisco: W.H. Freeman & Co., 1976), p. 409.
137. Ibid., p. 411.

CHAPTER 11

EQUALITY AND LIBERATION: PUBLIC OPINION, RACE, AND SEX

Two groups have been particularly involved in and affected by a changing political agenda — blacks and women. This chapter examines their opinions and also looks at public views about issues relevant to both groups. The focus is on political trust and efficacy, issues of public policy, and civil and political rights.

BLACK ATTITUDES AND BEHAVIOR

In every way, black opinions differ significantly from those of whites. Blacks are united on the issues of race and civil rights, and those issues guide their civic orientations, policy positions, and political participation. Whites, on the other hand, remain divided in their policy opinions, including racial issues.

Political Trust and Political Efficacy

The importance of political trust and efficacy has been stressed in earlier chapters. Cynicism and inefficacy may indicate unresponsive policymaking, a lack of citizen support for government programs, and a potential for either protest behavior or apathetic withdrawal. This section elaborates the earlier discussion of racial differences in political trust and efficacy. Although blacks have, since the late 1960s, proved substantially more distrustful of the political system than whites, the racial disparity in efficacy is not nearly so dramatic. Certainly, blacks have not always been less trustful than whites. In fact, the middle sixties saw blacks' positive evaluations of the political system exceeding those of whites. But black trust in government declined after 1966, and soon their evaluations had become more negative than those of whites.

Numerous studies mark the turning point for black trust in government as 1967. Joel Aberbach and Jack Walker, reporting results from a 1967 Detroit study, note that blacks were considerably less trustful than were whites.[1]

They found 52 percent of blacks to have low levels of trust in government, compared to 33 percent of Detroit whites. Schley Lyons's study of Toledo Public School System students in 1968 presents similar findings.[2] In a review of nine studies of black trust in government conducted after 1967, Paul R. Abramson found that seven showed lower trust among black children.[3] The evidence, he claims, "suggests that there was a time-series trend in which racial differences on political trust emerged during and after the summer of 1967."[4] Lower levels of political trust among blacks have persisted since the late sixties; in 1976, black respondents to the CPS American National Election Study were about 20 percent more likely to give distrustful responses (76 percent of blacks claimed to "never" trust government to do what is best compared to 58 percent of whites).

These findings are supported by a study of changes in black alienation from white society between 1968 and 1971. Howard Schuman and Shirley Hatchett surveyed Detroit blacks in 1968 and again in 1971, finding that blacks became more alienated during that period, more likely to view whites as hostile, and more willing to engage in violent protest.[5] These tendencies were most pronounced among the young, especially the best educated among the young. Another study of college students at three black southern colleges and at a predominately white university found black students to be more alienated than whites and over twice as likely to be cynical toward government.[6]

Certainly, the middle 1960s were years of rising hopes followed by severe disappointment for American blacks. The promises of the Kennedy and Johnson administrations and the passage of major civil rights legislation in 1964 and 1965 failed to bring rapid change. That cynicism and alienation would follow disappointment is not surprising, but an unexpected deviation from the normal relationship between political trust and education also occurred. Traditionally, higher levels of political trust have been linked to higher levels of education.[7] Although the trust-education relationship still held by the early 1970s for whites, Pomper notes that by 1972 college-educated blacks were "particularly prone to changing and downgrading their evaluation of government."[8] As Figure 11–1 indicates, the same held true in 1976. College-educated blacks were far more likely to be distrustful of government than were whites when asked, "How much of the time do you think the government in Washington can be trusted to do what is right?"

Aberbach and Walker suggest that political trust is strongly linked to race — specifically, to racial ideology — even when the effects of socioeconomic status are held constant. They examine the relationship between political beliefs and political trust for both whites and blacks, describing the relationship as "a process in which a set of beliefs influences the level of trust which in turn influences or deepens the beliefs."[9] For blacks, the beliefs most tied to political trust are racial pride and militance. For whites, variables that best predict trust are opinions on integration and spending directed at ghetto improvement.[10] In their Detroit study, Aberbach and Walker found distrustful blacks far more likely to respond affirmatively to the question, "Can you imagine a situation in which you would riot?" Distrustful whites were more prone to support an extremist (anti-integrationist) candidate. The result is

FIGURE 11–1   The Relationship Between Political Trust and Education by Race, 1976[a]

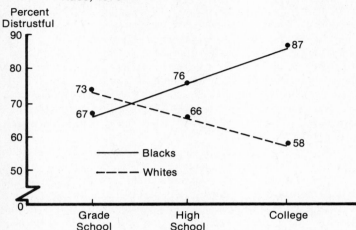

[a]How much do you think the government in Washington can be trusted to do what is right?
Source: Center for Political Studies. American National Election Study, 1976 [machine-readable data file].

that "many distrustful whites troop to the polls to vote for so-called 'law and order' candidates."[11]

In other words, both the sources and the impact of distrust in government vary from group to group. But racial attitudes are very important for all groups. Indeed, political trust depends on the impact of the political system on different groups. Aberbach and Walker stress the interaction between trust and system operation:

> *Our analysis shows that political trust is not merely a reflection of our respondents' basic personality traits, or a simple function of general social background factors. Our most important explanatory variables are those which arise from the workings of the social or political system, such as the citizen's expectations about the treatment he will receive from government officials, general feelings of deprivation and well-being, and beliefs about the status or acceptability of one's group in society. Levels of trust are determined by these factors and, in turn, are influenced by them in a chain of interactions which continues as the political system operates. Repeated setbacks or disappointments are necessary to dissipate trust when it is high and when trust is low, numerous successes are needed to increase it.*[12]

One might expect changes in trust to be accompanied by concurrent declines in political efficacy among blacks. There is no evidence of such a trend. Although most studies of political socialization of black children have supported lower levels of political efficacy and the slower development of efficacy among black youngsters, studies during the 1970s show only a narrow gap between adult black and white efficacy levels. Table 11–1 shows that by 1976, blacks were only slightly less efficacious than whites, the largest difference being that blacks are less convinced that officials care what they think.

TABLE 11-1   Political Efficacy among Blacks and Whites in 1976

Percentage Agreeing That	Whites	Blacks
Public officials care what people like me think	48%	32%
Politics and government not too complicated to understand	28	23
People like me have some say in what government does	58	56

Source: Center for Political Studies. American National Election Study, 1976 [machine-readable data file].

Although few studies of childhood socialization focus attention on blacks, those that have find wide agreement on the differential development of political efficacy between the races.[13] For example, both Dennis and Lyons note lower levels of political efficacy among blacks even when socioeconomic status is controlled.[14] Lyons found black children felt "less efficacious in high school than whites felt in junior high."[15]

This tendency for black children to display lower confidence in their potential to change the political system carries into adulthood. Analyzing a 1960 National Opinion Research Center Study, Dwaine Marvick noted that blacks were far less likely to feel that local government had been helpful, to feel that they could prevent a city council from passing unjust regulations, or to try to change a local law.[16] Although the difference between black and white efficacy levels persists, it apparently has decreased substantially. By 1972, blacks were only slightly less likely than whites to agree that "people like me have power."[17] Table 11-1 shows that the same was true in 1976.

Political efficacy has long been related to education, and that relationship holds for blacks as well as for whites. Even among young children, high achievement is positively related to efficacy.[18] Further, the more education a child receives, the higher is his or her efficacy. This is true for both blacks and whites, although Lyons found that racial differences persisted at all grade levels.[19] Thus, political efficacy, like political trust, is lower for blacks than for whites. But the racial differences in efficacy appear to be diminishing. Further, efficacy, unlike trust, is positively related to education for both races.

One could surmise that since efficacy and education are positively related for both races, and since blacks tend to attain lower education levels than do whites, education might have a leveling effect on political efficacy. In other words, we might expect education to reduce efficacy differences between the races. Pomper notes that this was the case in 1972, when college-educated blacks and whites were equally likely to give positive evaluations of their political power.[20] But the 1976 American National Election Study shows strikingly different results. Although blacks became more efficacious as their educational levels increased, college-educated blacks remained somewhat *less* efficacious than their white counterparts. Table 11-2 illustrates the racial differences in three efficacy items by education. What is particularly interesting is the fact that only among those blacks of high educational achievement do the consistent racial differences remain. In fact, among people with grade school and high school education, blacks tend to feel slightly *more* efficacious than do whites.

TABLE 11–2   Political Efficacy among Blacks and Whites in 1976, Controlling for Education

			Education	
Percentage Agreeing That		*Grade School*	*High School*	*College*
Public officials care what people like me think	White	23%	44%	63%
	Black	23	32	42
Politics and government not too complicated to understand	White	10	21	44
	Black	20	22	28
People like me have some say in what government does	White	35	54	72
	Black	50	55	63

Source: Center for Political Studies. American National Election Study, 1976 [machine-readable data file].

Equally important is that efficacy is apparently differentially related to political participation for blacks and whites. John S. Jackson notes that for blacks, efficacy is marginally related to conventional participation but not at all related to protest participation.[21] In his college samples, those students who feel a need to resort to protest activities instead of conventional participation are not, as might be expected, drawn simply from the ranks of the inefficacious. This finding corresponds to Pomper's analysis of 1972 national survey results. By combining responses to an efficacy question and to a political trust question (on the fairness of government), Pomper creates four categories: supporters (high trust, high efficacy), trustful (high trust, low efficacy), cynics (low trust, high efficacy), and oppressed (low trust, low efficacy).[22] Pomper observes that the cynic and oppressed categories increased markedly for blacks between 1964 and 1972. By 1972, cynics comprised a plurality among blacks, and together the cynics and the oppressed made up almost three-fourths of the blacks surveyed.[23] Table 11–3 shows that the same was true in 1976. Of all blacks surveyed in 1976, 42 percent were cynics, and another 32 percent were among the "oppressed."[24]

TABLE 11–3   A Typology of Black Feelings of Trust and Efficacy in 1976

		Political Trust	
		High	Low
Political Efficacy	High	*Supporters* 16%	*Cynics* 42%
	Low	*Trustful* 9%	*Oppressed* 32%
			N=192

Source: Center for Political Studies. American National Election Study, 1976 [machine-readable data file]. The category labels come from Gerald Pomper, *The Voters' Choice* (New York: Dodd, Mead & Co., 1975), p. 126.

Perhaps even more important than this prominence of cynics and the oppressed among black survey respondents is the tendency for the *best-educated*
blacks to fall into these categories. Pomper sees a new trend for well-educated
blacks:

> *Among whites, the college-educated group has always shown the highest
> degree of support and the most favorable ratio of supporters to cynics, and
> this remains true in 1972. In the past, the same relationship has been evi-
> dent among blacks as well, with the ratio of supporters to cynics among the
> college-educated reaching as high as 8:1. In 1972, by contrast, cynicism is
> particularly evident in this leadership group.*[25]

The same holds true in 1976. Table 11–4 shows the breakdown of the four
categories (supporters, trustful, cynics, and oppressed) for blacks and whites
within categories of education. Pomper's point is substantiated. Among
blacks with college education, 56 percent are cynics; among whites, 39
percent are cynics. Similarly, 30 percent of college-educated blacks feel
oppressed, while the corresponding figure for whites is 20 percent.

**TABLE 11–4   The Distribution of Alienation Types by Education
and Race, 1976**

Alienation Type	Grade School		High School		College	
	Blacks	*Whites*	*Blacks*	*Whites*	*Blacks*	*Whites*
Cynics	27%	25%	44%	35%	56%	39%
Supporters	26	10	13	20	12	33
Trusting	13	17	12	13	2	9
Oppressed	35	48	32	32	30	20
Total	101%	100%	101%	100%	100%	101%

Source: Center for Political Studies. American National Election Study, 1976 [machine-readable
data file]. The alienation type category labels are from Gerald Pomper, *The Voters' Choice* (New
York: Dodd, Mead & Co., 1975), p. 126.

Racial differences in both trust and efficacy persist through 1976: blacks
are substantially less trustful and slightly less efficacious. But the sources of
trust seem to differ across the races. For blacks the relationship between
trust and education is the reverse of the positive relationship found among
whites. In addition, efficacy, although similarly related to education for both
races, shows a much weaker relationship with education for blacks. And the
distance between college-educated blacks and whites is greater (in fact, the
direction is reversed) than that for blacks and whites at lower education
levels.

Attitudes Toward Black Civil Rights

One area of clear change is the network of attitudes toward civil rights issues. Over the past two decades, Americans have liberalized their positions
on such issues as integrated education (depending on whether the question
wording incorporates busing), housing, and interracial social contacts. Among
blacks, agreement on racial issues has been virtually unanimous (above 90
percent).[26] Among whites, support for integration has not been so dramatic.
Indeed, during the 1930s and 1940s, a large majority of whites opposed open

housing and equal job opportunity.[27] By the early 1960s support for these and other prointegration issues had climbed to over a majority in most instances.[28] Figure 11–2 shows that across several racial issues, liberalization has taken place — most rapidly in the interval between 1970 and 1972.

FIGURE 11–2   Changes in White Racial Attitudes, 1963–1976

TREIMAN SCALE of questions on racial attitudes was administered to a nationwide sample of about 1,350 whites in 1963, 1970, 1972 and 1976. The bars show for each year the percentage of respondents giving what is considered to be a prointegration response to each question.

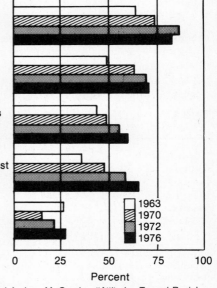

1. Do you think white students and black students should go to the same schools or to separate schools?

2. How strongly would you object if a member of your family wanted to bring a black friend home to dinner?

3. White people have a right to keep blacks out of their neighborhoods if they want to, and blacks should respect that right.

4. Do you think there should be laws against marriages between blacks and whites?

5. Blacks shouldn't push themselves where they're not wanted.

1963
1970
1972
1976

0   25   50   75   100
Percent

Source: From D. Garth Taylor, Paul B. Sheatsley, and Andrew M. Greeley, "Attitudes Toward Racial Integration," *Scientific American* 238 (June 1978), p. 43. Copyright © 1978 by Scientific American, Inc. All rights reserved.

Additional evidence of increased acceptance of integration is that the endorsement of the integration of public facilities has "now become so settled in the public mind that it [is] difficult to find whites who would not endorse the principle."[29]

Despite the increasing acceptance of integration, many whites remain reluctant to endorse full racial integration and equality. In particular, resistance seems to spring from the South, from less-educated members of the public, from older persons, and from persons less accepting of liberal values.[30]

Scholars differ some in their analysis of trends in support for integration, but there is general agreement that liberalization is accelerated among the younger and the more highly educated.[31] Clearly, the South still lags behind other regions, although that gap narrowed slightly during the 1970–1972 period.[32] Taylor et al. speculate that change may stem from a general liberalization in society, a "general movement toward a liberal position on several measures of personal and civil liberties."[33] These authors build a model to explain changing racial attitudes; the model incorporates generation, education, and general liberalism as causal factors.[34] As an indicator for general liberalism, they select willingness to support a qualified woman for president. The findings are informative. Age cohort clearly has the strongest effect on increasing racial liberalism, accounting for 37 percent of the change between 1963 and 1976. Of that explained change, 18 percent is accountable by age alone, the remaining 19 percent by the greater education and general liberalism of the young. Taylor et al. speculate that this age-specific liberalism is generated by exposure to "different values."[35] Younger cohorts have grown up in a more integrated society. Overall, the model accounts for more than half of the change in racial liberalism over the period.[36]

Even though public opinion increasingly supports racial integration, Pomper notes a clash between white America's general attitudes and its practical applications of those attitudes.[37] Support for racial issues has not been followed by support for the tactics used by blacks to attain the goal of equality. Not until 1972 did a simple majority of the public (including both blacks and whites) disagree that civil rights leaders have pushed too fast, that most black actions have been violent, and that the actions of blacks have hurt their cause.[38] Blacks and whites clearly disagree on the tactics appropriate to the struggle for equality, with 80 percent of blacks endorsing protest marches in 1972 (57 percent of whites), 71 percent of blacks endorsing civil disobedience (54 percent of whites), and 68 percent of blacks favoring demonstrations (38 percent of whites).[39]

Another area in which white support for civil rights has rarely exceeded 15 percent is school busing.[40] Using 1972 survey data, Sears et al. test two possible explanations for lagging white support for busing. One model explained positioning on busing in terms of self-interest, predicting that survey respondents with school-aged children living in areas where busing was occurring or threatened, and/or living in areas with all-white schools, would be most likely to oppose busing. A second model, the "symbolic politics model," "views anti-busing sentiment as primarily derived from long-standing political predispositions, specifically racial prejudice and political conservatism, which in turn can be traced to political socialization in preadult life."[41] The study points to the latter explanation as the significant one, concluding that attitudes toward busing are manifestations of generalized racial attitudes learned during childhood, rather than rational reactions to immediate situations.[42]

Like other dimensions of political tolerance, survey responses reflecting racial attitudes seem to depend upon the context and content of the question asked. Whites have found it increasingly easy to endorse the general principle of equal opportunity and to mix with blacks in formal relationships. But they still are reluctant to support "preferential treatment in the economic sphere or more intimate relationships" (forced on children by busing).[43] Racial tolerance is a complex set of attitudes, and liberalization appears to have proceeded at a much faster pace on its more general and less intimate dimensions.

Thus, although support for integration has grown substantially among the white public in recent years, Americans have been more accepting of the principles of equality than of the actual struggle for equality.

Attitudes on Policy Issues: Liberalization among Blacks

The gaps between blacks' and whites' opinions on several racial issues have indeed narrowed, but what about attitudes on nonracial issues? Is polarization of the races evident in other policy domains? The answer appears to be yes, increasingly so. Blacks are becoming more liberal than the population at large, not only on issues like school integration, but also on foreign policy and the size of the government. In fact, in each of five issue areas (economic welfare, size of government, black welfare, school integration, and foreign policy), blacks have enlarged their distance from the general population between the 1950s and the 1970s.[44] Indeed, "no other group in American society is as distinctively liberal as American blacks."[45]

The liberal consensus of American blacks (and the change in the distribution of the issue opinions of both blacks and the larger population) is illustrated in Figure 11-3. Note that 62 percent of blacks were located in the most liberal decile of the population by the early 1970s, while only 15 percent of the general population could be so classified. While the general population has moved from the center toward both extremes during the twenty-year interval, blacks have moved much more rapidly toward the extreme position and virtually all movement has been in a leftward direction.

The dramatic concentration of blacks on the left-most part of the attitude scale by the 1970s also indicates a remarkable level of attitude consistency; placement in the most liberal decile indicates virtually perfect consistency across issue areas.[46] Nie et al. point out, "The degree of liberal attitude consistency [for blacks] across such a diverse set of issues is greater than for any other group."[47] The implication of this may be that the increased salience of race on the political agenda has provided an organizing principle for American blacks, guiding choices not only on racial issues, but on other issues as well. The end product has been a group of people with very tightly organized, highly consistent issue beliefs.

Support for Black Political Candidates

Americans seem to be far more receptive to black candidates than they were two decades ago. In 1978, 77 percent of the public claimed that they would vote for a "generally well-qualified [black] man" if their party nominated him for president.[48] In contrast, in 1958 only 38 percent expressed a willingness to support a black candidate. Socioeconomic lines seem to guide these opinions in important ways. College-educated respondents are 25 percent more likely to give positive responses than are the grade-school educated (86 percent to 61 percent). Blacks are considerably more supportive than whites (91 percent to 75 percent). Support is lowest in the South (67 percent) and highest in the West (87 percent). And upper-income persons ($20,000 and over) are more positive than are respondents with incomes under $5,000.[49]

FIGURE 11 – 3   Liberal – Conservative Distribution of Blacks and General Population in 1950s and 1970s.

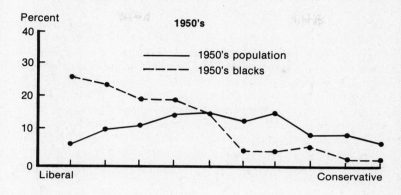

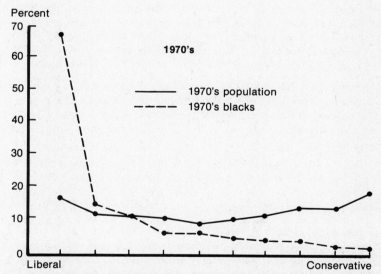

Source: Norman H. Nie, Sidney Verba, and John R. Petrocik, *The Changing American Voter,* enlarged edition (Cambridge: Harvard University Press, 1979), pp. 244, 254. Reprinted by permission. Copyright © 1976, 1979 by the Twentieth Century Fund.

Expressed support for black candidates should, however, be viewed with some skepticism. Richard Murray and Arnold Vedlitz report that although black political candidates *in five Southern cities* received 94 percent of the black vote, they received only 22 percent of the white vote.[50] Upper socioeconomic-status whites were somewhat more likely to support black candidates, but even this group gave them only 27 percent of the vote.

POLITICAL PARTICIPATION AND GROUP CONSCIOUSNESS

Although blacks manifest high levels of support for protest activity, that support does not preclude participation in those forms of political activity considered "legitimate" by the American populous. In a 1968 study of the participation of blacks and whites, Verba and Nie discovered that blacks did exhibit lower levels of activity than did whites on *some forms* of participation; but when socioeconomic status and/or group consciousness are held constant, those participation differences disappear and, in some cases, are reversed.[51]

In examining the lower participation levels of blacks, Verba and Nie raised the possibility that any relationship between race and political activism may be spurious. The slightly lower activity of blacks may stem from their lower socioeconomic status. Indeed, when the participation of blacks and whites is compared *within* socioeconomic groups, the picture changes: "at five out of the six socioeconomic levels, blacks participate more than whites."[52]

A second factor also proves powerful in explaining the political behavior of blacks. Those blacks who demonstrate high levels of group consciousness also exceed the political activity of whites.[53] Verba and Nie measured the level of group consciousness by counting references to race in response to open-ended questions about group conflict. They found that respondents who mentioned race — and thus showed an "awareness of their own status as a deprived group" — actually participated more than whites.[54] In short, blacks

participate less than whites but more than one would expect given their social and economic conditions. And among those blacks who manifest some consciousness of group identification, the rate of participation is as high as that of whites and higher than one would expect given their other social characteristics.[55]

Given equal socioeconomic footing, then, blacks exceed the activity levels of whites, particularly when they exhibit group consciousness.

WOMEN AND PUBLIC OPINION

A recent study of childhood socialization shows that children maintain rather inflexible attitudes about what men and women can and should do with their lives. The following are some excerpts from children's statements about the limitations placed upon the activities of men:

"Can't bake so good. They don't know how. Can't do housework. They get tired and feel like resting."   (second-grade boy)

"Can't clean house like a lady wants it. He doesn't know how."
                                                                (second grade boy)

"I don't think a male child would want to put on an apron (to learn cooking)."   (second-grade girl)[56]

Women, too, are restricted from performing traditionally male tasks:

"Women can't be doctors because they's probably faint in the middle of the operation, 'cause they'd be afraid."   (fourth-grade boy)

"She's not allows to (work). If a man saw her he's chase her."

(second-grade boy)

"We're not allowed to do that (be a truck driver)."   *(fourth-grade girl)*

"They don't have enough power."   *(fourth-grade girl)*[57]

The belief that certain types of work are off limits for women is still widespread among children, and included among the restricted occupations is political activism. Women traditionally have been less active in politics, they express less interest in politics, and they are less efficacious than men. Many adult women and men (some studies show more women than men) agree with the elementary school sample: politics is not, for many of the American public, a world that welcomes women.

Political Trust, Interest, and Efficacy

Sex differences in general civic orientations has been a theme of much literature. In particular, studies note that women are less interested in politics, less confident in their abilities to affect the political system, and perhaps more confident in authority figures to do what is right. *The American Voter* reported that "it is the sense of political efficacy that differs most sharply and consistently between men and women."[58] Even when controlling the effects of education and region, Campbell et al. saw significant sex differences in efficacy; they attribute lower levels of efficacy among women to sex-role orientations. The woman is expected to see the man (husband) as her link with the outside world.[59] Similarly, she guides her political decisions with "secondhand" information, leaving the "sifting of information up to her husband" and letting him guide her vote.[60] As a consequence, women have also shown lower levels of political sophistication.[61]

Studies of childhood political socialization point out that sex differences in political orientations surface long before adulthood. Fred Greenstein's study of New Haven children (grades 4 through 8) suggests that some of the differences noted in *The American Voter* were already present in his sample. Boys showed higher levels of political information; they were also more apt to respond to questions about the news with political references ("Can you think of a news story which made you feel happy?).[62] That these differences may be attributable to perceptions of "proper" behavior for men and women is underscored by a growing (and strong) tendency of children to rely on the father over the mother for political advice by the eighth grade.[63]

Another study of early political socialization by Robert Hess and Judith Torney provides additional evidence of the higher political information possessed by boys.[64] They find boys more interested in politics, more likely to discuss political issues, and better able to handle abstractions.[65] Although girls demonstrate an acceptance of the normative values attached to being a good citizen, they report lower levels of political interest than do boys.[66] Girls discuss political issues as frequently as do boys, but boys are reported much more likely to engage in political arguments. Girls tend to view politics in more personal terms; they focus on persons in government, while boys focus on institutions. And they are more strongly attached to the political system.

Hess and Torney's study, however, finds no political efficacy differences in the early grades. Children's perceptions of effectiveness of political action do not vary by sex.[67] The absence of sex-related differences in efficacy finds further support in the work of Easton and Dennis, who note

> *something must happen between childhood and later phases of the life cycle that leads females into becoming disenchanted with their earlier expected role in political life that they once shared with boys.*[68]

A more recent study of fourth- through twelfth-grade children challenges some findings of Hess and Torney and substantiates others. Orum et al. investigated the "political effect" of their sample.[69] In particular, they questioned the finding of a stronger attachment of females to government and of a greater personalization of government among girls. They found no significant differences between boys and girls on these characteristics; nor do measures of political benevolence and cynicism scales show sex differences. Similarly, no differences are reported in the political discussions of boys and girls.[70] Orum et al. did find that boys score consistently higher on political information than do girls, although these differences are significant only for white children.[71]

The finding of similar levels of efficacy in children is problematic. If sex-role orientations lead to political differentiation among both children and adults, then why do girls feel as competent as boys in their dealings with the political system, while women are less efficacious than men? Several possibilities seem obvious, and they will be explored below. First, it is possible that efficacy becomes differentiated during adulthood, as Easton and Dennis suggested. Women may *become* less efficacious because of *situational* factors (like, for example, motherhood) or because of more sophisticated applications of the sex-role models they learned as children. A second possibility is that early findings of sex-related efficacy differences were time-bound, that the socialization process has changed and with it adult differences.

The connection between women's political efficacy and situational variables has been sustained by recent research. In particular, female employment and childbearing are related to feelings of political competence. Kristi Andersen examined the political efficacy of men, working women, and housewives from 1952 to 1972.[72] Her study concludes that both working and nonworking women exhibited lower political efficacy than did men in 1952. But by 1960, working women's efficacy was very similar to that of men, while housewives widened the efficacy gap.[73] Andersen goes on to show that since 1960, employed women have shown efficacy levels similar to those of men. And those changes, according to Andersen, cannot be attributed to socioeconomic characteristics.[74] This trend continued in 1976, but Andersen's measurement of political efficacy may hide an important characteristic of female political efficacy. Andersen creates an efficacy scale, combining three efficacy items, and then uses that scale to look at sex differences. As Figure 11–4 shows, this procedure hides the exaggerated sex differences on the item "sometimes government and politics seem too difficult to understand." On this item even employed women remain less efficacious (by 16 pecent) than are men.

FIGURE 11 – 4   Political Efficacy Items for Working Males and Working Females, 1976

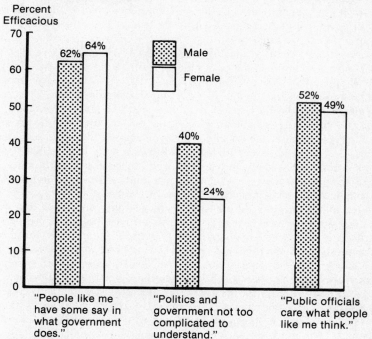

Source: Center for Political Studies. American National Election Study, 1976 [machine-readable data file].

Another adult characteristic is thought to affect the political efficacy of women and might help to explain the lack of differentiation among children. Cornelia Flora and Naomi Lynn report that mothers are less efficacious than nonmothers, again even when socioeconomic status is controlled.[75] In fact, women of higher socioeconomic status exhibit greater differences tied to motherhood than do those of lower status.[76] These differences may be attributable to "anticipatory socialization"—that is, women of lower education may have better anticipated motherhood status, while more highly educated women suffer more trauma and an accelerated sense of isolation with the birth of a child.[77]

One theory explaining lower political efficacy among women meshes well with reported efficacy differences along occupational and child-rearing lines for women. Rita Mae Kelly and Mary Boutilier build a theory of the political socialization of women in which the acquisition of political efficacy is a primary element.[78] Political efficacy, they note, is an outgrowth of general feelings of personal competence to control one's life space, or "the physical and social reality of an individual's day-to-day existence."[79] Some aspects of life (including the political) have, according to this theory, been excluded from female control.[80] In order to broaden the scope of female control in the political world, women must first broaden their control over nonpolitical aspects of their life. The nuclear family and the roles it generates have limited that control. An extension of these arguments might easily show that working women and women without children experience greater life-space control and thus exhibit higher levels of political efficacy. This theory is also linked to sex-role ideology or one's feelings about the appropriate roles for women and men to play. Sex-role ideology is thought to be strongly related to the political attitudes and behavior of women; it will be discussed more fully later in this chapter. For now, let it suffice to say that sex-role ideology may have defined the male as the "public" person and the female as the "private" person, thus limiting the "life space" available for the female to control.

Lest the reader believe that men and women are uniformly seen as radically different in their feelings of political competence, it should be noted that findings of adult differences in political efficacy have been subject to challenge. We noted above that the absence of childhood efficacy differences could point to changing patterns; early findings of adult efficacy differences may be time-bound. When analyzing 1968 National Election Study data, Judy Bertelson found significant sex differences in efficacy only on one of four efficacy items; women were more likely to find politics too complex to understand.[81] This finding fits with women's more general tendency "to find life overwhelmingly complicated and beyond control" and would certainly fit into the "life-space" theory presented above.[82] Nevertheless, on other aspects of efficacy women are not significantly lower than men.[83] Findings reported by John Soule and Wilma McGrath show that sex differences on political efficacy are not large (since 1956, never as great as 10 percent on any item other than that of government complexity).[84] Moreover, Soule and McGrath note that for women of higher education levels, sex differences are greater (not reduced, as suggested in *The American Voter*).[85]

Data from the 1976 American National Election Study support the claims of both Bertelson and Soule and McGrath. Table 11–5 shows that women in 1976 fit the pattern described by Bertelson. Women are only slightly less efficacious than men and then only on the government-complexity item.

TABLE 11–5   Responses to Political Efficacy Items by Sex, 1976

	Male	Female
People like me have some say in what government does	57%	58%
Government and politics not too complicated to understand	35	22
Public officials care what people like me think	48	45

Source: Center for Political Studies. American National Election Study, 1976 [machine-readable data file].

In summary, sex differences in efficacy may once have been large and significant, but by 1976 they were slight. Differences in political efficacy seem to be restricted to the perception of government complexity, and they seem to stem from a combination of situational factors and socialization.

Women and Political Participation

Closely connected to traditional views of lower levels of political efficacy among women are pictures of lower levels of political participation. Just as young children respond that women should not be truck drivers, so have adults stated similar views: "I have never voted. I never will ... A woman's place is in the home ... Leave politics to the men." Or, "Mama always thought politics was men's business."[86] Indeed, Verba and Nie found women to be slightly overrepresented among the "inactive" category among the public. (Inactives are citizens who "engage in no political activity." They have "little or no psychological involvement in politics, little or no skill and competence.")[87] Between 1944 and 1954 women voted at a rate about 10 percent lower than that of men.[88] That difference persisted through the 1960 presidential election; but by 1968 the difference was only 3 percent, and it has remained low in subsequent elections.[89] Similarly, Andersen reports that between 1952 and 1972 the sex gap in campaign activity has also narrowed.[90]

That women's political participation traditionally has lagged behind that of men should not be surprising. In the main, the difference has been attributed to political efficacy and feelings of political competence, which may be transmitted through the socialization process and limited by the life experiences of women.[91] But what has caused the narrowing of the gaps? To some extent, the participation gap seems to have narrowed because of (or at least simultaneously with) the reduction of other gaps. Also, the relationship between participation and sex seems to have been at least partly a function of socioeconomic differences between males and females. For example, Verba and Nie's study shows sex to have a much weaker effect on all types of participation than does socioeconomic status.[92] In particular, two changes in the socioeconomic status of women seem to reduce sex differences: increased education among women and the increase of women (particularly of professional women) in the work force.[93]

The education gap has long been a factor in differentiating male and female political behavior. Marjorie Lansing shows that beginning in 1952 there has been little, if any, difference in voting rates for males and females with high levels of education.[94] The fact that more and more women have reached higher educational levels has, not surprisingly, meant that the sex difference in participation has been reduced. Figure 11–5 shows that in 1976 sex differences in voting participation almost disappear for the college educated while they remain high (23 percent) for those with grade school education. Similarly, Hansen et al. report that "as of 1972, rates of voting, campaign activism, and political letter-writing among college educated or working women were equal to or greater than those of men of similar SES levels."[95]

In addition, the number of women in the work force has increased dramatically. The turn of women to the work force may provoke political participation in several ways:

> Not only do their jobs provide a growing number of women with a focus outside the home; their jobs can also offer them organizational bases for

political activity, such as trade unions and professional organizations. Finally, working women are more often the objects of the most obvious and measurable form of sex discrimination, unequal pay for equal work.[96]

In fact, Andersen finds that between 1952 and 1972 employed women not only reduced the participation differential with men, they eliminated it. By 1972 employed women were engaging in .85 campaign acts, men in .79, and housewives in .56.[97] Further, these changes cannot be attributed to education; the relative educational attainment of employed women and men has not changed since 1952.

FIGURE 11 – 5   Education and Sex Differences in Reported Voting Turnout, 1976

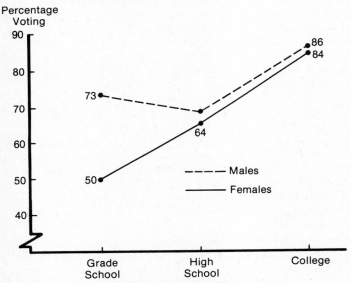

Source: Center for Political Studies. American National Election Study, 1976 [machine-readable data file].

Thus, the participation of women has increased relative to that of men, and the receding distance between the sexes can be attributed largely to two forces: education and employment status.

Although the political activity gap has narrowed, the possibility remains that female activists may still show important differences from their male counterparts. Edmond Constantini and Kenneth Craik suggest that the *political* division of labor among the sexes may approximate the division of labor in the home, with males playing "instrumental" roles (performing "those functions related to the external world") while females play more "expressive" roles (concentrating on internal, family affairs).[98] A recent study of party organization in two Georgia counties supports such a division of labor among activists:

Gender distinctions are particularly evident in two areas: ambition and activities. Activities such as attending meetings and telephoning can be understood as fulfilling the expressive support function and more commonly as "women's work." More importantly, the party's major goal — that of recruiting candidates and capturing office — is also gender-related. According to our research, men are more ambitious than women, an expressive/instrumental differential that comports well with recent evidence that the under-representation of women in elective office is more the result of a paucity of women candidates than discrimination against them at the polls.[99]

Still further support for a traditional political division of labor is found in a study of Republican and Democratic committee workers in a Connecticut town. Diane Rothbard Margolis reports that although women were more active in local party organizations, they played less visible roles and were more likely to engage in telephone work or solitary work.[100] She suggests that

the overriding reason men and women take on the roles they do is that these are the roles they play in our culture wherever men and women come together in any sort of social organization, the prototypical one being the family.[101]

Thus, even women who are active in politics are prone to perform the institutional maintenance functions, while men hold the more prominent external roles. Even though participation differentials have been reduced in recent years, women seem to participate differently than do their male counterparts. Moreover, the narrowing of the participation gap has not meant equal representation among political officeholders. We now turn to a consideration of the attitudes of both women and men toward women in politics, particularly toward female candidates for political office.

Attitudes toward Women in Politics: Support for Female Candidates

One item that has caused considerable concern among feminist commentators has been the noted tendency of men to give greater support to women in politics than do women. In particular, men gave more support to female candidates during the 1963–1972 interval, with women matching the support of men only in 1972.[102] Although little change was noted in the attitude of either sex toward female candidates between 1949 and 1964,[103] the post-1963 change for both sexes was dramatic, with support growing about 20 percent for each sex.[104] In addition, the trend for greater support for female candidates among men during the middle 1960s seems to have disappeared (or at least diminished) in subsequent years.[105] Change in support for female candidates has clearly occurred.

Attitudes toward female political candidates most often have been registered by asking survey respondents about their willingness to vote for a woman for president.[106] During the past three decades the level of support has ranged from around 50 percent to near 80 percent (in 1975) with the greatest changes taking place during and after the early 1970s.[107] Explanations for the dramatic rise in support vary widely. First, changes again may be attributable to changes in education and other socioeconomic characteristics. Change may be generational and due to the entry of a new cohort that is better educated and more affluent than older members of the public. Second, and closely related to the education-opinion connection, opinion change may have come from the media publicity given to the women's movement, the public's awareness of that movement, and the subsequent policy responses.[108] Third, it has been suggested that the "changes" are in part artifacts of methodological procedures. And finally, changing sex-role attitudes — attitudes about appropriate roles for men and women — may best explain changes in political orientations.

The connection between education and attitudes toward women candidates (like the connection between education and liberalism) has been widely noted.[109] Myra Marx Ferree shows that among the electorate, willingness to vote for women increased between 1967 and 1972 and that the increase was directly related to education.[110] Changes subsequent to 1972 show similar trends. Additionally, in a 1971 Pittsburgh study of *women* voters and party committee members, Audrey Wells and Eleanor Smeal show an association between support for more women in public office (not just the presidency) and education.[111] Higher levels of support also are found among younger cohorts (twenty- to twenty-nine-years old) and higher-income respondents. Another study conducted during a city council race sporting two male and two female candidates for at-large positions corroborates these findings. Robert Bernstein and Jayne Polly concluded that female candidates can "expect a readier acceptance among middle and upper class voters"; and especially within the lower class a readier acceptance among black voters.[112]

If the rising acceptance of female candidates is indeed largely attributable to changing socioeconomic-status characteristics — primarily education — then variations in support for women in politics since the early 1970s have probably resulted from generational shifts, the entry of a new cohort into the voting public. That new cohort, because of its increased educational attainment, may manifest more positive feelings toward female political actors.

But the generational explanation may oversimplify the situation. E.M. Schreiber notes that increases in willingness to vote for a women for president parallel increases in coverage of women in periodical literature. His theory views the relationship between education and these attitudes as time-bound and as part of the life cycle of women's issues. Egalitarian stances toward women in politics will, Schreiber notes, "trickle down" to the lower SES segments of society:

> The education-related results reflect not so much broad-mindedness, enlightenment, or the like acquired through higher education but rather a greater awareness of changes in norms that have been legitimized by such means as laws and court decisions. This in turn implies that over an issue's life history, the education-opinion relationship is variable and that it can be expected to diminish as the legitimized attitudes "trickle down" to the less educated.[113]

If Schreiber is correct, the relationship between education and support for women should be diminishing rather than remaining stable.

Still another explanation of changing attitudes is found in "sex-role attitudes" and "sex-role identities."[114] The former includes people's evaluations of what is "appropriate" and "inappropriate" in a given society for men and women to do, think, and seem."[115] The latter measures people's tendency toward (or away from) androgyny (sex-role identities that combine desirable male and female traits). Marjorie Hershey, reporting on a 1976 study of students at Indiana University, notes that "respondents' levels of sex-stereotyping are the best predictors of their attitudes toward women in politics."[116] In other words, respondents who find roles traditionally deemed appropriate to one sex (e.g., housecleaning) equally acceptable to either sex also express egalitarian attitudes about political candidates. Thus, change may be attributable to changing sex-role attitudes. This is not to say that education and media influence are unrelated to support for women. In this sense, education and media influence may prod changes in sex-role attitudes, which in turn explain change in attitudes toward candidates. Changes in sex-role attitudes — particularly in attitudes toward family roles (especially maternal employment) — have changed substantially since the mid-1960s. Those changes appear to be connected to higher educational levels and employment among women.[117]

A final explanation of change in opinions toward female candidates is methodological. Wells and Smeal point out that the wording of questions asked to elicit attitudes about female candidates varied through the years and might well have provoked unreliable responses.[118] For example, the original Gallup question asked if one would "vote for a woman for president if she was qualified in every *other* respect." Not only were unacceptably worded questions used, but Wells and Smeal also point out "the inadequacy of this single indicator for a complex cluster of attitudes."[119] Thus, it may be that some of the change in attitudes toward women candidates reflects unreliable or changed survey questions rather than true attitude change.

Sex Differences in Sex-Related Attitudes
It has often been noted that "women do not offer a natural constituency."[120] Women's political attitudes seem to be structured more by socioeconomic characteristics or by party preference than by sex. Perhaps most notable among the similarities between men's and women's political preferences are the distributions of responses on sex-related issues. As Figure 11 – 6 shows, men are at least as likely as women to give the liberal response on sex-related issues in 1976. The same trend has been noted for 1972, when men were more likely to favor equality for women in society, to favor equal treatment for employed women, to favor lenient abortion policy, and to disagree that "women should stay out of politics and government."[121]

The fact is that sex-related issues have deeply divided women. Certainly, the Equal Rights Amendment has found less than unanimous support among women. The ERA has been an issue around which many women have rallied; it has pushed many into pro-ERA activism, others into active opposition. Although it has been assumed that political activists are more likely to favor sexual equality,[122] activists on the ERA issue often defy that assumption as well as others about political activism. Pro-ERA activists fit common general-

FIGURE 11–6 Sex Differences in Opinions on Several Issues

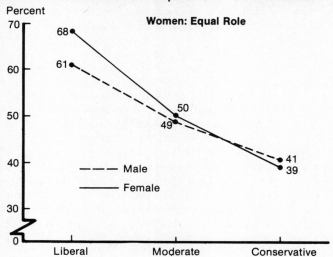

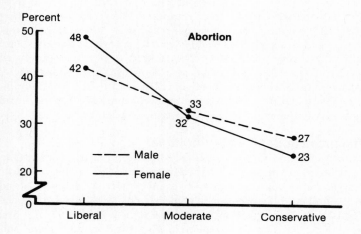

Source: Center for Political Studies. American National Election Study, 1976 [machine-readable data file].

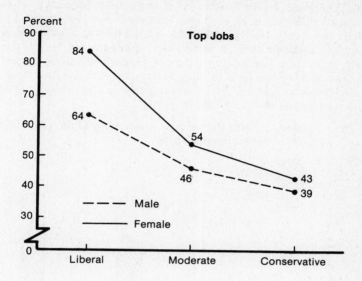

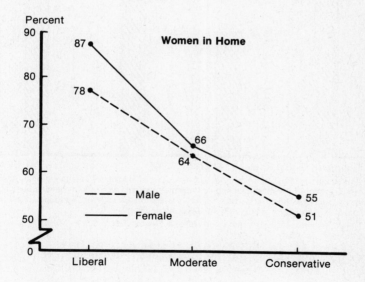

izations linking socioeconomic status and attitudinal characteristics to political activism.[123] They are more highly educated, younger, and more urban than their opponents. But the anti-ERA activists, or at least those surveyed in Texas during the ratification battle there, share a characteristic that helps them overcome their participatory disadvantages. They share a strong fundamentalist religious preference; they are members of the "religious right." Their motivation to political activism stems from a strong desire to preserve traditional life-styles and morality.[124]

FIGURE 11 – 7   Ideology and Percentage Supporting Liberal Positions on Sex-Related Issues, 1976[a]

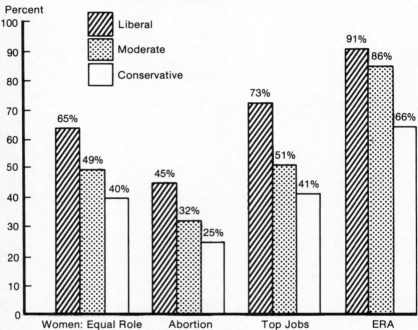

[a]Percentage supporting the "liberal" position on issues within ideological categories. The "liberal" position includes the belief that women should have an equal role with men in running business and government, support for abortion "anytime," belief that women are kept out of top jobs because of sex discrimination, and approval of the Equal Rights Amendment.
Source: Center for Political Studies. American National Election Study, 1976 [machine-readable data file].

If sex does not explain differences on sex-related issues, what factors are important in dictating these preferences? Ideological preference seems to be important in determining stances on these issues, with conservatives giving substantially less support to equality than do liberals.[125] Figure 11 – 7 shows that liberals are considerably more supportive of equal roles for women (abortion on demand, equal employment treatment, and the ERA). Perhaps the more important effect of ideology, however, is the impact it has on male/female differences on these issues. Ideology has a much stronger impact on the views of females than on the views of males. And among liberals, females give more support to sexual equality than do men. Table 11 – 6 notes these male/female differences. Although women who express liberal ideological preferences are more liberal than their male counterparts, moderate or conservative women are less distinct in their issue positions and sometimes give less support to sex-related issues than do men.

TABLE 11–6   Sex Differences on Sex-Related Issues by Ideology, 1976

| | | Ideology | |
Issue	Liberal	Moderate	Conservative
Women should have equal role	+ 7.6[a]	+ .9	−2.8
Abortion should be available anytime	+ 5.4	−1.6	−3.6
Women kept out of top jobs by discrimination	+19.7	+7.5	+3.9
Women don't necessarily belong in home	+ 9.0	+2.3	+3.8
Support for ERA	+ 3.9	−7.9	−4.6

[a]Percentage female at the most liberal position minus the percentage male at most liberal position.
Source: Center for Political Studies. American National Election Study, 1976 [machine-readable data file].

Thus, women have not been particularly distinctive in their sex-related issue positions; men have been equally likely to favor equality for women, to accept women in politics, and to favor liberal abortion policy. Some women have, in fact, worked actively against the "women's movement." Those women seem motivated by religious fundamentalism and basic conservatism. In fact, the liberal-conservative continuum seems to explain opinions on sex-related issues quite well. Further, there seems to be some interaction between sex and ideology, with liberal women giving the most support to sexual equality.

Sex Differences in Other Attitudes

Thus far we have dealt only with the political similarities between women and men. We now turn to the distinctive opinion characteristics of women, of which there appear to be few. Sexual differences in issue opinions are not notable in American politics, perhaps because there have been few long-term issues that have been perceived to affect men and women differently.[126]

There is, however, some evidence of sex-based policy differences. In particular, women have voiced stronger opposition to war and more generally to the use of force. For example, women were always more opposed to the Vietnam War than were men. They have also been more prone to vote for dovish candidates. Similar sex differences were evidenced after World War II and during the Korean intervention.[127] This reluctance toward war may stem from a general abhorrence of the use of force; and as such, it carries over into social policy. Pomper notes that women have been more likely to prefer "gentler methods" of dealing with civil rights problems rather than using force.[128] Additionally, women have favored stricter gun control than have men.[129] Figure 11 – 8 shows that these relationships still held in 1976. Women were approximately 15 percent more likely to favor stricter gun control and to favor solving the problems of urban unrest (rather than using force to alleviate urban unrest).

FIGURE 11–8   Sex Differences on the Issues of Gun Control and Solving Urban Unrest, 1976

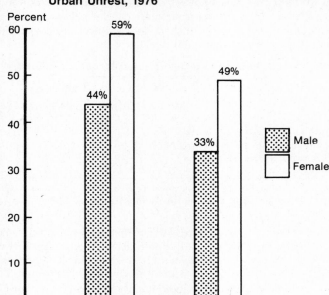

Source: Center for Political Studies. American National Election Study, 1976 [machine-readable data file].

In summary, the opinion characteristics of and toward women are much less distinctive than those of blacks. Women are slightly less efficacious and less interested in politics than are men. But their differences in efficacy are limited to one item, the perception of complexity in government. In addition, sex differences in efficacy are removed among working women and men.

Women also participate in politics less than do men. Although women have almost removed the gap in voting participation, they still lag behind men in campaign activity. The remaining gaps in political participation seem to disappear when socioeconomic status is controlled. In particular, working women and women with high levels of education participate at levels equal to those of men.

One area of fairly dramatic change has been the network of attitudes toward women candidates and toward sex-related issues. Since 1963, support for female candidates (as expressed in interviews) has increased by about 20 percent for both sexes, particularly among young, well-educated, and high-income survey respondents. Increases in more flexible sex-role attitudes have also led to support for women in politics. Surprisingly, however, support for women and for sex-related issues has not been higher among women than men.

Women have not distinguished themselves in their nonsexual attitudes. Although we have presented some evidence of sex differences in issues involving the use of force, those differences are few. By and large, women's positions on political issues are indistinguishable from those of men.

CONCLUSION

This chapter has discussed opinion characteristics relating to blacks and women. Clearly, there are strong similarities between the two groups. Both blacks and women are underparticipators in politics, and both groups are slightly less efficacious than their comparison groups (for blacks, whites; for women, men). A variety of explanations has been offered for the differences observed. For both groups, however, we can observe common threads. Theories developed to explain the reduced levels of efficacy among women and blacks, for example, tend to emphasize lower levels of feelings of "life-space control" and self-competence in both groups. Many in both groups, through life experiences, have lost confidence in their abilities to control their lives; a loss of confidence in their political abilities is a natural outgrowth of that. Increasing educational and employment opportunities for both groups have reduced the efficacy and participation gaps, but for blacks, the reduction has been accompanied by growing political distrust.

Perhaps the differences between blacks and women are more important than their similarities. Blacks are virtually unanimous in their issue opinions, both in racial issues and on other policy issues. Women, on the other hand, are very divided both on sex-related issues and on other issues. In addition, blacks are very distinct from whites in their positions on both types of issues. Women, on the other hand, are virtually indistinguishable from men in their preferences. Finally, group identification seems to push both groups toward political participation. But for blacks, that participation is directed toward common goals. For women, many participants direct their efforts toward issues like the Equal Rights Amendment and abortion; but that participation is directed at both sides of those issues. The fight to pass the ERA and the opposition to the ERA are both led by active women.

The implications for future political action are intriguing. For blacks, efficacy and participation seem to be on the rise. That may mean a stronger, united voice with which to express unified policy preferences in the policy arena. The question is whether those preferences will find expression. For women, increased participation probably means increased divisiveness.

NOTES

1. Joel D. Aberbach and Jack L. Walker, "Political Trust and Racial Ideology," *American Political Science Review* 64 (December 1970), pp. 1199–1219.
2. Schley R. Lyons, "The Political Socialization of Ghetto Children: Efficacy and Cynicism," *Journal of Politics* 32 (May 1970), pp. 287–304.
3. Paul R. Abramson, "Political Efficacy and Political Trust among Black School Children: Two Explanations," *Journal of Politics* 34 (November 1972), p. 1247.

4. Ibid., p. 1248.
5. Howard Schuman and Shirley Hatchett, *Black Racial Attitudes: Trends and Complexities* (Ann Arbor, Mich.: Institute for Social Research, 1974), p. 117.
6. John S. Jackson III, "Alienation and Black Political Participation," *Journal of Politics* 35 (November 1973), pp. 869 and 873.
7. See Chapter 9.
8. Gerald M. Pomper, *The Voters' Choice: Varieties of American Electoral Behavior* (New York: Dodd, Mead & Co., 1975), pp. 124–25.
9. Aberbach and Walker, "Political Trust," p. 1211.
10. Ibid., p. 1212.
11. Ibid., p. 1213.
12. Ibid., p. 1214
13. For a good review of this literature see Abramson, "Political Efficacy and Political Trust," p. 1246.
14. Jack Dennis, *Political Learning in Childhood and Adolescence: A Study of Fifth, Eighth, and Eleventh Graders in Milwaukee, Wisconsin* (Madison: Wisconsin Research and Development Center for Cognitive Learning, 1969); Lyons, "Political Socialization," pp. 296–97.
15. Lyons, "Political Socialization," p. 297
16. Dwaine Marvick, "The Political Socialization of the American Negro," *Annals of the American Academy of Political and Social Science* 361 (September 1965), pp. 120–21.
17. Pomper, *The Voters' Choice*, p. 124.
18. Lyons, "Political Socialization," p. 300.
19. Ibid., pp. 294–95
20. Pomper, *The Voters' Choice*, p. 124.
21. Jackson, "Black Political Participation," pp. 870–71.
22. Pomper, *The Voters' Choice*, pp. 125–26.
23. Ibid.
24. Both categories were also large for whites in 1976. Among whites, 35 percent were cynics, while 29.6 percent were oppressed. Overall, blacks were about 10 percent more likely than whites to fall into one of the two categories.
25. Pomper, *The Voters' Choice*, p. 125.
26. Ibid., p. 132.
27. Robert S. Erickson, Norman R. Luttbeg, and Kent L. Tedin, *American Public Opinion: Its Origins, Content, and Impact* (New York: John Wiley & Sons, 1980), p. 40.
28. Ibid., pp. 40–41.
29. D. Garth Taylor, Paul B. Sheatsley, and Andrew M. Greeley, "Attitudes toward Racial Integration," *Scientific American* 238 (June 1978), p. 43.
30. John G. Condran, "Changes in White Attitudes toward Blacks: 1963–1977," *Public Opinion Quarterly* 43 (Winter 1979), p. 466; Taylor et al., "Attitudes toward Racial Integration," p. 44.
31. Angus Campbell, *White Attitudes toward Black People* (Ann Arbor: Institute for Social Research, 1971), Chapter 5. See also Taylor et al., "Attitudes toward Racial Integration"; and Condran, "Changes in White Attitudes."
32. Taylor et al., "Attitudes toward Racial Integration," p. 44.
33. Ibid., p. 45.
34. Ibid., pp. 46–49.
35. Ibid., p. 48.
36. Ibid., p. 49.

37. Pomper, *The Voters' Choice*, p. 133.
38. Erickson et al., *American Public Opinion*, p. 42.
39. Pomper, *The Voters' Choice*, p. 127.
40. David O. Sears, Carl P. Hensler, and Leslie K. Speer, "Whites' Opposition to Busing: Self-Interest or Symbolic Politics," *American Political Science Review* 73 (June 1979), p. 371. In the case of school busing, black support is also less than unanimous, but whites are much more opposed than are blacks. See Jonathan Kelley, "The Politics of School Busing," *Public Opinion Quarterly* 38 (Spring 1975), p. 23.
41. Sears et al., "Whites' Opposition to Busing," p. 372.
42. Ibid., p. 381.
43. Ibid., p. 382.
44. Norman H. Nie, Sidney Verba, and John R. Petrocik, *The Changing American Voter*, enl. ed. (Cambridge, Mass.: Harvard University Press, 1979), p. 255.
45. Ibid.
46. Ibid., p. 254.
47. Ibid.
48. The Gallup Opinion Index, Report No. 160 (November 1978), p. 26.
49. Ibid.
50. Richard Murray and Arnold Vedlitz, "Voting Patterns in the South: An Analysis of Major Elections from 1960 to 1977 in Five Cities," *Annals of the American Academy of Political and Social Science* 439 (September 1978), p. 36.
51. Sidney Verba and Norman H. Nie, *Participation in America: Political Democracy and Social Equality* (New York: Harper & Row, 1972), chap. 10.
52. Ibid., p. 156.
53. Ibid., pp. 157–60.
54. Ibid., p. 157.
55. Ibid., p. 159
56. Gloria Morris Nemerowicz, *Children's Perceptions of Gender and Work Roles* (New York: Praeger, 1979), pp. 106–8.
57. Ibid., pp. 108–11.
58. Angus Campbell et al., *The American Voter* (New York: John Wiley & Sons, 1960), p. 490.
59. Ibid.
60. Ibid., p. 492.
61. Ibid., p. 491.
62. Fred I. Greenstein, *Children and Politics* (New Haven, Conn.: Yale University Press, 1969), pp. 115–18.
63. Ibid., p. 119.
64. Robert D. Hess and Judith V. Torney, *The Development of Political Attitudes in Children* (Chicago: Aldine, 1967), Chapter 8.
65. Ibid.
66. Ibid., p. 186.
67. Ibid.
68. David Easton and Jack Dennis, "The Child's Acquisition of Regime Norms: Political Efficacy," *American Political Science Review* 67 (March 1967), p. 37.
69. Anthony M. Orum et al., "Sex, Socialization and Politics," *American Sociological Review* 39 (April 1974), pp. 197–209.
70. Ibid., p. 204.
71. Ibid., pp. 200–3.
72. Kristi Andersen, "Working Women and Political Participation," *American Journal of Political Science* 19 (August 1975), pp. 439–53.

73. Ibid., p. 444.
74. Ibid.
75. Cornelia B. Flora and Naomi B. Lynn, "Women and Political Socialization: Considerations of the Impact of Motherhood," in *Women in Politics,* Jane S. Jaquette, ed. (New York: John Wiley & Sons, 1974), pp. 37–53.
76. Ibid., p. 40.
77. Ibid., pp. 44–45.
78. Rita Mae Kelly and Mary Boutilier, *The Making of Political Women* (Chicago: Nelson-Hall, 1978), Chapter 2.
79. Ibid., p. 52.
80. Ibid., Chapter 2.
81. Judy Bertelson, "Political Interest, Influence, and Efficacy: Differences between the Sexes and among Marital Groups," *American Politics Quarterly* 2 (October 1974), p. 419.
82. Ibid.
83. Ibid., p. 420.
84. John W. Soule and Wilma E. McGrath, "A Comparative Study of Male-Female Political Attitudes at Citizen and Elite Levels," in *A Portrait of Marginality,* Marianne Githens and Jewel L. Prestage, eds. (New York: David McKay, 1977), p. 183.
85. Ibid., pp. 183–84.
86. Robert E. Lane, *Political Life* (New York: Free Press, 1959), p. 211.
87. Verba and Nie, *Participation in America,* pp. 85–97.
88. Robert E. Lane, *Political Life,* p. 210.
89. Marjorie Lansing, "The American Woman: Voter and Activist," in *Women in Politics,* p. 8.
90. Andersen, "Working Women," p. 442.
91. Jane S. Jaquette, ed., *Women in Politics,* p. xv; Campbell et al., *The American Voter,* pp. 489–90.
92. Verba and Nie, *Participation in America,* p. 359.
93. Lansing, "The American Woman," pp. 8–9; Andersen, "Working Women," p. 444; and Susan B. Hansen, Linda M. Franz, and Margaret Netemeyer-Mays, "Women's Political Participation and Policy Preferences," *Social Science Quarterly* 56 (March 1976), p. 580.
94. Lansing, "The American Woman," p. 9.
95. Hansen et al., "Women's Political Participation," p. 581.
96. Andersen, "Working Women," p. 441.
97. Ibid., p. 443.
98. Edmond Constantini and Kenneth H. Craik, "Women as Politicians: The Social Background, Personality, and Political Careers of Female Party Leaders," in *A Portrait of Marginality,* p. 235.
99. Diane L. Fowlkes, Jerry Perkins, and Sue Tolleson Rinehart, "Gender Roles and Party Roles," *American Political Science Review* 73 (September 1979), p. 779.
100. Diane Rothbard Margolis, "The Invisible Hands: Sex Roles and the Division of Labor in Two Local Political Parties," *Social Problems* 26 (February 1979), pp. 315–24.
101. Ibid., p. 322.
102. Myra Marx Ferree, "A Woman for President? Changing Responses: 1958–1972," *Public Opinion Quarterly* 38 (Fall 1974), pp. 390–99.
103. Hazel Erskine, "The Polls: Women's Role," *Public Opinion Quarterly* 35 (Summer 1971), pp. 275–90.

104. E.M. Schreiber, "Education and Change in American Opinions on a Woman for President," *Public Opinion Quarterly* 42 (Summer 1978), p. 174.
105. Ibid.
106. Audrey Siess Wells and Eleanor Cutri Smeal, "Women's Attitudes toward Women in Politics: A Survey of Urban Registered Voters and Party Committeewomen," in *Women in Politics,* pp. 56–57.
107. Schreiber, "Education and Change in American Opinions," p. 174.
108. Ibid., pp. 176–80.
109. Ferree, "A Woman for President," p. 393; Wells and Smeal, "Women's Attitudes toward Women in Politics," p. 66; and Schreiber, "Education and Change in American Opinions," p. 176.
110. Ferree, "A Woman for President," p. 393.
111. Wells and Smeal, "Women's Attitudes toward Women in Politics," p. 66.
112. Robert A. Bernstein and Jayne D. Polly, "Race, Class and Support for Female Candidates," *Western Political Quarterly* 28 (December 1975), p. 736.
113. Schreiber, "Education and Change in American Opinions," p. 181.
114. Marjorie Randon Hershey, "Support for Political Woman: The Effects of Race, Sex and Sexist Roles," in *The Electorate Reconsidered,* John C. Pierce and John L. Sullivan, eds. (Beverly Hills: Sage Publications, 1980), pp. 179–99.
115. Ibid., p. 182.
116. Ibid., p. 191.
117. Karen Oppenheim Mason, John L. Czarjka, and Sara Arber, "Change in U.S. Women's Sex Role Attitudes, 1964–1974," *American Sociological Review* 41 (August 1976), pp. 573–97.
118. Wells and Smeal, "Women's Attitudes toward Women in Politics," p. 56.
119. Ibid., p. 57.
120. Hansen et al., "Women's Political Participation," p. 576.
121. Ibid., p. 580.
122. Hansen et al. lend some support for the position.
123. Kent L. Tedin et al., "Social Background Differences between Pro- and Anti-ERA Activists," *American Politics Quarterly* 5 (July 1977), pp. 395–407.
124. David W. Brady and Kent L. Tedin, "Ladies in Pink: Religion and Political Ideology in the Anti-ERA Movement," *Social Science Quarterly* 56 (March 1976), pp. 564–75.
125. Differences usually approach 30 percent. For example, CPS National Election Study Data for 1976 show that for females, 68 percent of the liberals favored an equal role for women, as compared to 38.6 percent of the female conservatives. The trend is similar, although not quite so dramatic, among males.
126. Pomper, *The Voters' Choice,* p. 68.
127. Ibid., pp. 77–81.
128. Ibid., p. 82.
129. Ibid., p. 83.

PART IV

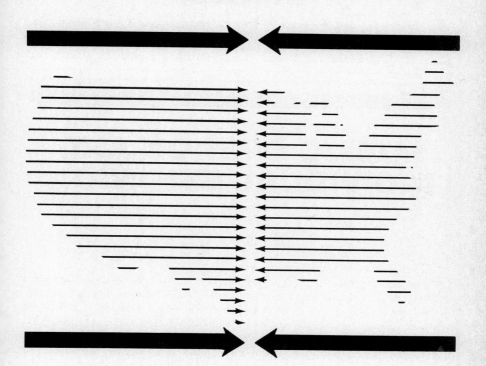

PUBLIC OPINION
AND POLITICAL
BEHAVIOR

CHAPTER 12

PUBLIC OPINION AND INDIVIDUAL BEHAVIOR

The last six chapters have dealt primarily with the expression of political opinions and the dynamics of political beliefs and attitudes. The last section of the book examines the relationship between public opinion and political behavior. This chapter concentrates on traditional patterns of political behavior of Americans, primarily within the context of elections and the influence of elected officials. This discussion also shows how political activists and nonactivists differ along demographic and attitudinal dimensions. Then the chapter turns to the extent to which political participation is motivated by concerns with political issues and events.

The discussion of political behavior and public opinion has been a minor but constant theme through many of the preceding chapters. Thus, to obtain a broader perspective than this chapter alone presents, one must review and reconsider those earlier discussions, especially party support, political trust, political tolerance, beliefs and issues, and equality and liberation. Similarly, the two chapters that follow this one carry on the relationship between public opinion and behavior.

POLITICAL PARTICIPATION

The concern with the nature of political participation in America is well placed. Within any form of representative democracy, there must exist established communication channels between the mass public and political and social elites. While these various channels are not used by everyone,[1] their presence is necessary to ensure mass/elite communication should the political need arise. The availability of multiple alternative channels of participation may be just as important, or even more so, to the stability of a system than the presence of a few effective participatory channels.[2] Indeed, some scholars argue that participation in politics can be an important element of a democratic polity even if the participatory act is not especially influential:

Participation is important not only because it communicates the citizen's needs and desires to the government, but because it has other, more direct benefits. Some have argued that it is, in itself, a prime source of satisfaction — satisfaction with the government and satisfaction with one's own role. Furthermore, it has been viewed as an educational device through which "civic virtues" are learned.[3]

Thus, while questions dealing with the impact or *effectiveness* of political participation are of extreme importance (and will be subjected to examination in Chapter 14), normative democratic theorists have argued that the participatory act itself helps to mold and educate the democratic citizen.[4]

In their 1972 book, *Participation in America,* Sidney Verba and Norman Nie offered the following definition of political participation:

Political participation refers to those activities by private citizens that are more or less aimed at influencing the selection of governmental personnel and/or the actions they take.[5]

As Verba and Nie point out,[6] this definition restricts the range of phenomena to be included under the rubric of "political participation." First, it is restricted to *political* acts, — i.e., those acts related to influencing government. While other spheres of political involvement will be discussed, such as school activities and voluntary organizations, the main concern is with participation in the broad area of electoral politics. Second, emphasizing *activities* isolates *behavior* as the focus of examination. Political participation, therefore, does not refer to psychological orientations to politics. Such things as political interest, efficacy, and trust are looked upon as antecedents to the behavioral act rather than as participatory acts themselves. Third, we examine participatory acts that nearly universally are recognized as legitimate within the American political system. There are other forms of participation, which could range from civil disobedience to assassinations and mob violence, that are directed at influencing governmental actions, but they are not usually considered to be viable tactics of influence for the vast majority of Americans.[7]

In their work on political participation, Verba and Nie begin with the assumption that citizens initiate participatory actions in order to achieve some end. They also assume that citizens are aware of both the potential payoffs of their acts and the amounts of effort the act would require:

Political acts differ in what they can get the citizen: some types of activity supply little more than the gratification from taking part; other political acts can lead to more specific and concrete payoffs. Political acts differ in what they get the citizen into: some activity is likely to bring him into open conflict with others; some is not. And political acts differ in what it takes to get into them: some activity calls for initiative, time, resources, skill; some does not.[8]

The main thrust of Verba and Nie's argument is that the dynamics of American political participation can be understood only *after* first understanding the dimensions of the political acts themselves. Reasons for political participation are not one-dimensional, meaning that there does not exist one common reason for a person to become actively involved in politics. There are many different reasons why someone would choose a particular mode of participating in politics, and these reasons are based upon the specific dimensions of that participatory act.

Verba and Nie identified four separate dimensions of a participatory act. The first dimension relates to the *type of influence* the act might have. How much pressure is applied to an elite to comply with the reason for the contact? Also, how much information about the wants and needs of the citizen is communicated by the act? Second, what is the probable *scope of the outcome* of the participatory act? Will the result of the participatory act affect an extended group of people, or only those who engage in the act itself? Third, what degree of *political conflict* is involved in the act? Is the participation of one person, or a group of persons, likely to be met by "counterparticipatory" attempts by others? And fourth, how much *initiative* is required on the part of the participants? Is the participatory act relatively easy to execute, or is it more complex, requiring coordination of personnel and activities?[9]

Based upon these dimensions of political participation, Verba and Nie described four different *modes of participation* — categories into which thirteen concrete political acts were classified. The first category they labeled *voting*. This is, of course, the most often utilized form of political participation. The second category, *campaign activities,* includes all participatory acts relating to the conduct of a political campaign (working for a candidate or party, attending political meetings, contributing money, and trying to convince another person, or group of persons, how to vote). The third category is called *citizen-initiated contacts*. This mode of participation includes activities such as writing letters to and other forms of individualized contact with governmental officials. The final category of participation is termed *cooperative activities*. Activities associated with this category include such things as membership in political organizations, work groups, or contacting officials on behalf of some group-related cause.

Verba and Nie then categorized each mode of participation across the four dimensions of political activity. The results of this categorization are presented in Table 12–1. As the table indicates, political participation is a varied phenomenon. Instead of thinking about political activities as being "more" or "less" participatory, one can more usefully consider them as discrete methods of influencing governmental officials.

This chapter focuses on the first three forms of participation — voting, campaign activity, and citizen-initiated contacts — with primary emphasis on voting and campaign activities. Cooperative, group-oriented activities are discussed in Chapter 13. The following subsections review the *extent* of participation in the first three modes of political activity. The second major section analyzes the characteristics of those who do, and those who do not, utilize these forms of participation.

American Voting Trends

As stated earlier, voting in elections is by far the most widespread act of political participation. The modern political campaign has come to be a form of interest stimulation, the main intent of which is to convince the citizen to

TABLE 12–1 Four Modes of Participation and the Dimensions of Participation

| Modes of Activity | Dimensions of Participation | | | |
	Scope of Influence	Conflict	Scope of Outcome	Initiative Required
Electoral Activity				
Voting	High pressure/ Low information	Conflictual	Collective	Little
Campaign Activity	High pressure/ Low to high information	Conflictual	Collective	Some
Nonelectoral Activity				
Citizen-Initiated	Low pressure/ High information	Nonconflictual	Collective or particularized	A lot
Cooperative	Low to high pressure/ High information	Usually nonconflictual	Collective	Some or a lot

Source: From *Participation in America,* p. 48 and p. 54, by Sidney Verba and Norman H. Nie. Copyright © 1972 by Sidney Verba and Norman H. Nie. Reprinted by permission of Harper & Row, Publishers, Inc.

go to the polls and vote a certain way. While it is accurate to state that the vote is the most prevalent mode of political participation in the United States, it should not be inferred from this that the level of voting in the United States is high. In fact, compared to voting participation in twenty-three other democratic nations, the United States ranks twenty-second out of twenty-four. Table 12–2 shows that of the other democratic nations listed, voter turnout in the United States is only higher than that of India and Botswana. Although the ethic of voting is the strongest form of participation, it is much stronger in many other democracies than it is in the United States. The fact that in 1976 only 53 percent of the American public voted in the presidential election should be a sobering one. It indicates that almost half of those people who could have voted in 1976 — i.e., those who were eligible to vote — chose not to do so.

How does this figure of 53 percent compare to past voting turnout? Figure 12–2 provides some answers. First, it can be seen that in the past sixty years, voting turnout seems to have followed a cyclical pattern. The beginning of a surge in turnout corresponded with the enfranchisement of women in 1920. This upswing prevailed until the midst of World War II and then far into the cold-war period. Since 1960, however, there has been a steady decline in the proportion of people who turn out for both presidential and congressional elections.[10] It is not possible to state with certainty, however, whether the pattern is truly cyclical or whether in later years the present low level will persist.[11] What can be safely stated on the basis of Figure 12–1 is that the

American public has demonstrated an ability in the past to turn out in high numbers; the trend in the past ten years, however, has been away from large-scale participation in elections.

TABLE 12-2   Vote Turnout in Democratic Nations for Elections Held Between 1969 and 1973

	Turnout Rates		
Over 90%	*Between 80% and 90%*	*70%–80%*	*Under 70%*
Australia[a]	Iceland	Israel	Switzerland (56%)
Italy[a]	Sweden	France	United States (55%)
Malta	Denmark	Ireland	India (54%)
Belgium[a]	Luxembourg	Canada	Botswana (34%)
Austria	Netherlands[a]	Japan	
West Germany	Finland	Great Britain	
New Zealand	Norway		

[a]Countries with compulsory voting and/or registration.

Source: Committee for the Study of the American Electorate, September 5, 1976, compiled by Hart Research Associates.

A second item of interest contained in Figure 12 – 1 is that turnout for off-year congressional elections usually runs a good ten to twenty percentage points below that of presidential elections.[12] It is apparent that without the mystique and excitement of the presidential races, less than 40 percent of the electorate participate in the selection of members of Congress. The turnout patterns for both presidential and off-year congressional races follow similar convolutions — an indication that the forces governing turnout over the past sixty years affect both types of election.

While the differences in the characteristics of voters and nonvoters are considered later in this chapter, one factor that affects turnout must be mentioned here. Understandably, the most important factor that determines whether someone will vote or not (outside of age restrictions) is whether that person is registered to vote. In a 1974 survey it was found that 55 percent of the sample did not vote. Of that 55 percent, 18 percent were registered to vote but chose not to. This means that, in 1974, over 80 percent of those not voting were not registered to vote. Now, consider the following facts:

- Between 1972 and 1976 there was a net gain in the total number of people eligible to vote of 9,055,707.
- Forty-eight states *loosened* residency requirements for registration between 1972 and 1976.
- Between 1972 and 1976, five states *loosened* the deadline for registration, thirty-two states stayed the same, and thirteen states tightened the deadlines.
- Between 1972 and 1976, six states *loosened* rules governing cancellation of registration, thirty-nine states stayed the same, and five states tightened their rules.

The balance sheet for this period, then, was conducive to a higher number of registered voters in 1976 than in 1972, from both the perspective of popula-

**FIGURE 12–1   Voter Turnout in the United States for Presidential and
Off-year Congressional Elections, 1920–1974**

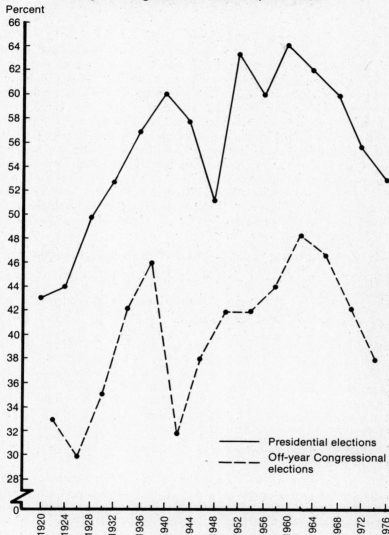

Source: U.S. Census Reports, *Statistical Abstract of the United States,* 1976.

tion increase as well as a general loosening of registration requirements. Actual registration figures, however, do not follow expectations. In 1972 there were 95,565,000 registered voters. In 1976, there were 90,305,000 people registered. So in this four-year period, there was a drop of 5,260,000 registered voters.[13] It is clear that the drop-off in registration, and consequently in voting, is not due to institutional barriers or unfavorable shifts in the potential voter base.

Participation in Political Campaigns

In light of the relatively low participation in the most basic of political acts, voting, one would assume that activities relating to campaign participation might show even lower levels of attendance. Table 12–3 shows that such an assumption is essentially correct. The percentage of American citizens who actively engage in campaign-related activities is very low. The least cited form of participation is contribution of funds, with an average of 5 percent of the public giving money. The form of campaign-related activity most often used is also the easiest: talking to friends about the campaign and attempting to sway them to a particular position. One remarkable thing about these data is their constancy. While turnout has been up and down across this period, the percentage of Americans engaged in campaign-related activities has remained fairly stable. Figure 12–2 shows that the level of campaign activity (the average of the five campaign-related acts shown in Table 12–3) has not changed appreciably over a twenty-two-year period.

TABLE 12–3   American Public Involvement in Campaign-Related Activities, 1956–1976

Campaign-Related Activity	1956	1960	1964	1968	1972	1976
Contribute money	10%	12%	11%	9%	10%	9%
Use political bumper sticker or wear political button	16	21	16	15	14	8
Work for political party or candidate	3	6	5	5	4	5
Attend political rally or meeting	10	8	8	9	9	7
Express political opinions to friends	29	33	31	29	31	37

Source: Center for Political Studies. American National Election Study, 1956–1976 [machine-readable data file].

What may account for the changes in voting and the consistency in other campaign activities during the same period? The patterns may stem from the differences in the strength of motivation leading to each. Voting is a relatively "easy" act, requiring only marginal commitment to a candidate or party or a feeling about one's "citizen duty." As a result, changes in the perceived attractiveness of candidates, fluctuations in support for political parties, and alterations in affect toward the system may easily influence the behavior of marginally committed citizens. As a result, they may move in and out of the voting public. On the other hand, it takes much greater commitment to give up one's money and extended periods of time. People with intense feelings about politics may be less affected by the temporal variations in the campaign stimuli.

FIGURE 12–2   Average Campaign Activity, 1956–1976

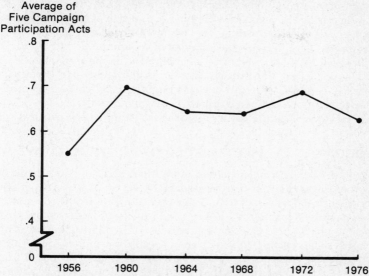

Source: Center for Political Studies. American National Election Study, 1956–1976.

Citizen-Initiated Contacts

In their 1972 analysis, Verba and Nie found that the percentage of people
who engaged in individual contact of public officials, either through letters or
in person, was quite small. Of the entire 1972 sample, 6 percent reported
having made particularized contacts (contacts with a scope of outcome limited
to the individual actor) with community officials, and roughly the same percentage had made contacts with governmental officials outside the local
community. Interestingly, when comparing the people who made particularized contacts, the researchers did not find an association with any other
form of political activity. In fact, they concluded that contacting governmental officials about individual problems is not really a true form of
political participation, as are voting, campaign work, and communal activities. Verba and Nie write,

> particularized contact has no general goal, which may explain why almost
> all types of political activity are somewhat intercorrelated except for such
> contacts. The rather unusual position of particularized contacts reinforces
> the importance of the "scope of outcome" dimension of political participa-
> tion. Contacting on a narrow personal issue stands at one extreme of that
> dimension.[14]

They conclude that the act of contacting public officials about personal problems is not a *political* act but rather, in Gabriel Almond and Sidney Verba's
term, an act of *parochial* participation.[15] In a sense it is no more political
than is the act of going to a bank to secure a loan. Surely, though, there

remains some political content in the feeling that government is a place, even
of last resort, that individual benefits can be obtained.

The next section continues with an investigation of individual-level political behavior by concentrating on two modes of participation: voting and
campaign activity. Again, the discussion of communal activity — the individual's involvement with a group — is addressed in the next chapter. To this
point it is clear that the most obvious forms of political participation are not
universally engaged in by all of those eligible to do so. Less than half vote
and fewer than one in four engages in campaign activity. The next section
reveals just who is participating and who is sitting on the political sidelines.

DEMOGRAPHIC CHARACTERISTICS OF POLITICAL ACTIVISM

Although the levels of participation in elections and campaigns is not high, if
those who do participate are representative of those who do not, then the
prescriptions of a representative democracy are at least approximated. Since
not everyone participates, it is important to identify the characteristics of
those who do. If, in opposition to the ideal of a representative democracy,
political activists come primarily from a specific stratum of American society,
their particular interests may receive greater degrees of attention from political elites for the basic reason that it is their particular voices that are being
heard.

Voters and Nonvoters

In 1976, the Committee for the Study of the American Electorate commissioned a poll of individuals who had not voted in 1972 but were eligible to do
so. Table 12–4 presents a demographic breakdown of the sample of nonvoters
(according to sex, age, race, income, and education). For comparison purposes,
a similar breakdown of people who voted in 1972 is also provided. The table
indicates the following:

- There is very little difference between the sexual composition of the voter
  and nonvoter samples.
- Younger citizens are more predominant in the nonvoter group.
- Minority groups tend to comprise more of the nonvoter sample.
- The lowest-income group is disproportionally represented in the nonvoter
  group.
- Nonvoters have significantly lower levels of education than do voters.

The overall impression from these figures is inescapable: persons who possess
higher-status characteristics are more likely to vote than those with lower-
status characteristics. Let us look more closely at the three demographic
areas that seem to show the greatest differences: age, race, and education.[16]

AGE. As Figure 12–3 indicates, younger people have reported that they
voted less often than any other age group for the last six presidential elections.[17] Those individuals between the ages of thirty-one and sixty-five show
consistently high levels of turnout across the twenty-year period. Older individuals — those over sixty-five — show turnout percentages that, although not
as low as the youngest group, are much lower than the middle-aged groups.

TABLE 12–4   Comparative Demographic Distributions of Voters and Nonvoters

Demographic Category		Voters in 1972	Nonvoters in 1972	Difference[a]
Sex:	Males	51%	48%	+ 3%
	Females	49	52	− 3
		100%	100%	
Age:	18–24	11%	23%	−12%
	25–34	19	23	− 4
	35–49	30	24	+ 6
	50–64	24	17	+ 7
	65	16	13	+ 3
		100%	100%	
Race:	White	89%	74%	+15%
	Black	8	18	−10
	Chicano	3	7	− 4
		100%	100%	
Income:	Under $5,000	16%	28%	−12%
	$5,000–$10,000	28	27	+ 1
	$10,000–$15,000	27	23	+ 4
	$15,000	29	21	+ 8
		100%	100%	
Education:	Grade school or less	14%	23%	− 7%
	High school	45	59	−14
	College	41	18	+23
		100%	100%	

[a]A positive sign indicates a voting tendency, a negative sign, a nonvoting tendency.

Source: Committee for the Study of the American Electorate, September 5, 1976, compiled by Hart Research Associates.

To some extent, the fact that younger and older citizens do not vote with the same frequency as those in the middle-aged categories, should not be too surprising once we consider the life-styles of the groups involved.[18] Verba and Nie refer to the life-style differences of younger and older citizens as the "start-up and slow-down" patterns:

> In the early years one has the problem of "start-up." Individuals are still unsettled, are likely to be residentially and occupationally mobile. They have yet to develop the stake in the politics of a particular locality that comes with extended residence, with home ownership, with children in school and the like ... In later years, the problem is one of "slow down." Old age brings with it sociological withdrawal as individuals retire from active employment. And it brings as well physical infirmities and fatigue that lower the rate of political activity.[19]

Verba and Nie did find, however, that when controlling for socioeconomic status and length of residence, the relationship between voting turnout and age becomes almost linear. This indicates that after confounding factors are taken into account, it appears that "the longer one is exposed to politics, the more likely one is to participate."[20] Additionally, it must be remembered that we are so far only considering the act of voting in national elections. In a recent study, M. Kent Jennings found that the rate of involvement of young parents in community activities is substantially higher than that of individuals of similar age but who have not yet established a family. While the "slow-start" phenomenon may apply to national political activities, it does not necessarily apply to *all* political activities.[21] In the same vein, it may be the case that younger citizens choose to participate in politics in ways other than voting. In the area of campaign-related activities we shall, in fact, see that this is indeed the case.

FIGURE 12 – 3   Reported Voter Turnout in Presidential Elections across Age Groupings, 1956 – 1976

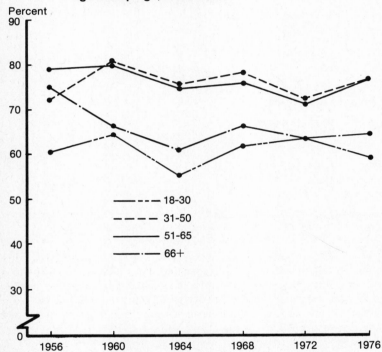

Source: Center for Political Studies. American National Election Study, 1956 – 1976.

RACE.   The pattern of turnout for black Americans during the past twenty years is a testament to the belief that if you make the rules of the game more equitable, then everyone will get a chance to play. As Figure 12– 4 indicates, there was a steady increase in black voting participation between 1956 and 1968. Of course, this period was marked by dramatic changes in black consciousness and in the pace of the civil rights struggle.[22] In the early sixties, the passage of the Voting Rights Act and the Civil Rights Act removed the legal obstacles to black voting participation. As of 1976, black turnout figures were still below those of whites, but the difference, when compared to the enormous gulf of an election just sixteen years earlier, has diminished encouragingly.[23]

FIGURE 12–4   Reported Voting Turnout in Presidential Elections for Blacks and Whites, 1956–1976

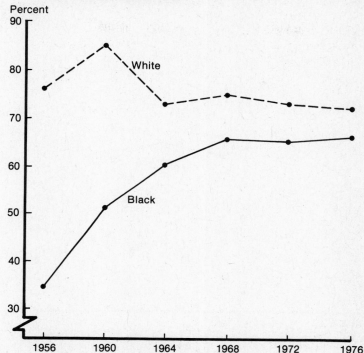

Source: Center for Political Studies. American National Election Study, 1956–1976.

EDUCATION. Nowhere is the relationship between demographic classification and voter turnout more clear than in the area of education.[24] Figure 12–5 plainly illustrates that as the level of education increases, the voting turnout follows suit. The patterns of turnout across the six-election period is very stable. Elsewhere, this book stresses that differences in information levels, feeling of political trust, levels of efficacy, and general involvement in political matters are all related to levels of educational attainment, as is higher socioeconomic status. Therefore, one would expect differences in beliefs and attitudes between voters and nonvoters. This is in fact the case, as we shall see.

Campaign Activists

We have seen that there are significant demographic differences between those who vote and those who do not. We would expect that those differences would persist among the characteristics of those who are and those who are not active in political campaigns. After all, working in political campaigns requires higher degrees of initiative, commitment, and resources. Figure 12–6 shows, however, that while some differences remain large between campaign activists and nonactivists, there are some important changes. Figure 12–6

FIGURE 12 – 5   Reported Voting Turnout in Presidential Elections across Levels of Education, 1956 – 1976

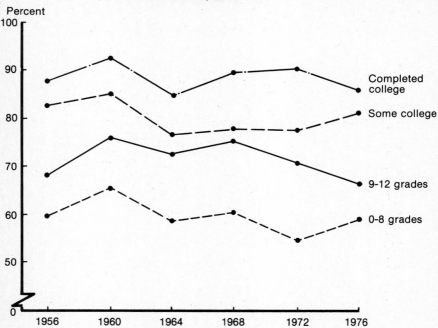

Source: Center for Political Studies. American National Election Study, 1956 – 1976.

presents a demographic profile of the campaign activist (those who had high frequencies of campaign-related activity). The Index of Representation used in Figure 12 – 6 merely tells us the degree to which a group is represented in the activist category.[25] For instance, while individuals under the age of thirty made up 16 percent of the sample, they made up 17 percent of the campaign activists. Therefore, they were overrepresented by 5 percent. That is, the difference between 17 percent and 16 percent is about 5 percent of the 16 percent.

Looking at Figure 12 – 6, we see that the earlier differences noted along education and income lines persist. While individuals with a high school education are represented in campaign activities according to their distribution in the public, lower-educated people are far less likely to be involved in campaigns, while those with higher education are greatly overrepresented. Lower-income groups also are not well represented in the campaign-activist group, while middle- and upper-income groups are. It is clear that the demands of time and resources required by campaign activity are too much for those of lower socioeconomic status.

It is in the areas of sex, age, and race that we see some interesting differences from the data presented earlier in connection with voting activists. While the turnout differences between males and females were not very great, males are overrepresented in the campaign-activist category. While

FIGURE 12-6   Demograpic Profile of Campaign Activists

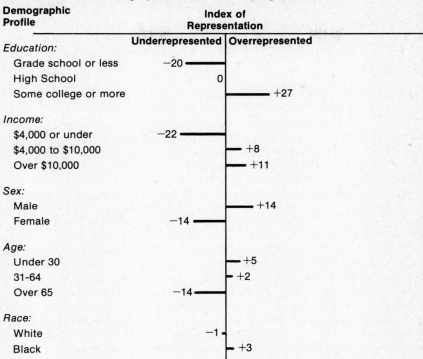

Demographic Profile	Index of Representation	
	Underrepresented	Overrepresented
Education:		
Grade school or less	−20	
High School	0	
Some college or more		+27
Income:		
$4,000 or under	−22	
$4,000 to $10,000		+8
Over $10,000		+11
Sex:		
Male		+14
Female	−14	
Age:		
Under 30		+5
31-64		+2
Over 65	−14	
Race:		
White	−1	
Black		+3

Source: From *Participation in America* by Sidney Verba and Norman H. Nie, p. 100. Copyright © by Sidney Verba and Norman H. Nie. Reprinted by permission of Harper & Row, Publishers, Inc.

this difference is probably not as great as it was in the decades before the seventies, there still appears to be some hesitancy on the part of females to enter into campaign activities and probably some resistance on the part of males fully to accept them.[26] Recall, too, that the chapter on sex and politics noted a tendency for women activists to take on particular forms of activity when involved in political parties. In the category of age there is a dramatic reversal of the voting figures. While young people do not engage in voting behavior to the same degree as other age groups, they are *overrepresented* in the area of campaign activism. Paul Beck and M. Kent Jennings found that in 1972 younger people tended to be more politically active than were their parents.[27] Perhaps the main reason for this upsurge in youth campaign activism was the McGovern candidacy and resistance to the war in Vietnam. Whatever the stimulus, it is clear that the "slow-start" hypothesis offered earlier has to be modified to exclude activities beyond voting. In the early seventies there seemed to be no tendency for young people to avoid involvement in politics. In terms of racial differences, the slight separation of white and black turnout patterns is erased in the area of campaign participation. Blacks are slightly more likely to engage in campaign activities than are whites. This is perhaps due to their perception of a greater payoff in terms of governmental policies.[28] Thus, the impact of demographic factors depends on the particular relevance of those factors to politics at the time of the participation. In some cases a demographic attribute associated with low voting (e.g., age) may actually increase campaign activity when the campaign is relevant.

The Demographic Basis of Political Participation — A Summary

Verba and Nie found that in 1972 about 11 percent of the sample could be classified as "complete activists." These were people who "engaged in all types of activity with great frequency."[29] As a conclusion, this section on the demographic bases of political participation looks at the demographic characteristics of this highly participative substratum of American society.

Figure 12 – 7 again employs the Index of Representation to compare the actual composition of the "complete-activist" group with their proportions in the public. The data show that the greatest differences are found in the educational and income strata. The activist stratum of American society is disproportionally composed of those individuals with upper-status characteristics.[30] Sexual and racial differences in the complete-activist group are very small. Although there still remain cultural barriers to minority and female participation, it is clear that those barriers are becoming much less of a deterrent. Nevertheless, one cannot assume that participation means political influence. Finally, although younger individuals tend to participate at disproportionate rates in campaigns, overall their activity level is still relatively lower than that of the middle-aged individuals. Older citizens also show a much lower predilection to engage in all forms of political activity.

It appears, then, that political participation is very much a class-related phenomenon. Individuals with lower socioeconomic status engage less frequently in all forms of political activity.[31] Using these findings as a basis for comparison, the analysis now turns to the attitudinal correlates of political activity.

POLITICAL ACTIVITY AND POLITICAL ATTITUDES

In the context of the demographic bases of participation, the examination now can proceed to the relationship between political attitudes and political participation. In this section three areas of political thinking are discussed: partisanship, political ideology, and system affect (trust and efficacy). We have seen that activists differ on the basis of socioeconomic characteristics, now we investigate whether they *think* differently.[32]

Partisanship

As early as 1960, the authors of *The American Voter* recognized that partisan attitudes have a significant impact upon political participation:

> *It is not accidental that the individual's general partisan orientation and the extent of his involvement in politics, either of which may influence a wide set of attitudinal and behavioral characteristics, are related to each*

other. Although our causal understanding of this relationship is far from sure, the fact of association is clear enough: the stronger the individual's sense of attachment to one of the parties, the greater his involvement in political affairs.[33]

FIGURE 12-7 Demographic Profile of Complete Activists

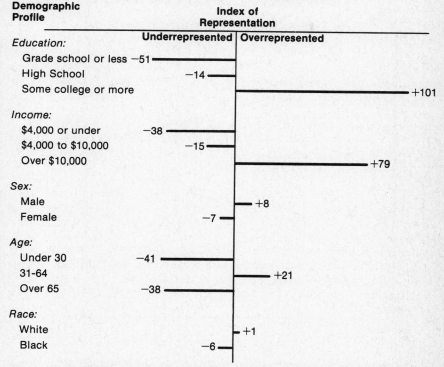

Demographic Profile	Index of Representation
	Underrepresented | Overrepresented
Education:	
Grade school or less	−51
High School	−14
Some college or more	+101
Income:	
$4,000 or under	−38
$4,000 to $10,000	−15
Over $10,000	+79
Sex:	
Male	+8
Female	−7
Age:	
Under 30	−41
31-64	+21
Over 65	−38
Race:	
White	+1
Black	−6

Source: From *Participation in America* by Sidney Verba and Norman H. Nie, p. 100. Copyright © 1972 by Sidney Verba and Norman H. Nie. Reprinted by permission of Harper & Row, Publishers, Inc.

The data for participation rates of strong as compared to weak party identifiers and Independents are quite plain (see Figure 12-8). While both strong and weak partisans have maintained fairly consistent turnout rates, the participation rate of Independents has shown a consistent decline over the past six presidential elections. As noted in Chapter 10, partisanship is associated with higher rates of psychological involvement in politics and higher rates of attentiveness. In general, people who self-identify as Independents are less involved in politics and show their disinterest through lower levels of political activity:[34]

The independent Independents are predominately disinterested nonparticipants in political affairs. Although some independent Independents are informed and involved citizens, independent Independents are generally among the least politicized, most indifferent members of the electorate. They are often those who, like the young, have recently entered the electorate. Their rates of participation are as unpredictable as their preferences.[35]

FIGURE 12 – 8   Strength of Party Identification and Voting Turnout in Presidental Elections, 1956 – 1976

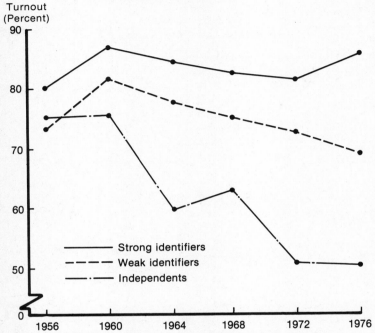

Source: Center for Political Studies. American National Election Study, 1956 – 1976.

Unlike the young, however, Independents do not demonstrate higher rates within any mode of political participation.[36] They exhibit lower levels of voting, campaign activity, and organizational activity. The implication of all of this is inescapable: affinity for one of the two major political parties is closely associated with higher levels of political participation. It is not clear, as the authors of *The American Voter* pointed out in the above quotation, whether people who are active in politics develop stronger partisan ties as a result of that activity, or if strong partisans are motivated to participate more as a result of their attachment. Since, as noted in the chapter on political socialization, party identification is formed in the early stages of life, it is more likely that higher levels of political participation flow from the stimulation of party affiliation.

Ideology

Since higher socioeconomic status has been associated with more conservative beliefs on certain kinds of issues[37] and higher levels of political activism, we should expect to see a relationship between political activism and conservatism on those issues. In 1967, Verba and Nie observed that while strong partisans participated at higher rates than weak partisans and Independents, strong Republican identifiers had higher participation rates than strong Democratic identifiers. To a certain extent, this was due to the higher socioeconomic status of Republicans. But, even after controlling for differences in socioeconomic status of the Democrats and Republicans, strong Republicans still turned out at higher levels and had higher levels of campaign activity. The reason, they concluded, was that the conservative beliefs of the Republicans induced higher levels of participation. When they controlled for *both* socioeconomic status and political beliefs, they found that the participation rates for both groups of identifiers were approximately equal. The authors concluded that the conservative beliefs of Republicans motivated them into higher levels of participation.[38]

Additional data from subsequent elections has, however, led to a modification, if not an outright reversal, of the theory of conservatism and higher levels of political activity.[39] Instead of being linked consistently to one political ideology, political participation tends to follow the prevailing ideology of the particular election. Figure 12–9 presents the relationship between the level of campaign activity (the average of five different campaign-related acts) and strong self-identified ideological stances for six elections. The patterns presented in this figure are striking and bear close attention. In the elections of 1956, 1960, and 1964, there was a clear difference between the two polar ideological stances and campaign activism. Conservative ideologues were much more likely to utilize the campaign mechanism to influence public policy.[40] In 1968, a remarkable change occurred: conservative participation dropped off and liberal activism rose. In a way it is fitting that the campaign, which occurred at one of the most highly polarized points in our nation's recent history, should have had equally high levels of liberal and conservative involvement. In 1972, the pattern continued its surprising revelation. Liberal activism was much more pronounced in the campaign to elect George McGovern. Conservatives, on the other hand, did not significantly change their campaign involvement from that of 1968. In 1976, we see a drop-off of liberal campaign activism and an increase in conservative activism. Strong liberals, however, continued to retain a participatory advantage over strong conservatives.

The indication from these patterns is that campaign-related activism is associated with the opportunity structure of the specific campaign. Strong liberals reacted to the McGovern candidacy by increasing their involvement in the campaign. Their involvement level dropped off sharply, however, during the campaign of Jimmy Carter, who, while plainly more liberal than Ford, did not risk his political fortunes by embracing some of the stands that endeared McGovern to the liberals. Using a slightly different measure of participation and ideology, Beck and Jennings reaffirmed the relationship between liberalism and campaign activity in 1972. Using two samples, one of parents and one of their voting-age children, they found that *for both groups* liberal ideology was connected to a more activist campaign orientation (see Figure 12–10).[41] Miller and Levitin also provide evidence of the increased

FIGURE 12-9   Average Campaign Activity of Self-Identified Strong Liberals and Strong Conservatives, 1956-1976

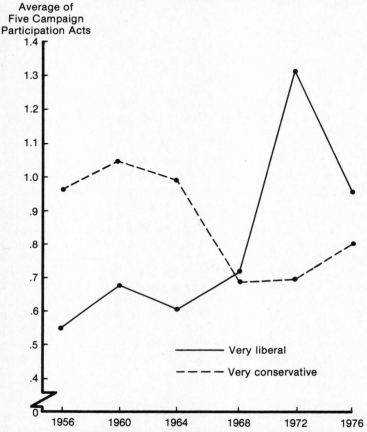

Source: Center for Political Studies. American National Election Study, 1956-1976.

activity of what they label as the "new liberals," and document the drop-off of participation in the subsequent campaign.[42]

The conclusions of the 1967 Verba and Nie study are, in a sense, time-bound. Their data were collected at a time when liberals did not see the presidential arena as a promising area in which to promote their causes. Political ideology and political activism are much better viewed as interactive processes. Seeking to promote ideological ends, party identifiers will increase their activism to take maximum advantage of those election environments that are seen as potentially supportive.[43]

System Affect

Chapter 9 covered the patterns of change in the public's political trust and its involvement within the political system. We noted the rise of political cynicism in recent years and documented some of the more important reasons for

**FIGURE 12–10   Comparison of Participation Rates and Political Ideology
for Parents and Their Children, 1973**

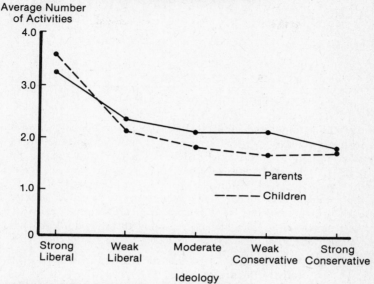

Source: Adapted from Paul Allen Beck and M. Kent Jennings, "Political Periods and Political
Participation," *American Political Science Review* 73 (September 1979), p. 742.

this rise. It should come as no large surprise that there exists a strong relationship between psychological involvement with the system and activity relating to that system's political apparatus.[44] Generally, those people who distrust governmental officials have high feelings of powerlessness, have little
faith in the mechanism of voting, and refrain from political activity. For instance, while 92 percent of those respondents in 1972 who had high feelings of
political efficacy voted, only 60 percent of those with low efficacy did the
same. It is even more striking that individuals who felt that elections made a
difference reported a turnout rate of 82 percent. Those who felt that people
should only vote if they are interested in the outcome evidenced a voting
turnout figure of only 20 percent.[45]

In 1968, 1972, and 1976 the Gallup organization asked nonvoters in each
election to give the most important reason for their nonparticipation. The
results are summarized in Table 12–5. Even under the most conservative
assumption that nonregistration was not due to psychological involvement,
and that the proportion who reported illness as a reason were, in fact, too ill
to vote, Table 12–5 nevertheless shows that political cynicism or plain disinterest accounts for a large chunk of the reasons given for not voting (27 percent in 1968 and 1972, and 34 percent in 1976).

In their 1967 study, Verba and Nie isolated four main types of political
participators: *voting specialists,* those whose only political activity is voting;
partisan activists, those who engage heavily in campaign-related activities;
complete activists, those who engage in all forms of political activity; and *inactives,* those who refrain from any sort of political activity. Verba and Nie

TABLE 12-5   Reasons for Not Voting, 1968-1976

	1968	1972	1976
Not Registered	34%	28%	38%
Don't Like Candidates	12	10	14
No Particular Reason	8	13	10
Not Interested	7	4	10
Illness	15	11	7
Other	24	34	21

Source: Gallup Opinion Index, No. 9, December 1972, and No. 137, December 1976. Reprinted by permission.

looked at the ratings for each group across the dimensions of level of psychological involvement in politics, level of political efficacy, level of political information, and level of civic-mindedness. Their results are summarized in Table 12–6. The table indicates that more complex and involved political activities are associated with higher levels of involvement, efficacy, and system affect. People who vote *and do nothing else,* do not differ in psychological characteristics from people who refrain from all forms of political activity. The clear indication is that, for many people, voting is done out of a sense of habit rather than of duty.

TABLE 12-6   Psychological Characteristics of Four Political Activity Patterns

Activity Type	Psychological Involvement	Efficacy	Information	Civic-Mindedness
Inactives	Low	Low	Low	Low
Voting Specialists	Low	Low	Low	Low
Partisan Activists	Medium	Medium	Medium	Low
Complete Activists	High	High	High	High

Source: From *Participation in America,* by Sidney Verba and Norman H. Nie, p. 87. Copyright © 1972 by Sidney Verba and Norman H. Nie. Reprinted by permission of Harper & Row, Publishers, Inc.

The Basis of Political Activism

We have covered both the demographic as well as some of the attitudinal characteristics of the different types of political activity prevalent in this political culture. Because of the strong relationship that exists between lower social status and such things as the degree of political involvement, information levels, and the like, it is not possible to state with certainty what factor is most important in determining the level of political activism. In a recent multivariate analysis of the characteristics of nonvoters in the 1976 election, William Maddox attempted to isolate the importance of socioeconomic and attitudinal factors upon the voting act.[46] His results, summarized in Table 12 – 7, illustrate the difficulty of the task. The table shows that the largest percentage of nonvoters have both low social status and low involvement. In the two categories in which one factor is high and the other low, however, each factor accounts for almost the same percentage of the nonvoting public. This information suggests that social status and psychological involvement may play equally important roles in nonparticipation. What is abundantly clear is that when the two factors are conjoined the result is a severe reduction in the incentive to participate.

TABLE 12–7 Classification of Nonvoters in 1972 by Social Status and Degree of Involvement

Social Status	Degree of Involvement	Percentage of Nonvoters
Low	Low	62%
Low	High	15
High	Low	16
High	High	7

Source: From "The Changing American Nonvoter, 1952–1978" by William S. Maddox in WATCHING AMERICAN POLITICS edited by Dan Nimmo and William Rivers. Copyright © 1981 by Longman, Inc. Reprinted by permission of Longman, Inc., New York.

POLITICAL PARTICIPATION AND ISSUES

By putting the above discussion into a broader context, the analysis of individual participation concludes by examining the relationship between participation and issue beliefs. Since the election of 1964, political scientists have observed that the public has been more inclined to base its voting decisions on a comparison of its positions on important issues with those of the candidates seeking its support.[47] Instead of basing their vote choice on party affiliation alone, voters have come at least to articulate issue concerns in their evaluations of candidates. As Figure 12–11 shows, issue mentions in candidate evaluations increased sharply in 1964, and while the level has dropped off, they continue to occupy a position that is much higher than that which was attained in the fifties. Specific mention of the candidate's party ties ("I like him because he's a Republican" and the like) have dropped off sharply over the past twenty years.

Likewise, studies have shown an increasing ability on the part of the mass public to identify the differences between both the parties and the candidates along relevant issue dimensions.[48] There has also been a marked increase in split-ticket voting and party switching on the basis of issue preferences.[49] In all, results between 1964 and 1972 especially have lent credence to the belief articulated by the late V.O. Key that the voters are indeed not fools.[50] When voters are given a distinct choice in an election, the findings indicate greater tendencies to make decisions that are independent of long-term predilections.[51] This pattern was reinforced by studies of the 1976 campaign contest between Carter and Ford. In that election the issues were not clearly defined, hence the strength of issues in the vote choice of the electorate dropped off from its level in 1972, and candidate evaluation and political party affiliation became more important.[52] In all, there has appeared throughout the general public a tendency that resembles the pattern Pomper identifies as "the responsive voter," in which the individual's vote is not predetermined but must be won by the candidate's articulation of relevant political issues.[53]

FIGURE 12–11   Frequency of Evaluations of Candidates in Terms of Party Ties, Personal Attributes, and Issue Positions, 1952–1972

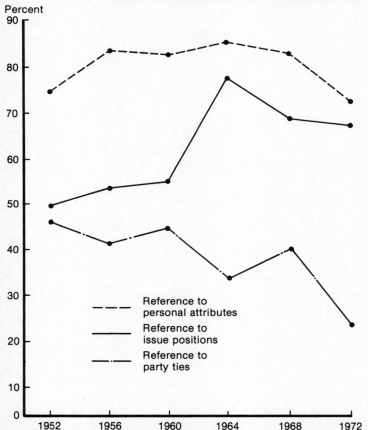

NOTES

1. Systems theorists would argue that too much utilization of demand channels would cause system overload. In this light, too much political attention would not be a desirable state for the stability of a system.
2. For a good discussion of the support dimension of participation, see Sidney Verba, *Small Groups and Political Behavior* (Princeton, N.J.: Princeton University Press, 1961), especially Chapter 7.

3. Sidney Verba and Norman H. Nie, *Participation in America: Political Democracy and Social Equality* (New York: Harper & Row, 1972), p. 5.
4. For two diametrically opposed views on the desirability of an informed and active electorate, see Dennis Thompson, *The Democratic Citizen* (New York: Cambridge University Press, 1970); and the last chapter of Bernard Berelson, Paul Lazarsfeld, and William McPhee, *Voting* (Chicago: University of Chicago Press, 1954).
5. Verba and Nie, *Participation in America,* p. 2.
6. Ibid., pp. 2–3.
7. This does not imply, however, that such tactics have not been rationally chosen as instruments of influence or at least to attract attention to societal problems. The riots in Miami in 1980 are examples of this attention-attracting use of extralegal activism.
8. Verba and Nie, *Participation in America,* p. 45.
9. Ibid., pp. 47–51.
10. For a fuller discussion of this, see William H. Flanigan and Nancy Zingale, *Political Behavior of the American Electorate,* 3rd ed. (Boston: Allyn & Bacon, 1975), pp. 14–19.
11. Extension of turnout data back into the nineteenth century is not reliable because the change to the Australian ballot form dramatically affected turnout and vote choice. See Jerrold Rusk, "The Effect of the Australian Ballot Reform on Split Ticket Voting: 1876 – 1908," *American Political Science Review* 64 (December 1970), pp. 1220 – 38. For the best treatment of voting trends in this period, see Walter Dean Burnham, *Critical Elections and the Mainsprings of American Politics* (New York: Norton, 1970).
12. The ebb and flow of vote turnout between presidential and off-year elections is examined in Angus Campbell, "Surge and Decline: A Study of Electoral Change," in *Elections and the Political Order,* (New York: John Wiley & Sons, 1966), pp. 40–62.
13. All figures reported were compiled by Peter Hart and Associates, *Non-Voter Study 1976,* Committee for the Study of the American Electorate, Press Release, September 5, 1976.
14. Verba and Nie, *Participation in America,* pp. 68–69.
15. Gabriel Almond and Sidney Verba, *The Civic Culture* (Princeton, N.J.: Princeton University Press, 1963), Chapter 1.
16. For a more in-depth examination of the relationship between demographic characteristics and vote turnout, see Raymond Wolfinger and Steven J. Rosenstone, *Who Votes?* (New Haven, Conn.: Yale University Press, 1980).
17. The reader should remember that public opinion surveys are not the most valid method of assessing turnout. First, being interviewed tends to make people more interested in politics; thus, they tend to participate more as a group than those not interviewed. (See Robert E. Kraut and John B. McConahay, "How Being Interviewed Affects Voting: An Experiment," *Public Opinion Quarterly* 37 (Fall 1973), pp. 398– 406.) Second, since there is no way to check the accuracy of self-reported voting, a percentage of those voting did not in fact vote. On this problem, see Aage Clausen, "Response Validity: Vote Report," *Public Opinion Quarterly* 32 (1968), pp. 588– 606; and Michael Traugott and John P. Katosh, "Response Validity in Surveys of Voting Behavior," *Public Opinion Quarterly* 43 (1979), pp. 359– 77.
18. Articles on the subject of age and turnout include Vern Bengston and Neal Cutler, "Generations and Intergenerational Relations: Perspectives on Time, Age Groups, and Social Change," in *The Handbook of Aging and Social Science,* Robert Binstock and Ethel Shanah, eds. (New York: Van Nostrand Reinhold, 1976); Nor-

val D. Glenn, "Aging, Disengagement and Opinionation," *Public Opinion Quarterly*
33 (Spring 1969), pp. 17–33; Norval D. Glenn and Michael Grimes, "Aging, Voting
and Political Interest," *American Sociological Review* 33 (August 1968), pp. 563–
75; and Matilda Riley, "Aging and Cohort Succession: Interpretations and Misin-
terpretations," *Public Opinion Quarterly* 37 (Spring 1973), pp. 35–49.

19. Verba and Nie, *Participation in America,* pp. 139.
20. Ibid., p. 148.
21. M. Kent Jennings, "Another Look at the Life Cycle and Political Participation,"
    American Journal of Political Science 23 (November 1979), pp. 755–71.
22. See Chapter 11 for more detailed information on important points in the civil
    rights movement.
23. Still the most useful reference on black voting patterns is Donald R. Matthews and
    James W. Prothro, *Negroes and the New South Politics* (New York: Harcourt Brace
    & World, 1966).
24. See also James Barber, Jr., *Social Mobility and Voting Behavior* (Chicago: Rand
    McNally, 1970); Norval D. Glenn, "Class and Party Support in the United States:
    Recent and Emerging Trends," *Public Opinion Quarterly* 37 (Spring 1973), pp. 1–
    20; Austin Ranney, "Turnout and Representation in Presidential Primary Elec-
    tions," *American Political Science Review* 66 (March 1972, pp. 21–37); and Eugene
    Declercq, Thomas Hurley, and N. Luttbeg, "Voting in American Presidential Elec-
    tions: 1952–1972," *American Political Quarterly* 3 (1975), pp. 17–23.
25. Verba and Nie, *Participation in America,* p. 96.
26. See Chapter 11 for a discussion of sexual differences in participation.
27. Paul Allen Beck and M. Kent Jennings, "Political Periods and Political Participa-
    tion," *American Political Science Review* 73 (September 1979), pp. 737–50.
28. While the Republicans began to actively court the black vote in 1972, blacks had
    never held out too much hope for a Nixon activist policy in the area of civil rights.
29. Verba and Nie, *Participation in America,* p. 80.
30. See Donald Devine, *The Attentive Public: Polyarchy and Democracy* (Chicago: Rand
    McNally, 1970).
31. For interesting examinations of these relationships between socioeconomic status
    and political activity, see R. Robert Huckfeldt, "Political Participation and the
    Neighborhood Societal Context," *American Journal of Political Science* 23 (August
    1979), pp. 579–92; and Lester Milbrath and M. Goel, *Political Participation*
    (Chicago: Rand McNally, 1977).
32. While we generally assume that the attitudinal characteristics of partisanship,
    ideology, and affect *precede* political participation, it is also reasonable to assume
    that for some, participation itself increases the level of political interest and issue
    and party affiliation.
33. Angus Campbell et al., *The American Voter* (New York: John Wiley & Sons, 1960),
    p. 143.
34. For references on the behavior of the American Independent, see Campbell et al.,
    The American Voter, chap. 6; Flanigan and Zingale, *Political Behavior of the Amer-
    ican Electorate,* chap. 4; and Norman H. Nie, Sidney Verba, and John R. Petrocik,
    The Changing American Voter (Cambridge, Mass.: Harvard University Press,
    1976), Chapter 4.
35. Warren E. Miller and Teresa Levitin, *Leadership and Change: The New Politics
    and the American Electorate* (Cambridge, Mass.: Winthrop Publishers, 1976), p. 99.
36. Verba and Nie, *Participation in America,* pp. 216–19.
37. For a review of the relationship between higher social status and conservative
    ideology, see Campbell et al., *The American Voter,* pp. 209–13; and Lloyd A. Free
    and Hadley Cantril, *The Political Beliefs of Americans* (New York: Simon & Schus-

ter, 1968), pp. 220 – 26. For changes in that relationship and in the meaning of "liberalism" and "conservatism," see Everett Carll Ladd, Jr., with Charles D. Hadley, *Transformations of the American Party System,* 2nd ed. (New York: Norton, 1978), pp. 217– 27.

38. Verba and Nie, *Participation in America,* pp. 225– 28.

39. In another place, Nie and Verba have modified their position on this issue; see Nie, Verba, and Petrocik, *The Changing American Voter,* pp. 202– 9.

40. See also, Herbert McClosky, "Consensus and Ideology in American Politics," *American Political Science Review* 58 (June 1964), pp. 361– 82.

41. Beck and Jennings, "Political Periods and Participation."

42. Miller and Levitin, *Leadership and Change,* pp. 259– 62.

43. Two recent works emphasize the role of the political environment in the shaping of the public's opinions: Benjamin Page, *Choices and Echoes in Presidential Elections: Rational Man and Electoral Democracy* (Chicago: University of Chicago Press, 1978); and John C. Pierce and Paul R. Hagner, "Changes in the Public's Political Thinking: The Watershed Years, 1956–1968," in *The Electorate Reconsidered,* John Pierce and John Sullivan, eds. (Beverly Hills: Sage Publications, 1980), pp. 69– 90.

44. See Chapter 9 for a full discussion of this area.

45. Data from the 1976 CPS National Election Survey.

46. William S. Maddox, "The Changing American Nonvoter, 1952 – 1978" (Paper delivered at the Annual Meeting of the Southern Political Science Association, Gatlinburg, Tennessee, November 1979).

47. Some recent sources on the rise of issue voting during this period are Eugene DeClercq, Thomas L. Hurley, and Norman Luttbeg, "Variability in Electoral Behavior," *American Journal of Political Science* 26 (February 1975), pp. 1– 18; Samuel Kirkpatrick, William Lyons, and Michael Fitzgerald, "Candidates, Parties and Issues in the American Electorate: Two Decades of Change," *American Political Quarterly* 3 (July 1975), pp. 247–83; Arthur H. Miller, "Partisanship Reinstated? A Comparison of the 1972 and 1976 U.S. Presidential Elections," *British Journal of Political Science* 8 (January 1978), pp. 129– 52; and Teresa Levitin and Warren E. Miller, "Ideological Interpretations of Presidential Elections," *American Political Science Review* 73 (September 1979), pp. 751– 71. The most complete overview of this area is found in Nie, Verba, and Petrocik, *The Changing American Voter,* Chapters 10 and 18.

48. See Chapter 10 for an overview of the relationship between party identification and individual opinion.

49. Some citations on split-ticket voting and party switching are V.O. Key, Jr., *The Responsible Electorate* (Cambridge; Mass.: Harvard University Press, 1966); Richard W. Boyd, "Presidential Elections: An Explanation of Voting Defection," *American Political Science Review* 63 (1969), pp. 498– 514; David Repass, "Issue Salience and Party Choice," *American Political Science Review* 65 (1971), pp. 389– 400; Samuel Kirkpatrick and Melvin Jones, "Issue Publics and the Electoral System: The Role of Issues in Electoral Change," in *Public Opinion and Political Attitudes,* Allen Wilcox, ed. (New York: John Wiley & Sons, 1974), pp. 537– 55; and Nie, Verba, and Petrocik, *The Changing American Voter,* Chapter 18.

50. V.O. Key, Jr., *The Responsible Electorate.*

51. The most forceful presentation of this argument is found in Benjamin Page and Richard Brody, "Policy Voting and the Electoral Process: The Vietnam Issue," *American Political Science Review* 65 (September 1972), pp. 979– 95.

52. See Arthur Miller, "Partisanship Reinstated?"

53. Gerald M. Pomper, *The Voters' Choice: Varieties of American Electoral Behavior* (New York: Dodd, Mead & Co., 1975), p. 8.

CHAPTER 13

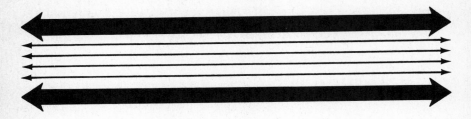

INTEREST GROUPS
AND
PUBLIC OPINION

Few question the central role of interest groups in American politics. Indeed, some scholars even suggest that government's primary function is to control and funnel into public policy the competition among the diverse political interests in society. As V.O. Key argued, "The exercise of the power of governance consists in large in the advancement of legitimate group objectives, in the reconciliation and mediation of conflicting group ambitions, and in the restraint of group tendencies judged to be socially destructive."[1] One aspect of interest groups that gives them importance is their central position in the understanding of public opinion. Many changes in public opinion — as well as much stability — are reflected in interest groups. Changes in public opinion have contributed to the growth of interest groups in areas of public policy where previously they had been moribund, and have been linked to the appearance of new kinds of interest groups — the "public" interest group and the "single-issue" interest group. Much of the recent alteration in the constellation of interest-group politics is a direct consequence of important shifts in public opinion about the political positions promoted by those groups.

Interest groups attempt to shape public opinion as one of their tactics in influencing public policy. In this context, we define an interest group as an organization of individuals who share a political opinion and who attempt to influence government in order to see that opinion reflected in public policy. As will become clear later in the chapter, the shared opinion may not be the only or even the major reason for the individual joining the group. Moreover, there are varying levels of involvement and agreement with an organization. The most familiar division is between the leaders or activists in the organization and the mass members or followers. Yet the relationship of individuals to interest groups does not stop at the boundary of formal membership. There usually exist a number of people who can be called "identifiers." They do not "belong" to the group in the sense of paying membership dues, and yet they think of themselves as members. They follow the successes and failures of the group, rooting from the sidelines, and look to the organization and its leaders for guidance in response to new issues and events.

Interest groups are central to the linkage aspect of the relationship between public opinion and democratic politics.[2] As groups play their role in promoting the shared opinions or interests of their members, they contribute to democratic politics; they increase the responsiveness of political leaders. Through the pooling of resources and the organization and articulation of shared opinions, the members of an interest group enhance their ability to achieve their goals. The ability of the society's interest-group universe to represent all interests and to respond to changes in public opinion — such as the birth and growth of newly shared political interests — is a telling gauge of its fundamental democratic character. If new interests develop and new sets of opinions form but no organizations respond to represent those opinions, then the public may need to employ other channels to influence the government.

Interest groups also are important in the formation and change of public opinion. Groups not only respond to changes in public opinion, but they also help to create that change. On the one hand, as groups attempt to increase the salience of their particular interest, as they press their claims on government, they define many of the issues on which public opinion is formed. One of the most important tasks of an interest group is to create a political climate in which the shared interest of its members achieves a place of priority on the public agenda. Interest groups bring to the attention of the public those issues, interests, and conditions about which they previously may have been unaware. As the public confronts those new issues they must form opinions or perhaps change previous opinions loosely held, or reinforce the opinions they already claim. At the same time, interest groups (and their leaders) are important referents or cue-givers to people who identify with them. That is, if the public is positively oriented toward a group, people may accept a d articulate the positions promoted by that group. If there is a negative orientation toward the group, people may automatically reject the group's interest and articulate opinions contrary to the group's position. The positive and negative cue-giving role of groups is especially important when the individual is confronted with unusual issues, ones that are not clearly within the range of previously held opinions. Indeed, in times of rapid change in society, interest groups may interpret events for people and thereby consequently create opinions. Groups also are important in opinion change, as they indicate to their cue-takers (members or identifiers) how the group interest is newly linked to a previously contrary opinion.

In summary, interest groups are important in some forms of democratic theory by representing segments of the public in the formation of policy. They are also important in the creation and change of public opinion. Interest groups are an important mechanism for aggregating and articulating the shared opinions of portions of the public. In the past several decades there have been some important changes in American interest groups that reflect directly on the public's political opinions. New groups have been created and the size of some others has grown exponentially. New kinds of groups have appeared. New group tactics have been employed, many of which are designed to influence public opinion. This chapter will discuss many of the important changes in the relationship between interest groups and public opinion: changes in the size, strength, and distribution of interest groups and how those changes might be explained; the role of opinions in the individual's decisions to join or abstain from interest groups promoting interests with which they agree; and changes in group tactics, focusing on the expression and creation of public opinion.

CHANGE IN THE GROUP UNIVERSE

The Nature of the Change

Interest groups serve as mechanisms for the articulation and organization of shared political opinions. Thus, it should not be surprising that during the same period that American public opinion underwent many changes, so did the characteristics of American interest groups.

As the issues in their policy area become generally more salient to the public, some groups experience rapidly growing membership. Rosenbaum notes, for example, that "between 1970 and 1971, membership in the five largest environmental groups jumped by 400,000, a 33 percent increase in one year."[3] Moreover, new environmental interest groups were formed, including the Environmental Defense Fund, the Friends of the Earth, Environmental Action, the Natural Resources Defense Council, and the Environmental Policy Center.[4] A similar growth took place in interest groups representing older Americans.[5] Founded in 1961, the Council of Senior Citizens now has a membership of more than 3 million people over the age of fifty-five. The American Association of Retired Persons (AARP), formed in 1958, has 7.5 million members, and the National Retired Teachers Association, affiliated with the AARP, has 500,000 members. Other organizations, while much smaller, also appeared. One example is the Gray Panthers, led by Margaret Kuhn. This group adopted many of the tactics of other organizations of the period (1970), "taking to the streets with banners and picket signs to protest nursing-home abuses."[6]

In the 1960s and early 1970s there also took place a radical change in the nature of the organizations in the women's movement. The National Organization for Women (NOW), the largest of the women's interest groups, was founded in 1966. By 1967 it had grown to 1,200 members, and by 1974 it had 700 chapters and 40,000 members.[7] Jo Freeman notes that the women's movement has also had numerous smaller organizations,

> the small group of from five to thirty women held together by an often tenuous network of personal contacts and feminist publications. These groups have a variety of functions but a very consistent style. . . . The thousands of sister chapters around the country are virtually independent of one another, linked only by numerous publications, personal correspondence and cross-country travelers. These form and dissolve at such a rate that no one can keep track of them.[8]

Some of the women's organizations have had more explicitly political purposes and hence greater public exposure and longevity. These include the Women's Equity Action League and the National Women's Political Caucus.

The mid and late 1970s witnessed the emergence of another organizational force — the "New Right" pressure groups.[9] Their purpose is to gain conservative control of political offices. The activism of the New Right's leaders stems from the mid-1970s, following the ill-fated Nixon administration. The New Right focuses on a rather narrow set of issues, related generally to "traditional American values." One man, Richard A. Viguerie, has received the greatest attention, primarily because of his ability to raise very large sums of money for conservative causes and candidates through mail requests. Among these groups are the Committee for the Survival of a Free Congress; the Heritage Foundation, Inc.; the Conservative Caucus; and the National Conservative Political Action Committee, Inc. The New Right groups also are linked to traditional conservative organizations: in some cases their leaders are products of such groups as Young Americans for Freedom, and in other cases they meet with those groups in planning joint efforts and exchanging information.

The 1960s, of course, exhibited many changes in black political organizations during that decade's civil rights movement. In addition to the major black organizations that had been extant for a number of years (the NAACP from 1910, the Urban League from 1916), Martin Luther King's Southern Christian Leadership Conference (SCLC) and Student Non-Violent Coordinating Committee (SNCC) achieved prominence. According to Hanes Walton, the black pressure groups during this period were basically single-tactic groups (e.g., the SCLC and King used mass nonviolent civil disobedience, while the NAACP worked through the judicial process).[10] While the groups represented the interests of many in the black community, according to Walton, "At present, conservative white majority opinion has badly crippled several of the major black reform pressure groups," because they wanted to make basic structural responses in society rather than concentrate on more narrowly defined public policies.[11]

Specific issues in recent years have stimulated the active involvement of traditional interest groups, but they also have given rise to groups whose sole purpose relates to that issue. Thus, during the Watergate period a number of familiar groups took positions either in support of or opposition to the impeachment of President Nixon. At the same time, however, many other organizations were formed specifically for the purposes of achieving or blocking impeachment and conviction. Among the impeachment opponents were the following groups: National Citizens' Committee for Fairness to the Presidency; Americans for the Presidency; Texas Committee in Support of the President; Citizens in Support of the President; and Friends and Neighbors of President Nixon in Whittier, California. On the other side, the pro-impeachment position, were such new groups as National Campaign to Impeach Nixon and the National Committee on the Presidency.[12]

Most of the major changes in the group universe took place in the turbulent politics of the 1960s and early 1970s — the civil rights struggle, the foundation of the women's rights movement, the source of the antiwar movement, and the roots of the environmental causes. In the decade of the 1970s, two rather distinct kinds of groups have come to play a very prominent role in the articulation and presentation of public opinion to the political system. These two kinds of groups provide a very interesting contrast, because in one sense they are found on very opposite ends of a spectrum. On the one hand, there is the development of the *public interest group,* and on the other, there is the rise of the *single-issue interest group.* Both have had very profound effects on politics.

A public interest group is defined by Jeffrey Berry as "one that seeks a public collective good, the achievement of which will not selectively and materially benefit the membership or activists of the organization."[13] Public interest groups seek to obtain goals that will, at least in their eyes, benefit everyone, regardless of whether they are members of the group. Such a definition does have some problems, for it is difficult to find groups that do not think of themselves as benefiting "everyone," although perhaps in some rather indirect ways. Another characteristic that often has been applied to public interest groups is the *generality* of their concerns, the broad range of issues with which they deal. Public interest groups tend to engage far-ranging sets of issues that are united by the generality of their impact on the public rather than by their more narrow impact on the group's members.

A number of groups have variously been included under the public interest rubric: environmental, consumer, civil rights, antiwar and peace groups, as well as others.[14] However, two public interest organizations have received the greatest attention and perhaps have had the greatest impact. These two are Common Cause and Ralph Nader's Public Citizen (Nader also heads a number of other organizations). Common Cause was born in 1970 of the efforts of John Gardner. It gained a membership of 100,000 in six months and reached a peak of 320,000 during the impeachment proceeding against Richard Nixon. Common Cause grew out of the political malaise of the late 1960s and early 1970s and seemed to many people of widely divergent political positions to be an opportunity for the "public" to have its voice heard. The goals of Common Cause are such that if they are achieved they are distributed to all Americans who want them regardless of whether or not they are members of the organization. Thus, when Common Cause is successful in achieving greater disclosure in campaign finance contributions, *all* citizens who prefer disclosure benefit from a more open political system.

Nader's organizations, or course, are most well-known for their consumer causes. In the 1970s his groups focused on the American government, especially the U.S. Congress. The exposure of consumer fraud and the critical examination of Congress are both public or collective goods; the positive results from them cannot be withheld from people who did not participate in the effort to achieve those goods.

Single-interest groups always have been present in American politics, but there seem to be many more of them recently, and there seem to be some changes in their activities. As their name implies, single-interest groups tend to focus on one goal or at least on an extremely narrow range of goals. As a result, they tend to have a very homogeneous membership.[15] What makes single-issue groups distinctive is their apparent unwillingness to compromise their goals. This confronts directly the traditional view of American democratic politics as compromise and interaction among groups, the trading of some benefits in order to acquire others, and then working together to achieve both.

Single-interest groups often are unable to work within the parameters of those American political parties that traditionally have been based on the aggregation of and compromise among diverse interests. In confronting political candidates, single-interest groups frequently either sharply defend or starkly condemn them — there rarely is middle ground. A politician is either a friend or a rival, and that determination is based on the one issue. Single-issue groups also tend to generate counterparts on the other side of the issue, perhaps as a result of their generally uncompromising, true-believer positions. Examples of single-interest groups include the following: Citizen's Committee on the Right to Bear Arms; National Organization for the Reform of Marijuana Laws (NORML); the Greenpeace Foundation; National Right to Work Committee; the Clamshell Alliance; the Right to Life Amendment Political Action Committee; ERA and anti-ERA groups; pro- and antihunting groups; the Committee on Handgun Control.

In summary, the constellation of interest groups in American politics — the organizations through which public opinion may be organized, articulated, and shaped — has changed radically in the past decade. Existing groups grew rapidly. In certain policy areas, many new groups were formed. New kinds of groups became influential in American politics, including the public interest group and the single-interest group. We turn to some alternative explanations for these changes.

Explanations for the Changes

According to Robert Salisbury, there are three major theories about the formation of new groups.[16] These three theories have their roots deep in the interest group literature, predating many of the more recent changes. Yet each of them has some relevance to contemporary events. These three are the equilibrium theory, the proliferation theory, and the entrepreneurial theory. As it will become clear, the three explanations are not mutually exclusive.

THE EQUILIBRIUM THEORY. This explanation posits that the natural state of affairs is a balance among the interests in a society. The relevant competing interests will have organizations for the pressing of their political demands, and a natural equilibrium will develop in the struggle among these groups. The balance or equilibrium means that competing interests are represented and that there is stability through time in the number of interests and in their relative strength. New groups form when something occurs that disturbs the balance, that creates a disequilibrium. Henry Pratt has argued that

> the general perspective . . . emphasizing interest group formation as arising out of a felt need to restore homeostasis following disruptive societal events, would seem to have value in accounting for the recent growth of senior-citizen activism.[17]

Pratt suggests that disequilibrium was introduced by rapid technological growth, with a special impact on the aged. Technological growth isolated the aged from the rest of society through the breakdown of the three-generation family unit and the *perceived* obsolesence of the older person's personal skills. Both of these generated frustration among the aged, frustrations that in many cases led to political action. Thus, the formation of the many groups representing the aged or retired was a reaction to the disequilibrium and a natural response to restore balance in society.

In the case of older Americans, then, we find environmental-level changes occurring that had a special relevance for a particular segment of society. The environmental (systemic) changes produced a shared position in society, a position characterized by relative social isolation and estrangement. The shared position in society generated similar political or classified interests and opinions. With no present political linkages seen as adequately articulating those opinions and interests, the natural response was for the formation of new organizations and the rapid expansion of existing groups. Those new organizations explicitly represent the shared opinions of the older Americans comprising their membership; their existence and their subsequent political activity reflect the changes in society and their impact on the political opinions of an important segment of the American public.

THE PROLIFERATION EXPLANATION. The proliferation explanation of changes in the group universe is linked to the equilibrium explanation. Both emphasize changes in the larger environment that cause a social disruption of some segment of society, and this segment then organizes to protect and articulate its interests. Yet the proliferation approach is somewhat more specific in identifying the sources of the disruption and linking the increase in the number of interest groups to the characteristics of an increasingly modern and technological society. There is a *"proliferation* growing out of the rapid pace of change, specialization, and diversity of interests in modern society."[18] In its simplest form, this approach suggests that as the economic and social diversity of society increases, the interests become more narrow and separable. People in particular locations in society come to share more with each other and less with those people in other locations. Moreover, there become more and more of these identifiable and distinct niches. Since people who share the social locations share interests, and should share public opinions designed to protect or enhance those interests, the groups form and form and form — as long as the process of proliferation and differentiation in society continues.

In a chapter entitled "The Mushrooom Effect," Jo Freeman examines the astounding increase in the number of feminist groups in the early 1970s.[19] Her analysis does not follow precisely the proliferation explanation, but the mushrooming of the organizations she describes has much in common with what proliferation would predict. Women's organizations have been active for a number of years.[20] However,

> *the women's liberation movement "took off" in 1970. It was during that year*
> *that the accelerating influx of new people became too great for the groups*

and organizations to handle, and that new groups were formed more quickly than anyone could keep count.[21]

The proliferation of women's groups took on a very clear pattern. That pattern was great heterogeneity among groups, with great homogeneity within groups. As it became clear that the issues of feminism have somewhat different implications for women in different situations, those women who shared a particular location in society formed their own organizations to represent their interests. Thus, in addition to some large national organizations (e.g., the National Organization for Women) there emerged organizations with specific ties to black women, older women, women in the labor movement, women in the federal service, and so on. While the rapid increase in the number of organizations may not have stemmed directly from differentiation and specialization in society, once the women's movement was kicked off by whatever forces account for it, the nature of the economic and social development in recent years seems to have guided the path taken in the formation of organizations.

THE ENTREPRENEURIAL EXPLANATION. The entrepreneurial explanation builds on the equilibrium and proliferation models. The latter two may describe the conditions and processes that lead to interest group formation, but there often is the implicit (and sometimes explicit) assumption that there is something automatic about group formation. That is, once disequilibrium exists, or once differentiation occurs, people who share interests, and hence opinions, will in some way automatically come together and form an organization to promote their common cause. Yet there must be some kind of catalyst, some vehicle for that organization. These catalysts "or entrepreneurs invest some form of capital resources in a set of selective benefits to be made available to those who join the organization."[22] That is, an organizer or "entrepreneur" invests his or her own resources and attempts to capture a market of potential group members. That market is captured, or at least members are attracted, through the offering of goods that cannot be obtained without belonging to the organization. These goods are called "selective benefits," as opposed to public goods (ones that are available to everyone). We return to this process in the section on joining groups.

Indeed, some of the most spectacular interest group successes of the 1970s are the direct result of entrepreneurship on the part of one person or a small group of people. One need go no farther than Common Cause to find an example. Common Cause was the direct outgrowth of the efforts (investment) of one man, John Gardner. In commenting on the exceptional growth of Common Cause in its early years, Berry says "Gardner was, simply, the right man at the right time."[23] And Andrew McFarland says "the founding of Common Cause in the summer of 1970 was an impressive feat of leadership on the part of John Gardner."[24] The entrepreneurial nature of Common Cause's beginning is starkly evident in this: "Gardner originally planned to raise $500,000 in 'start-up' capital that would be used until dues could begin to carry Common Cause expenses."[25] Thus, Gardner invested his personal resources, including his experience and his reputation, into the formation and growth of Common Cause, and the investment produced many profitable returns for the organization.

It should be apparent that the three explanations are not mutually exclusive. The disequilibrium and proliferation explanations focus on larger systemic sources of interest group formation. And the technological-differentiation sources of proliferation surely are indicative of a certain amount of disequilibrium. Disruption in itself will not automatically form groups; some interests will organize, and others will not. Entrepreneurs serve as catalysts for the formation of interest groups when the systemic conditions are appropriate, and when people can be induced to join.

JOINING GROUPS

During the 1960s and 1970s there occurred a number of changes in the groups operating in American politics; there were patterns of rapid growth and decline in many groups. New kinds of groups came to dominate certain areas of politics. In many cases, these changes in groups reflected concurrent changes in public opinion. The conditions for the formation and expansion of groups were provided by the generation of imbalance or disequilibrium in society, continuing the differentiation of society into narrow interest sectors, and by the activity of interest group entrepreneurs, investing their own resources to attract members. Yet, while these may define the environment within which the groups formed, it is clear that membership in those groups by people with shared opinions is less than automatic. Even in those cases where organizations have formed there are many people who share opinions who do not join the appropriate group. And, in other areas, there are people who share opinions yet no organization is successfully formed and maintained.

Incentive Theory

The question to be confronted in this section, then, is this: Why do people join (or choose not to join) organizations for the purpose of promoting their shared interest? In recent years, the most frequently forwarded explanation for participation in organizations (i.e., interest groups) is labeled "incentive theory." The individual's decision to participate in an organization is the consequence of a personal calculation of the costs to be absorbed from the participation and the benefits to be derived from it.[26]

A person will join an organization when the benefits of that participation outweigh the costs. The costs of interest group participation are evident — time, money, and emotional investment in the group's political life. Because of the costs of participation, the benefits available are held out to potential members as *incentives* to participation. Three major types of incentives (potential benefits) have been identified: material, solidary, purposive.

Material incentives, according to James Q. Wilson, are "tangible rewards: money, or things and services readily priced in monetary terms."[27] *Solidary* incentives relate to the psychological or emotional benefits of participation. On the one hand, there is the sense of belonging, "the fun and conviviality of coming together, the sense of group membership or exclusiveness, and such collective status or esteem as the group as a whole may enjoy."[28] Generally speaking, these rewards are available to all members of the organization. However, there are solidary incentives that are not available to everyone in the group. These include positions of status or authority within the organization; they are important to people precisely because not everyone can enjoy them. The third kind of incentive is *purposive*. Purposive incentives relate to the political or ideological goal of the organization. The incentive is the opportunity for the individual to participate in activity directed at achieving some worthwhile goal, presumably one with which the group member is in agreement. The purposive incentive is the one we usually think about when discussing groups of people sharing certain political opinions joining together to promote their shared opinions.

Most people join groups because they receive some mix of rewards or benefits. Or, to put it another way, most groups recruit members by offering a mix of incentives. Groups will differ in the relative emphasis they place on different kinds of incentives, and people will differ in the importance they attach to various incentives in their decision to participate in the organization. Thus, groups that are formed in order to promote a particular political goal — the shared political opinions of their members — will rely heavily on purposive incentives to attract members. Yet, those organizations will offer solidary and material incentives as well.

Why do organizations that are predominately purposive — their primary reason for existence being to achieve some identifiable political goal — provide material or solidary incentives to members? One answer is found in the distinction between collective and selective goods. Collective (or public) goods are ones that an individual can receive regardless of whether he or she participates in the activity to obtain it. Selective goods or incentives are those that are available only when the individual participates in the organization. For example, suppose an environmental organization actively lobbies government and achieves the establishment of a national park. The outcome is the provision of a public good, for access to and use of that park is not restricted to only those members of the organization that lobbied for it in the first place. Similarly, increases in Social Security benefits are not restricted only to those people belonging to organizations that actively lobbied on behalf of that increase. Rather, they are distributed to all individuals meeting the established qualifications, independent of organizational membership. On the other hand, *selective* goods are distributed only to people who participate in the organization. Membership is a condition for the receipt of selective benefits.

The reason for much of the mix in the incentives offered by organizations is found in the distinction between collective and selective benefits. It explains, for example, why some organizations must offer "special deals" to attract members to support their organization — even when those potential members are in complete agreement as to the worthiness of the organizational goal. How so? Remember that group membership may be explained in terms of a rational calculation by the individual. The rational individual wants to maximize benefits while minimizing costs. That is, he wants to get the most for the least cost. Thus, when an organization obtains a collective benefit there is no reason for an individual to participate in the organization's activities, for the person will receive the benefit anyway. The rational activity is to abstain from participation in organizations that are attempting to achieve public goods — policy goals with which one agrees and the benefits of which one will receive regardless of membership. The benefits will be provided without the costs. These people — those who obtain the benefits without the costs — have been called "free riders." Mancur Olson says that free-riding is a much bigger problem for large organizations.[29] In large organizations, he argues, the presence or absence of any single person will go unnoticed and will have an insignificant impact on the ability of the organization to achieve its goal. On the other hand, in small groups the absence of a single person will be noticed and will affect the organization's ability to achieve the collective good. With the diminished ability of the organization to achieve the public good, then, it becomes rational for the individual to participate in organizational efforts to achieve the goal, for without those efforts the good might not be provided at all.[30]

The question for the large organization then becomes, How do we stimulate people to membership? The answer is through the provision of selective incentives — benefits that are available only to group members. Thus, the goal of the National Rifle Association (NRA) is to protect the right to bear arms as well as to enhance hunting safety and hunting opportunities in the country. The NRA is a large organization, and its major goals — particularly the one of opposing gun controls — are collective goods. If they want, all people could benefit from the achievement of the purpose, regardless of their membership.[31] Thus, the NRA offers a number of other incentives, both material and solidary, available only to members. The material benefits are not of such a magnitude that they would make the difference between someone being able to satisfy fundamental needs. On the other hand, given that the cost of membership is relatively small (only $10 per year), the material benefits themselves need not be great. These include a subscription to the *American Rifleman,* low-cost gun insurance, game-availability bulletins, and a colorful Wildlife and Game Map "ready for framing." Solidary benefits offered are of both kinds (i.e., those derived from belonging to the group, and those obtained from position within the organization). The member is given the opportunity to become involved with NRA-related hunting and gun clubs and to display "NRA lapel emblem and an NRA decal for your car — FREE." The member also is offered the chance to compete for hunting awards, providing evidence of personal ability.

In contrast to the NRA mix of incentives is that offered by Common Cause. Common Cause's rewards or benefits to members are almost entirely purposive, dealing with the shared goal of enhancing public impact on government activity. To be sure, some solidary benefits may derive from participating in Common Cause activities, and the members do receive some publications. But those publications are designed to enhance citizen involvement and information levels. The flavor of the Common Cause appeal is captured in the following excerpt from a letter from John Gardner to potential members:

> *The identity of one person responsible for Watergate has never been disclosed.*
> *That person is you.*
> *Yes, you and every other American citizen is to blame. Whether Republican, Democrat, or independent. It doesn't make any difference whom you voted for. Watergate and all the corruption it symbolizes isn't restricted to any party. It reflects an undercurrent of political treachery that has become part of our very system itself. And because we, the people of this country, have tolerated corruption and let it grow to the point where it threatens our very existence as a democracy — we are all to blame for the consequences. Voting on Election Day isn't enough. We've got to do more.*
> *Yes, I know it's impossible for one person to correct what's wrong in our system. To do that takes clout. And clout calls for organized strength. And it seems that everybody but the people has been organized. So no matter how angry you become over what you saw happening in and to our government, chances are that like so many other Americans, you told yourself there was little you could do to stop it . . . until now.*
> *Now there is Common Cause.*

The purposive nature of the Common Cause appeal is clear. What also is evident is that if the goals are obtained the result will be the distribution of collective goods — available to everyone, regardless of whether they are members of Common Cause. This combination of purposive incentives and collective goods in a very large organization has caused some people to question Olson's "logic of collective action."[32] That is, in the absence of selective incentives (available only to members), why have so many participated in such a large organization where clearly one person's absence would make no difference. Does the participation mean that Common Cause members are "irrational" (in an economic sense)? Or does the perception of a clear threat to the political system comprise sufficient incentive to overcome the potential costs of the participation? Perhaps there was a view by many members during its height that if Common Cause were unsuccessful, there would be no benefits at all to distribute.

Incentive Theory and Recent Changes

What does this discussion of the foundations of group membership say about the changes in the interest group universe in the sixties and seventies and its relationship to changes in public opinion? Several things stand out.

First, as observers of politics we often label and group together into a single category organizations that appear to share a common goal of promoting a particular interest (e.g., environmental groups and civil rights organizations). The above discussion should alert us to the possibility that different groups in the same general policy area may actually have a very distinctive mix in incentives offered to potential members. Similarly, people who apparently share policy preferences because they belong to similar groups may actually be joining those groups for different reasons.

In the women's movement, for instance, some organizations may emphasize purposive incentives while others emphasize purely solidary incentives. Explicitly political organizations, such as the National Organization for Women, may focus more on the achievement of identifiable policy goals that are collective goods; that is, they will be available to all women regardless of whether or not they are members of the organizations. On the other hand, small "rap" groups — those in which there is intensive and sustained interaction among the participants — may satisfy psychological needs of the participants; they may exist primarily through their offering of solidary benefits that are selective. They are selective in the sense that they are available only upon participation in the organization. It is interesting to note, in this regard, that some women's organizations that offer primarily solidary benefits of the kind that come from a feeling of cohesion have attempted to explicitly reject those solidary benefits that come from particular status within the organizations, such as positions of authority.[33] To the contrary, the status positions that would lead to individual benefits are systematically rotated among all individuals. This would either eliminate those positions as sources of solidary benefits or ensure that all members receive them. Since positions of authority are expressly devalued in these cases, though, the sense is that solidary benefits from status within the organization are unacceptable.

Thus, the growth of both the number and the size of organizations within a particular sector of interest may reflect a rather diversified response of public opinion, rather than some apparently monolithic surge, responding to the same incentives.

Second, much of the rapid rise and fall of memberships in some interest groups in the last two decades might be attributed to their reliance on purposive incentives — those most directly related to the character of public opinions. While an issue is extremely important, highly salient politically, the purposive incentive can become very important, even for large groups striving to obtain collective goods. The salience of the issue — the immediacy of a Watergate, the perceived impending environmental doom, or the revulsion of a war — may strike deep into the political consciousness of people. However, as the immediacy of the goal or the threat fades, so may the effectiveness of the purposive incentive. It is the "true believer" whose membership in the organization is sustained through times of low salience by the promise of achieving some ultimate goal that will contribute to the good of all. Norman Ornstein and Shirley Elder cite Common Cause as an example of the unstable nature of membership in organizations relying on purposive incentives.[34] Common Cause's membership rose sharply during the impeachment proceedings of President Nixon but then fell off rapidly after his resignation. For members of purposive organizations, then, the incentive may become more effective in the face of immediate and rather concrete group objects — such as the impeachment of a president — as opposed to long-term purposive goals that are hard to identify precisely, such as "to correct what's wrong in our system."

Third, changes in public opinion will not automatically result in changes in the membership of groups representing the gains or losses in public opinion. The extent to which the interest group universe will reflect the changes in public opinion depends on the structures of benefits distributed by the organizations and the extent to which the avowed goal of the group results in a collective good. This works both in the face of increases in favorable opinions and increases in unfavorable opinions. A great leap forward in the public's support for the goals of a group may not automatically result in large increases in membership. The increase in membership is unlikely to result if the group's goal will result in the provision of public goods, unless there is either (a) selective incentives simultaneously offered, or (b) the presence of such an immediate and highly salient context for the goal that the individual cannot afford the risk of waiting for others to provide the good — the costs of the good not being provided are extremely high, or at least are seen to be quite high. On the other hand, a great decline in public support for the cause of an interest group may not necessarily result in a dip in the group's formal membership. Membership may remain stable even when the group's members lose the depth of their conviction about the desirability of the purpose. "Selective" incentives — those available only to group members, such as material and solidary benefits — may be sufficient to maintain the membership in the face of loss of purposive support. In such a case, whether the movement in public opinion will result in the movement of memberships will largely be a function of two things: the relative importance of the group goals to the individual; and the availability of alternative sources of the selective benefits without the costs of inconsistent group goals.

Fourth, there is the question of the relationship between the changes in public opinion and interest groups, and the explanations of changes in public opinion identified in the beginning chapters of the book. It will be recalled that the major explanations of changes in public opinion were classified into three major categories: environmental/systemic, leadership, and individual. Each of these has implications for public opinion and interest group involvement.

One of the major environmental changes has been the identification of the development of postindustrial values among a number of Americans. Postindustrial values are those that reflect the individual's position at the higher level of a need hierarchy — esteem and self-actualization needs. The kinds of opinions thought to stem from that value positioning seem central to a number of changes in interest group membership. That is, people at the higher levels (self-actualizing) are said to be more likely to support abstract values, such as equality, responsiveness and participation in government, and aesthetic qualities in the natural environment. Many of the changes in interest group membership relate directly to organizations promoting those political positions. The civil rights movements, the environmental movement, the antiwar movement, and the women's movement all have as their purpose the achievement of situations identified with the higher-level values of people.[35] Thus, the change in the environment may have led to changes in value structures, which led to changes in political opinions, which led to membership in particular kinds of groups, whose primary incentives were purposive.

The second category deals with the importance of leadership behavior in stimulating the response of the public. The earlier focus on the entrepreneurial theory of interest group formation should make clear the relevance of this class of explanation. The change in public opinion and interest group involvement is a twofold consequence of leadership behavior. First, it stems from political leaders' cues to the public as to the appropriate political positions and the links between different political issues. They help to define for the potential members of an organization the nature of the interest and its political implications. They articulate for the potential members the content of the shared concerns and identify their political relevance. Thus, they help to establish the market for the entrepreneur. At the same time, the political leaders create the incentive structures for the political organizations. They control organizational resources and play the major role in the decisions as to how those resources — purposive, solidary, and material — will be used to attract new members and to hold old ones. Many of the changes in interest groups were the consequence of leaders investing their own resources and offering incentives to prospective members. To be sure, the success of these group leaders was at least partially a function of events beyond their immediate control (e.g., Watergate). On the other hand, without the leaders plying their entrepreneurial skills in the market of public opinion, much of what occurred in the interest group arena may have never taken place.

The third category contains changes resulting from individual-level characteristics of individuals. Verba and Nie have shown that group participants (communalists) are more likely to come from people "with college education and high income."[36] The increases in college education levels corresponded to the increases in group participation. And much of that increase took place in those causes for which support also has been variously related to education — civil rights, environment, women's rights.

In summary, then, these changes in interest group membership seem part and parcel of the major changes throughout public opinion.

GROUP TACTICS: SHAPING PUBLIC OPINION

To this point, the major focus of this chapter has been the role of interest groups as *consequences* of public opinion. Interest groups form to express shared opinions and to make opinion-based claims on the political process. Opinion-based responses to purposive incentives proffered by groups act as one of several reasons for people joining groups. This section considers the public opinion–interest group relationship in the other direction — the role of groups in creating or activating public opinion. To be sure, the shaping of public opinion is only one of many tactics employed by interest groups. And, for many groups, influencing public opinion may even be a relatively minor task. Yet, from all appearances, political organizations have been very important in many of the recent changes in American public opinion. It may not always be clear whether groups actually changed public opinion or whether they capitalized on changes already in process. In either case, though, the link between the actions of interest groups and the responses of the public seems ever tighter.

Why Shape Public Opinion?

Interest groups have several very realistic reasons for wanting to shape public opinion. First, one constant concern of interest groups is the creation of a supply of new members. Convincing people to share the opinions of the organization may lead to those same people joining the group, thereby contributing to the resources of the organization. Thus, attempts to influence public opinion may increase the probability that the group will continue to grow, or at least survive, through the constant addition of new members. Second, interest groups attempt to influence public opinion because they believe that appropriate opinions in the public will contribute to the achievement of the group goal. Public opinion may influence public policy (see the following chapter). This influence may be direct, as when a ground swell of opinion leads to clear-cut and decisive demands for a particular policy. And it may be indirect, when their policy preferences influence the public's choices among electoral candidates.

The two reasons for group attempts to influence public opinion, preserving the life of the group and contributing to preferred policy, are possible because of a very important characteristic of American politics. Both the political conflict and the public are continually changing. New issues appear and old issues become newly interpreted in the changed political and social context. This changing and shifting of new and old issues provides the opportunity for the groups to influence the unsettled opinions. At the same time, there is a continual turnover in the composition of the public. New people enter the electorate with weakly held opinions, or opinions not yet formed. The groups have the chance to compete over the allegiances of these new segments of the public, to create new opinions or to interpret new issues.

How Groups Shape Public Opinion: The General Processes

Group attempts to shape public opinion may be either long term or short term in their goal. Three general processes are involved.

WITHIN-GROUP PROCESSES. In almost all groups there are a number of processes at work to create uniformity of opinion. In many groups, of course, a similarity in opinions is the prime reason for the shared membership. Yet people may join a group for reasons other than its stated goals. People may lose their initial commitment to the organization. People may be drawn to the organization by a specific issue but remain unfamiliar with the entire range of organizational concerns. And they may share the general philosophy of the organization but remain relatively untaught as to specific group concerns. All of these conditions lend themselves to *within*-group processes directed toward the creation of opinions consistent with those of the group.

Thus, the organization may engage in "educational" activities for its own members. There are orientation sessions in which the goals and activities of the group are explained. There are pamphlets and excursions, seminars and films. There also may be rewards and sanctions (solidary and material incentives withheld) distributed to members based on their expression of the "correct" opinions. People may be socially more integrated into the group when they share the group opinions. Achievement of formal positions of leadership and status in the organization may be blocked when individual opinions do not coincide with group interests. Conflict over group goals or the appropriate ways to achieve those goals may lead to schisms among the group members, to the revocation of membership, or to the establishment of new groups in the same policy area. Thus, it is in the self-interest of group leaders to try to shape and support the appropriate opinions of group members through both formal educational processes and through the informal socialization mechanisms. The increasing solidarity or cohesion in the group resulting from those efforts are important to the leader for two reasons. First, of course, the efforts may contribute to the maintenance of the leader's position within the organization. Second, the shared opinions will contribute to the ability of the organization to achieve its goals. Group energies can be directed at the policy goal rather than dissipated in internal struggles.

The direction of influence attempts at people already members of the group may seem an uneconomical use of group resources. Why try to convince people to support the group cause when they already belong to the group? Moreover, how can influence attempts pointed toward *members* be construed as attempts to affect *public* opinion? In many cases of large organizations, the members may be a significant portion of the relevant public. The policymakers may seem more responsive to the preferences of members when they are communicated independently, where the reference is the public rather than the organization. Also, cohesion among group members may impress other portions of the public; those group members may be used as sources of cues and information by many other people. In each case, influencing group members to support the group positions may be a highly important strategy.

CUE-GIVING PROCESSES. The educational processes operate primarily within the organization and often depend on the interaction of members with each other. However, many of the organization's activities work not only on the members of the organization, but on other people who identify with the group, who use the organization as the source of appropriate political positions even without formal membership. Thus, people who think of themselves as strong or committed environmentalists may look to the Sierra Club for guidelines as to how to respond to environmental issues.

What conditions may be necessary for this cue-giving to take place? First, the individual must perceive shared goals with the organization. Second, there must be some clear-cut and recognizable signal as to the organization's position on the issue. Third, there must be some perception that this is a legitimate issue for the group to be issuing cues on (i.e., even though the individual and the organization may share many goals, a particular policy area may be seen as off limits, such as an environmental group issuing foreign-policy statements). And fourth, the individual must have a cognitive structure that will admit the opinion advocated by the organization. That is, the position must fit consistently with the other opinions held by the person.

Cue-giving by groups is particularly important in opinion formation when the social and political worlds are in a time of rapid change. When new issues appear, or newly complex issues dominate the agenda, the individual is in a particularly appropriate cue-taking position. In a volatile environment it may be cognitively and intellectually impossible for any individual to systematically evaluate every important issue. One recourse is to turn to cue-givers who have specialized in the issue area, who have the time, the skills, and the motivation to evaluate the issues within a domain in detail. The individual who has been successfully guided in the past with relative confidence will accept future cues in that or closely related areas. The cue-taking role becomes even more important when the issues take on highly technical forms. How does the individual know who to trust when the content of the argument clearly is out of reach? The answer is either to forgo the argument or rely on someone or some organization that is trusted.

CLIMATE-SHAPING. Group socialization and cue-taking are based in rather well-defined relationships between the individual, the group or its leaders, and political issues. On the other hand, interest groups try to shape public opinion with no particular link between the individual, the group, and some specific issue. There is considerable "public relations" (some call it propaganda, while others call it education, depending on the relative perspective), the purpose of which is to create a general "climate of opinion." As Carol Greenwald notes, "groups use the broad brush, community-directed techniques of propaganda, publicity, and public relations to produce a favorable public opinion environment for their ideas."[37]

Very often no pressing issue is at hand. However, the group is preparing the way for the future. It is inevitable that issues crucial to the group will appear on the public agenda. The group needs to be ready, and it needs to have the public ready to respond appropriately (in the direction favored by the group). Thus, some groups may continually laud their particular conception of the "American way" or the "free-enterprise system" so that it is accepted by the general public. Then, when a specific issue arises, the group's position on the issue can be tied into the general orientation already cultivated.

How Groups Shape Public Opinion: Specific Techniques

The choice of techniques to influence public opinion will stem from at least three considerations. One factor is the goal or target of the group. Is it trying to educate and influence its own membership? Is it trying to communicate cues on specific issues to identifiers? Or is it trying to alter the long-term "climate" among the general public? Some techniques may be more appropriate for one goal than for another. A second factor is the nature of the resources available to the group. Group resources are many: large membership, strategic locations in the political system, a healthy financial structure, strong and visible leadership, and high social status or moral authority are some of them. The absence of a resource may restrict the ability of the group to employ a particular tactic, and the abundance of another resource may dictate a technique consistent with it.

The third consideration is the group's operating view or "theory" of public opinion. To what kinds of appeals does the group view the public to be susceptible? Does the group see the public open to the articulation of potential dangers? Are arguments framed in terms of economic gains or costs, in terms of patriotic feelings, or in terms of social justice? Do they think people want two sides of an argument or just one? Does the public want conclusions on the information leading to the conclusions? Do they see the change process as one of rationality, functionalism, or cognitive consistency? (See Chapter 2.)

Chapter 6 described in some detail how the development of the mass media, particularly the electronic media, has contributed to major shifts in the American political system. Interest groups clearly take advantage of the present permeation of society by the mass media. On television, on the radio, and in the magazines and newspapers, interest groups promote their general goals or specific policies, using many of the same approaches and techniques as other advertisers. Of course, any particular group's use of the media depends on having the kind of goal or policy that is acceptable for media communication, having the resources to exploit the media opportunities, and viewing the use of the media as an effective way of achieving the particular goal in mind.

Perhaps the most obvious use of the media is when interest groups explicitly advertise their positions. In times of environmental pressure, oil companies demonstrate their commitment to preservationist values with pictures of cows drinking from streams flowing by refineries; mineral companies show trees and grass growing on hills of a former strip mine; or timber companies picture wild animals cavorting in clear-cut forests on their way to a new verdancy. On the other side, environmentalists show pictures of burning rivers and of oil-covered waterfowl. In 1974, Mobil Oil placed a large advertisement in the *Christian Science Monitor* (September 3, 1974), with the title "Capitalism: Moving Target." That advertisement lauded the responsiveness of business to change in society, concluding

> *partly because of its ability to adapt — which is simply another word for responsive change — private business remains the most productive element in our society and on balance the best allocator of resources. If you decide to draw a bead on it, remember you're aiming at a moving target. Because, as we've said here before, business is bound to change.*

Mobil Oil was not combating a specific piece of legislation. Rather, it was trying to influence the political climate, trying to generate a positive feeling toward the business interest.

An organization in opposition to an initiative in Washington State recently headed its advertisement in a major regional paper, "Help Kids Walk Safely."[38] Supporters of the initiative were trying to rescind a two-cent increase in the gas tax. That tax was to be used to fund street improvements. Clearly, the opponents of the initiative had a theory about the nature of public opinion, about the kinds of values to which the public would respond. How could one vote against kids walking safely?

Interest groups also create news events. They plan events that they hope the media will wish to cover, and thereby bring attention to the group's cause. Protests, occupations, and sit-ins are well-known tactics, particularly for groups without the financial resources to use other tactics. Opposition to nuclear power, to the harvest of young seals for their fur, and to the hunting of whales are recent examples that achieved media coverage. The groups hope that public opinion will be aroused through that coverage. Groups may be involved in the media in other ways: they may act as a conduit for people leaking information to the press from sensitive government positions; they may have their own media that they use to attract members and to keep their own members informed.

Interest groups have become more and more sophisticated in the use of the media to influence public opinion. They employ many of the same techniques as advertisers and political campaigners. They recognize the central role of the mass media in modern political life and the dependence of the public on the media for much of their information about political events and conditions. They know that they may reach the most people in the public through television. Yet groups try to have an impact on the public in other ways. How else do groups try to influence public opinion? The list is long, and we will pass over it briefly. Groups monitor the actions of public officials and report on their activities to their members and to others who have an interest. Many groups count the votes of legislators and report the percentage of times the votes support the interest group position. These support scores are published in media and distributed as widely as possible. Interest groups engage in direct-mail advertising. This advertising is an attempt to recruit members and to influence opinions on general and specific issues. Mailing lists are obtained from a variety of sources, often from other groups to which people belong. Many groups engage in educational efforts in the schools by sending them materials or by sponsoring activities that may be related only generally to their goal. Groups may fund workshops, speaking contests, and summer camps, all with the purpose of informing and educating young people. Each investment in one of these is evidence of the importance groups give to the role of public opinion in achieving their goals.

CONCLUSION

This chapter has shown a number of links between interest groups and the understanding of changes in public opinion. The growth and decline of interest groups is one of the potential consequences of changes in public opinion. Groups also are one of the potential sources of that opinion change.

The changes in the interest group universe hold several implications for the relationship between public opinion and democracy. To be sure, however, those implications depend on the particular picture of democracy one visualizes. First, the rise of the public interest groups may have increased representation for some interests in society that previously were heard only faintly. Thus, the democratic linkage role of groups may have increased. Second, much recent group activity has had purposes that are directly linked to the achievement of certain democratic values — freedom, equality, and open government. On the other hand, not all of the changes are universally viewed as democratic in nature. At the same time that new groups may represent previously ignored interests, many of those groups have a deep-seated aversion to compromise and bargaining. This rigidity, of course, may run counter to some fundamental conceptions of democratic pluralism that focuses on the willingness of competitors to compromise and bargain.

NOTES

1. V.O. Key, Jr., *Politics, Parties and Pressure Groups,* 5th ed. (New York: Crowell, 1964), p. 17. For an understanding of the central role of groups in some theories of American politics, the reader should examine these two classics: Arthur F. Bentley, *The Process of Government* (Chicago: University of Chicago Press, 1908); and David B. Truman, *The Governmental Process* (New York: Knopf, 1951).
2. Carol S. Greenwald, *Group Power* (New York: Praeger, 1977), p. 24.
3. Walter A. Rosenbaum, *The Politics of Environmental Concern* (New York: Praeger, 1973), p. 75
4. D. Faye White, "Who's Who in the Environmental Movement," in *Interest Groups: Influence in a Changing Environment,* Robert H. Salisbury, ed. (Washington, D.C.: National Journal Reprints, 1979– 80), p. 63.
5. Norman J. Ornstein and Shirley Elder, *Interest Groups, Lobbying and Policymaking* (Washington, D.C.: Congressional Quarterly Press, 1978), p. 46.
6. Henry J. Pratt, *The Gray Lobby* (Chicago: University of Chicago Press, 1976), p. 52.
7. Jo Freeman, *The Politics of Women's Liberation* (New York: David McKay, 1975), p. 80.
8. Ibid., pp. 103– 4.
9. William J. Lanquette, "The New Right — 'Revolutionaries' Out after the 'Lunch-Pail' Vote," in *Interest Groups: Influence in a Changing Environment,* pp. 29–33.
10. Hanes Walton, Jr., *Black Politics: A Theoretical and Structural Analysis* (Philadelphia: J.B. Lippincott, 1972).
11. Ibid., p. 160.
12. *Congressional Quarterly Weekly Report,* May 25, 1974, pp. 1370–73.
13. Jeffrey M. Berry, *Lobbying for the People: The Political Behavior of Public Interest Groups* (Princeton, N.J.: Princeton University Press, 1977), p. 7.
14. Ornstein and Elder, *Interest Groups,* pp. 46– 47.
15. We are grateful to our colleague, Terry Cook, for his ideas that are reflected in this paragraph.
16. See Robert H. Salisbury, "An Exchange Theory of Interst Groups," *Midwest Journal of Political Science* 13 (February 1969), pp. 1– 32; and Robert H. Salisbury, "Interest Groups," in *Handbook of Political Science,* vol. 4, Fred I. Greenstein and Nelson W. Polsby, eds. (Reading, Mass: Addison-Wesley, 1975), pp. 171–228.
17. Pratt, *The Gray Lobby,* p. 74.
18. Salisbury, "Interest Groups," p. 191.
19. Freeman, *The Politics of Women's Liberation,* pp. 147– 69.
20. See Joyce Gelb and Marian Lief Pally, "Women and Interest Group Politics: A Comparative Analysis of Federal Decision-Making," *Journal of Politics* 41 (May 1979), pp. 362– 92.
21. Freeman, *The Politics of Women's Liberation,* p. 148.
22. Salisbury, "Interest Groups," p. 193.
23. Berry, *Lobbying for the People,* p. 29.
24. Andrew S. McFarland, *Public Interest Lobbies: Decisionmaking on Energy* (Washington, D.C.: American Enterprise Institute, 1976), p. 20.

25. Andrew J. Glass, "Common Cause," in *Political Brokers*, Judith G. Smith, ed. (New York: Liveright, 1973), p. 275.
26. Among the major works laying out economic or "rational" approaches to understanding why people join interest groups are Mancur Olson, *The Logic of Collective Action* (Cambridge, Mass.: Harvard University Press, 1965); James Q. Wilson, *Political Organizations* (New York: Basic Books, 1973); and Salisbury, "An Exchange Theory of Interest Groups."
27. Wilson, *Political Organizations*, p. 33.
28. Ibid., p. 34.
29. Olson, *The Logic of Collective Action*.
30. Various aspects of Olson's formulation have been critically examined in Brian M. Barry, *Sociologists, Economists and Democracy* (London: Collier-Macmillan, 1970); Norman Frohlich, Joe Oppenheimer, and Oran Young, *Political Leadership and Collective Goods* (Princeton, N.J.: Princeton University Press, 1971); and Salisbury "An Exchange Theory of Interest Groups."
31. Clearly, many people do not want the benefit, even though it is available to them.
32. See the sources in note 30.
33. Warren T. Farrell, "Women's and Men's Liberation Groups: Political Power Within the System and Outside the System," in *Women in Politics*, Jane S. Jaquette, ed. (New York: John Wiley & Sons, 1974), pp. 171–201.
34. Ornstein and Elder, *Interest Groups*, pp. 18–19.
35. See John C. Pierce, "The Role of Preservationist Identification in the Belief Systems of Water Resource Group Leaders," *Polity*, vol. 9 (Summer 1977), pp. 538–50.
36. Sidney Verba and Norman H. Nie, *Participation in America: Political Democracy and Social Equality*, (New York: Harper & Row, 1972), p. 98.
37. Greenwald, *Group Power*, p. 89.
38. Spokane *Spokesman Review*, October 29, 1977.

CHAPTER 14

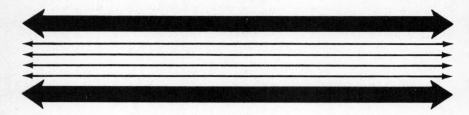

PUBLIC OPINION AND PUBLIC POLICY: THE QUESTION OF CORRESPONDENCE

The relationship between the public and policy is central to many conceptions of democratic representation.[1] One part of the representative relationship is the extent to which the public's preferences are mirrored in public policy or in the attitudes and behavior of public officials. Much of this chapter discusses the correspondence between public opinion and public policy. However, it is important to keep several caveats in mind. First, there is more to democracy than the extent to which public policy matches public opinion. While consistent shunting aside of public preferences would create doubt as to the democratic nature of a political system, so would public policy that reflected undemocratic public preferences.

Second, representation is more than policy-public opinion congruence. Heinz Eulau and Paul D. Karp, for example, suggest that representatives may be responsive in more than their reaction to public opinion; they may respond to their constituents through the allocation of "pork barrel" funds to their district.[2] Thus, the absence of congruence between policy and public opinion may not necessarily mean the absence of representation.

Third, correspondence between public preferences and public policy does not mean that the public has influenced that policy. A variety of influence mechanisms may have been at work. To be sure, one of those possibilities *is* that public opinion caused the public policy. However, several other possibilities are present. One is that public opinion and public policy are both responding to some third force. A major social crisis may generate a similar reaction among policymakers and the general public. Another possibility is that the correspondence occurs merely by chance. The public may hold preferences consistent with the policy but exert no influence on the policymakers. The policymakers may enact the policy with no regard to the public's preferences, believing that the public cares little one way or the other. Yet the public's preferences and the policy may be in the same direction. Of course, under those circumstances it is just as possible that the opinions and the preferences will be inconsistent. Still another seriously considered alternative explanation of opinion-policy correspondence is that public opinion is affected by policy. This possibility is considered later in the chapter.

Fourth, correspondence between public opinion and public policy may come from one or more in a whole set of linkage processes. That is, there may be several channels through which public opinion affects policy and policymakers. We cannot tell whether correspondence was produced by interest group pressures, by the actions of political parties, or through elections.

Fifth, the definitional and measurement problems involved in identifying and measuring public opinion are especially pertinent here. How one defines the public and how that public's opinions are measured will structure conclusions about the correspondence of those opinions with policy.

CONCEPTUALIZING AND MEASURING CORRESPONDENCE

Conceptualizing Correspondence

The impact of public opinion on public policy has been conceptualized from a number of perspectives. Various studies look at the responsiveness to public opinion among different levels and branches of government, different issue or policy areas, different kinds of people, and different kinds of policymakers. Overall, though, there exist three fairly distinct approaches to the study of correspondence. These can be labeled dyadic, collective, and systemic.

The distinction between the dyadic and the collective approaches to correspondence was developed by Robert Weissberg.[3] Dyadic and collective approaches focus on *representatives'* attitudes and behaviors. In the *dyadic* approach, the preferences of the public are grouped (usually within a constituency) and are compared to those of a *particular* representative — usually the one elected to represent them. That representative is judged to be more or less responsive, depending on the correspondence of his or her attitudes or behavior to those of the constituency.

Collective approaches maintain a focus on the correspondence between public opinion and the opinions of formal representatives; the opinions of individual representatives are not compared to those of their particular constituency. Rather, the focus is on "institutions collectively representing a people."[4] The *distribution* of opinions or behaviors in the institution (e.g., legislature) is compared to the distribution in the public.

Similar distributions of opinion in the public and in the institution may occur (collective representation) even when there is widespread absence of dyadic representation. Dyadic *mis*representation that is symmetrical (evenly balanced in the aggregate) may result in collective representation. For example, constituency A may be misrepresented by its legislator, who holds different beliefs on an issue; another constituency (B) with different preferences than its legislator also may be misrepresented. But the representative of constituency B may match the preferences of constituency A; and the same may be true for constituency B and representative A. Weissberg argues that the larger the number of representatives (hence, the greater the number of dyadic relationships) the more likely is symmetry in misrepresentation to occur, and hence, to result in collective representation. Thus, before judging the extent to which correspondence occurs, one should look both at the dyadic relationships between constituents and their own representative, and at the collective relationship across all constituencies and all representatives.

The *systemic* approach to correspondence moves beyond the comparison of the preferences of constituencies and those of formal representatives. Rather, within a particular system (nation, state, community) the policy preferences of the public are compared to the actual *policy outputs* of that system. The question here is whether actual government policy reflects what the public prefers that policy to be, regardless of the distribution of opinions and the behaviors of the intermediary representatives.

Measuring Correspondence

In studies of correspondence, three approaches to the measurement of public opinion surface most often. These approaches are used in dyadic, collective, and systemic studies alike. The first measurement approach is the most obvious: people are asked about their political preferences. But the obvious is not necessarily simple. If one wishes to compare the correspondence of constituents and congressional representatives across the United States, the preferences of the public in each congressional district must be assessed. Yet large samples are needed to make reliable estimates of public opinion. Large samples in each of the 435 districts would be prohibitively expensive. Thus, some studies have relied on very small congressional-district samples, then generated aggregate opinions (such as an average) and compared those averages to the representative's opinion.[5] Yet errors are likely to crop up in estimates of district opinions from very small samples. Consequently, studies based on small district samples have been criticized for the unreliability of their estimates.[6]

A second measure of public opinion is through *simulation*. Simulation measures have been developed to overcome some of the problems of small sample sizes.[7] The public is divided into "types" based on combinations of such demographic characteristics as race, income, age, education, and religion. National polls reveal the relationship between those characteristics and opinions about a particular policy issue. Through census data, the frequency of people with those demographic characteristics in each constituency is determined. Then, "artificial" opinions are created for that constituency according to the relative incidence of people with the characteristic and the relationship of that characteristic to the relevant opinion.

A third measure of constituency opinion is voting statistics on initiatives or referenda. Election results provide a perfectly accurate reflection of the public's behavior (assumed to reflect their preferences) on some very important issues before them and their representatives. The votes on initiatives and referenda are aggregated (counted or added) according to the formal electoral boundaries from which legislators are selected. Two problems are present in this estimate of public preferences. First, the issue on the ballot is not always the one in which the researcher is interested, and it may not be particularly important compared to some of the burning political disputes of the day. Second, voter turnout on initiatives and referenda often is low, particularly when they occur at a different time than elections for public officials. Thus, the opinions of many in the public may be excluded from the information used to judge the constituency's preferences. The portion of the public that votes in the referendum or initiative ballot may be quite different from that staying at home; and the researcher may not know the extent or the direction of that bias. The two groups may provide different constituencies for the representatives.[8]

No matter how accurately measured opinions reflect those actually in the public, there remains a further problem. How does one aggregate those responses to come up with *a* public opinion? With a distribution of responses on a question of policy, how do we decide whether to employ the average opinion, the modal (most frequent) opinion, the median opinion, or the majority opinion in a referendum? How do we make sure that the question alternatives reflect the alternatives available to policymakers? In order to have some kind of majority in the public, we may collapse and group categories, but that grouping may not respond to the alternatives in politics.[9]

Just as there are several approaches to measuring public opinion, so are there some options in the estimates of the representatives' responsiveness. As in the measurement of public opinion, a number of studies survey public officials, asking them questions similar to or identical with those asked of the public. In this case, the representatives' responses can be compared to those in the public on issues identified by the researcher as salient to the politics of the day. A second approach is to focus on behavior, such as the roll-call votes of representatives (if they are legislators). Where a vote corresponds closely to the opinions elicited from the public, the legislator's behavior can be compared directly. In many cases, however, there is no directly corresponding vote to which public opinions can be compared. One option is to analyze a series of legislative votes, all of which are in the same general policy area as the opinion. Through the examination of a set of behaviors with a common content (e.g., civil rights or foreign policy votes), representatives can be placed in relative positions on an attitudinal dimension (e.g., more or less pro-civil rights). Legislators' positions then can be compared to the relative positions of the public. Even though the specific stimuli generating the response are different for the public and the representative, the assumption is that the responses are comparable, and the degree of correspondence can be adequately measured.

Once the preferences of the public and the representatives have been measured, the question then becomes how to determine the degree of correspondence. In part, the answer depends on the particular measures of public opinion and representative responses. When one has votes on referenda or initiatives, the majority position of the public can be compared to the preference or the vote of the representative. Does the representative's position match the majority preference of his or her constituency? The aggregated measure of the constituency opinion (mean, modal, median) can be compared to that of the representative, and the two measures can be compared to each other across a series of publics and their representatives.[10] Is it possible, with the latter method, to obtain high correlations when the representatives are quite distant from their constituencies in an absolute sense? All that is required is that the constituencies and their representatives be ordered in a similar manner in relative magnitude and positioning. With the following distributions from 0 to 100 a very high correlation can exist, but responsiveness is hard to find, for the representatives are very distant from the public. Thus, more than the correlation is needed.

	Public	Representative
A.	2	92
B.	4	94
C.	6	96
D.	8	98

There also needs to be an inspection of the absolute position of the opinions and preferences of the groups being compared. Indeed, the correlation could be very low, but all representatives and all publics could be grouped very closely to each other, so that there can be no doubt as to the presence of responsiveness, as in the following:

	Public	Representative
A.	49	53
B.	53	49
C.	50	52
D.	52	50
E.	51	51

All of the opinions of the public and of the representative are within a very narrow range. Even if a particular representative is not ordered in the same priority as the corresponding public, and even if other representatives may be closer to the appropriate public, it is clear that the representative's opinion still corresponds very closely to that of the public.

DYADIC CORRESPONDENCE

As noted above, dyadic correspondence refers to the extent to which the preferences of a public, usually a formal constituency, are matched by the preferences and actions of that public's formal representative. The most widely cited study of dyadic correspondence between public and representative preferences was conducted by Miller and Stokes.[11] With congressional districts as the focus, they examined correlations among public preferences, representatives' perceptions of public preferences, the representatives' own preferences, and the representatives' roll-call behavior.[12] Warren Miller and Donald Stokes concluded that a "representative's roll-call behavior is strongly influenced by his own policy preferences and by his perception of preferences held by the constituency."[13] Yet they found that representatives' perceptions of constituency attitudes are "very imperfect." At the same time, there are variations in the patterns among different issue areas. Civil rights issues stand out as most productive of strong relationships between a constituency's attitude and its representative's perception of that attitude. This they attribute to the salience of civil rights in the period of their study — the late 1950s.

Most subsequent studies of dyadic relationships respond to or elaborate the representational structure defined and studied by Miller and Stokes.[14] Robert Erikson criticizes the Miller and Stokes study for its reliance on small, nonrandom samples of constituents. Instead, Erikson uses the "simulation" technique for estimating constituency attitudes. He finds "fairly strong" relationships (correspondence) between simulated constituency opinion and the voting of representatives."[15] Moreover, this relationship is stronger between the public's opinions and those of the winner than it is between the public and the loser in congressional elections. This suggests that elections may give the public some control over the degree to which their representative's attitudes and behavior correspond to their own.[16]

A number of studies focus on the legislator in the dyadic-correspondence relationship. The most frequently cited source of possible variation is the legislator's representational "role." The role is the preferred pattern of behavior with regard to the legislator's constituents. Three major representational roles have been defined: delegate, trustee, and politico. The *delegate* says the representative should do what the constituency wants. The *trustee* says that the representative should do what is best for the constituency. The *politico* says that the representative's behavior should vary with the issue and the circumstances.[17]

The obvious question is whether the legislator's role orientation influences the accuracy of his or her perception of the constituency's opinions and thus the level of correspondence between legislator and constituency. As Aage Clausen argues,

> *clearly the perceptual capabilities of leaders are very important in that form of government in which the representation of constituency attitudes and beliefs is the primary principle, the citizenry is the primary criterion by which leaders are judged.*[18]

The obvious expectation would be that "delegates" would exhibit more accurate perceptions and higher levels of correspondence. Yet most studies reject that hypothesis.

Ronald Hedlund and Paul Friesema asked Iowa legislators to predict their constituents' behavior on four referenda questions on the Iowa ballot.[19] They found substantial variation among issues, with 90 percent accuracy on one issue and 60 percent on another. Across all four issues, legislators with a delegate role orientation "were least able to predict constituency opinion."[20] Similarly, a study in Florida assessed the accuracy of legislators' predictions of constituency votes on three "straw ballots";[21] overall, the predictions were rather accurate. Again, however, delegate legislators were *less* able to predict the votes of their districts. In another study of votes on five constitutional amendments the delegates were less likely than trustees to vote with the majority of their district and were less likely to vote with their perceptions of their districts' majority vote.[22]

These findings clearly raise some serious doubts about the importance of representational roles in generating correspondence between the public and representatives. In a study of voting on referenda James Kuklinski and Richard Elling have tried to answer those questions.[23] Their results show that the effect of role orientation depends on the issue area. On two of three issue areas, delegates' correspondence was higher because of the salience of those issues. Indeed, a summary of these studies would say that correspondence depends on the interaction of issue salience and role orientation. Even on mundane issues, correspondence *can* be high. Overall, though, correspondence is usually higher on salient issues. Trustees exhibit greater correspondence on many issues, but on some very salient issues the delegates show more correspondence. Moreover, in legislative elections public correspondence often is higher with winners than with losers.[24]

COLLECTIVE CORRESPONDENCE

Collective correspondence refers to the match between the *distribution* of public preferences (or some summary figure representing that distribution) and the distribution of preferences among a group of representatives. Measures of this correspondence focus on the degree to which people with particular preferences (e.g., antiabortion) are over- or underrepresented, and on the total amount of misrepresentation in the entire public. Moreover, people with particular characteristics (e.g., race or sex) are segregated, and the distribution of their preferences can be compared to that of both the general public and the representatives. Thus, one might wish to identify a group of activists and determine the extent to which they "represent" the public in their activity, and the extent to which they are represented by the legislators.[25]

Charles Backstrom compared the attitudes of members of the U.S. Congress with those of the American public on six policy questions in 1970. The six issues are the Vietnam War, the antiballistic missile system (ABM), control of inflation, the family income maintenance program, social-welfare programs for blacks, and the role of the Supreme Court in the protections of the rights of the accused. Backstrom found that,

> on balance, opinions in the Ninety-Second Congress seemingly did not greatly differ from those in the public. Specifically the House differed by an average of only 11 percentage points, compared to the Senate's 20, fulfilling the constitutional expectation that the lower body reflects public opinion more closely.[26]

But again, there was some variation among issues. The House of Representatives was the closest to the public on the issue of Vietnam and relatively close on the issues of social welfare for blacks, the rights of the accused, and the antiballistic missile system. The Senate closely reflected the public's opinions on Vietnam and the ABM. On the other hand, the Senate was substantially more liberal than the public on the Supreme Court's actions and on aid to blacks. Overall, Backstrom concluded that this particular congress "reflected opinions in the public reasonably closely."[27]

One ambitious study compared the preferences of the public in each state to those of party leaders, bureaucrats, and legislators in those states.[28] The party leaders are somewhat to the "right" of the public, the bureaucrats the most liberal, and the legislators are the centrists among the elite.[29] Overall, however, party leaders exhibited preferences closest to public opinion, followed by bureaucrats and legislators. Part of this greater proximity by county party leaders is a result of their similarity to the public in demographic characteristics. One consequence of this pattern is that the elite group the farthest from actual policymaking is the most representative of the public's policy preferences. To those interested in enhancing collective correspondence, this might argue for increased party control over the processes through which public officials are selected.

Several studies here examined how well local leaders reflect the preferences of their citizens. Verba and Nie measured correspondence by the percentage of the leaders in a community that agreed with an individual in the definition of the important problems facing that community. They examined the effect of political participation on the correspondence rates and found that "the average percentage of concurrence doubles as one moves from the least active to the most active citizens."[30] This pattern remains even when taking into account the similarity of social backgrounds of the leaders and the high-level participants. Even within high socioeconomic categories, activists are more likely to obtain concurrence from leaders than are the nonactivists. Moreover, Susan Hansen has found that concurrence levels are higher in communities with higher rates of political participation.[31] Higher rates of voting and campaign activity seem to give the greatest boost to concurrence. Concurrence scores are also higher in communities with partisan elections; particularly in lower SES communities, highly competitive elections enhance concurrence scores.

SYSTEMIC CORRESPONDENCE

Assessing the level of systematic correspondence (public opinion and actual policy) presents some difficult problems. One of these problems is the task of systematically classifying public policy in a form that provides information equivalent to that provided by public opinion data. Public policy is detailed and complex, while public opinion usually is measured in very general terms. Yet the policy must be interpreted for its correspondence to public opinion. Another problem is the often questionable relationship between formal policy and implemented policy; the gap between the two may be considerable.

In one major effort to overcome the problem, Paul D. Schumaker and Russell W. Getter examined "the degree to which governments respond unequally to the preferences of various subpopulations in their communities."[32] They looked at policy responsiveness in fifty-one American cities. They measured policy through an analysis of the distribution of revenue-sharing funds provided to the city by the federal government. Public policy preferences in each community were simulated. "Bias" in systemic responsiveness was measured by comparing two subgroups' (e.g., blacks and whites) preferences to

the actual allocations of funds in nine policy areas. If two subgroups' preferences differ as to the uses of the allocations, then the conclusion is that there
is "bias" in the responsiveness. Thus, if the things whites prefer receive the
money while the things blacks prefer do not, then there is bias in policy. On
the other hand, if neither blacks nor whites obtain their preferences, there is
no bias, even though there is also no responsiveness.

Most cities are biased in favor of upper-income and white subgroups. And
the relative bias to race and economic and educational groups is strongly
related. Nevertheless, "there is substantial community-to-community variation in differential responsiveness."[33] As the city size increases so does responsiveness bias toward whites and upper-income groups. The bias decreases as
cities become more heterogeneous. Overall, then, the responsiveness of community public policy to public opinion depends on the attributes of the particular system in which the policy is produced (e.g., size) and on the characteristics of the citizens (race) whose opinions are used as the standard for the
comparison of public policy.

Several studies look at correspondence between opinions and policy at the
state level, even going back so far as data from the 1930s. Ronald Weber and
William Shaffer have attempted to "evaluate the relative impact of preference (public opinion and interest group strength), as well as political culture,
socio-economic environment upon . . . policy output."[34] They looked at the following policy areas: public accommodations, parochial-school aid, right-to-
work laws, teacher unionization, and firearms control. As in other studies,
they estimated state public opinion data from simulation. The relative impact
of public opinion depends on the policy area. State policy is most closely
aligned with the public's preferences in the area of public accommodations
policy — the desegregation of public accommodations. Public opinion has
a moderate impact on gun regulations, and it has no independent impact on
the remaining three. On two of the issues (parochial-school aid and right-to-
work laws) though, the size of the relevant interest groups in the state is
important.

In a closely related study, Richard Sutton compared simulated public opinion in the states to public policy in eleven policy areas.[35] He assessed the
percentage of the time the state policy in an area was congruent with (in the
same direction as) the *majority* public opinion. The states are "most responsive on issues involving civil rights, welfare policy, liquor and gambling laws,
and the unionization of public employees."[36] Sutton found that different state
characteristics are important in responsiveness in different areas of public
policy. As in other studies,

> It is suggested that when opinions about public issues are tied to basic
> socio-cultural values, citizen preferences are stable and intense and more
> easily identified and acted upon by lawmakers.[37]

The strong link between policy at the state level and public preferences is
no newcomer to American politics. Indeed, Erikson examined public opinion
and public policy in the 1930s and concluded that "the evidence tends to support the proposition that state legislators are rather responsive to public

opinion — at least on certain issues."[38] Those "certain" issues are the ones that are salient to the public, where the public articulates the clearest demand for policy.

There also are several major studies of public opinion and policy at the national level in recent years. Robert Weissberg has examined changes in the relationship of public opinion and public policy. As with other authors, he concluded that there is considerable variation among policy areas. However, unlike other studies that seem to reveal considerable concurrence, Weissberg concludes that

> *perhaps the most salient conclusion is that considerable variation occurs by policy area in the degree of congruence. However, this range is not from perfect congruence to perfect incongruity, but rather from limited concordance to a completely negative relationship between opinion and policy.*[39]

While Weissberg finds congruence in public opinion and policy to be the exception, rather than the rule, he does think the gap between the two might be even greater were it not for the demands of the public.

In contrast, Alan Monroe paints a fairly rosy picture.[40] Monroe examined public opinion from 1960 to 1974, focusing on identifiable questions of national policy. He found 248 cases where public opinion could be compared to public policy at the national level. Monroe classified both the public preferences and the policy as either supporting the "status quo" or supporting "change." He found that in 64 percent of the cases, public policy is consistent with public opinion. As one might expect, consistency was higher when the direction was pro status quo, rather than pro change (75 percent compared to 59 percent). Consistency rates were 92 percent for foreign policy and 79 percent for energy and environmental policy. On the other hand, two of the areas fell below 50 percent — reform (most of which would have required constitutional amendments) and defense (43 percent). Slightly lower consistency existed among policy areas of lower public salience. The greatest bias against change is found in reform cases: no change occurred in many cases when the public wanted that change. On the other hand, in some areas there is a bias *toward* change. For example, substantially more change occurred in civil rights policy than the general public wanted. Monroe concludes that

> *political decisionmakers are usually disposed to act in accordance with public opinion, but that institutional structures and the press of so many decisions to be made cause decisions to be long delayed and sometimes forgotten.*[41]

Monroe's data also provide the opportunity to compare the correspondence levels of the national policy formed within the legislature to that created within the executive branch of government.[42] The results are shown in Table 14-1.

Overall, executive policy is only marginally more consistent with public opinion than is legislative policy. However, this pattern varies by policy area. On foreign-policy questions, the executive is much more consistent with the public than is the legislature and, during that period, slightly more consistent on the question of Vietnam. On the other hand, the legislature is more consistent (although to a rather small degree) in the areas of economics and labor, civil rights, energy, and the environment.

TABLE 14 – 1   Consistency Between Public Preference and Positions Taken by Legislative and Executive Branches of Government (Nonspending Items), 1960 – 1974

	Legislative	Executive	N
All Cases	57%	60%	222
Policy Area			
Social Welfare	60	56	35
Economic and Labor	61	54	36
Defense	42	43	14
Foreign Policy	50	88	24
Civil Rights	46	39	24
Energy and Environment	78	71	14
Reform	46	47	30
Vietnam	57	68	28
Miscellaneous	76	82	17

Source: Alan D. Monroe, "Public Opinion and Public Policy, 1960 – 1974" (Paper prepared for delivery at the 1978 Meeting of the American Political Science Association, New York, August 31 – September 3). Copyright by the American Political Science Association, 1978. Used by permission.

OVERVIEW OF CORRESPONDENCE

First, the level of correspondence is highly variable; there are great differences in the level of correspondence under different conditions. As a consequence, statements about the degree to which correspondence exists cannot be simplistic; rather, they must be conditional. Some conditions enhance correspondence, while others may detract from it.

Second, correspondence seems to be greater for some kinds of issues than for others. Most studies agree that the greater the salience of the issue — the greater its prominence and its importance to the public — the greater is the correspondence. In the 1960s and 1970s, this meant that civil rights issues usually exhibited the greatest correspondence, at least between public opinion and representative opinion.

Third, correspondence is greater for some kinds of people than for others. The findings of bias in responsiveness fit general expectations. Correspondence is higher for those who participate more in politics generally and for those who are otherwise advantaged in society — white, better educated, higher income. A caveat is in order: it is clearly possible that certain kinds of participants are the *consequence* of correspondence levels rather than causes of it. In some contexts, people who see little correspondence or responsiveness may be moved to participate in order to attempt to alleviate that condition.

Fourth, the level of correspondence varies among representatives and systems. Some kinds of representatives are more likely to hold opinions similar to those of their constituents than are other kinds, and some kinds of systems (state or community, for example) are more likely to produce higher levels of correspondence. Trustees, for instance, generally exhibit greater similarity to the public in their opinions, although under some conditions delegates seem to do better. Legislators of different party affiliations may differ in the proximity of their opinions to those of their fellow partisans in the public. The national executive's policies show greater consistency with the public's opinions than do those of the national legislature (Congress). Responsiveness bias in communities increases as the size of the city increases, and concurrence levels are higher in communities with overall higher rates of participation. Nevertheless, even with these patterns of correspondence identified, much remains to be learned about the interdependence of public opinion and public policy.

THE QUESTION OF DIRECTION IN CORRESPONDENCE

The implicit assumption of this chapter has been that patterns of correspondence with public opinion stem from public opinion's influence on the beliefs or behaviors of leaders and through them on public policy. Public opinion presumably can exercise its influence over policy and policymakers in a variety of processes, identified earlier as linkage mechanisms — for example, through elections, interest groups, political parties, or direct legislation. Yet some people see little evidence that the concurrence patterns result from the influence of the public. Rather, it is suggested, the causal direction is reversed; concurrence probably is the result of the impact of policy and policymakers on public opinion.

The argument that concurrence results from the impact of policy and leaders on the public should sound familiar. Early in the book, and throughout a number of other chapters, a major explanation of recent patterns in public opinion is based in the dependence of the public on leaders for cues as to how to respond to politics. It takes little imagination to convert this into an explanation of policy-opinion correspondence. Simply put, the argument is that the public's opinions correspond to policy and to the preferences and behavior of leaders because the public is responding *to* the leaders. The public's response to leaders may stem from intentional manipulation by the government, creating public support or rationalization for the policies. Or it may be the consequence of the public's dependence on others for information and cues about policy questions relevant to their own interest.

Eulau and Karps have said that with respect to policy responsiveness, "the debate really turns on the competence of the citizenry in public policy."[43] A number of scholars conclude that many in the public are fundamentally incompetent to deal with the major issues of public policy to which public officials are called to respond.[44] If so, how then can one argue that the public is effectively communicating policy positions to the leaders who translate them into policy? In such a situation, the messages from the general public will take on the sound of cacophony. No clear policy messages will be transmitted from the public to leaders. The same kind of jumble will exist for many in the public, as they try to sort out the many issues and alternatives with few independent resources for making reasoned choices. The only recourse available to most people is to rely on favored cue-givers for appropriate positions on policy questions. With this reliance, then, correspondence can appear to be quite high. But the correspondence comes from the leaders and the policy, and not from the public's impetus.

There is little doubt that public officials attempt to influence public opinion in both direct and indirect ways. In cases where agreement with the policy is important to its successful implementation, there may be widespread dissemination of "information" about the policy and its favorable consequences. Witness government efforts to educate the public about fuel conservation and the benefits of reduced vehicle speed on highways. Most bureaucracies in government have public relations personnel whose purposes is to educate the public, to build acceptance of policy or proposed policy, and to generate support for the goals of the agency. In times of challenge to government policy proposals, administration representatives will head into the country's hinterlands, meet with local media people and organizations, and try to sell the policy.

Politics in the arena of public opinion is competition for the allegiance of citizens to particular points of view. Policymakers have their own views and enter into that competition. And the government has resources unavailable to many other interests in society. As Weissberg notes, political socialization "automatically provides leaders with an enormous reservoir of credibility competency and good will."[45] The recent decline in political trust among both adults and children, though, may signal a decline in that resource's importance for government in shaping public opinion. Indeed, in many cases, the failure (or perceived failure) of government and leaders to meet the standards created in political socialization may impose a burden on creating appropriate opinions in the public. In such cases, people may be particularly suspect of the government's information and positions. Moreover, the socialization process may identify outer boundaries or constraints beyond which the government may not go with its policy proposals. Policymakers may maintain their influence on public opinion only as long as they stay within those bounds.

There is evidence for the policy-public opinion influence process working in both directions. Barry Hughes presents data showing changes in public opinion on the Vietnam War involvement and changes in actual involvement (troop strength, costs of the war) for the period between 1965 and 1971.[46] The decline in public support for U.S. involvement *preceded* by several years the drop in the actual involvement. However, after the peak of U.S. involvement in Vietnam, the actual policy followed the decline in public support. Hughes argues that these data are an "instance in which public opinion clearly led public policy, and we have every reason to believe that in this case it strongly influenced policy."[47] On the other hand, Hughes also shows public support for U.S. intervention in Cambodia in 1970 both before and after the actual intervention. The policy decision to intervene in Cambodia resulted in substantial opinion change about that intervention. The changes occurred across all educational categories, but especially among those with higher education.

Weissberg has examined changes in public opinion from before and after nine policy decisions in the period from 1963 to 1971, focusing on policies that were discussed on television by the president.[48] In each case, public opinion responded favorably to policy change. However, the magnitude of the changes varied widely. At one extreme, when President Kennedy appealed for a tax cut from Congress, public support for that position increased only from 62 percent to 66 percent. On the other hand, when President Nixon announced the Cambodian invasion, support jumped from 7 percent to 50 percent.

In summary, what can be said about the impact of leaders and policy on public opinion? As with many other questions, the answer refuses to be simple. Indeed, the responsiveness of public opinion to leaders and policy seems to depend on some of the following:

1. *The characteristics of the public.* People with access to more information and who possess mainstream personal characteristics are more likely to respond immediately to policy.
2. *The availability of information.* Leaders and policymakers are more likely to shape public opinion when they control information and cues relevant to the policy, and when the public is less able to turn to alternative sources.
3. *The policy area.* Leaders and policymakers are more likely to shape public opinion in policy areas that are removed from the sources of political divisions that pervade domestic politics and that are more likely to reflect a "national interest" widely viewed as the legitimate purview of government, such as national defense and foreign policy.
4. *Public views of politics.* People with greater trust are more likely to respond to political leaders.

CORRESPONDENCE AND THE CHANGE OF PUBLIC OPINION

The correspondence of public opinion to public policy and to the orientations of political leaders is particularly crucial in a time of change in public opinion. The response of policy to change in opinion may be the real test of responsiveness in a political system. In times of great stability the development of correspondence surely is easier. It is less difficult to determine the dominant opinions of the public, and the pressure for correspondence generally will be in the direction of the maintenance of the status quo. In the American system, with its federal, separated, and decentralized structure, it is easier to prevent action than it is to formulate it.

In times of great opinion flux, it may be difficult for leaders to know what to do with policy. When public opinion is in a period of instability it will be hard to determine if the shifts are permanent or are temporary preludes to further change. Moreover, the *formal* control mechanisms built into the American system that enable the public to ensure correspondence provide only a delayed constraint. That is, except for extraordinary cases, the public's opportunity to punish nonresponsive public officials occurs at regular intervals (two, four, or six years). Yet changes in public opinion may respect no election timetables.

Correspondence also is difficult to achieve in a time of opinion change because of the usual absence of uniform movement across the public. That is, even with rapid change in opinions in much of the public, some segments of the society will not change at all, while others will change only slowly. The public official then has the difficult task of interpreting the competing signals, trying to distinguish the most appropriate opinion to respond to.

In times of rapid opinion change correspondence may be easier for public officials than for the policy they formulate. Leaders' attitudes, and even their behavior, may respond to many of the same forces as those that shape the public's own changes. Moreover, the forces that act as constraints on leaders, such as elections, may move them to articulate the corresponding attitudes even when they are not deeply felt. The shifting of opinions, or the articulation of opinions sufficiently ambiguous to appear responsive, is a fairly common occurrence among politicians. On the other hand, framing and enacting major change in *policy* clearly is a difficult task — even in the context of massive public support for policy change. Again, the structure of the system's policymaking process is oriented toward difficulty in making rapid change. *Creating* policy in a new area may even be easier than *changing* policy in a traditional area that has built up clientele with access to centers of power.

Many changes in public opinion may not be amenable to changes in public policy or in the policy orientations of leaders. Certain kinds of changes in public opinion may have no direct analogue in policy. For example, during the 1960s and 1970s there was a drop in public trust in the political system. These changes certainly were important. How does the system adjust and become concurrent with those opinions?

We have relatively little information available on the consistency of correspondence levels through time. How much change in correspondence levels has there been? Under what political and social conditions is correspondence likely to become greater or lesser? We do not really know, although some speculations can be made about the second question based in the patterns reviewed above. Of course, change in correspondence levels will occur with changes in public opinion. Correspondence levels will *decrease* when public opinion moves away from present policy; those levels will increase when public opinion follows and responds to public policy or to the preferences of public officials. Change in public policy may affect levels of correspondence. Policy may move either toward or away from public opinion, thereby either increasing or decreasing the levels of concurrence.

Changes in the mechanisms available to the public for the purpose of affecting political responsiveness to opinions may occur. On the one hand, the public may be moved to the greater use of the existing mechanisms for the control of public officials. The public may place greater emphasis on who to vote for in elections. The public may enforce its policy preferences through the defeat of the incumbent with the discordant preferences and the elevation of the challenger with positions more closely attuned to those of the public. Or there may be created new mechanisms to ensure or at least to enhance the public's impact on policy. Such processes as citizen advisory committees, talk-back cable TV, the class-action law suit, and mandated public hearings may change the level of concurrence. They may make the preferences of the public (or the activist segments of it) more clear to the policymakers; they may make the policymakers' actions more clear to the public, and they may make policies newly available to public influence where previously they had not been.

Finally, there may be changes in the variables associated with opinion-policy correspondence levels. These may be personal variables, systemic variables, public official variables, and policy variables; some kinds of each have been linked to greater or lesser levels of correspondence. Thus, if greater salience to the public is linked to greater correspondence, increases (decreases) in policy salience may generate increases (decreases) in correspondence. Or, if certain kinds of issues are more likely to lead to correspondence (or the absence of it), the increasing prominence of those issues on the country's policy agenda may increase (or decrease) the level of correspondence. Similarly, changes in community characteristics, in the distribution of individual characteristics, and in the orientations of public officials may lead to changes in correspondence if those characteristics are themselves producers of variations in correspondence.

Correspondence and Opinion Dynamics

Public opinion patterns can take on several forms, based on whether change or stability in opinion takes place at the aggregate and at the individual level. Four combinations result: both individual- and aggregate-level change are present; individual change occurs, but aggregate change does not; aggregate change is found, but individual change is not; and neither individual nor aggregate change occurs (although complete stability may not be the case). Each of these has some implications for the nature of the change in correspondence between public opinion and public policy.

Where there is (in the most common case) asymmetrical individual change (in a predominate direction), there is a change in the distribution of opinions across the public (aggregate change). This provides the clearest signals for corresponding adjustments in public policy or in the orientations of political leaders (representatives). The changes in opinion will be relatively widespread across the public; there will be fewer competing signals as to the appropriate direction for policy.

Individual change and aggregate stability occur when there is symmetrical individual change. That is, across the electorate the changes in individual opinions tend to balance out. This creates some particular problems for the analysis of changes in correspondence. Public policy may move away from an apparently stable public opinion, at least stable at the aggregate level. The conclusion may be that correspondence is decreasing because aggregate public opinion is unchanged while public policy is altered. Yet the public policy may simply be responding to changes among a particular segment of the public, a segment to which it always has been responsive. And that change may be counterbalanced by changes in the portions of society to which policy has been unresponsive. Thus, foreign policy may always have been responsive to the opinions of the most highly educated portions of the public. Both the greater educated and the lesser educated may change their opinions in oppo-

site directions, resulting in aggregate stability. The foreign policy may follow
the direction of the more highly educated. Relying only on aggregate change
would give the appearance of stability in *opinions* with change in *policy,*
when there may have been change in the opinions of the policy-determining
portions of the public. On the other side of the same coin, stability in policy
and aggregate stability in opinions may not reflect stability in correspondence levels. Again, public policy may reflect only a portion of the public
(group A, say), and that portion's opinions may be different from those of the
remainder of the public (group B). Both group A and group B may change in
their opinions, and that change may balance — be symmetrical. If policy remains unchanged, then correspondence has changed, for the policy reflects a
different segment of the public. That pattern may stem from inertia in the
political system or from changes in political realities — the newly represented
group may be newly powerful.

When there is no change in the opinions of individuals there still can be a
change in the aggregate distribution of opinions. Chapter 2 identified two
patterns through which this pattern is generated: replacement, when new
generations enter the electorate and replace older generations with different
opinions; and arousal, when substantial portions of the electorate acquire
opinions about an issue when previously they held none. In the first case,
change is long-term; in the second, it is more likely to be mercurial. What
does this pattern mean for correspondence levels and change? If aggregate
change is produced through generational replacement, it is likely that diminishing correspondence will be confined to those members of the new generation, those that have brought in the new opinions. Not only will they hold
opinions out of step with current leaders and policy, they also will be in the
least efficacious position for changing the policy through traditional linkage
mechanisms. That is, younger generations are traditionally the least involved
in electoral and interest group politics, and few of their members rapidly
reach positions of political authority. This may explain the movement of
many young people to nonelectoral forms of political action in the face of
noncorresponding policy during the 1960s and the 1970s.

Opinion arousal presents a different situation, although still within the
same boundaries. Opinion arousal may fit most appropriately when discussing the impact of policy on the opinions of the public. That is, opinion
arousal (the appearance of opinions on an issue by many people when previously they had none) seems most likely to take place when a new issue
suddenly appears, one on which the government has formed a definite
and clearly communicated position. This position becomes the only or the
predominate source of cues for the public. Thus, in the creation of their opinions they come into concurrence with the public policy.

The last pattern seems most conducive to the development of opinion-
policy correspondence over the long run; little change in public opinion occurs, either at the individual level or at the aggregate level. Policymakers
have a stable set of public cues to respond to. On the other hand, stability in
public opinion may inhibit correspondence in times of rapidly changing issue
agendas. Policy may change in order to respond to change in society, but the

opinions may remain the same. Policies and policymakers may move ahead of the public, creating gaps between the two.

Thus, clearly the dynamics of public opinion patterns have implications for the nature of opinion-policy correspondence. At the same time, it is important to recognize that the *kind* of public opinion pattern that occurs also will affect the nature of correspondence. That is, different kinds of patterns may have different implications for the nature of correspondence and for the sources of that correspondence.

Opinion/Policy Correspondence and the Sources of Opinions

Chapter 2 identified three kinds of explanations of recent patterns in public opinion: the characteristics of the larger environment within which politics takes place; the attitudes and behavior of political leaders; and the characteristics of individuals or groups of individuals in the American public. Each of these explanations has some special implications for the correspondence between public opinion and public policy or political leaders.

Environmental sources of opinions stem from the characteristics of the political, social, and economic systems in which people spend their lives. Changes in those systems cannot help but influence the relationship of individuals to politics as well as their opinions about it. At the same time, those changes in the larger environment have two other effects. One is to simultaneously work on the opinions and behaviors of the public's representatives, either directly or through the choices exercised by the public. To the extent that the responses of the public and of the leaders are similar, then changes in the environment will contribute to continued or increased correspondence. On the other hand, the assumption that leaders and the public will respond in the same way to environmental changes may be tenuous. The two groups will be responding from different positions in society, and those differences (and the correlates of them, such as SES) may dictate different responses. To the extent that different responses are generated, the level of correspondence will decline. The second effect is that the changes in the larger environment not only influence the opinions and behaviors of the public and the leaders, they also define the issues to which the opinions and the policies respond. Thus, the changes in the environment define the objects of potential correspondence. Some kinds of issues seem more or less likely to produce correspondence. The degree to which the environmental changes place correspondence-maximizing or -minimizing issues on the agenda will therefore affect the links between the public and policy, or its makers.

Opinions resulting from cues provided by political leaders clearly will affect the level of correspondence. To the extent that public responses to leader cues are in proportion, then correspondence will be increased. That is, if the public responds to cues for change in greater numbers than those cued positions are present in the leaders, then correspondence will not be enhanced. On the other hand, if the public merely follows the cue-givers always used, then no change in correspondence will occur. The public may look beyond its formally designated representatives as sources for the changes in opinions. Thus, a rapidly changing set of cues may disrupt the "dyadic" mode of correspondence. The public may not take the cues from its *own* "representative." Rather, a more nationally prominent source may provide the rationale for opinion change across a number of people. Indeed, major issues may first be argued among a small elite at the national level, influencing major portions of the public throughout the country and then having an impact on the political leaders and the policies those publics choose.

Individual characteristics that produce opinions may also influence correspondence levels. Changes in opinion may occur among people with distinct personal characteristics. If the change moves that group of people away from the rest of the public and away from policy, then correspondence levels have changed, at least for that group. Similarly, there may be a change in the relative incidence of people with a certain characteristic who share a particular opinion. If that opinion is similar to policymakers' views, then correspondence will increase. On the other hand, if that opinion is discordant with policy or policymakers' views, the increasing incidence of the personal characteristic will decrease the level of concordance.

CONCLUSION

To probe the nature and impact of public opinion's dynamics is to consider the most central theoretical and normative elements of public opinion. We cannot argue that we understand public opinion unless we can show that we know the dynamics of those opinions. A simple description of some of the major parameters of public opinion is insufficient; many of those parameters have changed, and some undoubtedly will continue to change in the coming decades. With a static sketch, students of public opinion will be confined to viewing the fixed image of the public's political orientations with no opportunity to picture where that image came from or where it is going.

NOTES

1. Hanna Pitkin provides the most widely cited discussion of representation in her work, *The Concept of Representation* (Berkeley: University of California Press, 1976).
2. Heinz Eulau and Paul D. Karps, "The Puzzle of Representation: Specifying Components of Responsiveness," *Legislative Studies Quarterly* 3 (August 1977), p. 241.
3. Robert Weissberg, "Collective vs. Dyadic Representation in Congress," *American Political Science Review* 72 (June 1978), pp. 535–47.
4. Ibid., p. 535.
5. Warren E. Miller and Donald E. Stokes, "Constituency Influence in Congress," *American Political Science Review* 57 (March 1963), pp. 45–56.
6. Robert S. Erikson, "Constituency Opinion and Congressional Behavior: A Reexamination of the Miller-Stokes Representation Data," *American Journal of Political Science* 22 (August 1978), pp. 511–35.

7. Erikson, "Constituency Opinion and Congressional Behavior." For a critical view of simulation measures, see James H. Kuklinski, "Constituency Opinions: A Test of the Surrogate Model," *Public Opinion Quarterly* 41 (Spring 1977), pp. 34–40.
8. For a discussion of different kinds of constituencies, see Richard F. Fenno, Jr., *Home Style* (Boston: Little, Brown & Co., 1978), especially Chap. 1.
9. For a discussion of the problems in aggregating preferences for purposes of assessing correspondence, see Anne L. Schneider, "Measuring Political Responsiveness: A Comparison of Alternative Methods," in *Water Politics and Public Involvement,* John C. Pierce and Harvey R. Doerksen, eds. (Ann Arbor, Mich.: Ann Arbor Science, 1976).
10. One frequently employed measure is the correlation coefficient. See Christopher H. Achen, "Measuring Representation," *American Journal of Political Science* 22 (August 1978), pp. 475–510; and Christopher H. Achen, "Measures of Representation: Perils of the Correlation Coefficient," *American Journal of Political Science* 21 (November 1977), pp. 805–15.
11. Miller and Stokes, "Constituency Influence in Congress."
12. Miller and Stokes estimated the opinions of a district's voters through the use of small samples derived from a procedure designed to provide a sample representative of the American public and not the public of particular congressional districts. The results of the study have been criticized on the basis of the sampling reliability problems.
13. Miller and Stokes, "Constituency Influence in Congress," p. 56.
14. For example, see Charles F. Cnudde and Donald J. McCrone, "The Linkage Between Constituency Attitudes and Congressional Voting Behavior: A Causal Model," *American Political Science Review* 60 (March 1966), pp. 66–72.
15. Erikson, "Constituency Opinion and Congressional Behavior," p. 524.
16. See also John L. Sullivan and Robert E. O'Connor, "Electoral Choice and Popular Control of Public Policy: The Case of the 1966 House Elections," *American Political Science Review* 6 (December 1972), pp. 1256—65.
17. For an important discussion of these representative role orientations, see John C. Wahke, et al., *The Legislative System* (New York: John Wiley & Sons, 1962), pp. 267–86.
18. Aage R. Clausen, "The Accuracy of Leader Perceptions of Constituency Views," *Legislative Studies Quarterly* 11 (November 1977), p. 362.
19. Ronald D. Hedlund and H. Paul Friesema, "Representatives' Perceptions of Constituency Opinion," *Journal of Politics* 34 (August 1972), pp. 730–52.
20. Ibid., p. 742.
21. Robert S. Erikson, Norman R. Luttbeg, and William V. Holloway, "Knowing One's District: How Legislators Predict Referendum Voting," *American Journal of Political Science* 19 (May 1975), pp. 231–46.
22. H. Paul Friesema and Ronald D. Hedlund, "The Reality of Representational Roles," in *Public Opinion and Public Policy,* Norman R. Lutbeg, ed. (Homewood, Ill: Dorsey Press, 1974), pp. 413–17.
23. James H. Kuklinski and Richard C. Elling, "Representational Role, Constituency Opinion, and Legislative Roll-Call Behavior," *American Journal of Political Science* 21 (February 1977), pp. 135–47.
24. In addition to the studies cited above, see the Miller and Stokes data cited in Robert S. Erikson and Norman R. Luttbeg, *American Public Opinion: Its Origins, Content and Impact* (New York: John Wiley & Sons, 1973), p. 259; and the propensity of winners to be more likely than losers to attribute the results to the voters' issue concerns (called the "congratulation-rationalization" effect) in John W. Kingdon, *Candidates for Office: Beliefs and Strategies* (New York: Random House, 1968), p. 31.

25. Several methods may be employed to assess the cumulative gap between the distribution of preferences in the public and the distribution in a leader sample. One of these methods is the Lorenz Curve and the Gini Index of Inequality based on it. For an introduction to this method, see Hayward R. Alker, Jr., *Mathematics and Politics* (New York: Macmillan, 1965), pp. 29–53. For two recent applications, see Kenneth J. Meier, "Representative Bureaucracy," *American Political Science Review* 69 (June 1975), pp. 526–42; and John C. Pierce, "Conflict and Consensus in Water Politics," *Western Political Quarterly* 32 (September 1979), pp. 307–19.

26. Charles H. Backstrom, "Congress and the Public: How Representative Is the One or the Other?" *American Politics Quarterly* 5 (October 1977), p. 422.

27. Ibid., p. 429.

28. See Eric M. Uslaner and Ronald E. Weber, "Public Opinion and Linkage Politics in the American States: Which 'Elite' Is Most Representative?" (Paper delivered at the 1977 Annual Meeting of the American Political Science Association, Los Angeles, March 16–18); and Eric M. Uslaner and Ronald E. Weber, "Policy Congruence in the American States: Descriptive Representation Versus Electoral Accountability" (Paper prepared for delivery at the 1979 Annual Meeting of the Midwest Political Science Association, Chicago, Illinois, April 19–21).

29. Uslaner and Weber, "Policy Congruence," p. 13.

30. Sidney Verba and Norman H. Nie, *Participation in America: Political Democracy and Social Equality* (New York: Harper & Row, 1972), p. 305.

31. Susan Blackall Hansen, "Participation, Political Structure and Concurrence," *American Political Science Review* 69 (December 1975), pp. 1181–99.

32. Paul D. Schumaker and Russell W. Getter, "Responsiveness Bias in 51 American Communities," *American Journal of Political Science* 22 (May 1977), p. 248.

33. Ibid., p. 257.

34. Ronald E. Weber and William R. Shaffer, "Public Opinion and American State Policy-Making," *Midwest Journal of Political Science* 16 (November 1972), p. 685.
35. Richard L. Sutton, "The State and the People: Measuring and Accounting for State Representativeness," *Polity* 5 (Summer 1973), pp. 451–76.
36. Ibid., p. 465.
37. Ibid., pp. 465–66.
38. Robert S. Erikson, "The Relationship Between Public Opinion and State Policy: A New Look Based on Some Forgotten Data," *American Journal of Political Science* 20 (February 1976), p. 35.
39. Robert Weissberg, *Public Opinion and Popular Government* (Englewood Cliffs, N.J.: Prentice-Hall, 1976), p. 137.
40. Alan D. Monroe, "Consistency Between Public Preferences and National Policy Decisions," *American Politics Quarterly* 7 (January 1979), pp. 3–19.
41. Ibid., p. 17.
42. Alan D. Monroe, "Public Opinion and Public Policy, 1960–1974" (Paper prepared for delivery at the 1978 meeting of the American Political Science Association, New York).
43. Eulau and Karps, "The Puzzle of Representation," p. 243.
44. See the extensive references to this position in the earlier chapters.
45. Weissberg, *Public Opinion and Popular Government*, p. 225.
46. Barry B. Hughes, *The Domestic Context of Foreign Policy* (San Francisco: W.H. Freeman, 1978), p. 113.
47. Ibid., p. 113.
48. Weissberg, *Public Opinion and Popular Government*, p.235.

CHAPTER 15

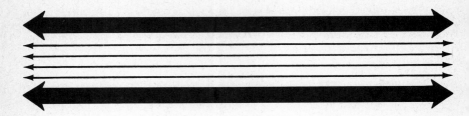

PUBLIC OPINION AND THE CONTINUING DYNAMIC

The preceding chapters have emphasized several central themes. These themes are the analysis of the dynamics of American public opinion and the implications of those dynamics for the character of American democracy. To recapitulate, opinion dynamics refers to stability and change in the interaction among opinion patterns, opinion explanations, and opinion processes. *Opinion patterns* refer to the distributions of aggregate and individual opinion characteristics at any particular time and the continuity or discontinuity in those characteristics across time. *Opinion explanations* refer to the causal sources of the patterns, the reasons *why* the public's opinions take their particular form and either hold or change that form. Three major kinds of explanations have been emphasized: those that underscore the public's dependence on, or responsiveness to, political leaders; those that focus on large-scale changes in the political, social, or economic environment; and those that are linked to the character of the individual's attributes. *Opinion processes* are the individual- and aggregate-level mechanisms through which the opinion dynamics — the stability and the change — take place. Dominant opinion processes include replacement of cohorts, the arousal of opinions in the public, and individual-level changes that may either be symmetrical or asymmetrical when aggregated across the electorate.

Many patterns of public opinion have changed over the last three decades; at the same time, many other patterns have shown substantial stability. In still other cases, there is so much dispute about the methods used to measure opinions and their patterns that we still are uncertain as to what has happened or what the fundamental character of public opinion really is. The patterns of public opinion are the outcome of a dynamic process, one in which opinion is produced as the result of the interaction between the individual and those causal forces to which that individual responds. Of course, it is difficult to know with great certainty whether the patterns we observe now are ones of stability or ones of change. Which of the various explanations is appropriate? This has many ramifications for the correct interpretation of American politics and for accurate predictions of future trends.

Assessment of the actual content of public opinion patterns, their explanations, and the processes through which they occur also has significant implications for the democratic quality of the policymaking process. The public's opinions, especially when they become highly visible and move individuals to political action, may provide a clear stimulus to government action. The public's opinions are one standard by which we judge the responsiveness of government. Opinions are an important stimulus to individual political action in democratic processes. The opinions individuals express reveal much about the extent to which the public meets the demands and standards established for it by democratic theorists.

The analysis of public opinion as a continuing dynamic seems again to take on special relevance in American politics. The decades of the 1960s and the 1970s revealed many apparent shifts in the aggregate- and the individual-level characteristics of American public opinion, shifts that seem to produce change in the fundamental character of much of the social and political systems. As a new decade begins — and some say a new political era with a potential shift in political power at all levels of government — it is important to examine the relevance and the substance of public opinion. What changes in the American public's opinions and behaviors will appear in the eighties? What are the causal explanations for what now is taking place with regard to public opinion and American politics? Through what individual and aggregate processes might we explain our judgments about the present and the future of public opinion? The following paragraphs identify some preliminary evidence about several possible changes in major patterns of public opinion and speculate on the explanations and the processes related to them. First, we examine the possibility of a partisan realignment in the 1980s. Then the chapter provides a brief overview of the apparent growth in conservatism in the American public and the relationship between ideological identification and important policy positions.

PARTISAN REALIGNMENT

It will be recalled that presidential elections frequently are classified in terms of their impact on and relationship to the distribution of partisan preferences in the American public.[1] The distribution of partisan preferences among the major political parties (that is, the relative size of the two parties' followings in the public) obviously affects the likelihood of either party's winning or losing an important election; it will influence the long-term stability and predictability of election outcomes; and it will influence the kinds of appeals that candidates make during their election campaigns.

Realigning elections generally are thought to be the most important kind, for a realigning election signals a substantial and an enduring shift in the relative public support for the two major political parties. That is, the aggregate distribution of party identification is so changed that the party previously in the majority now is a minority, and the minority party is thrust into dominance *in terms of the public's allegiances.* The change in the relative preponderance of the two parties' followers is linked to the environment of the electoral campaign — the nature of the issues at stake and the character of the stands on those issues of the two parties and their presidential candidates. The last apparent realigning election in the United States — one in which the majority/minority status of the two major parties was reversed — occurred in 1932, with the initial victory and the subsequent popularity of Franklin Roosevelt.[2] That election signaled the emergence of the Democratic party as the majority party (or at least the plurality party) in the public's allegiances for some fifty years. The major issue of that period, of course, was the onset of the Great Depression and the appropriate role for government in response to the financial troubles of the nation.

A common interpretation of the 1932 election of Roosevelt was that his subsequent presidency converted many Republicans into Democrats. In retrospect, that newfound dominance of the Democrats in the 1930s stemmed not from large-scale conversions at the individual level, but rather from asymmetrical distributions of partisan allegiances in replacement cohorts.[3] That is, the new generations (cohorts) coming of age in the 1930s matured politically in an overwhelmingly Democratic direction, primarily in response to the interaction between the nature of the political and social environment and the character of the country's political leadership.

Realigning elections are not the only type of presidential contest. Other types of elections have occurred since the 1930s. Lyndon Johnson's win in 1964 has been called a *converting* election. That is, there was a shift in the relative preponderance of the two major parties but no change in their majority or minority status. In the case of the 1964 election, the change benefited the Democrats, the victorious majority party. President Kennedy's election in 1960 has been labeled a *maintaining* election. That is, there was no aggregate-level change in the distribution of partisan allegiances, and the majority party (the Democrats) won the presidential contest. The 1968 and 1972 victories of Richard Nixon fall into the category of *deviating* elections. Deviating elections are those in which there is no disturbance of the fundamental distribution of party allegiances, but because of powerful short-term forces (issues or personalities specific to the election) the minority party claimed the contest.

In the late 1960s and through the 1970s there emerged another trend that fails to mesh with the traditional fourfold classification of elections just described. Rather than a partisan alignment or realignment centered around a spectacular victory, some scholars have identified a partisan *dealignment* — a withdrawal from and decomposition of the American public's support for both of the two major political parties.[4] Many more Americans now call themselves Independents (aligned with neither of the two major parties) than previously had taken that position. More important, that movement of the public as an aggregate from identification with the two major parties also seems in large part to have been a matter of generational replacement (much like the realignment of the 1930s). That is, relatively independent younger generational cohorts have been replacing the older more partisan generational cohorts.[5] Fully 51 percent of the new voters in 1972 and 47 percent of the new voters in 1976 called themselves Independents. On the other hand, that same label was taken by only 26 percent of those who entered the electorate before 1952 and only 32 percent of those entering the electorate in 1952.

When coupled with the generational/replacement basis of the last major realignment, the "dealignment" of the 1970s has suggested to some observers that Ronald Reagan's 1980 victory (along with Republican successes at the state and local levels and in the U.S. Senate) signals the beginning of another party realignment.[6] The argument goes that the realignment would lead to the eventual rise of the Republicans to a position as the dominant — if not majority — party in the feelings of the American electorate. The presence of a younger generation (cohort), substantial portions of which do not possess large-scale and deeply held party allegiances, would provide the potential reservoir from which the new Republicans could be drawn. The capture of this group in the coming years by the Republicans would constitute a replacement process similar in important ways to the two most recent major developments in aggregate party alignments — the realignments of the 1930s and the dealignments of the 1970s, both of them largely taking place through generational replacement processes.

Realignment producing Republican dominance through replacement, of course, would have to be a rather gradual process as the new cohorts enter the electorate and the youngest voting cohorts gradually turn to the Republican party. In a sense, such a realignment would come from a combination of replacement *and* partisan arousal among the most recently franchised cohorts. Some evidence of such a process has been cited in descriptions of the precursor to what has been called a "creeping realignment."[7] That is, in the period immediately following President Reagan's victory over Jimmy Carter, the number of Republican identifiers in the public apparently increased to a figure much closer to that for Democrats. The data do not yet reveal the generational location of those alleged shifts, nor of course do they reveal their permanence. Indeed, the problem in knowing for sure whether an enduring, replacement-produced alignment is on the way is that one can tell only with the passage of substantial time and many more studies. Replacement is a slow process, and to influence the partisan distributions requires significant political forces acting in the same direction on most members of the cohorts. Whether President Reagan's election and his postelection presidency are of that magnitude as a political force remains to be seen. And the "remains to be seen" caveat is the other problem. Realignment becomes clear only after the passage of time. Thus, while the opportunity seems present, and there are hints of a beginning of change, one must wait to see if the public opinion dynamic will produce a new partisan alignment.

CREEPING CONSERVATISM?

Just as there may be developing what some have called a creeping realignment, there have been suggestions that recent years — and those to come — will be identified as the time of the growth of conservatism in the American public. Much of this speculation, of course, stems from the victory of Ronald

Reagan. It also is based in the defeat of many liberal U.S. senators (e.g., Church, Bayh, McGovern), the heightened activity and success of conservative political action organizations, and the Moral Majority. How much of this apparent conservative tide is founded in the dynamics of American public opinion? And how much difference does it make in individuals' positions on issues of public policy if they think of themselves as conservatives rather than liberals?

Has there in fact been change in the aggregate distribution of the American public's ideological identifications? The answer is that it depends on what questions are used and who is reporting the findings. Indeed, there is not now general agreement on just how many liberals and conservatives there are in the public when people are asked to label themselves.[8] Surveys by the Gallup Organization in September of 1980 report that 31 percent call themselves conservative. Similarly, the National Opinion Research Center (NORC) reports 34 percent conservatives and 26 percent liberals. These two are relatively close in their estimates. However, a survey by Time/Yankelovich produced 44 percent of the public as self-identified conservatives and only 13 percent as self-identified liberals. And the Center for Political Studies found that "in early 1980, 45 percent of our representative sample said they were conservatives."[9] Given these studies' relatively wide range in the estimate of the number of conservatives, what is one to conclude? It is unlikely that great ideological volatility produced rather large shifts in the number of conservatives in the periods between these surveys, since the results with the greatest disparity were separated in time by only about a month. A more likely possibility is in the question wording. The way the question is formed or the kinds of alternatives given to the respondent may influence the willingness of the public to pick particular options. Thus, the survey producing the smallest number of conservatives (31 percent) actually used the terms *left* and *right* instead of liberal and conservative. Here is the question:

> *People who are conservative in their political views are referred to as being right of center and people who are liberal in their political views are referred to as being left of center. Which one of the categories [respondents handed a card: Far left, substantially left, moderately left, just slightly left of center, just slightly right of center, moderately right of center, substantially right of center, far right] best describes your political position?*[10]

Perhaps the terms *left of center* and *right of center* are more difficult for Americans to link to their own attitudes. While liberal and conservative may be traditional orientations in American politics, the left and the right may carry more extreme or negative connotations. People who are willing to call themselves "conservative" may be unwilling to give themselves the label of "substantially right of center" or "far right." Conflicting evidence also is found when we consider changes in ideological identification over the decade of the seventies. On the one hand, the Gallup Organization found a decline from 39 percent conservative in 1972 to 31 percent in 1980. And the National Opinion Research Center shows only a slight increase from 30 percent conservative in 1974 to 34 percent in 1980. On the other hand, the Center for Political Studies claims that "after 1978, there is clear evidence of a shift to the right."[11]

Finally, recent polling data show that the policy preferences of self identified liberals and conservatives are not clearly differentiated. That is, if there has been a shifting about of liberals and conservatives but without an *overwhelming* aggregate movement in a particular ideological direction, that shifting has not resulted in self-identified ideological groupings that differ widely on whole sets of political issues. Thus, in 1980, 72 percent of the liberals opposed a constitutional amendment banning abortions, while 57 percent of the conservatives did so. Although only 13 percent of the conservatives opposed a constitutional amendment that would permit prayers to be said in the public schools, only 23 percent of the liberals opposed it also. Of the liberals, 40 percent oppose the draft, while 26 percent of the conservatives do so. And on a number of issues the differences between conservatives of different educational attainment are much greater than the differences between conservatives and liberals. Thus, of the conservative college graduates about 75 percent say there is too much spending on welfare, but only 52 percent of the conservatives with less than a high school education take that position. Of the liberals, on the other hand, only 54 percent say there is too much spending on welfare.

Given the very ambivalent nature of the poll findings, why has there emerged a feeling that the country is experiencing a pronounced shift to the right? We suggest two reasons for this, both of which relate to the interaction of public opinion and elite sources of information. First, the emergence of many well-organized, articulate, and media-conscious conservative interest groups has enhanced the dispersion of conservative ideological positions through most of the important mass media channels. Groups such as the Moral Majority, which claim a large participatory membership, give the impression of a sweeping wave of organized conservative sentiment. The media-wise organizers of such groups are all the more powerful because there exists little comparably organized efforts on the other side of the political spectrum. With established forums for conservative issue articulation, and the lack of similar liberal organizations, the press, and a portion of the public, could well be responding to structural environmental cues. This echoing of rhetoric may not, in fact, make a lasting imprint on the shape of public opinion in the eighties. The second, and very much related, reason for an apparent conservative tide, lies less with long-term change but more with factors related directly to the electoral environment of the early 1980s. Ronald Reagan, having the control of his party secure, was able to articulate a more cohesive and consistent ideological platform during the campaign of 1980. Jimmy Carter, on the other hand, pursued a program of moderation rather than liberalism. Reagan, therefore, provided a more distinct and accessible point around which to coalesce opinions. His clearer articulation of the conservative creed allowed for a more distinct and unambiguous rallying point. If, as we frequently have argued in the book, public opinion responds to clear cues from the political environment, the emergence of a conservative shift is made much more understandable. If Reagan pursues a clear conservative direction, and if the Democrats do not provide a clearly drawn alternative, the notion of an "emerging Republican majority" may, indeed, come to pass.

CONCLUSION

While surely not the only possible patterns that will capture our attention in the coming year, partisan and ideological realignment are especially important because of what they may signal for central characteristics of the American political system. They show that the public opinion dynamic continues to work, but that the processes through which it operates are not always clear. They also reinforce the answers the first chapter gave as to why one should study public opinion. The dynamics of public opinion tell us about ourselves, about the formation and impact of public policy, and about the character and the quality of the American democracy.

NOTES

1. V. O. Key, Jr., "A Theory of Critical Elections," *Journal of Politics* 17 (February 1955), pp. 3–18; Angus Campbell, "A Classification of the Presidential Elections," in *Elections and the Political Order,* Angus Campbell et al., eds. (New York: John Wiley & Sons, 1966); and Gerald M. Pomper, "Classification of Presidential Elections," *Journal of Politics* 29 (August 1967), pp. 535–66.
2. Herbert B. Asher, *Presidential Elections and American Politics* (Homewood, Ill.: Dorsey, 1976), p. 298. To be sure, there is some dispute about the exact date to which the realignment should be attributed. See Jerome M. Clubb, William H. Flanigan, and Nancy H. Zingale, *Partisan Realignment: Voters, Parties and Government in American History* (Beverly Hills: Sage Publications, 1980), p. 21.
3. Kristi Andersen, "Generation, Partisan Shift, and Realignment: A Glance Back to the New Deal," in *The Changing American Voter,* Norman H. Nie, Sidney Verba, and John R. Petrocik, eds. (Cambridge, Mass.: Harvard University Press, 1976), p. 75.
4. Jack Dennis, "Trends in Public Support for the American Party System," in *Parties and Elections in an Anti-Party Age: American Politics and the Crises of Confidence,* Jeff Fishel, ed. (Bloomington, Ind.: Indiana University Press, 1978), pp. 3–21.
5. Nie et al., *The Changing American Voter,* p. 63.
6. See, for example, "Party Affiliation May Be Shifting to GOP," *Lewiston Tribune,* March 1, 1981.
7. Richard Wirthlin, quoted in "Party Affiliation May Be Shifting to GOP," *Lewiston Tribune,* March 1, 1981.
8. Unless otherwise noted, the data described in this section come from "Opinion Roundup" in *Public Opinion* (February/March 1981), pp. 20–31.
9. "Election '80 Reviewed," *ISR Newsletter* (Spring 1981), p. 3.
10. "Opinion Roundup," p. 20.
11. "Election '80 Reviewed," p. 3.

AUTHOR INDEX

SUBJECT INDEX